NT Server 4

The Cram Sheet

This Cram Sheet contains the distilled, key facts about Windows NT Server 4. Review this information last thing before you enter the test room, paying special attention to those areas where you feel you need the most review. You can transfer any of these facts onto a blank sheet of paper before beginning the exam.

INSTALLATION

1. Know these WINNT and WINNT32 switches:
   - **/OX** Creates three Setup disks; does not start install.
   - **/X** Installs Windows NT without creating the Setup boot floppies.
   - **/B** Installs Windows NT without making or using Setup boot floppies.

2. When upgrading an existing version of Windows NT, the following information stays intact:
   - Any edits made to the Registry using Registry Editor
   - Custom program groups, desktop layout, setting, and Control Panel preferences
   - Local security accounts (users and groups)
   - Network adapter, protocol, service configurations, and addresses (including Mac and RAS)
   - Preferences for Accessories and Administrative Tools

3. You cannot change server roles between member server and domain controller (PDC or BDC), or vice versa, without reinstalling Windows NT.

DISK MANAGEMENT

4. Network Client Administrator creates installation and startup disks for these operating systems:
   - Network Client 3.0 for MS-DOS and Windows
   - LAN Manager 2.2c for MS-DOS
   - LAN Manager 2.2c for OS/2
   - Windows For Workgroups 3.11

5. Review Disk Administrator menus and options (Table 4.1, page 79).

6. Only primary partitions can be active: Select Mark Active from the Partition menu in Disk Administrator.

FILE SYSTEMS AND FAULT TOLERANCE

7. Vital statistics for FAT and NTFS:

	FAT	NTFS
Maximum volume size	2 GB	16 EB
Maximum file size	2 GB	16 EB
File-level security	No	Yes
Long file name support	No	Yes
Self-repairing	No	Yes
Transaction logging capabilities	No	Yes
File-level compression	No	Yes

33. For a printer pool, all devices must connect to same print server and all printers should be identical.

34. Only Windows 95 and NT clients can use print drivers on NT print servers.

NETWARE

35. NWLink default frame type (auto) detection usually works OK, but some Ethernet adapters won't work with this setting. To communicate with older NetWare versions, manually enter all frame types.

36. Always consider frame type mismatch when Windows NT and NetWare (v3.12 and older) can't interact.

37. To give NetWare clients Windows NT access, install FPNW and NWLink. NWLink works without NetWare, too.

38. GSNW lets MS Network clients (Windows 3.x, 95, NT Workstation/Server) access NetWare resources.

39. Use the NWCONV.EXE utility to migrate NetWare users, groups, and resources to Windows NT.

40. WINS maps computer names to IP addresses and reduces broadcast traffic on network.

RAS

41. Important RAS facts:

- RAS supports PPP dialup clients only (not SLIP).
- RAS supports up to 256 incoming connections.

- NetBIOS gateway on server sustains standard Windows NT network operations for PPP-attached clients.
- RAS supports IP and IPX routing.
- RAS supports PPTP and Multilink PPP.
- RAS supports NetBIOS, NetBEUI gateway, and Windows Sockets applications.

42. RAS connection security settings are managed using the Security tab of the phonebook entry for outbound links and the Network Protocol Configuration dialog box for inbound links.

43. Put LMHOSTS files on RAS clients. Entries use #PRE tag to cache IP addresses locally, which speeds access.

44. RAS maintains a list of WAN resources. When resources are referenced, RAS attempts to AutoDial to regain the WAN connection.

PERFORMANCE MONITORING

45. Performance Monitor displays server characteristics. All data is viewable in Chart, Alert, Log, and Report Views.

46. Define administrative alerts by selecting Alert from the Options menu in Performance Monitor.

47. Look at Memory: Pages/Second to decide whether more RAM is needed.

48. The Performance Monitor Log option collects data to file to view later.

CORIOLIS
Certification Insider Press

8. Use FAT for 50 MB partitions or smaller and NTFS for partitions 400 MB or larger.

9. Rules for Permissions on NTFS Move and Copy operations:
   - If you move files within the same NTFS partition, they *retain* original permissions.
   - If you create, copy, or move files from one NTFS partition to another, they *inherit* parent folder permissions.
   - All NTFS permissions disappear when files are moved or copied from NTFS to FAT.

10. Convert FAT partitions into NTFS using CONVERT.EXE; HPFS is not supported in Windows NT 4.

11. NTBACKUP features and functions:
   - Do not back up temp files.
   - Back up the Registry on PDC and all BDCs.
   - NTBACKUP cannot back up the Registry across the network.

12. About disk striping with parity:
   - All partitions in set must be equal sizes (or close)
   - Partitions must be on different physical disks
   - Can be implemented with NTFS or FAT
   - 3 drives minimum; 32 drives maximum
   - Slower than striping without parity, faster than mirroring

13. If one drive in a set fails, missing data can be rebuilt from remaining devices and parity info.

14. If you lose a member of a volume set or stripe set without parity, everything is lost.

15. RAID levels and details:

Type	Fault Tolerant?	Speed	Includes
RAID 0	No	Fastest	Disk striping without parity, volume sets
RAID 1	Yes	Slowest RAID (faster)	Disk mirroring (slower), disk duplexing
RAID 5	Yes	Intermediate	Disk striping with parity

16. Neither boot nor system partitions can reside on a volume set or disk stripe set, even with parity.

USERS AND GROUPS

17. There are two types of groups: local and global. Local groups are created and available on local machines; global groups are available across domains. Local groups can contain users and global groups, global groups contain users only. You cannot place groups within global groups, nor can you place local groups within other local groups.

18. For group permissions, the least restrictive right takes precedence, except that No Access always wins. When combining NTFS and share permissions, the least restrictive wins for each kind (except No Access). When combining resulting NTFS and share permissions, the most restrictive wins.

19. You can perform the following in User Manager For Domains:
   - Produce, change, duplicate, and remove user and group accounts
   - Enable account policies (assign defaults for passwords, account lockouts, disconnect status, etc.)
   - Create user rights and audit policies
   - Establish trust relationships

BOOT FACTS

20. Boot and system partitions can reside on the primary disk in a disk mirror or duplex set. If the primary fails, you must hand-edit the BOOT.INI file on the boot drive to point to the ARC name for the remaining mirror or duplex drive instead.

21. Boot files—NTLDR, BOOT.INI, NTDETECT.COM, etc.—reside on the system partition. Windows NT OS files—including NTOSKRNL.EXE—reside on the boot partition. BACKWARDS!

22. The most important Windows NT boot process components:
   - **BOOT.INI** Boot initialization file: Describes Windows NT boot defaults, plus OS location, settings, menu selections. Resides in the root directory of the system partition. (Required for Windows NT boot floppy.)
   - **BOOTSECT.DOS** MS-DOS boot sector file: Used if NTLDR permits boot to some other Microsoft OS like DOS or Windows 95.

Resides in the root directory of system partition. (Not required.)

- **NTDETECT.COM** PC hardware detection: Reads device and configuration info before Windows NT boots. Resides in the root directory of system partition. (Required for NT boot floppy.)
- **NTLDR** OS loader program: Loads Windows NT or other designated OS. Relinquishes control once loading completes. Resides in the root directory of a system partition. (Required for Windows NT boot floppy.)
- **NTOSKRNL.EXE** Executable file for Windows NT OS: Includes all basic capabilities and items necessary to establish runtime environment. Resides in \Winnt\System32 on boot partition.
- **OSLOADER.EXE** RISC OS loader: Provides services and info equal to NTDETECT.COM, BOOTSECT.DOS, NTDETECT.COM, and NTLDR on PCs. Resides in the RISC boot PROM area.
- **NTBOOTDD.SYS** Used when system or boot SCSI drive has BIOS disabled. Replaces BIOS functions with software driver. Resides in the root directory of system partition.

23. ARC name information:

- **scsi(*) or multi(*)** Most ARC names begin with multi(*); scsi(*) appears only when SCSI has BIOS disabled. Multi(*) applies to IDE, EIDE, ESDI, and SCSI (where BIOS enabled). (*) indicates the address of the hardware adapter. Numbers start at zero, with controller seated closest to slot 0 in PC.
- **disk(*)** Applies only when scsi(*) keyword appears. Then, the value of (*) indicates SCSI bus ID, starting with zero, for drive where files reside. If multi(*) appears, disk(*) is always disk(0).
- **rdisk(*)** Applies only when multi(*) keyword appears. It indicates SCSI logical unit number (LUN) for the drive. Numbering begins with zero, so the first drive in the chain is named rdisk(0), the second is named rdisk(1), and so on.
- **partition(*)** Indicates the disk partition that contains designated files. Unlike other ARC numbering, partition numbers start at one, so the first partition is partition(1), the second partition(2), and so on.
- **\path** Indicates the directory on the partition for OS files. Default path for Windows NT is \winnt.

24. The ERD process often corrects boot sector problems. Otherwise, replace NTLDR or repair NTOSKRNL.

DOMAIN CONTROLLERS, TRUSTS, LOGINS, PROFILES, AND POLICIES

25. To promote BDC to PDC:

Launch Server Manager and select Promote To Primary Domain Controller from the Computer menu. Finally, confirm the promotion.

26. To allow workstations to log onto a domain:

(1) Add the computer names of all domain workstations using Server Manager.

(2) Add user accounts using User Manager For Domains.

(3) Configure each workstation to use the new domain within the Network applet.

27. Trusts between domains are one-way only. A two-way trust = two one-way trusts between domains.

28. User profiles are located in %systemroot%\Profiles\<username> directories.

29. The default export directory for logon scripts on domain controllers is Winnt\System32\Repl\Export\Scripts.

30. To manage Windows NT Server shares remotely, use Server Manager, not Windows NT Explorer.

PROTOCOLS AND SERVICES

PRINTING

31. DLC or LPR must be installed to enable communication with network-attached printers.

32. To fix a stalled print spooler, select Services in Control Panel, stop Spooler Service, then restart it.

MCSE
NT Server 4
Third Edition

Ed Tittel
Kurt Hudson
James Michael Stewart

MCSE Windows NT Server 4 Exam Cram, Third Edition

Limits of Liability and Disclaimer of Warranty

Trademarks

The Coriolis Group, LLC
14455 N. Hayden Road, Suite 220
Scottsdale, Arizona 85260

480/483-0192
FAX 480/483-0193
http://www.coriolis.com

Library of Congress Cataloging-in-Publication Data
Tittel, Ed
    MCSE NT server 4 exam cram/by Ed Tittel, Kurt Hudson, and James Michael Stewart.-- 3rd ed.
        p. cm.
    Includes index.
    ISBN 1-57610-618-7
    1. Electronic data processing personnel--Certification.   2. Microsoft software--Examinations--Study guides.   3. Microsoft Windows NT Server.   I. Hudson, Kurt.   II. Stewart, James Michael.   III. Title.
QA76.3.T57369   2000
005.4'4769--dc21   99-058381
                                                                          CIP

Printed in the United States of America
10 9 8 7 6 5 4 3 2 1

President, CEO
Keith Weiskamp

Publisher
Steve Sayre

Acquisitions Editor
Shari Jo Hehr

Marketing Specialist
Cynthia Caldwell

Project Editor
Sharon Sanchez
McCarson

Technical Reviewer
Bob Flynn

**Production
Coordinator**
Kim Eoff

Cover Design
Jesse Dunn

Layout Design
April Nielsen

CORIOLIS

14455 North Hayden Road • Suite 220 • Scottsdale, Arizona 85260

Coriolis: The Training And Certification Destination™

Thank you for purchasing one of our innovative certification study guides, just one of the many members of the Coriolis family of certification products.

Certification Insider Press™ has long believed that achieving your IT certification is more of a road trip than anything else. This is why most of our readers consider us their *Training And Certification Destination*. By providing a one-stop shop for the most innovative and unique training materials, our readers know we are the first place to look when it comes to achieving their certification. As one reader put it, "I plan on using your books for all of the exams I take."

To help you reach your goals, we've listened to others like you, and we've designed our entire product line around you and the way you like to study, learn, and master challenging subjects. Our approach is *The Smartest Way To Get Certified™*.

In addition to our highly popular *Exam Cram* and *Exam Prep* guides, we have a number of new products. We recently launched *Exam Cram Audio Reviews*, which are audiotapes based on *Exam Cram* material. We've also developed *Practice Tests Exam Crams* and *Exam Cram Flash Cards*, which are designed to make your studying fun as well as productive.

Our commitment to being the *Training And Certification Destination* does not stop there. We just introduced *Exam Cram Insider*, a biweekly newsletter containing the latest in certification news, study tips, and announcements from Certification Insider Press. (To subscribe, send an email to **eci@coriolis.com** and type "subscribe insider" in the body of the email.) We also recently announced the launch of the Certified Crammer Society and the Coriolis Help Center—two new additions to the Certification Insider Press family.

We'd like to hear from you. Help us continue to provide the very best certification study materials possible. Write us or email us at **cipq@coriolis.com** and let us know how our books have helped you study, or tell us about new features that you'd like us to add. If you send us a story about how we've helped you, and we use it in one of our books, we'll send you an official Coriolis shirt for your efforts.

Good luck with your certification exam and your career. Thank you for allowing us to help you achieve your goals.

Keith Weiskamp
President and CEO

Look For These Other Books From The Coriolis Group:

MCSE Networking Essentials Exam Cram, Third Edition
Ed Tittel, Kurt Hudson, James Michael Stewart

MCSE NT Server 4 in the Enterprise Exam Cram, Third Edition
Ed Tittel, Kurt Hudson, James Michael Stewart

MCSE NT Workstation 4 Exam Cram, Third Edition
Ed Tittel, Kurt Hudson, James Michael Stewart

About The Authors

Ed Tittel is a 20-year veteran in the computing business who owes his high-tech career to an ongoing affection for beautiful Austin, Texas. Ed covers numerous Windows subjects, with over 30 Windows-related titles to his credit. He also teaches for NetWorld + Interop and The Internet Security Conference (TISC) on Windows security and performance tuning. Prior to starting a company in 1994, Ed worked at Novell for six years, where he started out as a field engineer and left as Director of Technical Marketing.

Ed has contributed to over 105 computer books, including many Exam Preps and Exam Crams, for which he is series editor. Ed has also written articles for *Certification Magazine*, *InfoWorld*, *Windows NT Magazine*, and *PC Magazine*.

In his spare time, Ed likes cooking homemade stock and the many good things that it makes possible. He also walks the company Lab, Blackie, at least five times a day. Reach Ed via email at **etittel@lanw.com**.

Kurt Hudson, president of HudLogic, Inc, has earned MCSE, MCSE+Internet, MCT, CCNA, and COMPTIA Network+ and A+ Certified Technician ratings. He began his technical career with the U.S. Air Force, earning medals for systems efficiency, training excellence, and national security. He has worked for Unisys, where he helped launch two Windows 95 support operations for Microsoft and Compaq, and for Productivity Point International, where he trained hundreds of computer support engineers and system administrators. Today, he writes commercial technical publications, trains computer professionals, and troubleshoots networking problems. He has authored or co-authored several publications, which are listed at **www.hudlogic.com**. You can reach Kurt via email at **kurt@hudlogic.com**.

James Michael Stewart is a full-time writer focusing on Windows NT and Internet topics. Most recently, he has worked on several titles in the *Exam Cram* and *Exam Prep* series. Michael has been developing Windows NT 4 MCSE-level courseware and training materials for several years, including both print and online publications, as well as classroom presentation of NT training materials. He has been an MCSE since 1997, with a focus on Windows NT 4. You can reach Michael by email at **michael@lanw.com**, or through his Web page at **www.lanw.com/jmsbio.htm**.

Acknowledgments

Thanks to the team at Haights-Cross, particularly Kevin McAlily, and to the whole crew at Coriolis, particularly Keith Weiskamp, Shari Jo Hehr, and Paula Kmetz, for making Exam Cram build upon its successes. Once again, we are glad for the opportunity to refresh and replenish these titles, and to add more information and value for our readers.

Many thanks are due to the people who make these books happen. On the LANWrights side, I want to thank Dawn Rader, project manager, and Mary Burmeister, project editor, for superhuman efforts to meet an insane sequence of entirely necessary deadlines. I'd also like to thank James Michael Stewart for his herculean efforts to update the content on this book and to create a battery of scenario questions and online resources. And finally, oodles of thanks to Chelsea Valentine, who has helped us to organize and manage our reading feedback and online updates to these books better than ever before.

On the Coriolis side, special thanks to all the people involved in this project, especially Sharon McCarson, who shepherded this third edition through the process, plus Kim Eoff, our production coordinator for this title. We'd also like to thank Cynthia Caldwell, Neil Gudovitz, and Gary Hull, among many others, for their efforts to make these books show up in as many places around the world as possible.

Finally, thanks to my friends and family for their support. To Robert Wiggins: Thanks for showing me that no matter how bad things get, they could always be worse! To Quge and the gang: Hang in there, relief is nigh! To Mom and Dad: Thanks for listening to me kvetch when nobody else would. And finally, to Blackie: Thanks for making me get up and walk around occasionally. It's helped me stay (relatively) sane.

—*Ed Tittel*

I would like to thank the following people for their professional contributions to this book: Julie A. Hudson, Doug Dexter, and Lori Marcinkiewicz.

—*Kurt Hudson*

Acknowledgments

Thanks to my boss and co-author, Ed Tittel, for including me in this book series. Thanks to Dawn Rader; without you, this book would never have been complete. A warm howdy to Mary Burmeister (our other work slave). To my parents, Dave and Sue: Thanks for always being there and making it clear how much you care. To Dave and Laura: Buy the $20,000 home theater and I'll camp on your couch and cook your meals! To Mark: The cult of the Pocketgods will come back to haunt you—it is already noted in your permanent record. To HERbert: Please stop digging your claws into the back of my neck while I'm asleep. And finally, as always, to Elvis—I've been looking high and low for a glittery white jumpsuit of my own, but it seems that Wal-Mart is always sold out!

—*James Michael Stewart*

Contents At A Glance

Table Of Contents

Introduction

Welcome to *MCSE NT Server 4 Exam Cram, Third Edition*! This book aims to help you get ready to take—and pass—the Microsoft certification Exam 70-067, titled "Implementing and Supporting Microsoft Windows NT Server 4.0." This introduction explains Microsoft's certification programs in general and talks about how the *Exam Cram* series can help you prepare for Microsoft's certification exams.

Exam Cram books help you understand and appreciate the subjects and materials you need to pass Microsoft certification exams. *Exam Cram* books are aimed strictly at test preparation and review. They do not teach you everything you need to know about a topic (such as the ins and outs of installing Windows NT Server 4.0, or all the nitty-gritty details involved in using Performance Monitor). Instead, we (the authors) present and dissect the questions and problems we've found that you're likely to encounter on a test. We've worked from Microsoft's own training materials, preparation guides, and tests, and from a battery of third-party test preparation tools and practice exams. Our aim is to bring together as much information as possible about Microsoft certification exams.

Nevertheless, to completely prepare yourself for any Microsoft test, we recommend that you begin by taking the Self-Assessment included in this book immediately following this Introduction. This tool will help you evaluate your knowledge base against the requirements for an MCSE under both ideal and real circumstances.

Based on what you learn from that exercise, you might decide to begin your studies with some classroom training or some background reading. On the other hand, you might decide to pick up and read one of the many study guides available from Microsoft or third-party vendors on certain topics, including The Coriolis Group's *Exam Prep* series (for which a title on Windows NT Server 4.0 is also available).

We also strongly recommend that you install, configure, and fool around with the software that you'll be tested on, because nothing beats hands-on experience and familiarity when it comes to understanding the questions you're likely to encounter on a certification test. Book learning is essential, but hands-on experience is the best teacher of all!

The Microsoft Certified Professional (MCP) Program

The MCP Program currently includes the following separate tracks, each of which boasts its own special acronym (as a would-be certificant, you need to have a high tolerance for alphabet soup of all kinds):

➤ **MCP (Microsoft Certified Professional)** This is the least prestigious of all the certification tracks from Microsoft. Passing any of the major Microsoft exams (except the Networking Essentials exam) qualifies an individual for MCP credentials. Individuals can demonstrate proficiency with additional Microsoft products by passing additional certification exams.

➤ **MCP+SB (Microsoft Certified Professional + Site Building)** This certification program is designed for individuals who are planning, building, managing, and maintaining Web sites. Individuals with the MCP+SB credential will have demonstrated the ability to develop Web sites that include multimedia and searchable content and Web sites that connect to and communicate with a back-end database. It requires one MCP exam, plus two of these three exams: "Designing and Implementing Commerce Solutions with Microsoft Site Server, 3.0, Commerce Edition," "Designing and Implementing Web Sites with Microsoft FrontPage 98," and "Designing and Implementing Web Solutions with Microsoft Visual InterDev 6.0."

➤ **MCSE (Microsoft Certified Systems Engineer)** Anyone who has a current MCSE is warranted to possess a high level of expertise with Windows NT (version 3.51 or 4.0) and other Microsoft operating systems and products. This credential is designed to prepare individuals to plan, implement, maintain, and support information systems and networks built around Microsoft Windows NT and its BackOffice family of products.

To obtain an MCSE, an individual must pass four core operating system exams, plus two elective exams. The operating system exams require individuals to prove their competence with desktop and server operating systems and networking components.

You must pass at least two Windows NT-related exams to obtain an MCSE: "Implementing and Supporting Microsoft Windows NT Server" (version 3.51 or 4.0) and "Implementing and Supporting Microsoft Windows NT Server in the Enterprise" (version 3.51 or 4.0). These tests demonstrate an individual's knowledge of Windows NT in smaller, simpler networks and in larger, more complex, and heterogeneous networks, respectively.

Note: The Windows NT 3.51 version will be retired by Microsoft on June 30, 2000.

You must pass two additional tests as well. These tests are related to networking and desktop operating systems. At present, the networking requirement can be satisfied only by passing the Networking Essentials test. The desktop operating system test can be satisfied by passing a Windows 95, Windows NT Workstation (the version must match the NT version for the core tests), or Windows 98 test.

The two remaining exams are electives. An elective exam may fall in any number of subject or product areas, primarily BackOffice components. However, it is also possible to test out on electives by taking advanced networking topics like "Internetworking with Microsoft TCP/IP on Microsoft Windows NT 4.0" (but the version of Windows NT must match the version for the core requirements). If you're on your way to becoming an MCSE and have already taken some exams, visit **www.microsoft.com/mcp/certstep/mcse.htm** for information about how to complete your MCSE certification.

In September 1999, Microsoft announced its Windows 2000 track for MCSE, and also announced retirement of Windows NT 4.0 MCSE core exams on 12/31/2000. Individuals who wish to remain certified MCSEs after 12/31/2001 must "upgrade" their certifications on or before 12/31/2001. The details are too complex to discuss here; to obtain those details, visit **www.microsoft.com/mcp/certstep/mcse.htm**.

Whatever mix of tests is completed toward MCSE certification, individuals must pass six tests to meet the MCSE requirements. It's not uncommon for the entire process to take a year or so, and many individuals find that they must take a test more than once to pass. Our primary goal with the *Exam Cram* series is to make it possible, given proper study and preparation, to pass all Microsoft certification tests on the first try. Table 1 shows the required and elective exams for the MCSE certification.

➤ **MCSD (Microsoft Certified Solution Developer)** The MCSD credential reflects the skills required to create multitier, distributed, and COM-based solutions, in addition to desktop and Internet applications, using new technologies. To obtain an MCSD, an individual must demonstrate the ability to analyze and interpret user requirements; select and integrate products, platforms, tools, and technologies; design and implement code and customize applications; and perform necessary software tests and quality assurance operations.

Table 1   MCSE Requirements*

Core

All 3 of these are required	
Exam 70-067	Implementing and Supporting Microsoft Windows NT Server 4.0
Exam 70-068	Implementing and Supporting Microsoft Windows NT Server 4.0 in the Enterprise
Exam 70-058	Networking Essentials
Choose 1 from this group	
Exam 70-064	Implementing and Supporting Microsoft Windows 95
Exam 70-073	Implementing and Supporting Microsoft Windows NT Workstation 4.0
Exam 70-098	Implementing and Supporting Microsoft Windows 98

Elective

Choose 2 from this group	
Exam 70-088	Implementing and Supporting Microsoft Proxy Server 2.0
Exam 70-079	Implementing and Supporting Microsoft Internet Explorer 4.0 by Using the Internet Explorer Administration Kit
Exam 70-087	Implementing and Supporting Microsoft Internet Information Server 4.0
Exam 70-081	Implementing and Supporting Microsoft Exchange Server 5.5
Exam 70-059	Internetworking with Microsoft TCP/IP on Microsoft Windows NT 4.0
Exam 70-028	Administering Microsoft SQL Server 7.0
Exam 70-029	Designing and Implementing Databases on Microsoft SQL Server 7.0
Exam 70-056	Implementing and Supporting Web Sites Using Microsoft Site Server 3.0
Exam 70-086	Implementing and Supporting Microsoft Systems Management Server 2.0
Exam 70-085	Implementing and Supporting Microsoft SNA Server 4.0

* This is not a complete listing—you can still be tested on some earlier versions of these products. However, we have included mainly the most recent versions so that you may test on these versions and thus be certified longer. We have not included any tests that are scheduled to be retired.

To become an MCSD, you must pass a total of four exams: three core exams and one elective exam. Each candidate must also choose one of these three desktop application exams—"70-016: Designing and Implementing Desktop Applications with Microsoft Visual C++ 6.0," "70-156: Designing and Implementing Visual FoxPro 6.0," or "70-176: Designing and Implementing Visual Basic 6.0"—*plus* one of these three distributed application exams—"70-015: Designing and Implementing Distributed Applications with Microsoft Visual C++ 6.0," "70-155: Designing and Implementing Visual FoxPro 6.0," or "70:175: Designing and Implementing Visual Basic 6.0." The third core exam is "70-100: Analyzing Requirements and Defining Solution Architectures."

Elective exams cover specific Microsoft applications and languages, including Visual Basic, C++, the Microsoft Foundation Classes, Access, SQL Server, Excel, and more.

➤ **MCDBA (Microsoft Certified Database Administrator)** The MCDBA credential reflects the skills required to implement and administer Microsoft SQL Server databases. To obtain an MCDBA, an individual must demonstrate the ability to derive physical database designs, develop logical data models, create physical databases, create data services by using Transact-SQL, manage and maintain databases, configure and manage security, monitor and optimize databases, and install and configure Microsoft SQL Server.

To become an MCDBA, you must pass a total of five exams: four core exams and one elective exam. The required core exams are "Administering Microsoft SQL Server 7.0," "Designing and Implementing Databases with Microsoft SQL Server 7.0," "Implementing and Supporting Microsoft Windows NT Server 4.0," and "Implementing and Supporting Microsoft Windows NT Server 4.0 in the Enterprise."

The elective exams that you can choose from cover specific uses of SQL Server and include "Designing and Implementing Distributed Applications with Visual Basic 6.0," "Designing and Implementing Distributed Applications with Visual C++ 6.0," "Designing and Implementing Data Warehouses with Microsoft SQL Server 7.0 and Microsoft Decision Support Services 1.0," and two exams that relate to NT: "Internetworking with Microsoft TCP/IP on Microsoft Windows NT 4.0" and "Implementing and Supporting Microsoft Internet Information Server 4.0".

Note that the exam covered by this book is a required core exam for the MCDBA certification. Table 2 shows the requirements for the MCDBA certification.

➤ **MCT (Microsoft Certified Trainer)** Microsoft Certified Trainers are deemed able to deliver elements of the official Microsoft curriculum, based on technical knowledge and instructional ability. Thus, it is necessary for an individual seeking MCT credentials (which are granted on a course-by-course basis) to pass the related certification exam for a course and complete the official Microsoft training in the subject area, and to demonstrate an ability to teach. MCT candidates must also possess a current MCSE.

This teaching skills criterion may be satisfied by proving that one has already attained training certification from Novell, Banyan, Lotus, the Santa Cruz Operation, or Cisco, or by taking a Microsoft-sanctioned workshop on instruction. Microsoft makes it clear that MCTs are important cogs in the Microsoft training channels. Instructors must be MCTs before Microsoft will allow them to teach in any of its official

Table 2 MCDBA Requirements

Core

All 4 of these are required	
Exam 70-028	Administering Microsoft SQL Server 7.0
Exam 70-029	Designing and Implementing Databases with Microsoft SQL Server 7.0
Exam 70-067	Implementing and Supporting Microsoft Windows NT Server 4.0
Exam 70-068	Implementing and Supporting Microsoft Windows NT Server 4.0 in the Enterprise

Elective

Choose 1 from this group	
Exam 70-015	Designing and Implementing Distributed Applications with Microsoft Visual C++ 6.0
Exam 70-019	Designing and Implementing Data Warehouses with Microsoft SQL Server 7.0 and Microsoft Decision Support Services 1.0
Exam 70-059	Internetworking with Microsoft TCP/IP on Microsoft Windows NT 4.0
Exam 70-087	Implementing and Supporting Microsoft Internet Information Server 4.0
Exam 70-175	Designing and Implementing Distributed Applications with Microsoft Visual Basic 6.0

training channels, including Microsoft's affiliated Certified Technical Education Centers (CTECs) and its online training partner network.

Microsoft has announced that the MCP+I and MCSE+I credentials will not be continued when the MCSE exams for Windows 2000 are in full swing because the skill set for the Internet portion of the program has been included in the new MCSE program. Therefore, details on these tracks are not provided here; go to **www.microsoft.com/train_cert/** if you need more information.

Once a Microsoft product becomes obsolete, MCPs typically have 12 to 18 months in which to recertify on current versions. (If individuals do not recertify within the specified time period, their certifications become invalid.) Because technology keeps changing and new products continually supplant old ones, this should come as no surprise. This explains why Microsoft has announced that MCSEs have 12 months past the scheduled retirement date for the Windows NT 4.0 exams to recertify on Windows 2000 topics. (Note that this means taking at least two exams, if not more.)

The best place to keep tabs on the MCP Program and related certifications is on the Web. The URL for the MCP program is **www.microsoft.com/mcp/ certstep/mcps.htm**. But Microsoft's Web site changes often, so if this URL doesn't work, try using the Search tool on Microsoft's site with either "MCP" or the quoted phrase "Microsoft Certified Professional Program" as a search string. This will help you find the latest and most accurate information about Microsoft's certification programs.

Taking A Certification Exam

Alas, testing is not free. Each computer-based MCP exam costs $100, and if you don't pass, you may retest for an additional $100 for each additional try. In the United States and Canada, tests are administered by Sylvan Prometric and by Virtual University Enterprises (VUE). Here's how you can contact them:

➤ **Sylvan Prometric** Sign up for a test through the company's Web site at **www.slspro.com**. Or, register by phone at 800-755-3926 (within the United States or Canada) or at 410-843-8000 (outside the United States and Canada).

➤ **Virtual University Enterprises** Sign up for a test or get the phone numbers for local testing centers through the Web page at **www.microsoft.com/train_cert/mcp/vue_info.htm**.

To sign up for a test, you must have a valid credit card, or contact either company for mailing instructions to send them a check (in the U.S.). Only when payment is verified, or a check has cleared, can you actually register for a test.

To schedule an exam, call the number or visit either of the Web pages at least one day in advance. To cancel or reschedule an exam, you must call before 7 P.M. Pacific Standard Time the day before the scheduled test time (or you may be charged, even if you don't appear to take the test). When you want to schedule a test, have the following information ready:

➤ Your name, organization, and mailing address.

➤ Your Microsoft Test ID. (Inside the United States, this means your Social Security number; citizens of other nations should call ahead to find out what type of identification number is required to register for a test.)

➤ The name and number of the exam you wish to take.

➤ A method of payment. (As we've already mentioned, a credit card is the most convenient method, but alternate means can be arranged in advance, if necessary.)

Once you sign up for a test, you'll be informed as to when and where the test is scheduled. Try to arrive at least 15 minutes early. You must supply two forms of identification—one of which must be a photo ID—to be admitted into the testing room.

All exams are completely closed-book. In fact, you will not be permitted to take anything with you into the testing area, but you will be furnished with a blank sheet of paper and a pen or, in some cases, an erasable plastic sheet and an erasable pen. We suggest that you immediately write down on that sheet of paper all the information you've memorized for the test. In *Exam Cram* books, this information appears on a tear-out sheet inside the front cover of each book. You will have some time to compose yourself, to record this information, and take a sample orientation exam before you begin the real thing. We suggest you take the orientation test before taking your first exam, but because they're all more or less identical in layout, behavior, and controls, you probably won't need to do this more than once.

When you complete a Microsoft certification exam, the software will tell you whether you've passed or failed. Results are broken into several topic areas. Even if you fail, we suggest you ask for—and keep—the detailed report that the test administrator should print for you. You can use this report to help you prepare for another go-round, if needed.

If you need to retake an exam, you'll have to schedule a new test with Sylvan Prometric or VUE and pay another $100.

 The first time you fail a test, you can retake the test the next day. However, if you fail a second time, you must wait 14 days before retaking that test. The 14-day waiting period remains in effect for all retakes after the first failure.

Tracking MCP Status

As soon as you pass any Microsoft exam other than Networking Essentials, you'll attain Microsoft Certified Professional (MCP) status. Microsoft also generates transcripts that indicate which exams you have passed and your corresponding test scores. You can order a transcript by email at any time by sending an email to **mcp@msprograms.com**. The address for the official MCP site is **www.microsoft.com/mcp**. This site allows registered MCPs to download and print their transcripts.

Once you pass the necessary set of exams (one for MCP or six for MCSE), you'll be certified. Official certification normally takes anywhere from four to six weeks, so don't expect to get your credentials overnight. When the package for a qualified certification arrives, it includes a Welcome Kit that contains a number of elements:

➤ An MCP or MCSE certificate, suitable for framing, along with a Professional Program Membership card and lapel pin.

➤ A license to use the MCP logo, thereby allowing you to use the logo in advertisements, promotions, and documents, and on letterhead, business cards, and so on. Along with the license comes an MCP logo sheet, which includes camera-ready artwork. (Note: Before using any of the artwork, individuals must sign and return a licensing agreement that indicates they'll abide by its terms and conditions.)

➤ A subscription to *Microsoft Certified Professional Magazine*, which provides ongoing data about testing and certification activities, requirements, and changes to the program.

➤ A one-year subscription to the Microsoft Beta Evaluation program. This subscription will get you all beta products from Microsoft for the next year. (This does not include developer products. You must join the MSDN program or become an MCSD to qualify for developer beta products.)

Many people believe that the benefits of MCP certification go well beyond the perks that Microsoft provides to newly anointed members of this elite group. We're starting to see more job listings that request or require applicants to have an MCP, MCSE, and so on, and many individuals who complete the program can qualify for increases in pay and/or responsibility. As an official recognition of hard work and broad knowledge, one of the MCP credentials is a badge of honor in many IT organizations.

How To Prepare For An Exam

Preparing for any Windows NT Server-related test (including Windows NT Server 4.0) requires that you obtain and study materials designed to provide comprehensive information about the product and its capabilities that will appear on the specific exam for which you are preparing. The following list of materials will help you study and prepare:

➤ The Windows NT Server 4.0 product CD includes comprehensive online documentation and related materials; it should be a primary resource when you are preparing for the test.

➤ Microsoft offers a Resource Kit for Windows NT Server 4.0 (and supplements). It comes in two forms: a book/CD combination product from Microsoft Press, or an electronic version that's included with the

TechNet CDs. It's a "must-have" resource when preparing for this exam. We provide more details on the ResKit, as it's affectionately known, later in this and other chapters.

➤ The exam prep materials, practice tests, and self-assessment exams on the Microsoft Training And Certification Download page (**www.microsoft. com/train_cert/download/downld.htm**). Find the materials, download them, and use them!

In addition, you'll probably find any or all of the following materials useful in your quest for Windows NT 4.0 expertise:

➤ **Microsoft Training Kits** Microsoft Press includes coverage of Windows NT Server 4.0 in several training kits. For more information, visit: **http://mspress.microsoft.com/prod/books/1046.htm** and **http://mspress.microsoft.com/prod/books/1047.htm**. These training kits contain information that you will find useful in preparing for the test.

➤ **Microsoft TechNet CD** This monthly CD-based publication delivers numerous electronic titles on Windows NT 4.0 on the Technical Information (TechNet) CD. Its offerings include product facts, technical notes, tools and utilities, and information on how to access the Seminars Online training materials for Windows NT 4.0. A subscription to TechNet costs $299 per year, but it is well worth the price. Visit **www.microsoft.com/technet/** and check out the information under the "TechNet Subscription" menu entry for more details.

➤ **Study Guides** Several publishers—including Certification Insider Press—offer Windows NT Server 4.0 titles. The Certification Insider Press series includes:

➤ The *Exam Cram* series These books give you information about the material you need to know to pass the tests.

➤ The *Exam Prep* series These books provide a greater level of detail than the *Exam Cram* books and are designed to teach you every-thing you need to know from an exam perspective. *MCSE Windows NT Server 4 Exam Prep* is the perfect learning companion to prepare you for Exam 70-067, "Implementing and Supporting Microsoft Windows NT Server 4.0." Look for this book in your favorite bookstores.

Together, the two series make a perfect pair.

➤ **Multimedia** These Coriolis Group materials are designed to support learners of all types—whether you learn best by listening, reading, or doing:

➤ *Practice Tests Exam Cram* series Provides the most valuable test preparation material: practice exams. Each exam is followed by a complete set of answers, as well as explanations of why the right answers are right and the wrong answers are wrong. Each book comes with a CD that contains one or more interactive practice exams.

➤ *Exam Cram Flash Card* series Offers practice questions on handy cards you can use anywhere. The question and its possible answers appear on the front of the card, and the answer, explanation, and a valuable reference appear on the back of the card. The set also includes a CD with an electronic practice exam to give you the feel of the actual test—and more practice!

➤ *Exam Cram Audio Review* series Offers a concise review of key topics covered on the exam, as well as practice questions.

➤ **Classroom Training** CTECs, online partners, and unlicensed training companies (like Wave Technologies, American Research Group, Learning Tree, Data-Tech, and others) all offer classroom training on Windows NT Server 4.0. These companies aim to help you prepare to pass the Windows NT Server test. Although such training runs upwards of $350 per day in class, most of the individuals lucky enough to partake (including your humble authors, who've even taught such courses) find them to be quite worthwhile.

➤ **Other Publications** You'll find direct references to other publications and resources in this book, but there's no shortage of materials available about Windows NT Server 4.0. To help you sift through some of the publications out there, we end each chapter with a "Need To Know More?" section that provides pointers to more complete and exhaustive resources covering the chapter's information. This should give you an idea of where we think you should look for further discussion.

By far, this set of required and recommended materials represents a nonpareil collection of sources and resources for Windows NT Server 4.0 and related topics. We anticipate that you'll find that this book belongs in this company. In the section that follows, we explain how this book works, and we give you some good reasons why this book counts as a member of the required and recommended materials list.

About This Book

Each topical *Exam Cram* chapter follows a regular structure, along with graphical cues about important or useful information. Here's the structure of a typical chapter:

➤ **Opening Hotlists** Each chapter begins with a list of the terms, tools, and techniques that you must learn and understand before you can be fully con-versant with that chapter's subject matter. We follow the hotlists with one or two introductory paragraphs to set the stage for the rest of the chapter.

➤ **Topical Coverage** After the opening hotlists, each chapter covers a series of topics related to the chapter's subject title. Throughout this section, we highlight topics or concepts likely to appear on a test using a special Exam Alert layout, like this:

 This is what an Exam Alert looks like. Normally, an Exam Alert stresses concepts, terms, software, or activities that are likely to relate to one or more certification test questions. For that reason, we think any information found offset in Exam Alert format is worthy of unusual attentiveness on your part. Indeed, most of the information that appears on The Cram Sheet appears as Exam Alerts within the text.

Pay close attention to material flagged as an Exam Alert; although all the information in this book pertains to what you need to know to pass the exam, we flag certain items that are really important. You'll find what appears in the meat of each chapter to be worth knowing, too, when preparing for the test. Because this book's material is very con-densed, we recommend that you use this book along with other re-sources to achieve the maximum benefit.

In addition to the Exam Alerts, we have provided tips that will help you build a better foundation for Windows NT Server knowledge. Although the information may not be on the exam, it is certainly related and will help you become a better test-taker.

 This is how tips are formatted. Keep your eyes open for these, and you'll become a Windows NT Server guru in no time!

➤ **Practice Questions** Although we talk about test questions and topics throughout each chapter, this section presents a series of mock test questions and explanations of both correct and incorrect answers. We also try to point out especially tricky questions by using a special icon, like this:

Ordinarily, this icon flags the presence of a particularly devious inquiry, if not an outright trick question.

Trick questions are calculated to be answered incorrectly if not read more than once, and carefully, at that. Although they're not ubiquitous, such questions make regular appearances on the Microsoft exams. That's why we say exam questions are as much about reading comprehension as they are about knowing your material inside out and backwards.

➤ **Details And Resources** Every chapter ends with a section titled "Need To Know More?". This section provides direct pointers to Microsoft and third-party resources offering more details on the chapter's subject. In addition, this section tries to rank or at least rate the quality and thoroughness of the topic's coverage by each resource. If you find a resource you like in this collection, use it, but don't feel compelled to use all the resources. On the other hand, we recommend only resources we use on a regular basis, so none of our recommendations will be a waste of your time or money (but purchasing them all at once probably represents an expense that many network administrators and would-be MCPs and MCSEs might find hard to justify).

➤ Your authors have also prepared adaptive exams for NT Server 4 that are available online. To take these practice exams, which should help you prepare even better for the real thing, visit **www.coriolis.com/cip/ core4rev/**, follow the instructions from there, and pick the Windows NT Server 4 book.

The bulk of the book follows this chapter structure slavishly, but there are a few other elements that we'd like to point out. Chapters 14 and 16 each contain a sample test that provides a good review of the material presented throughout the book to ensure you're ready for the exam. Chapters 15 and 17 contain answer keys to the sample tests that appear in Chapters 14 and 16, respectively.

Following the sample tests is the Scenarios section, which gives you extra practice answering real-world questions of the type frequently found on Microsoft exams. And after that, the Online Resources section points you to some useful certification Web sites.

Additionally, you'll find the Glossary, which explains terms, and an index that you can use to track down terms as they appear in the text.

Finally, the tear-out Cram Sheet attached next to the inside front cover of this *Exam Cram* book represents a condensed and compiled collection of facts and tips that we think you should memorize before taking the test. Because you can dump this information out of your head onto a piece of paper before taking the exam, you can master this information by brute force—you need to remember it only long enough to write it down when you walk into the test room. You might even want to look at it in the car or in the lobby of the testing center just before you walk in to take the test.

How To Use This Book

If you're prepping for a first-time test, we've structured the topics in this book to build on one another. Therefore, some topics in later chapters make more sense after you've read earlier chapters. That's why we suggest you read this book from front to back for your initial test preparation. If you need to brush up on a topic or you have to bone up for a second try, use the index or table of contents to go straight to the topics and questions that you need to study. Beyond helping you prepare for the test, we think you'll find this book useful as a tightly focused reference to some of the most important aspects of Windows NT Server 4.0.

Given all the book's elements and its specialized focus, we've tried to create a tool that will help you prepare for—and pass—Microsoft Exam 70-067, "Implementing and Supporting Microsoft Windows NT Server 4.0." Please share your feedback on the book with us, especially if you have ideas about how we can improve it for future test-takers. We'll consider everything you say carefully, and we'll respond to all suggestions.

Send your questions or comments to us at **cipq@coriolis.com**. Our series editor, Ed Tittel, coordinates our efforts and ensures that all questions get answered. Please remember to include the title of the book in your message; otherwise, we'll be forced to guess which book you're writing about. And we don't like to guess—we want to *know*! Also, be sure to check out **www.certificationinsider.com** where you'll find information updates, commentary, and certification information.

Thanks, and enjoy the book!

Self-Assessment

Based on recent statistics from Microsoft, as many as 400,000 individuals are at some stage of the certification process but haven't yet received an MCP or other Microsoft certification. We also know that three or four times that number may be considering whether or not to obtain a Microsoft certification of some kind. That's a huge audience!

The reason we included a Self-Assessment in this *Exam Cram* book is to help you evaluate your readiness to tackle MCSE certification. It should also help you understand what you need to know to master the topic of this book—namely, Exam 70-067, "Implementing and Supporting Microsoft Windows NT Server 4.0." But before you tackle this Self-Assessment, let's talk about concerns you may face when pursuing an MCSE, and what an ideal MCSE candidate might look like.

MCSEs In The Real World

In the next section, we describe an ideal MCSE candidate, knowing full well that only a few real candidates will meet this ideal. In fact, our description of that ideal candidate might seem downright scary. But take heart: Although the requirements to obtain an MCSE may seem formidable, they are by no means impossible to meet. However, be keenly aware that it does take time, involves some expense, and requires real effort to get through the process.

More than 200,000 MCSEs are already certified, so it's obviously an attainable goal. You can get all the real-world motivation you need from knowing that many others have gone before, so you will be able to follow in their footsteps. If you're willing to tackle the process seriously and do what it takes to obtain the necessary experience and knowledge, you can take—and pass—all the certification tests involved in obtaining an MCSE. In fact, we've designed these *Exam Crams*, and the companion *Exam Preps*, to make it as easy on you as possible to prepare for these exams. But prepare you must!

The same, of course, is true for other Microsoft certifications, including:

➤ MCSD, which is aimed at software developers and requires one specific exam, two more exams on client and distributed topics, plus a fourth elective exam drawn from a different, but limited, pool of options.

➤ Other Microsoft certifications, whose requirements range from one test (MCP or MCT) to several tests (MCP+SB, MCDBA).

The Ideal MCSE Candidate

Just to give you some idea of what an ideal MCSE candidate is like, here are some relevant statistics about the background and experience such an individual might have. Don't worry if you don't meet these qualifications, or don't come that close—this is a far from ideal world, and where you fall short is simply where you'll have more work to do.

➤ Academic or professional training in network theory, concepts, and operations. This includes everything from networking media and transmission techniques through network operating systems, services, and applications.

➤ Three-plus years of professional networking experience, including experience with Ethernet, token ring, modems, and other networking media. This must include installation, configuration, upgrade, and troubleshooting experience.

➤ Two-plus years in a networked environment that includes hands-on experience with Windows NT Server, Windows NT Workstation, and Windows 95 or Windows 98. A solid understanding of each system's architecture, installation, configuration, maintenance, and troubleshooting is also essential.

➤ A thorough understanding of key networking protocols, addressing, and name resolution, including TCP/IP, IPX/SPX, and NetBEUI.

➤ A thorough understanding of NetBIOS naming, browsing, and file and print services.

➤ Familiarity with key Windows NT-based TCP/IP-based services, including HTTP (Web servers), DHCP, WINS, DNS, plus familiarity with one or more of the following: Internet Information Server (IIS), Index Server, and Proxy Server.

➤ Working knowledge of NetWare 3.x and 4.x, including IPX/SPX frame formats, NetWare file, print, and directory services, and both Novell and

Microsoft client software. Working knowledge of Microsoft's Client Service For NetWare (CSNW), Gateway Service For NetWare (GSNW), the NetWare Migration Tool (NWCONV), and the NetWare Client For Windows (NT, 95, and 98) is essential.

Fundamentally, this boils down to a bachelor's degree in computer science, plus three years' experience working in a position involving network design, installation, configuration, and maintenance. We believe that well under half of all certification candidates meet these requirements, and that, in fact, most aspiring candidates meet less than half of these requirements—at least, when they begin the certification process. But because all 200,000 people who already have been certified have survived this ordeal, you can survive it too—especially if you heed what our Self-Assessment can tell you about what you already know and what you need to learn.

Put Yourself To The Test

The following series of questions and observations is designed to help you figure out how much work you must do to pursue Microsoft certification and what kinds of resources you may consult on your quest. Be absolutely honest in your answers, or you'll end up wasting money on exams you're not yet ready to take. There are no right or wrong answers, only steps along the path to certification. Only you can decide where you really belong in the broad spectrum of aspiring candidates.

Two things should be clear from the outset, however:

➤ Even a modest background in computer science will be helpful.

➤ Hands-on experience with Microsoft products and technologies is an essential ingredient to certification success.

Educational Background

1. Have you ever taken any computer-related classes? [Yes or No]

   If Yes, proceed to question 2; if No, proceed to question 4.

2. Have you taken any classes on computer operating systems? [Yes or No]

   If Yes, you will probably be able to handle Microsoft's architecture and system component discussions. If you're rusty, brush up on basic operating system concepts, especially virtual memory, multitasking regimes, user mode versus kernel mode operation, and general computer security topics.

If No, consider some basic reading in this area. We strongly recommend a good general operating systems book, such as *Operating System Concepts*, by Abraham Silberschatz and Peter Baer Galvin (Addison-Wesley, 1997, ISBN 0-201-59113-8). If this title doesn't appeal to you, check out reviews for other, similar titles at your favorite online bookstore.

3. Have you taken any networking concepts or technologies classes? [Yes or No]

If Yes, you will probably be able to handle Microsoft's networking terminology, concepts, and technologies (brace yourself for frequent departures from normal usage). If you're rusty, brush up on basic networking concepts and terminology, especially networking media, transmission types, the OSI Reference Model, and networking technologies such as Ethernet, token ring, FDDI, and WAN links.

If No, you might want to read one or two books in this topic area. The two best books that we know of are *Computer Networks*, *3rd Edition*, by Andrew S. Tanenbaum (Prentice-Hall, 1996, ISBN 0-13-349945-6) and *Computer Networks and Internets*, by Douglas E. Comer (Prentice-Hall, 1997, ISBN 0-13-239070-1).

Skip to the next section, "Hands-On Experience."

4. Have you done any reading on operating systems or networks? [Yes or No]

If Yes, review the requirements stated in the first paragraphs after questions 2 and 3. If you meet those requirements, move on to the next section. If No, consult the recommended reading for both topics. A strong background will help you prepare for the Microsoft exams better than just about anything else.

Hands-On Experience

The most important key to success on all of the Microsoft tests is hands-on experience, especially with Windows NT Server and Workstation, plus the many add-on services and BackOffice components around which so many of the Microsoft certification exams revolve. If we leave you with only one realization after taking this Self-Assessment, it should be that there's no substitute for time spent installing, configuring, and using the various Microsoft products upon which you'll be tested repeatedly and in-depth.

5. Have you installed, configured, and worked with:

   ➤ Windows NT Server? [Yes or No]

If Yes, make sure you understand basic concepts as covered in Exam 70067 and advanced concepts as covered in Exam 70-068. You should also study the TCP/IP interfaces, utilities, and services for this test, Exam 70-059, plus Internet Information Server capabilities for Exam 70-087.

You can download objectives, practice exams, and other data about Microsoft exams from the Training and Certification Web page at **www.microsoft.com/train_cert/**. Use the "Find an Exam" link to obtain specific exam info.

If you haven't worked with Windows NT Server, TCP/IP, and IIS (or whatever product you choose for your final elective), you must obtain one or two machines and a copy of Windows NT Server. Then, learn the operating system, and do the same for TCP/IP and whatever other software components on which you'll also be tested.

In fact, we recommend that you obtain two computers, each with a network interface, and set up a two-node network on which to practice. With decent Windows NT-capable computers selling for about $500 to $600 apiece these days, this shouldn't be too much of a financial hardship. You may have to scrounge to come up with the necessary software, but if you scour the Microsoft Web site you can usually find low-cost options to obtain evaluation copies of most of the software that you'll need.

➤ Windows NT Workstation? [Yes or No]

If Yes, make sure you understand the concepts covered in Exam 70-073.

If No, you will want to obtain a copy of Windows NT Workstation and learn how to install, configure, and maintain it. You can use *MCSE NT Workstation 4 Exam Cram* to guide your activities and studies, or work straight from Microsoft's test objectives if you prefer.

For any and all of these Microsoft exams, the Resource Kits for the topics involved are a good study resource. You can purchase softcover Resource Kits from Microsoft Press (search for them at **http://mspress.microsoft.com/**), but they also appear on the TechNet CDs (**www.microsoft.com/technet**). We believe that Resource Kits are among the best preparation tools available, along with the *Exam Crams* and *Exam Preps*, that you can use to get ready for Microsoft exams.

You have the option of taking the Window 95 (70-064) exam or the Windows 98 (70-098) exam, instead of Exam 70-073, to fulfill your desktop operating system requirement for the MCSE. Although we don't recommend these others (because studying for Workstation helps you prepare for the Server exams), we do recommend that you obtain Resource Kits and other tools to help you prepare for those exams if you decide to take one or both of them for your own reasons.

6. For any specific Microsoft product that is not itself an operating system (for example, FrontPage 98, SQL Server, and so on), have you installed, configured, used, and upgraded this software? [Yes or No]

If the answer is Yes, skip to the next section. If it's No, you must get some experience. Read on for suggestions on how to do this.

Experience is a must with any Microsoft product exam, be it something as simple as FrontPage 98 or as challenging as Exchange Server 5.5 or SQL Server 7.0. For trial copies of other software, search Microsoft's Web site using the name of the product as your search term. Also search for bundles like "BackOffice" or "Small Business Server."

 If you have the funds, or your employer will pay your way, consider taking a class at a Certified Training and Education Center (CTEC) or at an Authorized Academic Training Partner (AATP). In addition to classroom exposure to the topic of your choice, you get a copy of the software that is the focus of your course, along with a trial version of whatever operating system it needs (usually, NT Server), with the training materials for that class.

Before you even think about taking any Microsoft exam, make sure you've spent enough time with the related software to understand how it may be installed and configured, how to maintain such an installation, and how to troubleshoot that software when things go wrong. This will help you in the exam, and in real life!

Testing Your Exam-Readiness

Whether you attend a formal class on a specific topic to get ready for an exam or use written materials to study on your own, some preparation for the Microsoft certification exams is essential. At $100 a try, pass or fail, you want to do everything you can to pass on your first try. That's where studying comes in.

We have included two practice exams in this book, so if you don't score that well on the first test, you can study more and then tackle the second test. We also have built adaptive exams that you can take online through the Coriolis Web site at **www.coriolis.com/cip/core4rev/**. If you still don't hit a score of at least 70 percent after these tests, you'll want to investigate the other practice test resources we mention in this section.

For any given subject, consider taking a class if you've tackled self-study materials, taken the test, and failed anyway. The opportunity to interact with an instructor and fellow students can make all the difference in the world, if you can afford that privilege. For information about Microsoft classes, visit the Training and Certification page at **www.microsoft.com/train_cert/** (use the "Find a Course" link).

If you can't afford to take a class, visit the Training and Certification page anyway, because it also includes pointers to free practice exams and to Microsoft Certified Professional Approved Study Guides and other self-study tools. And even if you can't afford to spend much at all, you should still invest in some low-cost practice exams from commercial vendors, because they can help you assess your readiness to pass a test better than any other tool. All of the following Web sites offer practice exams online for less than $100 apiece (some for significantly less than that):

➤ Beachfront Quizzer at **www.bfq.com/**

➤ Hardcore MCSE at **www.hardcoremcse.com/**

➤ LANWrights at **www.lanw.com/books/examcram/order.htm**

➤ MeasureUp at **www.measureup.com/**

7. Have you taken a practice exam on your chosen test subject? [Yes or No]

   If Yes, and you scored 70 percent or better, you're probably ready to tackle the real thing. If your score isn't above that threshold, keep at it until you break that barrier.

   If No, obtain all the free and low-budget practice tests you can find (see the list above) and get to work. Keep at it until you can break the passing threshold comfortably.

When it comes to assessing your test readiness, there is no better way than to take a good-quality practice exam and pass with a score of 70 percent or better. When we're preparing ourselves, we shoot for 80-plus percent, just to leave room for the "weirdness factor" that sometimes shows up on Microsoft exams.

Assessing Readiness
For Exam 70-067

In addition to the general exam-readiness information in the previous section, there are several things you can do to prepare for the "Implementing and Supporting Microsoft Windows NT 4.0" exam. As you're getting ready for Exam 70-067, visit the MCSE mailing list. Sign up at **www.sunbelt-software.com** (look for the "Subscribe to…" button). You will find a great source of questions and related information at the CramSession site at **www.cramsession.com**. These are great places to ask questions and get good answers, or simply to watch the questions that others ask (along with the answers, of course).

You should also cruise the Web looking for "braindumps" (recollections of test topics and experiences recorded by others) to help you anticipate topics you're likely to encounter on the test. The MCSE mailing list is a good place to ask where the useful braindumps are, or you can check Shawn Gamble's list at **www.commandcentral.com** (he's also got some peachy—and free—practice tests on this subject) or Herb Martin's Braindump Heaven at **http://209.207.167.177/**.

 You can't be sure that a braindump's author can provide correct answers. Thus, use the questions to guide your studies, but don't rely on the answers in a braindump to lead you to the truth. Double-check everything you find in any braindump.

Microsoft exam mavens also recommend checking the Microsoft Knowledge Base (available on its own CD as part of the TechNet collection, or on the Microsoft Web site at **http://support.microsoft.com/support/**) for "meaningful technical support issues" that relate to Windows NT Server. Although we're not sure exactly what the quoted phrase means, we have also noticed some overlap between technical support questions on particular products and troubleshooting questions on the exams for those products.

As you review the material for Exam 70-067, you'll realize that hands-on experience with Windows NT Server 4.0 is not only invaluable, it's absolutely essential. You must be familiar with installing this operating system, configuring protocols, using Performance Monitor and Network Monitor, working with users, groups, and trust relationships, and so forth. In short, the more time you spend with the product, the better you'll do when you take the test!

Onward, Through The Fog!

Once you've assessed your readiness, undertaken the right background studies, obtained the hands-on experience that will help you understand the products and technologies at work, and reviewed the many sources of information to help you prepare for a test, you'll be ready to take a round of practice tests. When your scores come back positive enough to get you through the exam, you're ready to go after the real thing. If you follow our assessment regime, you'll not only know what you need to study, but when you're ready to make a test date at Sylvan or VUE. Good luck!

Microsoft Certification Exams

Terms you'll need to understand:

√ Radio button

√ Checkbox

√ Exhibit

√ Multiple-choice question formats

√ Careful reading

√ Process of elimination

√ Fixed-length tests

√ Adaptive tests

√ Short-form tests

√ Combination tests

√ Simulations

Techniques you'll need to master:

√ Assessing exam-readiness

√ Preparing to take a certification exam

√ Practicing (to make perfect)

√ Making the best use of the testing software

√ Budgeting your time

√ Guessing (as a last resort)

Exam taking is not something that most people anticipate eagerly, no matter how well prepared they may be. In most cases, familiarity helps offset test anxiety. In plain English, this means you probably won't be as nervous when you take your fourth or fifth Microsoft certification exam as you'll be when you take your first one.

Whether it's your first exam or your tenth, understanding the details of exam taking (how much time to spend on questions, the environment you'll be in, and so on) and the exam software will help you concentrate on the material rather than on the setting. Likewise, mastering a few basic exam-taking skills should help you recognize—and perhaps even outfox—some of the tricks and snares you're bound to find in some exam questions.

This chapter, besides explaining the exam environment and software, describes some proven exam-taking strategies that you should be able to use to your advantage.

Assessing Exam-Readiness

Before you take any more Microsoft exams, we strongly recommend that you read through and take the Self-Assessment included with this book (it appears just before this chapter, in fact). This will help you compare your knowledge base to the requirements for obtaining an MCSE, and it will also help you identify parts of your background or experience that may be in need of improvement, enhancement, or further learning. If you get the right set of basics under your belt, obtaining Microsoft certification will be that much easier.

Once you've gone through the Self-Assessment, you can remedy those topical areas where your background or experience may not measure up to an ideal certification candidate. But you can also tackle subject matter for individual tests at the same time, so you can continue making progress while you're catching up in some areas.

Once you've worked through an *Exam Cram*, have read the supplementary materials, and have taken the practice tests, you'll have a pretty clear idea of when you should be ready to take the real exam. Although we strongly recommend that you keep practicing until your scores top the 70 percent mark, 75 percent would be a good goal to give yourself some margin for error in a real exam situation (where stress will play more of a role than when you practice). Once you hit that point, you should be ready to go. But if you get through both practice exams in this book and the sample adaptive online exam (discussed in the Self-Assessment, the Introduction, and later in this chapter) without attaining that score, you should keep taking practice tests and studying the materials until you get there. You'll find more information about other practice test vendors in the Self-Assessment, along with even more pointers on how to study and prepare. But now, on to the exam itself!

The Exam Situation

When you arrive at the testing center where you scheduled your exam, you'll need to sign in with an exam coordinator. He or she will ask you to show two forms of identification, one of which must be a photo ID. After you've signed in and your time slot arrives, you'll be asked to deposit any books, bags, or other items you brought with you. Then, you'll be escorted into a closed room. Typically, the room will be furnished with anywhere from one to half a dozen computers, and each workstation will be separated from the others by dividers designed to keep you from seeing what's happening on someone else's computer.

You'll be furnished with a pen or pencil and a blank sheet of paper, or, in some cases, an erasable plastic sheet and an erasable pen. You're allowed to write down anything you want on both sides of this sheet. Before the exam, you should memorize as much of the material that appears on The Cram Sheet (in the front of this book) as you can, so you can write that information on the blank sheet as soon as you are seated in front of the computer. You can refer to your rendition of The Cram Sheet anytime you like during the test, but you'll have to surrender the sheet when you leave the room.

Most test rooms feature a wall with a large picture window. This permits the exam coordinator to monitor the room, to prevent exam-takers from talking to one another, and to observe anything out of the ordinary that might go on. The exam coordinator will have preloaded the appropriate Microsoft certification exam—for this book, that's Exam 70-067—and you'll be permitted to start as soon as you're seated in front of the computer.

All Microsoft certification exams allow a certain maximum amount of time in which to complete your work (this time is indicated on the exam by an on-screen counter/clock, so you can check the time remaining whenever you like). All Microsoft certification exams are computer generated and most use a multiple-choice format. Although this may sound quite simple, the questions are constructed not only to check your mastery of basic facts and figures about Windows NT Server 4.0, but they also require you to evaluate one or more sets of circumstances or requirements. Often, you'll be asked to give more than one answer to a question. Likewise, you might be asked to select the best or most effective solution to a problem from a range of choices, all of which technically are correct. Taking the exam is quite an adventure, and it involves real thinking. This book shows you what to expect and how to deal with the potential problems, puzzles, and predicaments.

In the next section, you'll learn more about how Microsoft test questions look and how they must be answered.

Exam Layout And Design

Some exam questions require you to select a single answer, whereas others ask you to select one or more correct answers. The following multiple-choice question requires you to select a single correct answer. Following the question is a brief summary of each potential answer and why it is either right or wrong.

Question 1

To track the level of processor usage, which Performance Monitor object and counter should you watch?

○　a. System: Interrupts/Second

○　b. Memory: Pages/Second

○　c. Processor: %Processor Time

○　d. Processor: Interrupts/Second

The correct answer to this question is c. The object you must watch is the Processor object, and utilization is reported by the %Processor Time counter. Answers a and b are incorrect because they choose the wrong object to watch. Answer d is incorrect because it measures the number of interrupts per second that the processor handles, which does not provide a direct measure of CPU utilization as does %Processor Time.

This sample question format corresponds closely to the Microsoft certification exam format—the only difference on the exam is that questions are not followed by answer keys. To select an answer, you would position the cursor over the radio button next to the answer. Then, click the mouse button to select the answer.

Let's examine a question where one or more answers are possible. This type of question provides checkboxes rather than radio buttons for marking all appropriate selections.

Question 2

Which of the following items describe disk striping without parity? [Check all correct answers]

- ❏   a. Requires at least 3 physical drives
- ❏   b. Can be implemented with FAT
- ❏   c. Provides fault tolerance
- ❏   d. Has faster read-write performance than disk mirroring
- ❏   e. Cannot recover data if a single drive within the set fails

Answers b, d, and e are correct. Disk striping without parity can indeed be implemented with FAT (or NTFS), so answer b is correct. Disk striping without parity offers faster read-write performance than disk mirroring, so answer d is correct. Because disk striping without parity is not fault-tolerant, it cannot recover if any drive in the set fails; thus, answer e is also correct. Answer a is incorrect because disk striping without parity requires only two drives. Answer c is incorrect because the "without parity" part in its name means that disk striping without parity is not fault tolerant.

For this particular question, three answers are required. As far as the authors can tell (and Microsoft won't comment), such questions are scored as wrong unless all the required selections are chosen. In other words, a partially correct answer does not result in partial credit when the test is scored. For Question 2, you have to check the boxes next to items b, d, and e to obtain credit for a correct answer. Notice that picking the right answers also means knowing why the other answers are wrong!

Although these two basic types of questions can appear in many forms, they constitute the foundation on which all the Microsoft certification exam questions rest. More complex questions include exhibits, which are usually screenshots of some kind of network diagram or topology.

For some of these questions, you'll be asked to make a selection by clicking on a checkbox or radio button on the screenshot itself. For others, you'll be expected to use the information displayed therein to guide your answer to the question. Familiarity with the underlying utility is your key to choosing the correct answer(s).

Other questions involving exhibits use charts or network diagrams to help document a workplace scenario that you'll be asked to troubleshoot or configure. Careful attention to such exhibits is the key to success. Be prepared to toggle frequently between the exhibit and the question as you work.

Microsoft's Testing Formats

Currently, Microsoft uses four different testing formats:

➤ Fixed-length

➤ Adaptive

➤ Short-form

➤ Combination

Some Microsoft exams employ more advanced testing capabilities than might immediately meet the eye. Although the questions that appear are still multiple choice, the logic that drives them is more complex than older Microsoft tests, which use a fixed sequence of questions, called a *fixed-length test*. Other exams employ a sophisticated user interface, which Microsoft calls a *simulation*, to test your knowledge of the software and systems under consideration in a more or less "live" environment that behaves just like the original.

For some exams, Microsoft has turned to a well-known technique, called *adaptive testing*, to establish a test-taker's level of knowledge and product competence. Adaptive exams look the same as fixed-length exams, but they discover the level of difficulty at which an individual test-taker can correctly answer questions. At the same time, Microsoft is in the process of converting some of its fixed-length exams into adaptive exams as well. Test-takers with differing levels of knowledge or ability therefore see different sets of questions; individuals with high levels of knowledge or ability are presented with a smaller set of more difficult questions, whereas individuals with lower levels of knowledge are presented with a larger set of easier questions. Two individuals may answer the same percentage of questions correctly, but the test-taker with a higher knowledge or ability level will score higher because his or her questions are worth more.

Also, the lower-level test-taker will probably answer more questions than his or her more-knowledgeable colleague. This explains why adaptive tests use ranges of values to define the number of questions and the amount of time it takes to complete the test.

Adaptive tests work by evaluating the test-taker's most recent answer. A correct answer leads to a more difficult question (and the test software's estimate of the test-taker's knowledge and ability level is raised). An incorrect answer leads to a less difficult question (and the test software's estimate of the test-taker's knowledge and ability level is lowered). This process continues until the test targets the test-taker's true ability level. The exam ends when the test-taker's level of accuracy meets a statistically acceptable value (in other words, when his or her performance demonstrates an acceptable level of knowledge and ability) or when the maximum number of items has been presented (in which case, the test-taker is almost certain to fail).

Microsoft has also introduced a short-form test for its most popular tests (as of this writing, all of the Core Four exams, plus TCP/IP, can appear in this format). This test delivers 30 questions to its takers, giving them exactly 60 minutes to complete the exam. This type of exam is similar to a fixed-length test, in that it allows readers to jump ahead or return to earlier questions, and to cycle through the questions until the test is done. Microsoft does not use adaptive logic in this test, but claims that statistical analysis of the question pool is such that the 30 questions delivered during a short-form exam conclusively measure a test-taker's knowledge of the subject matter in much the same way as an adaptive test. You can think of the short-form test as a kind of "greatest hits exam" (that is, the most impor-tant questions are covered) version of an adaptive exam on the same topic.

A fourth kind of test you might encounter is what we've dubbed the com-bination exam. Several test-takers have reported that some of the Microsoft exams, including Windows NT Server (70-067), NT Server in the Enter-prise (70-068), and Windows NT Workstation (70-073), can appear as combination exams. Such exams begin with a set of 15 to 25 adaptive ques-tions, followed by 10 fixed-length questions. In fact, many test-takers have reported that although some combination tests claim that they will present both adaptive and fixed-length portions, when the test-taker finishes the adaptive portion (usually in exactly 15 questions), the test ends there. Be-cause such users have all attained passing scores, it may be that a high enough passing score on the adaptive portion of a combination test obvi-ates the fixed-length portion, but we're not completely sure about this, and Microsoft won't comment. Most combination exams allow a maximum of 60 minutes for the testing period.

Microsoft tests can come in any one of these forms. Whatever you encoun-ter, you must take the test in whichever form it appears; you can't choose one form over another. Currently, the Windows NT Server 4.0 exam may be adaptive (especially if you're taking it in a language other than English), in which case you'll have 90 minutes to answer between 15 and 30 ques-tions (on average), or short-form, in which case you'll get 60 minutes to answer exactly 30 questions. If anything, it pays more to prepare thoroughly for an adaptive or combination exam than for a fixed-length or a short-form exam: The penalties for answering incorrectly are built into the test itself on an adaptive exam or the first part of a combination exam, whereas the layout remains the same for a fixed-length or short-form test, no mat-ter how many questions you answer incorrectly.

The biggest difference between an adaptive test and a fixed-length or short-form test is that on a fixed-length or short-form test, you can revisit questions after you've read them over one or more times. On an adaptive test, you must answer the question when it's presented and will have no opportunities to revisit that question thereafter.

Strategies For Different Testing Formats

Before you choose a test-taking strategy, you must know if your test is fixed-length, short-form, adaptive, or combination. When you begin your exam, the software will tell you that the test is adaptive, if in fact the version you're taking is an adaptive test. If your introductory materials fail to mention this, you're probably taking a fixed-length test. If the total number of questions involved is exactly 30, you're taking a short-form test. Combination tests announce themselves by indicating that they will start with a set of adaptive questions, followed by fixed-length questions, but don't actually call themselves "combination tests" or "combination exams"—we've adopted this term purely for descriptive purposes.

You'll be able to tell for sure if you are taking an adaptive, fixed-length, short-form, or combination test by the first question. If it includes a checkbox that lets you mark the question for later review, you're taking a fixed-length or short-form test. If the total number of questions is 30, it's a short-form test; if more than 30, it's a fixed-length test. Adaptive test questions (and the first set of questions on a combination test) can be visited (and answered) only once, and they include no such checkbox.

The Fixed-Length And Short-Form Exam Strategy

A well-known principle when taking fixed-length or short-form exams is to first read over the entire exam from start to finish while answering only those questions you feel absolutely sure of. On subsequent passes, you can dive into more complex questions more deeply, knowing how many such questions you have left.

Fortunately, the Microsoft exam software for fixed-length and short-form tests makes the multiple-visit approach easy to implement. At the top-left corner of each question is a checkbox that permits you to mark that question for a later visit.

> *Note: Marking questions makes review easier, but you can return to any question by clicking the Forward or Back button repeatedly.*

As you read each question, if you answer only those you're sure of and mark for review those that you're not sure of, you can keep working through a decreasing list of questions as you answer the trickier ones in order.

> There's at least one potential benefit to reading the exam over completely before answering the trickier questions: Sometimes, information supplied in later questions sheds more light on earlier questions. At other times, information you read in later questions might jog your memory about Windows NT Sever facts, figures, or behavior that helps you answer earlier questions. Either way, you'll come out ahead if you defer those questions about which you're not absolutely sure.

Here are some question-handling strategies that apply to fixed-length and short-form tests. Use them if you have the chance:

➤ When returning to a question after your initial read-through, read every word again—otherwise, your mind can fall quickly into a rut. Sometimes, revisiting a question after turning your attention elsewhere lets you see something you missed, but the strong tendency is to see what you've seen before. Try to avoid that tendency at all costs.

➤ If you return to a question more than twice, try to articulate to yourself what you don't understand about the question, why answers don't appear to make sense, or what appears to be missing. If you chew on the subject awhile, your subconscious might provide the details you lack, or you might notice a "trick" that points to the right answer.

As you work your way through the exam, another counter that Microsoft provides will come in handy—the number of questions completed and questions outstanding. For fixed-length and short-form tests, it's wise to budget your time by making sure that you've completed one-quarter of the questions one-quarter of the way through the exam period. For a short-form test, as you may experience with the Windows NT Server 4.0 exam, this means you must complete one-quarter of the questions one-quarter of the way through (the first 8 questions in the first 15 minutes) and three-quarters of the questions three-quarters of the way through (24 questions in 45 minutes).

If you're not finished when only five minutes remain, use that time to guess your way through any remaining questions. Remember, guessing is potentially more valuable than not answering, because blank answers are always wrong, but a guess may turn out to be right. If you don't have a clue about any of the remaining questions, pick answers at random, or choose all a's, b's, and so on. The important thing is to submit an exam for scoring that has an answer for every question.

> **TIP** At the very end of your exam period, you're better off guessing than leaving questions unanswered.

The Adaptive Exam Strategy

If there's one principle that applies to taking an adaptive test, it could be summed up as "Get it right the first time." You cannot elect to skip a question and move on to the next one when taking an adaptive test, because the testing software uses your answer to the current question to select whatever question it plans to present next. Nor can you return to a question once you've moved on, because the software gives you only one chance to answer the question. You can, however, take notes, because sometimes information supplied in earlier questions will shed more light on later questions.

Also, when you answer a question correctly, you are presented with a more difficult question next, to help the software gauge your level of skill and ability. When you answer a question incorrectly, you are presented with a less difficult question, and the software lowers its current estimate of your skill and ability. This continues until the program settles into a reasonably accurate estimate of what you know and can do, and takes you on average through somewhere between 15 and 30 questions as you complete the test.

The good news is that if you know your stuff, you'll probably finish most adaptive tests in 30 minutes or so. The bad news is that you must really, really know your stuff to do your best on an adaptive test. That's because some questions are so convoluted, complex, or hard to follow that you're bound to miss one or two, at a minimum, even if you do know your stuff. So the more you know, the better you'll do on an adaptive test, even accounting for the occasionally weird or unfathomable questions that appear on these exams.

Because you can't tell in advance if a test is fixed-length, short-form, adaptive, or combination, you will be best served by preparing for the exam as if it were adaptive. That way, you should be prepared to pass no matter what kind of test you take. But if you do take a fixed-length or short-form test, remember our tips from the preceding section. They should help you improve on what you could do on an adaptive test.

If you encounter a question on an adaptive test that you can't answer, you must guess an answer immediately. Because of how the software works, you may suffer for your guess on the next question if you guess right, because you'll get a more difficult question next!

The Combination Exam Strategy

When it comes to studying for a combination test, your best bet is to approach it as a slightly longer adaptive exam, and to study as if the exam were adaptive only. Because the adaptive approach doesn't rely on rereading questions, and suggests that you take notes while reading useful information on test questions, it's hard to go wrong with this strategy when taking any kind of Microsoft certification test.

Exam-Taking Basics

The most important advice about taking any exam is this: Read each question carefully. Some questions are deliberately ambiguous, some use double negatives, and others use terminology in incredibly precise ways. The authors have taken numerous exams—both practice and live—and in nearly every one have missed at least one question because they didn't read it closely or carefully enough.

Here are some suggestions on how to deal with the tendency to jump to an answer too quickly:

➤ Make sure you read every word in the question. If you find yourself jumping ahead impatiently, go back and start over.

➤ As you read, try to restate the question in your own terms. If you can do this, you should be able to pick the correct answer(s) much more easily.

Above all, try to deal with each question by thinking through what you know about Windows NT Server, protocols, administrative utilities, installation, configuration, management—the characteristics, behaviors, facts, and figures involved. By reviewing what you know (and what you've written down on your information sheet), you'll often recall or understand things sufficiently to determine the answer to the question.

Mastering The Inner Game

In the final analysis, knowledge breeds confidence, and confidence breeds success. If you study the materials in this book carefully and review all the practice questions at the end of each chapter, you should become aware of those areas where additional learning and study are required.

Next, follow up by reading some or all of the materials recommended in the "Need To Know More?" section at the end of each chapter. The idea is to become familiar enough with the concepts and situations you find in the sample questions that you can reason your way through similar situations on a real exam. If you know the material, you have every right to be confident that you can pass the exam.

After you've worked your way through the book, take the practice exams in Chapters 14 and 16. You'll also want to check the Scenarios part of this book (immediately following the two sample tests), which includes our newly added scenario questions. The sample tests and scenarios provide a reality check and help you identify areas to study further. Make sure you follow up and review materials related to the questions you miss while practicing before scheduling a real exam. Only when you've covered that ground and feel comfortable with the whole scope of the practice questions should you take the online exam. Only if you score 75 percent or better should you proceed to the real thing (otherwise, obtain some additional practice tests and keep trying until you hit this magic number).

> **TIP**
>
> If you take a practice exam and don't score at least 75 percent correct, you'll want to practice further. Microsoft provides free Personal Exam Prep (PEP) exams and also offers self-assessment exams from the Microsoft Certified Professional Web site's download page (**www.microsoft.com/train_cert/download/downld.htm**). If you're more ambitious or better funded, you might want to purchase a practice exam from a third-party vendor. Check the Online Resources section of this book (right before the Glossary) for pointers.

As a special bonus to readers of this book, your authors have created an adaptive practice exam on Windows NT Server 4.0. Coriolis offers this practice exam on its Web site at **www.coriolis.com/cip/core4rev**.

Additional Resources

A good source of information about Microsoft certification exams comes from Microsoft itself. Because its products and technologies—and the exams that go with them—change frequently, the best place to go for exam-related information is online.

If you haven't already visited the Microsoft Certified Professional site, do so right now. The MCP home page resides at **www.microsoft.com/mcp/certstep/mcps.htm**.

> *Note: This page might not be there by the time you read this, or may be replaced by something new and different, because things change regularly on the Microsoft site.*

Installing Windows NT Server

2

Terms you'll need to understand:

✓ Hardware Compatibility List (HCL)

✓ Windows NT Hardware Qualifier (NTHQ)

✓ File systems

✓ Licensing

✓ Primary Domain Controller (PDC)

✓ Backup Domain Controller (BDC)

✓ Member server

✓ Emergency Repair Disk (ERD)

✓ NetBIOS names

✓ Network names

✓ Network clients

✓ FDISK

✓ Network share

Techniques you'll need to master:

✓ Installation and configuration of Windows NT Server

✓ Creating an ERD

✓ Troubleshooting a Windows NT installation

As network operating systems go, Windows NT usually is a breeze to install. But before a successful installation is possible, it's necessary to understand Windows NT's requirements and to learn how to evaluate your target systems for suitability. After the preliminaries are dispensed with, you'll need to decide exactly how you want to install Windows NT. And because you never can be sure that everything will work the first time, it's a good idea to understand some common causes of potential difficulty and their well-known workarounds or outright solutions.

Because we intend for our materials to help you plan for and install Windows NT Server on a computer, we don't cover the installation process itself in great detail, other than to illuminate those aspects of the process that are noteworthy. If you're concerned about understanding the process in depth, or want to pursue more details than we cover here, we suggest that you consult the "Need To Know More?" section at the end of this chapter—the materials listed there should tell you everything you'd ever possibly want to know about the minutiae of Windows NT Server installation.

Planning The Configuration

Before you install Windows NT, it's a good idea to analyze and understand how you want to use your Windows NT Server in some detail. This will help you select new hardware or decide if the hardware you've got is suitable for use with Windows NT Server. Table 2.1 lists "bare minimum" and "recommended" machine configuration data for Windows NT Server.

Minimum Requirements Vs. Recommendations

When it comes to the minimum requirements in Table 2.1, there's no getting around them. For instance, we've tried installing Windows NT Server on a PC with only 12 MB of RAM: Unfortunately, everything goes quite well until the install program tries to load the Windows NT kernel, and then quits after issuing an error message that reads "insufficient RAM to run Windows NT Server." Thus, the minimum requirements represent hard

Table 2.1 **The minimum and recommended requirements for running Windows NT Server.**

Item	Minimum	Recommended	Discussion
CPU	Intel 486	Pentium or better	Windows NT Server works with non-Intel processors (e.g., MIPS R4x00, DEC Alpha AXP, IBM PPC), and supports up to four CPUs in the standard edition.
Display	VGA	VGA or better	Unless someone plans to work at the server console, plain vanilla VGA is all you'll need.
Hard Disk	124 MB free	200+ MB free	The more components (or BackOffice elements) you install on your server, the more disk space you'll need; if you install straight from a CD, you need only 10 MB of disk space for boot and temp files.
Floppy Disk	3.5" or 5.25"	3.5" or 5.25"	Floppies may be used during installation for setup disks.
CD-ROM	local or network	8X or better	Because NT ships on a CD, either direct- or network-based access to a CD-ROM is required.
Network	one	one or more	Without network access, Adapter networking features are disabled and cannot be configured.

(continued)

Table 2.1	The minimum and recommended requirements for running Windows NT Server *(continued)*.		
Item	**Minimum**	**Recommended**	**Discussion**
Memory	16 MB	64 MB or more	Testing has proved that "more is better" for RAM. Be sure to fully load the motherboard with L2 Cache memory as well. In general, put as much memory into a Windows NT Server as you can afford.
Pointing Device	mouse, etc.	mouse, etc.	A pointing device makes working with the GUI portion of the install program (and most of NT's utilities) much easier.

and fast limitations on the software. The recommended values are another story—they can be approached with a healthy skepticism, but should still be taken seriously. Windows NT runs much better if it has lots of system resources to work with, and a server is not a machine you'd want to shortchange on such resources anyway. As with most things, it's better to have the resources and not need them than to need them and not have them.

Assessing Hardware Compatibility

When it comes to setting up or buying a computer that will run Windows NT Server, "more is better" is an unwritten rule that's worth heeding for everything from CPU (or even the number of CPUs in the machine), to memory, disk space, and more. If you're buying a new machine, be sure to ask the vendor if the equipment is fully Windows NT compatible. Any answer other than a resounding "Yes" probably means that you should find another vendor.

Whether you're buying a new machine or reusing one you already own, Microsoft provides an invaluable tool that can save hours of frustration and unnecessary expense when installing Windows NT Server. On the Windows NT distribution medium—that is, the CD labeled "Windows NT Server 4"—you'll find a file named MAKEDISK.BAT in the \Support\Hqtool directory. This utility will create a bootable DOS floppy that runs a program named "NTHQ" (which stands for NT Hardware Qualifier) upon bootup.

> **TIP**
>
> By itself, NTHQ is a useful program, because it can:
>
> ➤ Produce a detailed report to document the configuration it finds.
>
> ➤ Troubleshoot, if installation fails because of hardware problems (the program includes online help and trouble-shooting data).
>
> ➤ Show all the hardware it detects when a computer will run DOS but won't load Windows NT (if something isn't detected, it's likely to be involved—if not the culprit).
>
> But NTHQ's real "intelligence" comes from its incorporation of compatibility information that Microsoft also publishes separately in a document called the "Hardware Compatibility List," usually abbreviated HCL.

The HCL is updated monthly, whereas the version that's incorporated into the NTHQ represents the HCL at the time the latest version of the software was produced. Because this is August 1996 for Windows NT Server 4, the corresponding HCL in the NTHQ is aging rapidly. For machines newer than August 1996, it might be necessary to check a newer edition of the HCL to assess component compatibility.

The latest HCL is always available on Microsoft's Web site (**www.microsoft.com**) and on its anonymous FTP server (**ftp.microsoft.com**). It's also published monthly on the TechNet CD. Given a current HCL, you could still use the NTHQ to document what it finds on a system, and then use the HCL to make sure that elements that the program marks as unsupported have since joined the latest HCL.

When it comes to assessing the results from NTHQ, or similar results by inspection of a more current HCL, there's only one thing to say about unsupported hardware: "If the item is not on the HCL, and the vendor does not have a known good, working Windows NT driver for the item, remove the offending item and replace it with something equivalent that *does* appear on the HCL." In most cases, trying to use incompatible hardware with Windows NT results in a failed installation or an unusable device. Save yourself some grief; do the homework in advance, and use only compatible system components.

Preparing The System

Before installing Windows NT, most experts—including Microsoft—recommend that you install DOS on the target machine (or machines), where that makes sense. Then, make sure you get the system's hardware components working. This includes all hard disks, CD-ROM drives, floppy disks, video cards, network interfaces, tape drives, and anything else that might make up part of your server.

Here's why: Because DOS is a much more forgiving operating system than Windows NT, making components work with DOS is merely a positive indication of potential success, rather than any kind of guarantee that those same components will work with Windows NT. But because DOS is more compact and easier to install, and a great many high-quality, DOS-based troubleshooting and diagnostic tools are available, bringing a system up under DOS first is your best shot at a successful Windows NT installation—assuming, of course, that all system components are on the latest HCL (or you've obtained the necessary drivers for items that are missing).

For similar reasons, the same experts that recommend you get your server up and running under DOS first also recommend leaving at least a small DOS partition on your Windows NT Server machine. If hardware or software problems ever prevent the machine from booting into Windows NT, there's still a good chance that you'll be able to boot it up under DOS and perform a variety of diagnostic tests and "idiot checks." In many cases, you'll be able to fix your problems and get the server back up much more quickly than otherwise. At a cost of a little extra preparation time and 20 to 100 MB of disk space, many system administrators find this approach quite worthwhile.

 Remember that Windows NT runs on several other CPU types besides the Intel x86 processor family (including MIPS, DEC Alpha AXP, and IBM PowerPC). But only Intel-compatible CPUs can run DOS. When reading test questions—or working with real machines—be sure that the hardware will run DOS before making any further assumptions about using DOS for diagnosis or troubleshooting. Just because over 95 percent of Windows NT installations run on Intel-compatible CPUs doesn't mean that Microsoft doesn't expect you to know about non-Intel installation and other issues, or that you'll never encounter such a machine in your work with the operating system. The Windows NT Server 4.0 CD is bootable and can be used to install the NOS, even if no operating system is currently on the computer.

Installing Windows NT

Because some installation decisions must be worked out in advance, it's a good idea to know what happens during the Windows NT installation process. This helps prior planning, so here's a high-level, step-by-step version of the Windows NT Server 4 installation process (we provide some discussion and pointers to other chapters in this book, where applicable):

1. Boot the machine under any operating system that can access the network and communicate with a source of Windows NT installation files, or under any Microsoft operating system that can access a local CD-ROM drive.

2. Run the Windows NT installation program that's appropriate for the platform: WINNT.EXE for DOS, Windows 3.x, or Windows 95 and 98 machines; WINNT32.EXE for Windows NT machines running Workstation or Server 3.5 or better. This copies the files from the distribution media (or network drive) to local hard disk space.

3. Verify the software and hardware components recognized by the installation program, and make changes if necessary (and repeat Steps 1 through 3 to restart the process).

   If your hard disk controller is not on the HCL (i.e., hardware raid disk controller), during the setup process, strike the F6 key when the message "setup is inspecting your hardware" appears. This will interrupt mass storage detection and give you the opportunity to load the controller's driver in the initial phase of setup. Failure to do this results in installation failure when setup reboots because the setup program will not be able to find the hard drive attached to the controller.

 If the hardware you need to add isn't essential to the installation (like a CD-ROM that works with DOS or Windows 95, but isn't recognized by Windows NT, or a hard disk that you want to put the system files on), wait until the initial installation is complete, and add the hardware later. That way, unforeseen problems won't impede the installation.

4. Select the hard disk partition where the Windows NT system files will reside. That partition can be either FAT or NTFS, but most experts recommend it be NTFS if at all possible (see Chapter 3 for a discussion of these file systems).

5. Format the selected partition. Do not create more than one partition during the installation process. After the installation is complete, use Disk Administrator to create any other required partitions.

6. Select the Windows NT default directory (most installations use the default \winnt directory).

7. Enter name and organization when prompted.

8. Select the licensing mode for the server; the options are Per Server (for small networks or Internet-attached machines), or Per Seat (for larger networks or private machines). Microsoft charges for licenses, and you may

change from Per Server to Per Seat only once (it can't be changed back). Because of potential expense issues, most organizations with more than one server elect Per Seat licensing (which allows users to connect to many servers without requiring a separate license for each connection). For single-server networks, it's okay to choose Per Server licensing, because it can be changed to Per Seat later.

9. Enter up to a 15-character name for the computer; it must be unique on your network (for large networks, this may take some planning or coordination).

10. Set the machine's security role. It may be either a Primary Domain Controller (PDC), a Backup Domain Controller (BDC), or a Stand-Alone Server (called a member server in Microsoft documentation, but not in the installation utility). Only one machine can be a PDC for a given domain, so only the first domain controller for a domain is installed as a PDC; all other domain controllers for the domain will be installed as BDCs. Member servers usually play other roles on a network, such as database server, communications server, or some other service. For more information about domain controllers, see Chapter 5.

11. Enter a password for the Administrator account (write it down; you'll need it again).

12. Select the options to create an Emergency Repair Disk (unless you're doing an extremely vanilla installation, we recommend against this—it's smarter to wait until the system is fully configured and generate the ERD then).

13. Select from the Components To Install checkboxes; choices include Accessibility Options, Accessories, Communications, Games, MS Exchange, and Multi-media. It's best to install everything (it's easier to delete

extraneous stuff later than to rerun the install program to add more stuff).

14. Establish networking role; choices are Wired To The Network and Remote Access To The Network. The first choice is the overwhelming favorite for most server machines.

15. Install Microsoft Internet Information Server 2.0 (IIS). This is optional, and should be chosen only for systems that plan to run a Web server.

16. Detect network adapters; choices are Auto-detect or Manual setup. Most network cards can be automatically detected, but some must be configured manually. Be sure to have drivers on hand for your network interfaces, should the latter condition prevail.

17. For each network interface, select the protocols to be used; choices are TCP/IP, NWLink IPX/SPX Compatible Transport, and NetBEUI. For most networks, TCP/IP is the predominant choice.

18. Select Network services; choices are Microsoft Internet Information Server (if installed in Step 15), RPC Configuration, NetBIOS Interface, Workstation, and Server. All are chosen by default; there is seldom any need to make changes here.

19. Supply network interface settings. These include IRQ number, memory base address, DMA settings, and more. A successful DOS installation documented by NTHQ can supply all this information, if you don't already have it recorded somewhere.

20. If either NWLink or TCP/IP protocols were selected in Step 17, you'll have to configure them now. This will take some preparation, especially for TCP/IP: Be sure to obtain the machine's IP address, one or more DNS server addresses, the IP gateway (router) address, and the WINS server address (if applicable).

21. If the machine was designated a PDC in Step 10, you must now supply its computer and domain names; otherwise, it just gets a computer name.

22. If you elected to install Internet Information Server in Step 15, you will select and configure its component options at this point.

23. You will be prompted for Date/Time properties; set the local date, time, and time zone information as requested.

24. You will be prompted for Display Properties; be sure to click the Test button (not just to make sure the display is working properly, but to be able to proceed with— and complete—the installation).

25. Create an Emergency Repair Disk (if selected in Step 12).

Based on the steps where user input or foreknowledge is required, some items deserve a bit more discussion. Here is additional information regarding the following steps in this preceding 25-step process:

4. Select FAT or NTFS for the Windows NT partition.

   Chapter 3 covers this subject in some detail, and provides other sources of further details and information. FAT is more accessible to different types of operating systems than NTFS, but NTFS is more robust and secure than FAT. Most production installations elect to store operating system files under NTFS for those reasons. It is important to note that the maximum size for the installation partition is 4,096 MB on a disk that is being formatted during setup. To overcome this limit, place a hard drive with a preformatted NTFS partition of 7.8 GB in the system and install on it. For more information, see Microsoft Technet article Q114841.

10. Select the security role for the server: PDC, BDC, or Stand-Alone Server.

Three important observations apply here (more details are covered in Chapter 5):

a. There can be only one PDC for any given domain. When installing domain controllers, only the first one can be a PDC (that's why including the domain name is an important part of the configuration information here—Windows NT won't permit a second PDC to be installed).

b. If there's any chance you might want to use the machine being installed as a domain controller, you must designate it as one now, or reinstall Windows NT later for it ever to attain such status.

c. A member server (Stand-Alone Server in the installation dialog) plays no role in domain management. The only way to convert a member server to a domain controller (and vice versa) is to reinstall Windows NT Server and change the designation in Step 10.

17. Choose Protocols: TCP/IP, NetBEUI, NWLink.

Microsoft has been deemphasizing NetBEUI for a while, and is pushing TCP/IP strongly. NWLink is recommended primarily for networks where interaction with NetWare-based resources is required (NWLink supports NetWare's native IPX/SPX protocols).

Most network administrators choose protocols for compatibility with existing installations, but Microsoft has this to say about possible rationales for choosing the aforementioned protocols:

a. NetBEUI is now recommended only for small, single-server networks. It's nearly completely self-configuring and self-tuning, and requires little or no administrative effort for installation and up-keep. It's also limited in scope and capability, and not at all routable, which is why it's best used only on small networks.

b.   NWLink makes it easy for Microsoft networking
clients to access NetWare-based resources or
applications, or NetWare networking clients to
access Windows NT-based resources or applications. NWLink thus provides the foundation for
NetWare interactions of all kinds (from simple
application access to making NetWare servers look
like Windows NT, or Windows NT Servers look
like NetWare). NetWare does a good job of
managing node addresses automatically, but
requires management of network addresses as the
number of physical networks increases. It's much
simpler than TCP/IP to manage, but more work
than NetBEUI.

c.   TCP/IP is the protocol of the Internet—and by
extension, for intranets as well—and represents
Microsoft's primary emphasis for large, complex, or
geographically dispersed networks. TCP/IP
supports global access and reach, and the richest
set of address and network management services.
It's also the most work to manage, and takes
ongoing effort and involvement from network
administrators. Microsoft has done an excellent job
of providing good infrastructure elements for
TCP/IP—including services like WINS, DNS,
and DHCP. Information about TCP/IP may be
found in Chapter 6.

19.   Supply network interface settings.

To configure a network interface card (NIC) properly,
you must determine which of the many settings that
can be involved will work on your system. If you get
the NIC working with DOS, you'll be forced to
resolve those issues in advance. Just be sure to record
all the relevant information, in case Windows NT's
network detection software can't puzzle all the details
out for itself.

For any PC adapter to work properly, it must be set to use a unique (and available) interrupt request line (IRQ), memory base address (and associated block of memory), and, in some cases, I/O port addresses and direct memory addresses (DMA) must also be supplied. It's imperative to understand how to resolve NIC configurations and how to install them successfully to make Windows NT work on a network.

20.   Configure NWLink and/or TCP/IP.

Each of these two protocols has its own special configuration issues.

For NWLink, it's important to understand that the NWLink Auto Frame Type Detection setting picks the predominant IPX frame type as its default. This makes it necessary to configure mixed NetWare 3.x (for versions older that 3.12) and 4.x networking environments manually, so that network addresses for the segments that carry the older 802.2 frame types can be distinguished from those that carry newer 802.3 frame types. (We'll cover this in detail in Chapter 7.)

For TCP/IP, it's essential to understand and obtain the following address information for a successful Windows NT installation:

a.   The IP addressing scheme in use on your network

b.   The subnetworking approach in use, and the subnet mask for each subnet to which the Windows NT Server will be attached

c.   The IP address for the server itself (and for each additional NIC that will handle IP)

d.   The IP address for at least one Domain Name Service (DNS) server, if not a primary and a secondary server address

e. The IP address for at least one Windows Internet Names Service (WINS) server, if not a primary and a secondary address

If you're working with an Internet Service Provider (ISP) in a small-to-medium-sized network, you should be able to get most if not all of this information from them. On larger networks, you'll need to work with your WAN or organization-wide networking authorities to obtain this information. We will discuss TCP/IP concepts and information further in Chapter 6.

21. Select a computer name.

Part of Microsoft's NetBIOS networking heritage is its use of 15-character names for computers, user accounts, and shared network resources. You should be knowledgeable about how to evaluate naming schemes, so it's wise to consider carefully how to create names that are easy to read and understand, and also easy for users to deduce. Because asking for things by name is a very human way to behave (but computers require that names be unique and conform to certain rules), naming is of utmost importance.

23. Supply Date/Time properties.

During installation, you must set the Time and Date for the new Windows NT Server, and indicate the time zone where the server operates. Time helps Windows NT format dates and timestamps, and is particularly essential on domain controllers and replication servers. You also can set locale (and associated language) information for Windows NT at this point that formats date displays and currency information as well.

With all these steps completed, you will have installed Windows NT Server, along with whatever options for protocols and services you selected along the way. Because the next step for most network administrators is to press on and define user accounts, groups, and install other applications to make a server ready for production use, we recommend against making an Emergency Repair Disk (ERD) at this point.

If you wait until the rest of the predeployment installation and configuration work is done before building an ERD, the ERD will contain all the work you've done on the system. On the other hand, if the post-Windows NT install work is complex or significant, making an ERD at this point prevents you from having to reenter all the information you entered during the first install. This will help if any problems occur after the OS has been installed, but before other predeployment installation and configuration work is complete (and the final ERD is created).

A successful Windows NT installation in and of itself doesn't represent a complete Windows NT Server installation by any means. There's usually quite a bit of additional work to do after Windows NT is installed before a system is completely ready for use. We'll cover the topics and utilities involved in this post-installation, predeployment work in Chapter 5.

The WINNT/WINNT32 Commands Demystified

The programs that drive Windows NT installation come in two flavors:

➤ **WINNT.EXE** This version of the install program is a 16-bit program, built to run on machines with DOS, Windows 3.x, or Windows 95 or 98 installed.

➤ **WINNT32.EXE** This version of the install program is a 32-bit program, built to run on machines running some version of Windows NT already. Most often, it's used to upgrade an existing operating system from a previous version, or to change the status of a Windows NT machine from Workstation or member server to a Windows NT Server of some kind (perhaps even a domain controller).

Other than the difference between 16- and 32-bit operating environments, the two programs are identical. That's why we can discuss the switches and options to both commands in the following Help message, which may be produced by entering WINNT /? or WINNT32 /? at the command prompt (remember, you have to be in the context of the \i386 directory):

```
WINNT [/S[:]sourcepath] [/T[:]tempdrive] [/I[:]inffile]
      [/OX] [/X | [/F] [/C]] [/B]
/S[:]sourcepath
          Specifies the source location of Windows NT files.
          Must be a full path of the form x:\[path] or
          \\server\share[\path].
          The default is the current directory.
/T[:]tempdrive
          Specifies a drive to contain temporary setup files.
          If not specified, Setup attempts to locate a drive for
          you.
/I[:]inffile
          Specifies the file name (no path) of the Setup information
          file.
          The default is DOSNET.INF. Microsoft documentation refers to
          this as the "inf_file".
          The /B switch may also require the /S switch.
/OX       Create boot floppies for CD-ROM or floppy-based
          installation.
/X        Do not create the Setup boot floppies.
/F        Do not verify files as they are copied to the Setup boot
          floppies.
/C        Skip free-space check on the Setup boot floppies you
          provide.
/B        Floppyless operation
/U        Unattended operation and optional script file
          (requires /S).
/R        Specifies optional directory to be installed.
/RX       Specifies optional directory to be copied.
/E        Specifies command to be executed at the end of GUI setup.
```

Following are some notes about the syntax used above:

1. Square brackets ([ ]) enclose optional terms. Among other things, this indicates that all the parameters and associated attributes are optional for both WINNT and WINNT32.

2. The string /S[:]sourcepath indicates that the value of sourcepath is optional, but if it appears, the colon must

appear also (that is, /S:X:\bin\source is legal, but /SX:\bin\source is not).

3. The vertical bar character (|) separates mutually exclusive options, so [/X | [/F] [/C]] means that if /X appears, neither /F nor /C can appear, and that if either /F or /C appears, then /X cannot appear, in any single invocation of WINNT or WINNT32.

4. The notation used in the sourcepath explanation \\server\share[\path] is a NetBIOS network name, called a UNC (Universal Naming Convention) name. Here, \\server is the NetBIOS computer name of the machine where the source files reside, \share is the NetBIOS name for the network share within which the files reside, and the optional \path designation can point to a subdirectory beneath the share itself. UNC names are quite common in Microsoft networks; they go back to MS-Net's origins.

Relevant Switches And Options

A significant number of the switches and options for these commands relate to unattended installations that can be ordered up across the network by an administrator to install Windows NT on servers elsewhere on a network. These switches are the ones you need to remember:

➤ /S   Must be used when reading source files from any drive other than the current default drive.

➤ /T   Must be used when the compressed files that WINNT or WINNT32 copies locally from the source directory is any drive other than the current default drive.

➤ /OX Appears occasionally; used to create boot floppies for a CD ROM installation, but does not start the install process.

➤ /X If you want to install Windows NT on a computer, but not to create a set of boot floppies, this is the switch to use.

➤ /F Used to skip the verify step after copying files to a set of boot floppies. Speeds the process, but not recommended. Only used with WINNT.

➤ /C Use only if using blank, preformatted floppies when creating a set of boot floppies. Only used with WINNT.

➤ /B Use when installing from a network drive or a CD-ROM drive, without using floppies.

Common Uses And Combinations

Remember that WINNT32 may be used only with machines running some version of Windows NT (3.5 and higher), and that WINNT must be used with DOS, Windows 3.x, and Windows 95 and 98. As for command and switch combinations, these are the most important:

➤ **WINNT /OX** Use this to create a set of boot floppies, sometimes called Setup disks, after an installation is complete.

➤ **WINNT /B** Use this to install Windows NT without using setup floppies, whether from a network drive or a (local) CD-ROM. Although you can map a CD-ROM drive as a network share, and read files directly across the network, this is painfully slow, and not recommended. For network installs, copy the files from the CD to a directory on a hard drive, and create a share for that directory.

Of course, the same switches can be used with WINNT32, but only on machines running Windows NT 3.5 or higher.

NetBIOS Names And Network Naming Schemes

By design, NetBIOS names are limited to 15 characters in length. The first character in a NetBIOS name must be alphabetic, but all other characters can be letters, numbers, or certain punctuation marks. It's not a good idea to put spaces in NetBIOS names, either. Table 2.2 lists those characters that should not appear within NetBIOS names; they're not necessarily illegal, but they often cause problems on networks, especially those with DOS or Windows 3.x clients.

Some additional caveats and information about NetBIOS names are required. Neither DOS nor Windows 3.x users can handle NetBIOS names longer than eight characters. Therefore, when working in a hybrid environment, you should either define NetBIOS names eight characters or shorter, or define aliases eight characters or shorter for those resources that DOS or Windows 3.x users must access. It's a good idea to stay away from punctuation marks of all kinds in NetBIOS names, if only because some applications may otherwise have trouble with them.

Finally, it's time to reveal that dollar signs are legal in NetBIOS names, but should be used for one purpose only: When a dollar sign appears in the final position of a NetBIOS share name, that name will not appear in network browser lists or in response to NetBIOS network survey commands like **net view**. Such shares are called "hidden shares" and are used by Windows NT itself to create a class of administrative shares that only adminis-

Table 2.2 Problem characters for NetBIOS names.

Character Name	Character	Key Combination
Bullet	•	Alt+0419
Dollar sign	$	Alt+0164
Vertical bar	|	Alt+0166
Section sign	§	Alt+0167
Paragraph marker	¶	Alt+0182

trators can access (and no one can see on the network). Only those who know such shares exist, and know their exact names, can access them.

Networking Clients With Windows NT

When installing a network server, it's usually desirable to make that server's resources available to clients elsewhere on the network. Sometimes, the software that enables desktop machines to communicate with the network must be installed from scratch—especially when bringing up a network for the first time, or when adding new clients to an existing network. To that end, Microsoft has included a utility, called the "Network Client Administrator," that creates installation and startup disks. These disks enable a variety of operating systems to become clients on a Windows NT network, including:

➤ Network Client 3.0 for MS-DOS and Windows 3.x

➤ LAN Manager 2.2c for MS-DOS

➤ LAN Manager 2.2c for OS/2

➤ Windows For Workgroups 3.11

For more information on the Network Client Administrator, see Chapter 5.

The process of creating an installation or startup disk is quite simple: Once inside the Network Client Administrator utility, select the Make Network Installation Diskette option, and it will pilot you through the process. It's also necessary to point the utility at the proper subdirectory where the source files for the various operating systems reside.

The official use for the Network Client Administrator is to make it easy for network administrators to create disks that can enable networking for workstations running any of the aforementioned operating systems. The second DOS option is provided to provide backward compatibility with MS-DOS users who wish to maintain existing batch files built for LAN Manager networks. In practice, this utility makes it easy to set up multiple clients at the same time, and builds install disks that make the best use of DOS's limited memory management and networking capabilities.

Another excellent "guerrilla application" of this tool, however, makes it easy to install Windows NT Servers onto a bare machine. Here's how this is done:

1. Use a bootable DOS disk, with FDISK included, to create and format a DOS partition on the new server's boot disk. For best results (if space isn't too precious), 200 MB is plenty of room to handle all the Windows NT files during installation; after that, you'll have plenty of room for DOS, diagnostics, and even Windows 95 or 98, if you're so inclined.

2. Install DOS on the boot partition and make it bootable. Install a network interface card, and make sure the computer continues to boot (if a test or diagnostics disk is included, make sure your work passes its tests).

3. Use the Network Client Administrator to create a DOS Network Client disk; install the software on the new server (you must have access to a working machine running Windows NT Server).

4. Create a share on the working server that points to a copy of the \i386 directory taken from the Windows NT distribution media (this directory includes subdirectories, so use the **xcopy** command, or some other utility that handles recursive copy).

5. Once the Microsoft Network Client is running on your new server, simply map a drive to the \i386 share. For example, **net use x:\\server\i386** does the job quite nicely. Then, enter X: at the command prompt to point to the mapped drive where the install files reside.

6. At that point, you need only invoke WINNT to start a network install of Windows NT, as follows:

```
winnt /b
```

Remember, this performs a floppyless install, right across the network. It may take a while to copy all the files (15 to 30 minutes is normal) but it's the easiest method of Windows NT installation we've tried.

Common Install Dilemmas

There are two major parts of a Windows NT installation:

1. The initial portion of the install, until all the files are copied to the target machine, occurs inside a blue-screen, character mode interface that's familiar to anyone who's ever installed any version of Windows. This is called the character mode portion of the install.

2. The second portion of the install occurs about midway through the process. At this point, enough of Windows NT has been installed that the machine reboots itself and uses a graphical user interface to complete the rest of the process. This is called the GUI mode portion of the install.

When problems occur during the character mode portion of the install, it's frequently necessary to restart the process and begin afresh. If the install program has begun copying files when it fails, one or two temporary directories will be present on the computer:

1. **WIN_NT.~LS:** where the install program stores all the compressed Windows NT system files.

2. **WIN_NT.~BT:** where the install program stores compressed boot files for Windows NT (this directory appears only if the /B switch has been selected for the WINNT or WINNT32 command that launched the failed installation; otherwise, these files are written to the three boot disks created during the installation process).

If you begin a reinstall of Windows NT without removing these directories and their contents, the install program will remove them for you. Experience has shown that it's faster to delete the files yourself—provided that you include the DOS program DELTREE.EXE on the DOS boot disk that you use to restart the machine (or in the DOS partition on the hard drive). Without DELTREE, it can take more than half an hour to delete these files; with DELTREE it seems to go somewhat faster (but be prepared to lose some time here).

Beyond the need to restart the process from time to time, there are a few other well-known dilemmas that may show up during a Windows NT installation. In the sections that follow, we'll cover two of the most common situations that you may encounter during installation.

To Upgrade Or Install Anew?

Windows NT can capture and use information from other, preceding Windows installations with degrees of success and fidelity that vary according to the difference between the information that's already on the machine, and the structure of Windows NT 4's native environment. According to the Microsoft literature, it's possible to instruct Windows NT Server 4 to capture configuration information from any of the following Microsoft operating systems (listed in decreasing order of difference):

➤ Windows 3.1, 3.11, or Windows For Workgroups (WFW)

➤ Windows 95 or 98

➤ Windows NT 3.5 and 3.51

As always, there are a few interesting terminological distinctions. Windows NT is not really considered an upgrade of Windows 3.x, WFW, or Windows 95 or 98, but if you install Windows NT in the same directory where the "earlier" version of Windows resides, the install program will grab as much configuration information as it can from either the .INI files (Windows 3.x) or from the Windows 95 or 98 Registry files. Most experts agree, however, that unless you have compelling reasons to leave parts of the previous installation alone (like no access to the application disks), you're better off backing up such a system, reformatting the drive, installing Windows NT, and then reinstalling the applications you want to keep on the machine. Because some 16-bit applications won't run under Windows NT anyway, this is by far the safest course of action.

The term "upgrade" really applies only to prior versions of Windows NT. The easiest upgrade is from a prior Windows NT Server installation (3.5 or 3.51) to 4; in that case, the bulk of the configuration information, the security and accounts database, and most services will transfer intact into the new environment. If you're upgrading multiple servers, and one or more is a domain controller, always upgrade the PDC first to keep the domain database correct and intact.

If you're upgrading an older version of Windows NT Server to a newer version, the following information is left intact:

➤ Any edits made to the Registry using the Registry Editor

➤ Custom program groups, desktop layout, settings, and preferences set through the Control Panel

➤ Local security accounts (users and groups)

➤ Network adapter settings, protocols, and service configurations and addresses (including Macintosh and RAS services, if applicable)

➤ Preferences set for Accessories and Administrative Tools. But the upgrade process does copy new versions of system files and change settings and program groups to reflect new utilities, capabilities, and organization. During an upgrade, it's necessary to provide the following information:

The directory where system files will reside (the default for 3.5 and 3.51 is \winnt35, which differs from 4's \WINNT default)

Some new parameters (if you're already using TCP/IP, they will be requested). You'll want to create a new Emergency Repair Disk as part of the upgrade process. Also, as with any major system changes, we recommend you begin the upgrade process by making a complete system backup of the current installation.

When it comes to upgrading from Windows NT Workstations to Windows NT Server, there's one well-known gotcha: If the resulting Server is to be used as a domain controller, it's necessary to reinstall Windows NT Server software from scratch. In other words, you can't use the upgrade option and obtain the desired result. If you do upgrade Windows NT Workstation to Windows NT Server, it can only be a member server; in that case, to be able to use the new version of User Manager that comes with Windows NT Server, you also must delete your old user profile. Even if you want to convert a Windows NT 4 Workstation machine to a Windows NT Server 4 machine, all of these restrictions still apply. Likewise, if you are upgrading a Stand-Alone (member) server from an earlier version of Windows NT to 4, you must reinstall from scratch if it is to become a domain controller.

The Hardware Works Now, But Not With Windows NT

You'll sometimes run into a situation where hardware that works fine with DOS, Windows 3.x, or Windows 95 or 98 is not on the HCL. This is especially common for older CD-ROM drives, many of which use proprietary interface cards and require custom drivers. Windows NT recognizes most SCSI CD-ROM drives, and many of the newer IDE CD-ROM drives, but it doesn't recognize all of them.

If this happens on a machine on which you're trying to install Windows NT, don't despair. You can always insert the Windows NT CD and simply copy the files from the \i386 directory to your hard drive, and use the copied files to perform the installation. If that doesn't work, as long as your machine can still access the network, you can always perform a network install by reading the necessary files from a mapped network drive.

Be sure to build the install floppies, though, just to make sure you can continue the process should the installation fail for some reason along the way. You'll want to be sure to back up the original system first, so you can always get back to where you started if you can't complete the installation for some reason.

You may sometimes encounter situations where Windows NT doesn't recognize hardware elements on your system during installation. If those elements aren't essential to the installation, you can always skip the problem-solving (or supplementary driver installation) that's usually required. But during the installation process, Windows NT will show you a list of the drives it recognizes on your system, and the overall system components; in both cases, it does give you options to install additional hardware, assuming that you've got the necessary driver software in hand.

Practice Questions

Question 1

> Which of the following elements of this PC's configurations do not meet Windows NT Server's minimum installation requirements for a network installation where source files will be copied to the machine's FAT partition? [Check all correct answers]
>
> ❑   a. 95 MB free disk space on the FAT partition
>
> ❑   b. 12 MB RAM
>
> ❑   c. 486/100 DX4 CPU
>
> ❑   d. Paradise VGA card
>
> ❑   e. CD-ROM drive

Answers a and b are correct. Because Windows NT Server requires 124 MB of free disk space for all the files, plus room to decompress them, answer a is insufficient and should be checked. Windows NT Server requires a minimum of 16 MB of RAM; therefore, answer b should be checked. Windows NT Server works on any Intel-compatible processor greater than or equal to a 486; answer c should not be checked. Indeed, Windows NT requires a VGA graphics card or better to work; answer d is correct, and should not be checked. Finally, Windows NT does not require a CD-ROM—but it's a good idea to have one, especially on machines for which a network install isn't possible—so having one is not a problem; answer e also should be unchecked.

Question 2

Which of the following tools or techniques can you use to assess the suitability of a Pentium PC built in early 1996 for Windows NT installation? [Check all correct answers]

❑ a. Microsoft Windows NT Diagnostics

❑ b. System Sleuth

❑ c. NTHQ disk

❑ d. Obtain a current copy of the Hardware Compatibility List, and check every system component to be sure it appears therein.

Answers c and d are correct. The Windows NT Hardware Qualifier disk may be constructed by running the MAKEDISK.BAT program in the \Support\Hqtool directory on the Windows NT CD ROM. Because NTHQ checks the machine against a built-in version of the HCL, it will do the job (except on machines with hardware newer than August 1996, which the software may not recognize). But because the machine is older than NTHQ, NTHQ should work correctly. This makes answer c correct. Finally, the HCL is indeed the source of the latest information on what works with Windows NT; even though checking by hand is more work than using NTHQ, it will produce a correct assessment of the machine, making answer d correct as well. Windows NT Diagnostics aren't available until Windows NT is installed successfully on a machine, nor does the program perform hardware checking on its own (rather, it reports the contents of the Registry written by the NTDETECT.EXE program that runs at bootup). This means answer a is incorrect. System Sleuth is an old PC diagnostics program that doesn't perform Windows NT hardware compatibility checks of any kind, making answer b incorrect as well. We call this a trick question because it slyly mentions that the machine is built in early 1996, which means that the HCL included on the distribution CD for Windows NT should be able to recognize all its components.

Question 3

Which of the following statements are true? When upgrading from Windows NT Workstation 3.51 to Windows NT Server 4 you can: [Check all correct answers]

❑   a. Transfer Registry edits from the old version to the new.

❑   b. Designate the machine as a domain controller.

❑   c. Maintain custom program groups.

❑   d. Maintain desktop layout, icon spacing and placement, and color scheme.

❑   e. Maintain local groups and accounts.

Answers a, c, d, and e are correct. The upgrade process maintains direct Registry edits, transfers any existing custom program groups, maintains the desktop as before, and preserves any existing local groups and accounts defined for that machine. Answer b is the only incorrect answer. A Windows NT Workstation upgraded to a Windows NT Server only can be designated as a Stand-Alone Server (member server elsewhere in Microsoft's documentation) in the install program (a complete reinstall is necessary to change this status).

Question 4

Even though Windows 95 can recognize the CD-ROM drive on a machine, it's not supported for Windows NT Server 4. How can you install Windows NT Server 4 on that machine anyway? [Check all correct answers]

❑   a. Create a set of installation disks from another Windows NT Server machine, and use the disks to perform the install.

❑   b. Use the xcopy command to copy the files from the \i386 directory onto the Windows 95 machine's hard disk, and run WINNT.EXE from there.

❑   c. While running Windows 95, change to the \i386 directory on the Windows NT CD, and run WINNT32.EXE.

❑   d. Copy the installation files from \i386 to a server, map a drive from the Windows 95 machine to that directory, and run WINNT.EXE from there.

Answers b and d are correct. Because the machine can recognize and use the CD-ROM while it's still running Windows 95, the easiest approach is to copy the files from the \i386 directory to a directory on the machine's hard disk. But this will work only if the drive is formatted to permit creation of another partition for NTFS, or if the FAT partition where the files are deposited may later be converted to NTFS (see Chapter 3 for a discussion of FAT and NTFS). That's why b is a correct answer. Answer d also is correct, because if the drives on the machine need to be completely reformatted—as often will be the case when upgrading from Windows 95 to Windows NT—it might be smarter to copy the installation files to a server, and perform a network install. This leaves the drives on the machine free to be reformatted completely, but it will require a boot floppy (that you might build using the Network Client Administrator). Answer a is incorrect because the install disks alone don't convey all the Windows NT installation files; there's still a need to gain access to the CD-ROM or a copy of its contents. Answer c is incorrect because the 16-bit installation program, WINNT.EXE, works with Windows 95; WINNT32.EXE only works with versions of Windows NT 3.5 and higher.

Question 5

> During Windows NT installation, Setup fails to recognize one of your SCSI drives, but this affects neither the boot nor the system drive. How can you solve this problem? [Check all correct answers]
>
> ❏　a. Use the Search For Devices option during installation, right after the hardware detection phase is complete.
>
> ❏　b. Press S to specify additional devices during installation, at the phase when the list of "Mass Storage Devices"appears.
>
> ❏　c. Complete the installation, and then add the missing SCSI drive, using the Control Panel afterwards.
>
> ❏　d. Stop the installation, remove the problem drive, and replace it with one that's listed on the HCL.

Answers b, c, and d are correct. During the phase when the list of Mass Storage Devices appears, it is possible to press S to specify additional devices, which makes answer b correct, but it requires that you have a copy of the driver software on hand. A better approach is described in answer c, where the option of installing the drive for the errant device in the SCSI Devices applet in Control Panel is mentioned. Because the drive is not essential to a successful installation, it's probably best to wait until installation is complete to add it to a working Windows NT Server. Thus, answer c is not only correct, it's recommended. Finally, answer d also is correct. If you remove an unsupported device, install a supported replacement, and restart the installation, it should complete successfully. In fact, answer c is recommended because it lets you complete the installation immediately, and helps you make sure a driver is available for the errant drive; if not, d becomes the only viable alternative. If some particular disk drive is indeed an essential part of an installation, and no driver for that device is to be had, then installation must be stopped until a replacement device with a working driver can be installed in its place. There is no Search For Devices option during installation, so this is patently false, as is answer a.

Question 6

> Select the installation recipe that permits you to install Windows NT Server across the network onto a Windows 95 computer.
>
> ○ a. Connect to the network directory that contains the Windows NT installation files and run WINNT32.EXE.
>
> ○ b. Connect to the network directory that contains the Windows NT installation files and run WINNT.EXE.
>
> ○ c. Connect to the network directory that contains the Windows NT installation files and run SETUP.EXE.
>
> ○ d. Create a client installation disk using Network Client Administrator, boot the machine with that disk, and run NETWORK.EXE.

Answer b accurately describes a network install scenario, and cites the correct version of the install program, so it is correct. WINNT32.EXE works with Windows NT only, not with Windows 95; this disqualifies answer a. SETUP.EXE is not the name of a program used to install Windows NT, so answer c is incorrect. Likewise, d is incorrect because NETWORK.EXE will not perform a networked Windows NT installation.

Question 7

> A RAID array and its SCSI controller must be installed on a new Windows NT Server machine. Which of these activities is required to make these devices available on your system? [Check all correct answers]
>
> ❑ a. Install the driver for the SCSI controller.
>
> ❑ b. Install the driver for the RAID array.
>
> ❑ c. Use the Services applet in Control Panel to start the SCSI controller and RAID array.
>
> ❑ d. Restart the machine.

Answers a, b, and d are correct. For any hardware components to work on a Windows NT machine, drivers must be installed and operating. Answer d is correct because hardware changes are recorded in the Registry and such changes cannot take effect until the next time a system boots; it's necessary to restart Windows NT anytime you add new hardware components to the system. Devices are started by the operating system itself when the computer boots up, so there's no way to start a SCSI controller or a RAID array in the Services applet in Control Panel. Therefore, answer c is incorrect and should be left unchecked.

Question 8

> What is the correct way to upgrade a computer running Windows For Workgroups to Windows NT Server 4?
>
> O   a. Install Windows NT in a separate directory and reinstall all applications.
>
> O   b. Install Windows NT in a separate directory and import WIN.INI and SYSTEM.INI into the Registry.
>
> O   c. Run WINNT32.EXE and install Windows NT into WFW's home directory, c:\windows.
>
> O   d. Run WINNT.EXE and install Windows NT into WFW's home directory, c:\windows.

Answer d is corect. Strictly speaking, upgrading from Windows For Workgroups (WFW) to Windows NT Server is not an installation option. But by installing Windows NT Server into the same directory where WFW resides, the install program is smart enough to grab what information it can carry into the Windows NT environment by detecting and reading the WIN.INI and SYSTEM.INI files, and converting program and group information into corresponding Windows NT Registry entries. It's a trick question because this really isn't an upgrade, per se, but rather a new installation that's smart enough to preserve some old configuration information. Answer a does not give the install program the implicit directive to convert the WFW.INI files and fails the "upgrade" requirement. Answer b apparently assumes that some magic import function for .INI files is available; because there isn't one, this answer also is incorrect. Finally, answer c provides the correct directory placement, but calls the 32-bit version of the install program, which works only with Windows NT, not with WFW.

Question 9

Windows NT permits creation of a network startup installation disk. Which of these activities is necessary to create such a disk? [Check all correct answers]

❑ a. Create the disk using Client Manager.

❑ b. Create the disk using User Manager For Domains.

❑ c. Specify the shared directory where the installation files reside.

❑ d. Choose Make Network Installation Startup Disk within the Network Client Administrator utility.

Answers c and d are correct. To build a network installation startup disk using Windows NT Server, it's necessary to identify the proper directory where the installation files reside, and to choose the Make Network Installation Startup Disk option immediately after launching the Network Client Administrator utility. There is no Client Manager utility in Windows NT Server; therefore, answer a is incorrect. User Manager For Domains has nothing to do with network installation, making answer b incorrect as well.

Question 10

There are 25 Windows 95 machines on your network. You want to upgrade them to Windows NT Workstation with a minimum amount of effort. The installation files reside in a shared directory named \\Server5\Wks4. What is the best way to handle the installation across the network?

○   a.   Attach to the shared directory and run WINNT.EXE across the network.

○   b.   Attach to the shared directory and run SETUP.EXE across the network.

○   c.   Install the Windows NT Workstation client using Network Client Administrator.

○   d.   Use Network Client Administrator to create a DOS Installation Startup Disk, attach to the shared directory, and run SETUP.EXE across the network.

Answer a is correct. To perform a network installation of Windows NT on a computer running Windows 95, it is necessary to obtain access to and run the WINNT.EXE program. Both answers b and d refer to SETUP.EXE, which is the install program for Windows 3.x and Windows 95, not for Windows NT (you must choose WINNT.EXE because it is the only version of the Windows NT installation program that works on non-Windows NT systems). Answer c is incorrect because it assumes that NCA includes support for installing Windows NT Workstation; because this is not the case, this answer is wrong.

Question 11

> When you installed Windows NT Server 4, you opted not to make a set of startup disks. How can you make a set of startup disks on that machine, now that the operating system's already installed?
>
> ○ a. You can't; you have to reinstall Windows NT Server 4 again.
>
> ○ b. Run WINNT.EXE /OX from the installation CD-ROM.
>
> ○ c. Run WINNT32.EXE /OX from the installation CD-ROM.
>
> ○ d. Run the System applet in Control Panel.

Answer c is the correct answer. To build a set of startup disks only, both WINNT.EXE and WINNT32.EXE support the /OX switch, which instructs these programs to build only a set of startup disks, nothing more. Thus, answer a is patently false. Answer b comes very close, but invokes the 16-bit version of the install program, which won't work on a machine running Windows NT. Finally, answer d is incorrect because the System applet includes no options to create a set of startup disks for Windows NT.

Need To Know More?

 Heywood, Drew: *Inside Windows NT Server, 2nd Edition.* New Riders, Indianapolis, IN, 1998. ISBN 1-56205-860-6. Chapters 3 through 5 provide all kinds of planning and installation information and advice, along with some useful troubleshooting tips.

 Siyan, Karanjit S.: *Windows NT Server 4 Professional Reference, 2nd Edition.* New Riders, Indianapolis, IN, 1997. ISBN 1-56205-805-3. Chapters 3 and 4 cover basic and advanced installation topics; all of this information is valuable. The detailed description of a Windows NT installation on pp. 82 through 94 is the best we've ever seen in print.

 Strebe, Matthew, Charles Perkins, and James Chellis: *MCSE: NT Server 4 Study Guide, 2nd Edition.* Sybex Network Press, San Francisco, CA, 1998. ISBN 0-7821-2222-1. Chapters 2 through 4 cover planning, hardware, and installation respectively. Chapter 17, "Troubleshooting," includes an informative section entitled "New Windows NT Installations."

The Windows NT Server 4 manuals cover planning, configuration, and installation issues quite well. Both the *Start Here Manual* and the *Concepts and Planning Manual* are worth perusing, at least once.

 The *Windows NT Server Resource Kit* contains lots of useful information about Windows NT system planning and installation. You can search the TechNet CD or the CD accompanying the *Resource Kit*, using keywords like "installation" and "hardware compatibility." In the *Resource Guide* volume, Chapter 1, "Deploying Windows NT Server," and Chapter 4, "Planning a Reliable Configuration," include information that is both germane and useful.

File Systems

Terms you'll need to understand:

√ File Allocation Table (FAT)

√ New Technology File
System (NTFS)

√ High Performance File
System (HPFS)

√ Compact Disk File
System (CDFS)

√ Long file names (LFNs)

√ Virtual FAT (VFAT)

√ FAT32

√ Share

√ No Access

√ Read

√ Change

√ Full Control

√ Add

√ Add & Read

√ List

√ CONVERT.EXE

Techniques you'll need to master:

√ Selecting a file system for
Windows NT

√ Securing system resources

√ Establishing access
permissions

√ Creating shares and
implementing share
permissions

√ Understanding the difference between copying and
moving files

√ Using CONVERT.EXE to
convert FAT to NTFS

Windows NT supports two primary file systems to save and retrieve data from storage systems of all kinds (primarily hard disks):

➤ File Allocation Table (FAT)

➤ New Technology File System (NTFS)

In this chapter, we'll review these file systems and explore the key aspects of features, functions, and behavior that you're likely to encounter. We'll also examine a couple of other special-purpose file systems that work with Windows NT, so that you're familiar with all the Microsoft Windows NT file systems alphabet soup. Then we'll conclude with some example file-system-related questions and some good places to go looking for more information on this fascinating subject.

FAT Comes In Many Flavors

FAT stands for File Allocation Table and refers to a linear table structure used to represent information about files. The information represented includes file names, file attributes, and other directory entries that locate where files (or segments of files) are stored in the FAT environment; this information points to the actual location on disk where the beginning of a physical file resides.

Original FAT

FAT is the file system originally used with DOS. FAT represents a nearly unbroken chain of capability back to the earliest days of the first DOS-based PCs. The file allocation table from which FAT draws its name stores directory information in a simple table structure that must be searched from beginning to end, one entry at a time, when users access directories or the files that reside within them.

 Although FAT is both primitive and simple, FAT implementations abound: A variety of versions for DOS, Windows 3.x, Windows NT, many flavors of Unix, and Macintosh are available. Numerous other, more exotic operating systems also support FAT file structures. For this reason, Microsoft recommends using FAT volumes with Windows NT Server or Workstation whenever many different types of clients must exchange data through a single file system. (Volumes are discussed in more detail in Chapter 4.)

One of the most important characteristics of original FAT is its use of so-called 8.3 (pronounced "eight-dot-three") file names, where the name of a file can be up to eight characters long, all extensions must be preceded by a period, and file extensions can be up to three characters long. This latter specification has led to the proliferation of many common three-character file extensions, such as .TXT for text files, .DOC for word processing files, .XLS for Excel spreadsheet files, and more. For many users, this is a defining characteristic for MS-DOS, but it's really a requirement of the FAT file system.

Because the size of files and partitions that FAT can manage has grown with each new version of MS-DOS, FAT uses two kinds of pointers in its allocation tables. Partitions smaller than 50 MB use 12-bit pointers, whereas larger partitions require the use of 16-bit pointers. That's why sometimes you'll see FAT volumes labeled as either "FAT12" (the volume's FAT uses 12-bit pointers) or "FAT16" (the volume's FAT uses 16-bit pointers). As shown in Figure 3.1, a FAT12 or FAT16 label appears in disk partition management utilities like the FDISK command that ships with most versions of MS-DOS. For versions of MS-DOS from 3.0 to 6.22, all FAT drivers are 16-bit only (but this does not affect whether a volume is called FAT12 or FAT16—that's purely a function of the size of the FAT volume itself).

Today, in addition to ordinary FAT, there are two other flavors of FAT in use in most modern Microsoft operating systems (Windows 95, 98, and

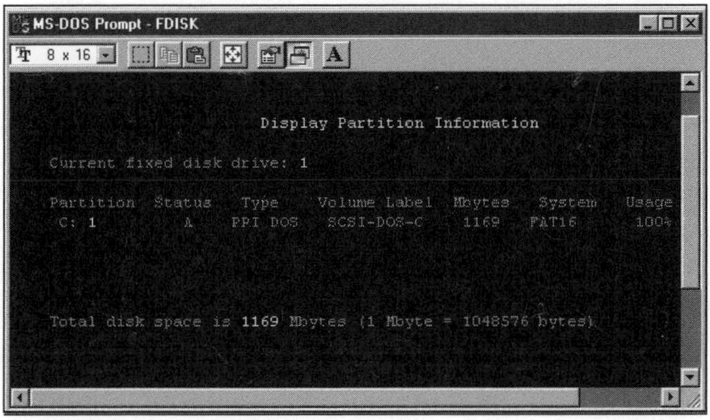

Figure 3.1   The MS-DOS FDISK utility indicates whether a FAT volume is FAT12 or FAT16.

Table 3.1 Vital statistics for the FAT file system.

Feature	Capability/Maximum
Maximum volume size	2 GB
Maximum file size	2 GB
Maximum files in root directory	512
Maximum files in nonroot directory	65,535
File-level security	No
Long file name support	No
Self-repairing	No
Transaction logging capabilities	No
File-level compression	No
Dual file fork support (Macintosh)	No
POSIX support	No

Windows NT, to be precise): Virtual FAT (VFAT) and the FAT32 File System. We'll cover those in the sections that follow.

Virtual FAT (VFAT)

The Virtual FAT file system was first introduced with Windows For Workgroups 3.11 to process file I/O in protected mode. With the introduction of Windows 95, VFAT added support for long file names (LFNs). Nevertheless, VFAT remains backward compatible with original FAT, which means that it supports access using 8.3 file names as well as LFNs, and in fact, maintains an equivalence mechanism that maps 8.3 names into LFNs, and vice versa.

VFAT is the version of FAT that the original releases of Windows 95 and 98, Windows NT 3.51, and Windows NT 4 currently support. When using VFAT file systems, it's absolutely essential to use file management utilities that understand VFAT in general and LFNs in particular. That's because earlier DOS file management utilities will happily reorganize what appears to them as an original FAT structure, and will often lose or damage any LFN information that the FAT table maintained by VFAT (or FAT32 for that matter) contains. Therefore, with VFAT volumes, you must be certain to use file management utilities that can understand and preserve VFAT file structures.

In the initial release of Windows 95, the 32-bit VFAT file system is the primary file system. VFAT can use either 32-bit, protected-mode drivers or 16-bit real-mode drivers. Actual allocation on disk is still 12- or 16-bit (depending on the size of the volume), so VFAT on the disk uses the same structure as earlier implementations of FAT. VFAT handles all hard drive requests, and uses 32-bit code for all file access to hard disk volumes.

As Table 3.2 should illustrate, the primary differences between VFAT and original FAT are an increase in maximum volume and file sizes, an increase in nonroot directory container size, and addition of long file name support to 8.3 file names. VFAT also supports both 16- and 32-bit calls, whereas original FAT supports only 16-bit calls.

The FAT32 File System

FAT32 is a 32-bit successor to VFAT that was introduced with Microsoft Windows 95 OEM Service Release 2, in September 1996. You sometimes will see this release called Windows 95 OSR2 in Microsoft publications. FAT32 is a completely native 32-bit file system (much like NTFS) and supports numerous updates and enhancements compared to other FAT implementations.

Table 3.2 Vital statistics for the VFAT file system.	
Feature	**Capability/Maximum**
Maximum volume size	4 GB
Maximum file size	4 GB
Maximum files in root directory	512
Maximum files in nonroot directory	No limit
File-level security	No
Long file name support	Yes
Self-repairing	No
Transaction logging capabilities	No
File-level compression	No
Dual file fork support (Macintosh)	No
POSIX support	No

Most importantly, FAT32 uses disk space more efficiently than other FAT implementations. FAT32 can use smaller disk clusters than earlier implementations, which were limited to a maximum of 65,635 clusters per volume (so as drives got bigger, cluster sizes had to increase as well). This means that even for drives larger than 4 GB in size, FAT32 can use 4 K clusters. The resulting savings grows as disk capacity grows and disk space is more efficiently used compared to FAT16 drives.

FAT32 also can relocate the root directory and use a backup copy of the FAT, rather than the default copy. FAT32 supports an expanded boot record to include copies of critical data structures, making FAT32 drives less susceptible to failures owing to FAT corruption than earlier implementations. FAT32 even represents the root directory as an ordinary cluster chain, which means that the directory can be located anywhere on a drive, and the prior limitation of 512 entries on a root directory no longer applies (as it does to earlier FAT implementations). Planned implementations of FAT32 may even support dynamic resizing of FAT32 partitions, but this is not supported in Windows 95 OSR2.

Windows 95 OSR2 and Windows 98 are the only current Microsoft operating systems that support FAT32. This means that not even Windows NT 4, with the latest service pack applied, supports this file system. If you create a multiboot configuration on a machine with Windows 95 OSR2 or Windows 98 and Windows NT installed, Windows NT will not be able to access any files that reside in a FAT32 partition. Windows 95 OSR2 and Windows 98 can, however, access the VFAT partitions that Windows NT creates.

The same proviso about using VFAT utilities on VFAT volumes applies to FAT32 volumes. Because earlier FAT utilities (including both FAT and VFAT, where FAT32 is concerned) can damage or lose critical disk information, *never* use anything but FAT32 file management utilities on FAT32 volumes.

In addition to increasing FAT's storage capacity (to a whopping 4 terabyte maximum for files and volumes), FAT32 makes some much-needed improvements to the root directory structure for FAT. Previous implementations required that all information in a FAT root directory fit into a single disk cluster. For all intents and purposes, this limited the number of files in the root to a maximum of 512 entries.

Table 3.3   Vital statistics for the FAT32 file system.

Feature	Capability/Maximum
Maximum volume size	4 TB
Maximum file size	4 TB
Maximum files in root directory	No limit
Maximum files in nonroot directory	No limit
File-level security	No
Long file name support	Yes
Self-repairing	Yes*
Transaction logging capabilities	No
File-level compression	No
Dual file fork support (Macintosh)	No
POSIX support	No

 The introduction of LFNs further limited what the root directory could hold. Because the maximum length of an LFN is 255, a single full-length LFN can consume 25 entries in a FAT (1 for the 8.3 name, 24 more for the LFN itself). This reduces the number of entries possible in a VFAT root directory to 21. Microsoft recommends that LFNs be avoided in FAT root directories unless FAT32 is in use.

Then, too, full file specifications, which require both path names and file names (whether LFNs or 8.3 names), are limited to a total of 260 characters. FAT32 does away with the problems that LFNs in root directories can pose, but it does nothing to increase the 260-character limit on full file specifications. For that reason, Microsoft recommends that even LFNs not be allowed to exceed 75 to 80 characters in length, to leave plenty of room for path designations (up to 180 to 185 characters).

Finally, FAT32 delivers several improvements to FAT's fault tolerance. For one thing, FAT32 boot records now capture important file system data (such as partition table information). For another, FAT mirroring can be enabled in FAT32, so that another copy of the FAT can be used to drive file lookup and access. That's why the Vital Statistics table for FAT32 includes a "Yes" under the Self-repairing category. (It gets an asterisk, though, because these characteristics, although useful, fall short of NTFS's broader set of self-repair capabilities.)

The New Technology File System (NTFS)

In keeping with the New Technology part of its name, NTFS incorporates significant improvements and changes to the file system native to Windows NT. From a user's point of view, files remain organized into directories (often called "folders" in the Windows environment). But unlike FAT, there is no special treatment for root directories, nor limitations set by underlying hardware (such as the ability to access only a maximum number of disk sectors or clusters, as is the case with FAT). Likewise, there are no special locations on an NTFS volume, like the file allocation table that gives FAT its name.

NTFS was designed to provide the following characteristics:

> ➤ **Reliability** Desirable on high-end or shared systems, such as file servers, reliability is a key element of NTFS design and behavior.

> ➤ **Added functionality** NTFS is designed to be extensible and incorporates advanced fault tolerance, emulates other file systems easily, supports a powerful security model, handles multiple data streams, and permits addition of user-defined attributes to files.

> ➤ **POSIX support** Because the U.S. Government requires minimal POSIX compliance in all systems it buys, NTFS provides them. Basic POSIX file system capabilities include optional use of case-sensitive file names, an additional timestamp for time of last file access, and an aliasing mechanism called "hard links" that lets two or more file names (potentially in different directories) point to the same file.

> ➤ **Flexibility** NTFS supports a highly flexible clustering model, with cluster sizes from 512 bytes to 64 K, based on a multiple of the hardware's built-in disk allocation factor. NTFS also supports LFNs, the Unicode character set, and maintains 8.3 file names for all files for backward compatibility with FAT.

NTFS Advantages

NTFS is constructed to handle large collections of data particularly well (see Table 3.4 for the details), and also works well for volumes of 400 MB or greater. Because the directory structure for NTFS is based on a highly efficient data structure called a "B-tree," search time for files under NTFS does not degrade as the number of files to be searched increases (as it does for FAT-based systems).

NTFS also has been designed with sufficient recoverability so that users never should need to employ any kind of disk repair utility on an NTFS partition. Among other things, NTFS maintains a Recycle Bin so that users ordinarily can retrieve their own deleted files without having to run an undelete utility of any kind. But NTFS also supports a variety of file system integrity mechanisms, including automatic transaction logging, which permits all file system writes to be replayed from a special system log.

Table 3.4   Vital statistics for the NTFS file system.

Feature	Capability/Maximum
Maximum volume size	16 EB
Maximum file size	16 EB
Maximum files in root directory	No limit
Maximum files in nonroot directory	No limit
File-level security	Yes
Long file name support	Yes
Self-repairing	Yes
Transaction logging capabilities	Yes
File-level compression	Yes
Dual file fork support (Macintosh)	Yes
POSIX support	Yes

NTFS also supports Windows NT's native object-level security, and treats all volumes, directories, and files as individual objects. Every time users request a file system object, they will be subjected to a security check that matches their right to access the requested object against a list of permissions for that object. Requests from users with sufficient rights will be granted; requests from users with insufficient rights will be denied. This security applies whether users are logged into a Windows NT machine locally or they make their requests across a network.

The vital statistics for NTFS show it as the powerhouse it is. In addition to a staggering capacity of 16 exabytes for volumes or files (an exabyte is 2^{64}, or approximately 16 gigabytes' worth of gigabytes), NTFS offers built-in compression that can be applied to individual files, entire directories, or complete volumes (and selectively removed or applied thereafter).

NTFS offers file-level security, which means that access to volumes, directories, and files can be controlled by an individual's account and the groups to which that account belongs. LFNs are customary with NTFS, but NTFS can map to 8.3 names to maintain support for FAT-based users. In addition to maintaining multiple copies of file system information, Windows NT offers multiple mechanisms to repair and restore an NTFS volume, should problems arise. Likewise, NTFS's transaction logging helps minimize the potential for data loss.

Finally, NTFS supports a much richer file structure, which means it's easy to graft support for other file systems onto an NTFS foundation. Microsoft exploits this capability to provide native support for the Macintosh Hierarchical Filing System (HFS) in NTFS, when Windows NT's Services for Macintosh are installed. Likewise, third parties have built native implementations of Sun's Network Filing System (NFS) that run on top of NTFS (NFS is a popular distributed file system on Unix networks).

Differences Between FAT And NTFS

Where file system overhead is concerned, FAT is more compact and less complex than NTFS. Most FAT volumes impose an overhead of less than

1 MB for the file allocation table structures that represent the directory entries for all files stored in the volume. Because of this low overhead, it is possible to format small hard disks and floppy disks with FAT. NTFS, on the other hand, requires a higher-end system than FAT, partly because each directory entry requires 2 K (this has the advantage, however, of enabling NTFS to store files of 1,500 bytes or less entirely within their directory entries).

NTFS cannot be used to format floppy disks, and shouldn't be used to format partitions smaller than 50 MB. Its relatively high overhead means that for small partitions, directory structures would consume as much as 25 percent of the available storage space.

 Microsoft recommends always using FAT for partitions of 50 MB or smaller, and NTFS for partitions of 400 MB or larger. In the "gray area" between 50 and 400 MB, other factors come into play. Chief among these is file-level security: If this is important, NTFS is the way to go, although FAT will work as well (but gets slower as the size increases).

In relation to file size, FAT partitions can be up to 2 GB, VFAT 4 GB, and FAT32 4 TB; however, FAT partitions work best when they are 200 MB or less, because of the way the FAT itself is organized. NTFS partitions can be as much as 16 EB; however, they currently are restricted to 2 TB by hardware and other system constraints.

FAT partitions may be used by Windows 95, Windows 98, Windows NT, MS-DOS, and WFW, not to mention other operating systems with added FAT support (for example, both Unix and Macintosh can accommodate such add-ons). With a few notable exceptions, NTFS partitions may be accessed directly only using Windows NT. NTFS information is readable across the network by many operating systems (including DOS, Windows 3.X, 95, 98, and other operating systems), partly because of its backward compatibility with FAT, and because of its ability to host other file systems. Also, a utility called NTFSDOS makes it possible to read NTFS data on a PC booted into DOS.

Local security is not an option when you are using FAT partitions (see the next section for more details). NTFS partitions, on the other hand, allow both files and directories to be secured locally. Another difference is that

FAT partitions are required for Windows NT to dual boot with other operating systems; likewise, at least one FAT partition is required to install and operate Windows NT on RISC-based systems.

Securing FAT And NTFS Resources

FAT partitions cannot support local security. This helps explain why the default for Windows NT Server is to disallow all local logins except for accounts with administrative or operator privileges. However, FAT partitions can use share permissions, which may be imposed when directories are shared on a network. This does not prevent someone who is logged on locally from accessing files located on a particular machine, but it can protect even FAT-based files from unauthorized network access.

For security purposes, NTFS is the wiser choice. NTFS partitions can lock out or limit access both for remote and local users. All files and directories on an NTFS partition can be locked using NTFS security. This means that the only people who can access protected files are the users that have been granted explicit access to them.

Directory shares and NTFS security are controlled by security properties associated with a directory to be shared, or with any NTFS file system object (which may be either a directory or an individual file). By selecting the Properties entry in the File menu, or right-clicking on a file name and selecting the Properties entry in the resulting context menu, users can examine Sharing (for directories only) and Security (for files and directories) tabs, shown in Figures 3.2 and 3.3.

The default for the system group Everyone is Full Control for both shares and secured resources. Only a network administrator, the owner, or a user who has been granted the Change Permissions permission can reset the access levels on an NTFS or shared resource because Change Permissions is inherent in Full Control, Security attributes on new shares should be changed to reflect resource requirements as soon as possible.

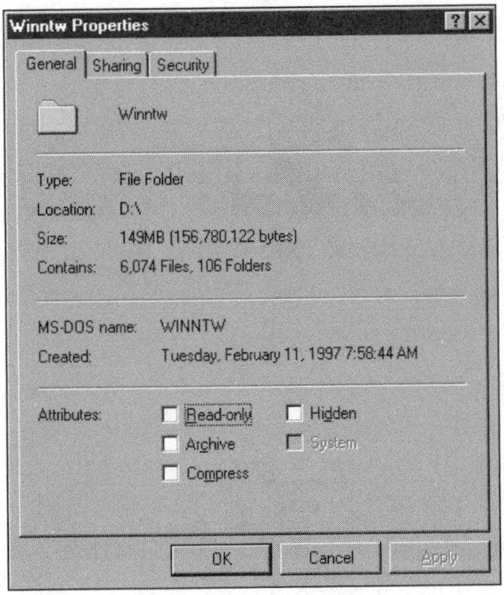

Figure 3.2   Only directories show both the Sharing and Security tabs.

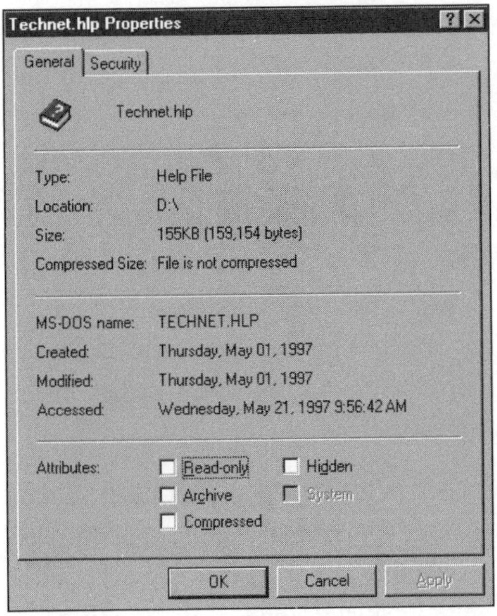

Figure 3.3   Files have only a Security tab (only directories can be shared).

Access Permissions

It is possible for a single user to belong to more than one named group in Windows NT. Access to resources may be assigned to groups or individual users. This makes it possible for a single user or group to be assigned different levels of access for any particular resource. For example, User A may be a member of two different groups—one that assigns User A **Read** access, and the other that assigns User A **Change** access. We explain how to resolve this apparent conflict in the sections that follow.

Share Permissions

A share may be created for a directory that will be given a share name, so users can connect to this directory across the network. The following list names the share permissions that can be assigned in the Windows NT environment:

➤ **No Access** Users can see the directory name, but have no access to its contents.

➤ **Read** Users can see the directory name, and read and execute files within the directory, but can make no changes.

➤ **Change** Users can read, write, execute, and delete files within the directory, but cannot change permissions for the directory or the files within it.

➤ **Full Control** Users can read, write, execute, and delete files within the directory, delete the directory, and change permissions for the directory and the files it contains, as long as the permissions in the contents haven't been restricted further.

For users that belong to more than one group, these permissions are cumulative, except the No Access permission. When the No Access permission is assigned, it overrides all other permissions. In other words, the broadest permission always will apply, unless No Access appears anywhere; when that happens, No Access always "wins."

For example, assume that User A belongs to both GroupOne and GroupTwo. Assume further that a ForEveryone directory exists and has been shared under the same name. Finally, assume that members of GroupOne have Read permission and members of GroupTwo have Change permission for the ForEveryone share.

In this scenario, User A has both Read (by virtue of membership in GroupOne) and Change (by virtue of membership in GroupTwo) access to the ForEveryone share. Because Change is a broader right than Read, this translates into Change permission for User A to ForEveryone.

If we assume that, instead, GroupOne was assigned No Access to ForEveryone, even though User A still has Change access by virtue of his or her membership in GroupTwo, User A cannot access the contents of the ForEveryone share because of the No Access assignment.

NTFS Permissions

NTFS treats directories (folders) and files as different types of objects and maintains a separate (but overlapping) set of permissions for each type. Here is a list of the NTFS permissions that can be assigned to folders (the corresponding permissions for files appear on the next page):

➤ **No Access** (None)

➤ **Full Control** (All) (All)

➤ **Add** (WX)

➤ **Add & Read** (RWX) (RX)

➤ **List** (RX)

➤ **Change** (RWXD) (RWXD)

➤ **Read** (RX) (RX)

Where two sets of values appear in parentheses after a permission name, the first value applies to the folder itself, and the second applies to any files that may be created within the folder. For instance, Full Control grants all rights to a folder, but it also means that for any file created within that folder, a user with Full Control to the folder will also have Full Control over files created within that folder (unless a file's permissions are reset explicitly by an administrator or the file's owner). In other words, NTFS works like this: Files and folders inherit the permissions set for their parent folders by default, but they can be overwritten by any user with the right to change permissions for the NTFS objects in question.

Here is the list of NTFS permissions for files:

> ➤ **Full Control** (All)

> ➤ **No Access** (None)

> ➤ **Change** (RWXD)

> ➤ **Read** (RX)

Like share permissions, NTFS permissions are cumulative, except the No Access permission which overrides all others. NTFS permissions and share permissions are used together when users connect over a network. When share and NTFS permissions combine, the most restrictive permission applies.

When accessing a resource locally (from the computer where the resource resides), a combination of share and NTFS permissions determine the actual resulting permission. By first taking the most liberal of NTFS permissions and the most liberal of share permissions, and by taking the most restrictive of those, one can calculate the resulting permission to the resource. Keep in mind that in all cases No Access is a trump card over all other access permissions.

For example, through the NTFS Security tab, User A is assigned Full Control permission to the ForEveryone folder. Through the Sharing tab, however, User A is assigned Read permission for the same folder.

This means that if User A tries to access the ForEveryone folder across the network, he or she will have Read permission only, because it is the most restrictive of the combination of share and NTFS permissions. However, if User A were to access the folder from the computer where the file resides, he or she would have Full Control. That's because share permissions apply to network access only.

Moving NTFS Secured Files

Higher-level folders usually share NTFS permissions with the files and folders that they contain. For example, if you create a folder within a folder where administrators have Full Control and backup operators have Read Only permission, the new folder will inherit those same permissions. The same goes for files that are copied from another folder or moved from a different NTFS partition.

However, if you move a folder or a file into another folder on the same NTFS partition, security attributes are not inherited from their new container object. For example, if you move a file from a folder with Read permissions for the Everyone group to a folder on the same partition with Full Control for the Everyone group, the moved file retains its original Read permission. That's because an NTFS move operation within the same partition changes only the object's location pointer, not any of the object's other attributes (including security information).

These three important rules will help you decide if permissions will be inherited or retained when performing move or copy operations on NTFS objects:

1. If you move files within the same NTFS partition, they will *retain* their original permissions.

2. Other operations such as file creation, file copy, and moves from one NTFS partition to another will *inherit* the parent folder's permissions.

3. All NTFS permissions are lost when files are moved or copied from NTFS to a FAT partition.

For remote users, both share and NTFS permissions apply (pick the most restrictive). For users logged on locally (interactively), only NTFS permissions apply (pick the least restrictive). But remember, No Access always wins. Because Windows NT's default NTFS permission is Full Control, the default is to deny anyone except administrators or operators local access to a Windows NT Server machine (no other user has log on locally right by default).

A Matter Of Conversion

Windows NT includes a utility named CONVERT.EXE that converts FAT volumes to NTFS equivalents, but there is no utility to perform a conversion from an NTFS volume to a FAT version. To do this, you'd have to create a FAT partition, copy the files from an NTFS partition to that FAT partition, and then delete the NTFS originals. Remember that when files are copied from NTFS to FAT, they lose all their NTFS security attributes (FAT lacks the ability to associate and store security attributes with the files under its care). When installing Windows NT, files are copied to a FAT partition, and the install program automatically invokes the CONVERT.EXE utility just before the install switches from character mode to the GUI interface (which occurs about halfway through the Windows NT installation process provided that NTFS was chosen as the file system).

What About HPFS?

HPFS stands for High Performance File System. Originally introduced with OS/2 1.2 and LAN Manager, HPFS was the first PC-compatible file system that supported LFNs. Like FAT, HPFS maintains a directory structure, but it adds automatic sorting of the directory and includes support for special attributes to better accommodate multiple naming conventions and file-level security.

With the introduction of Windows NT 4, Windows NT no longer supports HPFS directly. Also, HPFS file security is not directly compatible with NTFS security. The version of CONVERT.EXE from Windows NT 3.51 can be used to convert HPFS volumes (from LAN Manager, LAN Server, or Windows NT 3.51 or earlier Windows NT versions) to an NTFS equivalent. The utility's readme file also explains how HPFS security is mapped into an NTFS near-equivalent.

 Remember, HPFS is no longer supported in Windows NT 4.

CDFS

Windows 95, Windows 98, and Windows NT 3.51 and higher-number versions (including 4) support a special read-only file system called the Compact Disk File System (CDFS) to permit easy access to CDs in these operating systems. Because all of these operating systems primarily are distributed in that format, it should come as no surprise that CDFS is an important, if limited, file system in the Windows NT environment. One interesting enhancement that CDFS confers is the ability to boot a PC directly from the CD that contains the Windows NT distribution media.

Practice Questions

Question 1

> You have a 50 MB partition you wish to use as a share for users to store document files. What is the best file system type to format this partition with?
>
> ○ a. FAT
>
> ○ b. CDFS
>
> ○ c. NTFS
>
> ○ d. HPFS

Answer a is correct. FAT is the best choice because it requires much less overhead than NTFS, and Microsoft does not recommend NTFS on partitions smaller than 400 MB. CDFS is not a file system type that can be used to format a hard drive; it is the format of a CD-ROM. Therefore, answer b is incorrect. NTFS has too much overhead for a partition of this size. Therefore, answer c is incorrect. HPFS is not supported by Windows NT 4.0. Therefore, answer d is incorrect.

Question 2

> As you install Windows NT Server 4 on a brand-new machine, you decide to set up two 500 MB partitions, one where Windows NT and other server software will reside, the other where your users will keep their personal files, some of which are confidential. You would do which of the following?
>
> ○ a. Set up both partitions using VFAT.
>
> ○ b. Set up both partitions using NTFS.
>
> ○ c. Set up the system partition using NTFS and the user partition using FAT.
>
> ○ d. Set up the system partition using FAT and the user partition using NTFS.

The correct answer is b—to set up both partitions using NTFS. That's because file-level security is just as important for NT's own files as it is for user files that must be kept confidential (that is, secure). The first answer provides no file-level security, and answers c and d omit file-level security for the user and system partitions, respectively.

Question 3

While configuring a new 8 GB drive for Windows NT Server 4, your manager requests that you set up a large FAT partition for exchanging extremely large desktop publishing and graphics files with a print bureau. He asks you to configure the entire drive for such use, because your monthly newsletter and advertisements routinely require as much as 6 GB of uncompressed space. To meet his requirements, what is your best choice?

- ○ a. Set up a single 8 GB FAT partition.
- ○ b. Set up two 4 GB FAT partitions.
- ○ c. Set up four 2 GB FAT partitions.
- ○ d. Set up sixteen 500 MB FAT partitions.

Answer b is the best choice, because you know the files in question are extremely large (and therefore there will not be a large number of them). The only wrong answer is a, because Windows NT's FAT implementation is limited to a maximum partition size of 4 GB. If there were a lot of small files, answer c would be the best choice. Answer d, although theoretically possible, would require searching too many partitions to locate individual files (and the partitions might be too small for "extremely large" files as well).

Question 4

> You're upgrading a Windows NT Server from 3.51 to 4. The H:
> partition on the 3.51 server is formatted using HPFS. After up-
> grading Windows NT, you can use the CONVERT utility to convert
> H: from HPFS to NTFS.
>
> O   a. True
>
> O   b. False

The correct answer is b, false. Because Windows 4 no longer supports HPFS, you'll have to obtain the ACLCONV utility from Microsoft to convert the HPFS partition into NTFS. For Windows 4, you can only switch FAT partitions into NTFS partitions. Because Windows NT 3.51 CONVERT will switch HPFS to NTFS, it might be even better to convert HPFS to NTFS before installing the upgrade to 4.

Question 5

> User JimBob is a member of the Accounting, Managers, and
> PrintOperators groups. For a share named SalesFeb, these groups
> have the following permissions:
>
> • Accounting: Change
>
> • Managers: Read
>
> • PrintOperators: Full Control
>
> In addition, JimBob's NTFS permissions for the SalesFeb direc-
> tory are Read. JimBob can do the following with files in the
> SalesFeb share:
>
> O   a. Nothing; he has no access.
>
> O   b. Read and execute the files in the SalesFeb directory
>   only.
>
> O   c. Read, write, execute, and delete files in the SalesFeb
>   directory, but not change permissions for the directory
>   or its contents.
>
> O   d. Read, write, execute, delete, and change permissions
>   for SalesFeb and its contents.

The correct answer is b. To calculate share and NTFS permissions combined, take the most permissive of each kind and then the least permissive of the remaining share and NTFS permissions. If **No Access** appears anywhere, the resulting permission will always be **No Access.** Of the three share permissions that pertain to SalesFeb by virtue of JimBob's group memberships, **Full Control** is the most permissive, so that becomes his share permission. His NTFS permission is **Read.** The less permissive of **Read** and **Full Control** is **Read,** so Bob's effective permission to SalesFeb is **Read.** This makes b the only correct answer.

Question 6

User JimBob remains a member of the Accounting, Managers, and PrintOperators groups as before, but is added to the Dangerous group. For a share named SalesFeb, these groups have the following share permissions:

- Accounting: Change
- Managers: Read
- PrintOperators: Full Control
- Dangerous: No Access

In addition, JimBob's NTFS permissions for the SalesFeb directory are READ. JimBob can do the following with files in the SalesFeb share:

○ a. Nothing; he has no access.

○ b. Read and execute the files in the SalesFeb directory only.

○ c. Read, write, execute, and delete files in the SalesFeb directory, but not change permissions for the directory or its contents.

○ d. Read, write, execute, delete, and change permissions for SalesFeb.

Answer a is correct. Because No Access always takes precedence over everything, poor JimBob has no access to SalesFeb and its contents. Remember, No Access always wins.

Question 7

> If you put confidential data onto a FAT partition on a Windows NT
> Server 4 machine, any user can access the data from that parti-
> tion, providing that: [Check all correct answers]
>
> ❏   a. the user can log into the machine remotely.
>
> ❏   b. a share is defined for the folder that contains the
>   confidential materials.
>
> ❏   c. the user has READ permissions for that share (or
>   better).
>
> ❏   d. the user's file permissions are also READ (or better).

The correct answers are a, b, and c. If users cannot log into the machine
across the network, they can't get to any partitions on that machine, whether
FAT or NTFS. If a share is not defined where the confidential data resides,
no user can obtain access to the data across the network. Finally, the user's
share permissions must permit them at least to Read the data in that share,
or they still won't be able to access it. The final element, d, is irrelevant
because FAT partitions do not support file-level security—hence, they have
no associated permissions.

Need To Know More?

 Heywood, Drew: *Inside Windows NT Server, 2nd Edition*. New Riders, Indianapolis, IN, 1998. ISBN 1-56205-860-6. Chapter 11, entitled "Sharing Drives, Directories, and Files," deals very nicely with issues relating to shares and NTFS permissions and access information.

 Siyan, Karanjit S.: *Windows NT Server 4 Professional Reference, 2nd Edition*. New Riders, Indianapolis, IN, 1997. ISBN 1-56205-805-3. Chapter 3 contains a section entitled "Comparing the FAT and NTFS"; Chapter 9 is entitled "Managing Network Files and File-System Security." Both of these sections contain materials germane to this discussion.

 Strebe, Matthew, Charles Perkins, and James Chellis: *MCSE: NT Server 4 Study Guide, 2nd Edition*. Sybex Network Press, San Francisco, CA, 1998. ISBN 0-7821-2222-1. Chapters 4 and 5 both contain useful information about FAT and NTFS, including descriptions of their characteristics and differences.

Search the TechNet CD (or its online version through **www.microsoft.com/technet**) using the keywords "FAT," "VFAT," "FAT32," and "NTFS". KnowledgeBase articles Q154997 "Description of the FAT32 File System" and Q100108 "Overview of FAT, HPFS, and NTFS File Systems" are particularly informative.

 The *Windows NT Server Resource Kit* contains lots of useful information about NTFS and share permissions. Here again, you can search the TechNet CD or the CD accompanying the *Resource Kit*, using keywords like "NTFS permissions," and "share permissions." The section in Chapter 3, "Disk Management Basics," of the *Resource Guide* entitled "Windows NT File Systems" is a particularly good resource.

Windows NT
Fault Tolerance

4

Terms you'll need to understand:

✓ Fault tolerance

✓ Disk partition

✓ RAID (Redundant Array of Inexpensive Disks)

✓ Disk mirroring

✓ Disk duplexing

✓ Disk striping

✓ Disk striping with parity

✓ Disaster recovery

✓ UPS (uninterruptible power supply)

Techniques you'll need to master:

✓ Using Disk Administrator to implement fault tolerance

✓ Creating a volume set

✓ Creating a disk mirror

✓ Implementing disk striping (with and without parity information)

Fault tolerance embraces a wide variety of system capabilities and functionality. This topic is covered broadly in this chapter, across all subject areas.

The specific topics that fall under the general heading of fault tolerance for Windows NT Server include: disk mirroring, disk duplexing, and disk striping (with parity). Other relevant fault tolerance topics include disaster recovery (using Windows NT's built-in Disk Administrator utility) and several general storage, controller, and bootup matters. Some of the information in this chapter repeats information from other chapters. This should help you correlate various aspects of fault tolerance as implemented in Windows NT's overall system design and architecture.

Disk Administrator

All the fault tolerant features of Windows NT are focused on, or at least related to, the Disk Administrator utility. That makes it imperative to examine this tool thoroughly, so you may understand Microsoft's implementation of fault tolerance for Windows NT Server 4. The better your knowledge of Disk Administrator's tools and menus (see Figure 4.1), the more likely it is that you will understand fault tolerance. Remember, Disk Administrator appears beneath the Start menu, in the Programs| Administrative Tools (Common) fly-open menu.

Take time to familiarize yourself with the layout of Disk Administrator's menus, the locations of commands, and resulting dialog boxes. If you are visually inclined, you may be able to work with the tool for a short time and then be able to "see" it in your mind's eye. Those of you unable to visualize the utility must memorize its menus. Table 4.1 is a chart that will help you with that task. (*Note:* We omitted the Help menu.)

One important command is Commit Changes Now. This command instructs Windows NT to make your requested changes to the affected storage devices. In other words, partitions and drives will not be created or changed in Disk Administrator until this menu option is chosen.

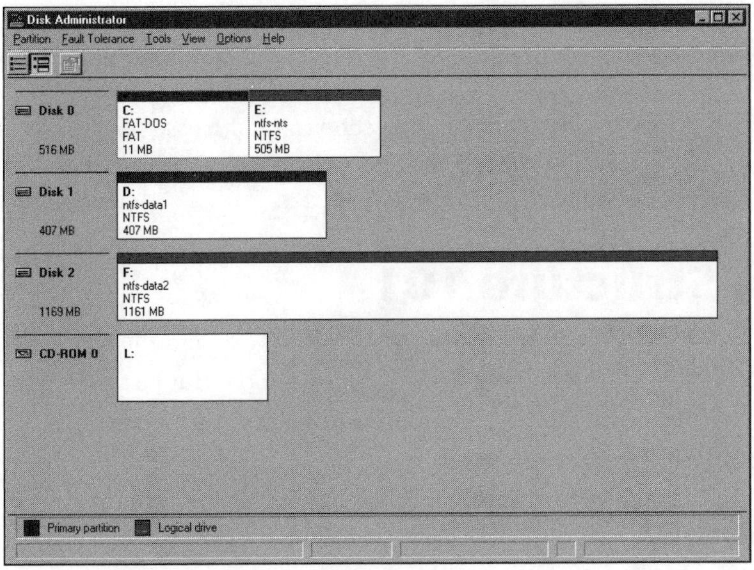

Figure 4.1   The Disk Administrator utility.

Table 4.1   Disk Administrator's menus and options.

Partition	Fault Tolerance	Tools	View	Options
Create	Establish Mirror	Format	Volumes	Toolbar
Create Extended	Break Mirror	Assign Drive Letter	Disk Configuration	Status Bar
Delete	Create Stripe Set with Parity	Eject	Refresh	Legend
Create Volume Set	Regenerate	Properties		Colors and Patterns
Extend Volume Set				Disk Display
Create Stripe Set				Region Display
Mark Active				Customize Toolbar
Configuration				
Commit Changes Now				
Exit				

Obviously, there are many commands in the five menus found in Disk Administrator. Many of these commands are discussed in further detail when a specific fault tolerance issue warrants such a discussion. But if a menu selection is not discussed further in this text, it's safe to assume you need know little (if anything) about it.

Disk Structure 101

Hopefully, you are already familiar with storage devices and the terminology used to describe their configuration and operation. But just to be sure you're equipped with the bare minimum of such information, a short refresher follows.

Partitions

A hard drive can contain one or more file systems, such as FAT or NTFS, each of which enables a NOS or OS to store and retrieve files. Each file system must reside on a different section of the disk. This is enabled by subdividing the disk into partitions. Even though Windows NT only supports FAT and NTFS natively, partitions that support other file systems can reside on a machine that runs Windows NT (even if Windows NT cannot access them). For instance, it's possible that a drive on a dual-boot machine running Windows 95 OEM release 2 and Windows NT Server 4 could contain a FAT32 partition; in that case, only Windows 95 or Windows 98 could access that partition (see Chapter 3 for more information).

In general, a hard drive can contain between 1 and 32 separate partitions. Thus, a single physical hard drive can appear as multiple logical drives. Hard drives should be partitioned to maximize their usage by the underlying NOS and its applications. If you attempt to change a partition, any information stored in that space on disk will be destroyed. If there is free unpartitioned space on a drive, you may create new partitions without damaging existing partitions. Likewise, deleting any one partition does not affect other partitions on a drive.

The NTFS file system supports a variety of partition schemes. A single drive may contain up to four primary partitions, or one to three primary partitions and a single extended partition. An extended partition can be subdivided further into multiple logical drives. The total number of primary partitions plus logical drives, however, cannot exceed 32 on any one physical hard drive under Windows NT's control.

Volumes

An NTFS volume is an organizational structure imposed upon one or more partitions that supports file storage. Under Windows NT, volumes can span multiple partitions on one or more physical drives.

An NTFS volume set is a logical disk drive comprised of 2 to 32 partitions. A volume set may be extended at any time by adding another partition to the set without damaging existing stored data. However, a volume set and its data must be destroyed to reduce the size of a volume. All the partitions in a volume set must use the same file system, and the entire volume set is assigned a single drive letter. Volume sets may span physical drives. A volume provides no fault tolerance for its data. If any one of the partitions or drives within a volume set fails, all of the data is lost.

The best way to remember the impact of losing a volume set element is the phrase "You lose one, you lose them all." This also means that the only way to recover the data in a damaged volume set is to restore the data from a backup.

Drive Letters

Every volume on a Windows NT machine must have an associated drive letter; in fact, Windows NT cannot access a volume unless it has an associated drive letter. Drive letters simplify the identification of an exact physical drive, partition, and volume for any referenced folder or file. Windows NT can assign drive letters to storage devices using the letters C through Z (A and B are reserved for floppy drives). Because this only covers 24 potential drives, and Windows NT supports as many as 32, the assumption is that some volumes will span multiple physical drives (which all share a single drive letter).

Windows NT automatically assigns the next available drive letter to each new volume that is created. You can reassign dynamically or shuffle drive letters using the Assign Drive Letter option on the Tools menu in Disk Administrator.

Another exception to association of volumes with drive letters applies to volumes formatted with file systems not supported by Windows NT. These volumes generally are not assigned drive letters because Windows NT cannot access them. Only the partition containing Boot.ini may be set to active or Windows NT will not boot.

Master Boot Record

The Master Boot Record (MBR) is a BIOS bootstrap routine used by low-level hardware-based system code stored in read-only memory (ROM), to initiate the boot sequence on a PC. This in turn calls a bootstrap loader, which commences loading the machine's designated operating system. The MBR directs the hardware to a so-called "active partition" from which the designated operating system may be loaded (for more information on this topic, consult Chapter 13).

 Only a primary partition can be made active, by using the Mark Active command on Disk Administrator's Partition menu. The system partition is where the MBR and boot loader reside; for Windows NT, the boot partition is where the Windows NT system files reside. It's backwards!

Fault Tolerance

The resilience of a system in the presence of errors, mistakes, or disasters without causing damage or loss to its data is its fault tolerance. Windows NT's fault tolerance features vary from disk partition organization to high-level file system operations to backup techniques. When all of these are combined, they make Windows NT a reliable and solid NOS.

The NTFS file system supports internal and automatic fault tolerance. Using a method called "hot fixing," every storage device write is monitored and written sectors are checked for integrity. If any verification fails, the questionable sectors are flagged and the data is rewritten to another working location on disk. This is performed automatically by the file system and does not report error messages to any applications. NTFS also logs all changes to the file system so that changes may be undone or reapplied if a discrepancy is found, or if damage is caused by a system failure or power loss.

Windows NT Server 4 supports three types of fault-tolerant disk structures—disk mirroring, disk duplexing, and disk striping with parity. These structures may be implemented using the Fault Tolerance menu in the Disk Administrator utility. But, as you'll soon learn, only disk striping with parity mirroring/duplexing qualifies as fault tolerant; disk striping without parity does not qualify, even though it's another legal way to aggregate multiple partitions in Disk Administrator.

The following sections refer only to software fault tolerance, because that is all that is required for the exam.

Disk Mirroring

Disk mirroring creates an exact duplicate of one physical storage device on a separate physical storage device. Both the primary drive and the backup (mirrored drive) are attached to the same hard drive controller. If the primary drive fails, there is no loss of data because everything written to the original disk also is written to the mirror. Barring other physical component problems, when the original drive fails, the system automatically switches to the mirrored drive to continue operation.

Disk mirroring's drawbacks include:

> **Slow performance** The act of writing the same data twice takes longer than writing it just once.

> **Increased cost** Every mirror must be a separate physical device; therefore, you must purchase twice the storage capacity.

> **No protection from controller failure** If the disk controller fails, the mirrored drive is just as inaccessible as the original drive.

 The boot and system partitions can be the primary disk in a disk mirror set. However, if the primary fails, it's necessary to hand-edit the BOOT.INI file on the boot drive to point to the ARC (Advanced RISC Computing) name for the mirror instead. (ARC names and BOOT.INI editing are both covered in Chapter 13.)

Chapter 4

Disk Duplexing

Disk duplexing is similar to disk mirroring, but more robust. Like mirroring, disk duplexing uses duplicate physical drives; unlike mirroring, the drives are connected to the system via a separate controller. If the original drive or controller fails, the system continues to operate using the duplexed drive. There is no system performance degradation, because writing the same data twice through two disk controllers requires no additional time, and both writes occur simultaneously.

One significant drawback to disk duplexing is the cost: It requires double the storage space and a second disk controller.

 As with mirroring, the boot and system partitions can be the primary disk in a disk duplexing set. If the primary fails, however, you must edit the BOOT.INI file by hand to point to the ARC name for the duplexed drive. Also, a custom boot floppy could be used to boot to the mirrored or duplexed drive.

Disk Striping

Disk striping stores data across multiple physical storage devices. In a stripe set, multiple blocks of equal size on separate devices are combined into a single logical device. When data is stored to a stripe set, it is written in 64 K chunks—stripes—across the drives, starting at the drive on the left with data block 1, then on the middle drive with data block 2, and so on (see Figure 4.2 for an example of a stripe set).

Disk striping is fast, especially when the individual storage devices are attached to separate disk controllers. Disk striping does not have the same

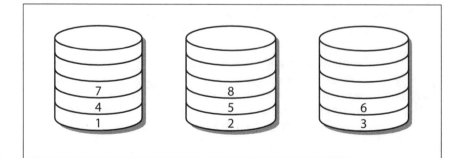

Figure 4.2 A stripe set using three physical disks.

cost drawbacks as mirroring and duplexing, because all or most of the storage space you purchase is fully available to you. You only need two devices to create a stripe set without parity, and such a stripe set can include as many as 32 devices. Disk striping can be implemented using either FAT or NTFS.

 However, disk striping without parity provides no fault tolerance. Should any one of the drives in a stripe set without parity fail, all of the data on all disks is lost (once again, it's "Lose one, lose them all!"). If any of the drive controllers fails, none of the data is accessible until that drive controller is repaired.

The boot and system partitions cannot be part of a disk stripe set without parity (or with parity, either, as you'll see in the next section). If the Windows NT documentation includes a stripe set without mention of parity, you must assume that this means a stripe set without parity.

Disk Striping With Parity

Disk striping with parity offers most of the benefits of parity-free disk striping without the same risk of data loss. Parity is a calculation based on the data. That calculated value is written to an additional stripe. Should a physical disk fail, the parity information is used in conjunction with the remaining data to calculate the the data that is on the failed drive. Then, if any one of the drives in a parity stripe set fails, that data can be rebuilt from the parity information on the remaining devices without loss.

To record parity information within a stripe set, additional space is required. Unfortunately, this means that the total amount of storage capacity is smaller than the sum of the capacity of all drives in the stripe set. To calculate the total capacity (T) of a stripe set with parity, use the following formula (where P is the size of any single partition and n is the number of partitions in the set):

```
T = P * (n - 1)
```

i.e., in a RAID set consisting of four 9 GB hard drives, T = 9(4 - 1) or 9(3) = 27 GB of usable data space. When you create a stripe set using the Create Stripe Set With Parity option on the Disk Administrator's Fault Tolerance menu, you will be presented with a dialog box that displays the total size of the set. This number is P * n, which equals the size of the smallest drive multiplied by the total number of drives. This number does not reflect the amount of actual usable storage space of a stripe set with parity. That number is determined by the preceding formula, which takes the space requirements for parity information into account.

Here are a few important items to remember about a software implementation of disk striping with parity:

➤ All partitions within a stripe set must be of equal size (or nearly so).

➤ Each partition must be on a separate physical disk.

➤ NTFS or FAT can be used as the file system on a stripe set with parity.

➤ A minimum of three devices is required to build a stripe set with parity; as before, the maximum number of devices remains set at 32.

➤ Writing performance is slightly slower than disk striping without parity, but faster than software disk mirroring.

➤ If one drive in a set fails, the data set can be regenerated from the remaining devices.

➤ Neither the boot nor system partitions can reside in a disk stripe set, even with parity.

RAID

The four disk storage organizations we've described for Windows NT represent software implementations of RAID (Redundant Array of Inexpensive—or Individual—Disks). In other words, RAID is a storage method that uses numerous devices in combination to store large amounts of data.

RAID also addresses various levels of fault tolerance and recoverability for specific configurations and storage techniques. There are six distinct levels recognized in RAID subsystems, starting with 0 (zero) and ending with 5 (five). Windows NT Server software supports RAID Levels 0, 1, and 5. Here's an explanation of these levels:

➤ **RAID 0 is disk striping without parity.** This level provides no fault tolerance, but it is the fastest data access method.

➤ **RAID 1 is disk mirroring.** This level provides a reasonable level of data protection, but has some performance consequences. Disk duplexing also is categorized as RAID 1 because it provides the same level of data protection with improved performance. Both mirroring and duplexing require twice as much physical storage as the data to be stored (because there are two identical copies of everything).

➤ **RAID 5 is disk striping with parity.** RAID 5 can outperform RAID 1; however, its real strength is its cost relative to RAID 1. As a RAID 5 array grows, it actually gets cheaper because only the space equivalent to one drive is used for parity, regardless if the array consists of 3 or 32 drives.

Remember that Windows NT's software implementation of RAID requires additional system overhead, especially when large numbers of devices are involved. Software RAID is convenient and inexpensive (it is included with Windows NT), but hardware RAID is faster and offers more options and reliability (like "hot-swappable" drives and controllers). Hardware RAID controllers make the implementation of RAID transparent to Windows NT.

Comparing RAID Levels

You must fully understand RAID levels before you can designate a level of fault tolerance for a particular system or configuration. Remember first and foremost that disk striping without parity (RAID 0) offers no fault tolerance whatsoever. In addition to the RAID levels and fault tolerance features of the various partition organizations, remain aware of expense and hardware requirements.

When comparing disk mirroring (or duplexing) to disk striping with parity, remember:

➤ Two physical disks per mirror set are required for disk mirroring or duplexing.

➤ No less than 3 or more than 32 physical disks may be used with disk striping with parity.

➤ You can mirror (or duplex) the partition where system and boot files for Windows NT are stored (these are the Windows NT boot and system partitions, respectively).

➤ You cannot use disk striping (with or without parity) for Windows NT system and boot partitions.

➤ Disk striping with parity uses $1/n$ of the total disk space available to store parity information (where n is the number of disks in the stripe set).

➤ If a disk stripe set with parity or a mirror set loses more than one physical drive, data from the entire set will be lost; the set then must be repaired, rebuilt, and the data restored from backup.

Recovery

As long as the physical disk(s) that contain the system and boot partitions do not fail, recovery from disk failure is relatively simple. However, recovery without resort to a backup is possible only with a disk mirror, disk duplex, or stripe set with parity. All other partition structures offer no "live recovery" for the data they store.

Fixing Broken Mirrors And Duplexes

When the primary member of a disk mirror (or duplex) set fails, Windows NT can use the other member of the set to continue operation. But whenever a member of a mirror or duplex set fails, you must replace the failed member and re-establish the mirror or duplex, or you no longer will benefit from the data protection. In fact, the Windows NT Server will be unable to reboot at all if the primary set member fails, because the BOOT.INI file points to that member (that's why it's necessary to hand-edit the ARC name in the boot file to point to the other member of the set to restart the system at all).

The first step in repairing a mirrored set is to break the mirror. This is accomplished in the Disk Administrator utility, using the Break Mirror option in the Fault Tolerance drop-down menu. Once the mirror is broken, you must reassign the drive letter to the remaining member of the (now broken) mirror set. For example, if Drives 1 and 2 are mirrored and assigned drive letter D, and Drive 1 fails, you must break the mirrored set, and then assign drive letter D to Drive 2.

The second step is to replace the failed drive. The replaced drive will show up as free space in Disk Admininistrator. From inside Disk Administrator, first check on the partition you want to mirror, then while holding the Ctrl button down, click on the free space (the drive that was replaced). Then with both drives highlighted, select Fault Tolerance|Create Mirror. For the exam, remember if one half of a mirror set fails—break mirror/replace drive/ re-establish mirror.

If the mirror set includes a boot partition, and the drive that failed was the original member of the set, you must boot with a floppy to regain access to the system to run the Disk Administrator utility to repair the set. You must create an up-to-date boot floppy for the system so this process can work. That boot floppy should contain the following files:

➤ BOOT.INI—edited version to point to the mirror drive

➤ NTLDR

➤ NTDETECT.COM

➤ NTBOOTDD.SYS—only if you are using a SCSI controller with BIOS translation disabled (or missing)

➤ BOOTSECT.DOS—only if you need to boot into MS-DOS or another operating system present on your system

You will need to edit the BOOT.INI file to match new parameters and the new location of the boot partition. For further information, read "Special Boot Considerations" later in this chapter.

Restoring With Parity Information

Recovering from a device failure with disk striping with parity is easy. After the device fails, the system is able to rebuild data on the fly from parity information stored on the still-operational devices. Because regeneration is CPU-intensive, performance slows dramatically. However, the system continues to operate, even with a failed set member.

After a set member fails, it's important to replace it quickly to restore fault tolerance and system performance levels to normal. From Disk Administrator, the replaced disk will show up as free space. Click on one of the partitions of the stripe set, then while holding the Ctrl button down, click on the free space, and the

> remaining partitions of the stripe set. With all partitions and the free space highlighted, select Fault Tolerance|Regenerate. Windows NT will rebuild the new drive into the disk array using the parity to calculate the missing data.

Special Boot Considerations

If the partition that contains Windows NT's system files fails, you will find where those mirrored system files are mapped in BOOT.INI, which uses ARC name syntax to map a path to the system files. This path designation starts by identifying the hard disk controller, and finishes with the name of the folder that contains the Windows NT system files.

Here are some examples of BOOT.INI entries:

```
multi(1)disk(0)rdisk(1)partition(2)\WINNT=
  "Windows NT Server Version 4.00"
scsi(0)disk(0)rdisk(0)partition(1)\WINNT=
  "Windows NT Server Version 4.00"
```

Should a system partition on a primary device in a mirror set fail, these entries will need to be changed. However, the changes should take place on a boot floppy, not the mirror device. Remember that if you choose to mirror the system partition using Windows NT Disk Administrator, it is most prudent to create a boot floppy for just such an instance.

If the original drive in a mirror set fails and that drive was the boot partition, BOOT.INI on the mirror drive (which must now function as the boot partition) must be edited to reflect the new, correct location of these files. You might also edit the BOOT.INI file on a boot floppy to perform the same function, especially if you plan to restore the original drive quickly and return the system to its previous state.

BOOT.INI lives in the system partition, usually on drive C, on your Windows NT machine. BOOT.INI is a text file, which means you can edit it with any text editor. BOOT.INI attributes are set as a system and read-only file; therefore, you must turn off these attribute settings before you can edit the file, and then reset them once your changes are complete. Here's an example of a BOOT.INI file:

```
[boot loader]
timeout=10
default=scsi(0)disk(0)rdisk(0)partition(1)\WINNT
[operating systems]
scsi(0)disk(0)rdisk(0)partition(1)\
   WINNT="Windows NT Server Version 4.00"
scsi(0)disk(0)rdisk(0)partition(1)\WINNT="Windows NT
   Server Version 4.00 [VGA mode]" /basevideo /sos
C:\="MS-DOS 6.22"
```

To edit the BOOT.INI file properly, you must know the following about ARC names:

➤ To change the BOOT.INI file to point to the proper location, you must edit both the default= line and the main NOS line (which is scsi(0)disk(0)rdisk(0)partition(1)\WINNT= "Windows NT Server Version 4.00" in the preceding example). Both ARC names must match exactly.

➤ The first four elements of an ARC name are always lowercase in the BOOT.INI file. We use uppercase in this discussion to set them off from normal body text

➤ The first element in an ARC name, either SCSI or MULTI, is the controller type. SCSI indicates that a SCSI disk controller is being used that does not support BIOS translation. If SCSI appears, it also means that a driver file named NTBOOTDD.SYS must appear in the system partition to handle BIOS translation for the controller. MULTI indicates any other controller type that supports BIOS translation, including IDE and SCSI (among others).

➤ The number immediately following SCSI or MULTI identifies the position of the controller within the system, numbered ordinally. Thus, the first controller is numbered zero (0), the second is one (1), and the third is two (2).

➤ The second element in an ARC name, DISK, designates the device number for a SCSI controller with no BIOS translation abilities. The string "DISK" always appears in an ARC name, but only if SCSI is the first element in the name, does the number that follows DISK identify a storage device. Such devices are also numbered ordinally. Thus, the first device also is numbered zero (0), the second is one (1), and so on. If MULTI appears first in an ARC name, DISK is ignored and will always be set to a zero (0).

➤ The value associated with RDISK is significant only if MULTI is the first keyword in an ARC name. If that is the case, the value associated with RDISK identifies the device number for some drive attached to whatever controller is specified. Here again, the first device is numbered zero (0), the second is numbered one (1), and so forth. If an ARC name begins with SCSI, the value of RDISK is ignored and is always set to zero. But because MULTI identifies the vast majority of controllers (except those SCSI controllers that do not offer BIOS translation), RDISK usually identifies the boot drive for Windows NT.

➤ The fourth element in an ARC name identifies a disk partition. PARTITION indicates the partition where system files reside, numbered cardinally. Unlike the other terms, the first partition is one (1), the second is two (2), the third is three (3), and so on.

➤ The fifth element in an ARC name is the name of the folder where the system files reside. "\WINNT" indicates that the folder (or directory) on the specified partition named "WINNT" is where system information may be found. Whatever the directory is named, this element must reflect that exact name.

➤ The data following the folder name provides the information that appears in the Windows NT boot menu. The equals sign and the quotes that enclose the text string must follow the folder name without any additional spaces outside the quotes.

➤ After the Boot Menu name, additional command line parameter switches may be added to control how Windows NT boots. These switches include /SOS and /BASEVIDEO. /SOS causes Windows NT to display the names of drivers on screen as they are loaded during system boot. /BASEVIDEO puts Windows NT into VGA mode, which is useful when troubleshooting video configuration problems.

One important item to remember is that Microsoft reversed what you might expect the terms "boot partition" and "system partition" to mean. As it happens, boot files are stored on the system partition, that is, the active partition where BOOT.INI and NTLDR reside. System files are stored on the boot partition, where the default WINNT directory resides. When you come across a request for the ARC name of a partition that contains boot files, remember that these boot files reside on the system partition, and the system files reside on the boot partition. We can only guess at Microsoft's thinking—that system files are for low-level hardware initiation of the boot process, and thus reside on the boot partition, and boot files supply bootup intelligence for Windows NT itself, and therefore reside on the system partition. Just remember that it's the opposite of common sense, and you'll do just fine.

Practice Questions

Question 1

> Using free unpartitioned space on a SCSI drive, you create a new partition. You highlight the free space, select Create from the Partition menu, specify the size of the partition, and click OK. Now the new drive appears in the Disk Administrator display. What should you do next in your endeavor to create a new place to store data?
>
> ○ a. Assign drive letter
>
> ○ b. Select Configuration, Save
>
> ○ c. Format
>
> ○ d. Commit Changes Now

Answer d is correct. You must use the Commit Changes Now command to save the partition creation changes as your next step; then you can proceed to format the partition and assign it a drive letter. It is not possible to assign a drive letter to a partition unless it is formatted; therefore, answer a is incorrect. The Configuration, Save command stores the current configuration status as stored in the Registry to an Emergency Repair Disk; this is not a step toward creating a usable volume, so answer b also is incorrect. Formatting a partition to create a volume is required, but this cannot occur until partition creation changes are committed, making answer c incorrect as well.

Question 2

> You have two IDE hard drives on a single drive controller in your Windows NT Server computer. There is only one partition on each of the two drives. The first drive's partition is formatted with FAT, and the second drive's partition is formatted with NTFS. The boot files are located on the second drive. What is the ARC name for the system partition?
>
> O a. multi(0)disk(1)rdisk(0)partition(1)
>
> O b. multi(0)disk(0)rdisk(1)partition(1)
>
> O c. multi(1)disk(0)rdisk(1)partition(1)
>
> O d. multi(0)disk(0)rdisk(1)partition(0)
>
> O e. multi(1)disk(0)rdisk(0)partition(1)

Answer b indicates the first partition of the second hard drive on the first multitype drive controller; because this is indeed the location of the system partition for this configuration, answer b is correct. Answer a displays an improperly composed ARC name: When MULTI is used, the disk(n) number must be set to zero. Therefore answer a is incorrect. Answer c points to a second drive controller that doesn't exist in this example, and consequently must be incorrect. Answer d supplies an incorrect number for the partition element—because partitions are numbered cardinally, a partition number never can be zero. Answer d is incorrect because the first partition is numbered one. Answer e names a second, nonexistent drive controller, and points to the first drive on that controller. Because the system partition for this question is attached to the first—and only—disk controller, on the second hard drive, answer e is incorrect. Remember that the system partition must be active, but it does not have to be on the first drive or the first partition on a drive.

Question 3

> What is the best method for implementing fault tolerance on a Windows NT Server computer with two high-speed SCSI drives, each on a separate controller card?
>
> ○ a. Disk duplexing
> ○ b. Disk striping without parity
> ○ c. Disk mirroring
> ○ d. Create a volume set across both drives.

Answer a is correct. Disk duplexing is the fault tolerance method that utilizes two drives, each on separate controllers. Disk striping without parity offers no fault tolerance, making answer b incorrect. Disk mirroring utilizes two drives on the same controller, making answer c incorrect as well. Finally, a volume set offers no fault tolerance either, making answer d incorrect.

Question 4

> Which items below describe disk striping with parity?
> [Check all correct answers]
>
> ❑ a. Requires three physical drives.
> ❑ b. Can be implemented with FAT.
> ❑ c. Provides fault tolerance.
> ❑ d. Has faster read-write performance than disk mirroring.
> ❑ e. Data cannot be recovered if a single drive within the set fails.

Answers a, b, c, and d are correct. Disk striping with parity requires a minimum of three physical drives, so answer a is correct. Disk striping with parity can be implemented with either NTFS or FAT. Therefore, answer b is correct. Because disk striping with parity is indeed a fault tolerant storage method, answer c also is correct. Because it spreads the load across more drives, disk striping with parity offers better performance than disk mirroring. Thus, answer d is correct as well. And because disk striping with parity can recover from a single drive failure, answer e is incorrect.

Question 5

> Which of the following ARC names indicates the third partition of
> the fourth SCSI drive on the second controller that has its BIOS
> disabled?
>
> ○　a. multi(1)disk(3)rdisk(0)partition(3)
>
> ○　b. multi(1)disk(0)rdisk(3)partition(3)
>
> ○　c. scsi(1)disk(3)rdisk(0)partition(3)
>
> ○　d. scsi(1)disk(3)rdisk(0)partition(4)

Answer c indicates the third partition on the fourth drive on a non-BIOS
SCSI controller, so this answer is correct. Answer a indicates a BIOS-
enabled controller, which makes this answer incorrect. Answer b indicates the same condition and is equally wrong. Answer d is close, but
indicates the fourth partition, and therefore is incorrect.

Question 6

> You want to implement fault tolerance on your Windows NT Server
> computer so your data will be protected in the event of a power
> failure or hardware malfunction. Which of the following techniques
> will provide you some type of fault tolerance? [Check all correct
> answers]
>
> ❑　a. RAID 1
>
> ❑　b. Disk duplexing
>
> ❑　c. Volume set
>
> ❑　d. Disk striping without parity
>
> ❑　e. RAID 5

The complete set of correct answers to this question is a, b, and e. RAID 1
indicates disk mirroring, which provides some fault tolerance; therefore,
answer a is correct. Disk duplexing is another fault tolerant storage method,
so answer b also is correct. RAID 5 is the same thing as disk striping with
parity; because this scheme provides fault tolerance, answer e is also correct.
A volume set is not fault tolerant, making answer c incorrect. Disk striping
without parity is not fault tolerant, either; therefore, answer d is incorrect.

Question 7

Your Windows NT Server computer has two physical disks. What
forms of storage can be implemented with only two drives?
[Check all correct answers]

❑   a. Disk striping with parity

❑   b. Disk mirroring

❑   c. Disk duplexing

❑   d. Volume set

❑   e. Disk striping without parity

Answers b, c, d, and e are correct. Disk mirroring uses only two drives, but they
must be on the same controller, so answer b is correct. Disk duplexing uses only
two drives, but as both must be on different controllers, answer c also is correct.
A volume set can consist of from 2 to 32 partitions on any number of drives, so
answer d also is correct. Disk striping without parity requires a minimum of
two drives; therefore, answer e also is correct. Disk striping with parity requires
a minimum of three drives, which makes answer a wrong.

Question 8

Which of the following drive sets supported by Windows NT Server
can contain the system and/or boot partitions? [Check all correct
answers]

❑   a. Disk mirroring

❑   b. Disk striping without parity

❑   c. Volume set

❑   d. Disk duplexing

Answers a and d are correct. Disk mirroring can contain either system or
boot partitions, or both, on the original disk. Therefore, answer a is correct.
Disk duplexing can accommodate either the system or boot partitions, or
both, on the original disk, so answer d also is correct. No kind of stripe set
can contain either system or boot paritions, so disk striping without parity

cannot contain the system or boot partitions. Of course, this means that answer b is incorrect. A volume set cannot contain either system or boot partitions, making answer c incorrect.

Question 9

What files should be placed on a boot disk to boot to the duplicate drive of a disk duplex from a floppy in the event of a failure of the original drive? Assume the drive controller is SCSI that does not support BIOS translation. [Check all correct answers]

❑   a. NTDETECT.COM

❑   b. BOOT.INI

❑   c. NTLDR

❑   d. WINA20.386

❑   e. NTBOOTDD.SYS

The full set of correct answers to this question is a, b, c, and e. NTDETECT.COM is required on the boot floppy, so answer a is correct. BOOT.INI is required on the boot floppy; therefore answer b also is correct. Answer c is correct because NTLDR is required on the boot floppy. NTBOOTDD.SYS is the driver for SCSI translation required for non-BIOS controllers, making answer e correct as well. WINA20.386 is a Windows device driver that is not needed on the boot floppy, so answer d is incorrect.

Question 10

The primary disk of a disk mirror fails. The mirror did not contain the system or boot partitions. What steps are required to restore the mirror set?

○ a. Replace the failed disk, reformat both drives, re-create a mirror set, and restore the data from a backup tape.

○ b. Replace the failed disk; Windows NT Server will automatically restore the mirror set.

○ c. Break the mirror set, replace the failed drive, and re-create the mirrored drive.

○ d. Replace the failed disk, select the mirror set and the replaced drive, and select Regenerate from the Fault Tolerance menu.

The steps in answer c will restore a mirror set properly, with the roles of the drives reversed, making answer c correct. Answer a causes you to perform many long and unnecessary steps: Neither formatting the two drives nor restoring from tape backup is required; therefore, answer a is incorrect. Windows NT will not automatically restore a mirror set, so answer b also is wrong. The steps in answer d are used to repair a stripe set with parity, so answer d is incorrect.

Question 11

You have a Windows NT Server where the system partition is the primary drive of a disk duplex set. If your system partition fails, what modification should you make to a boot floppy to boot to the mirrored partition?

○ a. Add the /MIRROR switch to the default line of the BOOT.INI file.

○ b. Edit the ARC name in the BOOT.INI file to reflect the location of the mirrored partition.

○ c. A boot floppy is not needed.

○ d. Change the PATH statement in AUTOEXEC.BAT.

Answer b is correct. Editing the ARC name enables you to boot the mirrored partition. The /MIRROR switch is not a valid command parameter, so answer a is incorrect. A boot floppy is required, so answer c is incorrect. There is no AUTOEXEC.BAT file on a Windows NT boot floppy, making answer d incorrect.

Question 12

You add four new drives to your Windows NT Server computer of sizes 800, 600, 500, and 300 MB. You want to establish a disk stripe set with parity. What is the total size of the largest set you can create using any or all of these drives?

- ○ a. 1200 MB
- ○ b. 1000 MB
- ○ c. 800 MB
- ○ d. 1500 MB

Answer d is correct. 1500 MB is the total size of the largest set that may be created from these drives, using only the 800, 600, and 500 MB drives. 1200 MB would be the size of the set if you used all four drives with 300 MB on each one. Because this is not the largest possible sum using this set of drives, answer a is incorrect. 1000 MB is indeed the amount of data that could be stored on the largest set created from these drives, but the question requested the total size of the set, making answer b incorrect. Although 800 MB represents the size of the largest individual drive, you must use three drives to create a disk stripe set with parity. This means answer c is incorrect as well.

Question 13

> Your Windows NT Server computer has four hard drives: a 1200 MB drive that supports the system partition, an 1800 MB drive with two unformatted partitions of 900 MB each, and two empty 800 MB drives. How much data can you store on a disk stripe set with parity created on this system? Choose the largest and best performing.
>
> ○   a. 2400 MB
> ○   b. 3400 MB
> ○   c. 1600 MB
> ○   d. 3200 MB

Answer c is correct. Always assume the simplest configuration. Although this question did not state the 1800 MB drive was partitioned into two equal segments, this is the easiest and most common sense arrangement. In addition, you're not given the option to repartition. 1600 MB represents the amount of data that can be stored on a stripe set with parity created using all of the two 800 MB drives plus 800 MB from one of the 900 MB partitions from the 1800 MB drive. 2400 MB is the total size of a set created using both of the 800 MB drives and 800 MB from one of the 900 MB partitions on the 1800 MB drive. Because a stripe set with parity requires one third of the space for parity data in this case, answer a is incorrect—it neglects to account for this reduction in actual storage capacity. 3400 MB is the size of a volume set created using both 800 MB drives and both 900 MB partitions on the 1800 MB drive. But the question requested creation of the fastest possible stripe set with parity; selecting two partitions on the same drive slows performance and is not legal with disk striping with parity configurations, so answer b is incorrect. 3200 MB is a set size that's not possible with these drives (because it would require five 800 MB partitions on five drives); therefore, answer d is wrong.

Question 14

If you do not care about fault tolerance, what is the best method to maximize your data storage space on your Windows NT Server computer?

○ a. Disk mirroring

○ b. Disk striping with parity

○ c. Volume set

○ d. Disk stacking

Answer c is correct. A volume set maximizes storage capacity and allows you to add additional space as needed. Disk mirroring cuts storage capacity in half to implement fault tolerance, making answer a incorrect. Disk striping with parity reduces storage capacity by one full partition to implement fault tolerance, making answer b incorrect also. Disk stacking is not a valid Windows NT storage technology, so answer d is incorrect. Although volume sets can be dynamically increased, it is important to remember that a volume set is the slowest performing disk configuration. Although it cannot grow dynamically, RAID0 is the best performing disk configuration and also is not fault tolerant.

Need To Know More?

 Heywood, Drew: *Inside Windows NT Server, 2nd Edition*. New Riders, Indianapolis, IN, 1998. ISBN 1-56205-860-6. Chapter 10 discusses fault tolerance issues, implementation tips, and troubleshooting techniques for storage under Windows NT Server.

Massiglia, Paul: *The Raid Book*. ISBN 1-57398-028-5. Available at **www.raid-advisory.com**.

Siyan, Karanjit S.: *Windows NT Server 4 Professional Reference, 2nd Edition*. New Riders, Indianapolis, IN, 1997. ISBN 1-56205-805-3. Chapter 9 has extensive coverage of Windows NT's storage capabilities and fault tolerant features.

Strebe, Matthew, Charles Perkins, and James Chellis: *MCSE: NT Server 4 Study Guide, 2nd Edition*. Sybex Network Press, San Francisco, CA, 1998. ISBN 0-7821-2222-1. Chapter 5 takes a detailed look into the file systems and storage features of Windows NT; it's well worth reading.

The Windows NT Server 4 manuals cover planning, configuration, and installation issues quite well. The *Concepts and Planning Manual* contains useful fault tolerance issue discussions.

The *Windows NT Server Resource Kit* contains lots of useful information about Windows NT's fault tolerance. The TechNet CD or the CD accompanying the *Resource Kit* can be searched using keywords like "fault tolerance," "disk mirror," and "stripe set." In the *Resource Guide* volume, Chapter 3, "Disk Management Basics," Chapter 4, "Planning a Reliable Configuration," and Chapter 5, "Preparing for and Performing Recovery," contain useful background, implementation, and reference information on Windows NT's fault tolerance features.

Managing
Windows NT
Resources

5

Terms you'll need to understand:

√ User accounts

√ User rights and permissions

√ Primary Domain Controller (PDC)

√ Backup Domain Controller (BDC)

√ Policies

√ Profiles

√ Logon scripts

√ Replication

Techniques you'll need to master:

√ Setting up and maintaining user accounts

√ Setting up user rights and permissions

√ Establishing system policies and user profiles

√ Implementing directory replication

The main impetus behind setting up a network is to share resources among users. Windows NT makes managing such resources fairly intuitive. In this chapter, we examine what you need to know to maintain resource management. We begin with a discussion of how to manage user accounts, which is where you assign rights to individual users. From there, we move on to examine domains, domain controllers, and local and global groups. For further user management, we explore how to set up user policies, profiles, and logon scripts to accommodate special needs for users. Finally, we turn to server-oriented topics such as replication, managing shared resources, and setting up client-based management.

Managing Users And Accounts

For most networks, user management on a per-user basis is frustrating. To relieve this administrative burden, Windows NT 4 comes equipped with an administrative tool for managing users. This tool is the User Manager For Domains (accessed from the Start menu—Start|Programs|Administrative Tools (Common)|User Manager For Domains).

The User Manager For Domains (for simplicity's sake, referred to hereafter as the User Manager) is where administrators create and manage user and group accounts. After you have familiarized yourself with this tool, the User Manager will be your primary access control tool for users and groups.

To simplify management—and to save your wits—the trick for managing users is the group administration philosophy. Rather than managing users one-by-one, it's easier to place individual users into groups and assign rights to the groups, not the users. Once a user is a member of a group, he or she inherits the access rights and restrictions assigned to that group.

To simplify matters further, Microsoft had the foresight to provide built-in groups (both local and global) for user management. Please note that you cannot delete or rename the built-in groups. It is a good idea to make use of these groups for administering users rights and restrictions. In addition, these built-in groups have certain users assigned to them by default. You may add or remove users from these groups as needed. Group concepts, as well as Windows NT's built-in local and global groups, are discussed later in this chapter.

Working With The User Manager For Domains

The User Manager is the primary tool for controlling users' rights. Here are the various functions and tasks of User Manager:

➤ Produce, change, duplicate, and remove group accounts

➤ Produce, change, duplicate, and remove user accounts

➤ Enable account policies (this establishes defaults for password requirements, account lockouts, disconnect status, etc.)

➤ Create user rights and audit policies

➤ Establish trust relationships

Creating New Users And Groups

To create a new user or group account in User Manager, perform the following steps:

1. Open User Manager, then click the User menu.

2. Select New User (or New Group, as desired).

3. Complete the New User dialog box by performing the following steps: Type the Username, Full Name (optional), Description (optional), Password, and Confirm Password.

4. Select the relevant buttons from the four checkboxes at the bottom of the New User dialog box if:

   ➤ The user must change password at next logon.

   ➤ The user cannot change password.

   ➤ The password never expires.

   ➤ The account is disabled.

In addition to these checkboxes, there are six option buttons at the bottom of the dialog box. These buttons govern many of the user's capabilities, as described in the following list:

➤ **Groups** This button enables you to add and remove users that are to be members of a certain group or groups.

➤ **Profiles** This button enables you to define the path to the user profiles for individual users, to logon scripts, and to a user's home directory.

➤ **Hours** This button allows you to set the hours during which a user can log on to the network. By default, if a user is already logged on when the restricted time is reached, the user may remain on the network, but may not log off and back on until the allowed time. You can change this to log the user off forcibly at a specific time. This is done through the user's account policy (discussed later in this chapter).

➤ **Logon To** This button restricts the user to log on to the network only from certain machines. However, because users tend to move around, it's a good idea to leave it set at the default (to log on to all workstations).

➤ **Account** Here you can set expiration dates for accounts (useful for temporary or contract workers). The default is Never, but you can type in a specific date. You also can assign the account as local (for users from untrusted domains) or global (for regular user accounts in the domain).

➤ **Dialin** This is where you establish the right for a user to dial in to the network, as well as establish callback security if desired.

Modifying Existing User Accounts

A common action for network administrators is setting up accounts for users. Often, new users take the place of existing users—it is easier to rename an account for an employee who is taking the place of another than to create a new account. To do this, simply select User, Rename from the User Manager. Just be sure to instruct the new employee to change the account's password at first logon because the old employee's password will be retained along with all other settings.

It is (unfortunately) common to accidentally delete a user's account. The only way to remedy this is to start anew and create a user account with the same name, rights, and restrictions. This is not as bad as it sounds because you can create user templates for departments or groups. Then, from the User menu, you can copy the template, rename it for the new user, and go from there if additional rights or restrictions are needed.

If you change the access rights for a user, that user must log off and then log back on for the new rights to take effect.

A Simple Look At Domains And Controllers

Put simply, a domain is a collection of networked workstations and servers that are managed as a group. In Windows NT, each domain must have a domain controller to administer user rights for that domain. The first Windows NT Server installed in a domain is the Primary Domain Controller (PDC); this means that the server is responsible for authenticating that domain's users at logon, because the PDC houses the security policy and database for the domain.

The next server to be installed should take on the role of Backup Domain Controller (BDC). The BDC maintains a copy of the security policy and domain database (it synchronizes with the PDC at specified intervals to maintain up-to-date copies of these security features). If the PDC goes down for any reason, the BDC is not automatically promoted to a PDC. However, users can continue to log on to the network. Although it is not required that you have a BDC, it is highly recommended.

You can promote a BDC to a PDC manually if you need to take the PDC down for maintenance purposes. It is important, however, to promote the BDC *before* downing the PDC, or else some account information that may not have yet been replicated between the controllers may be lost. BDC promotion is performed with the Server Manager tool (Start|Programs| Administrative Tools (Common)|Server Manager).

To promote a BDC, follow these steps:

1. Launch Server Manager.

2. Select the Computer menu.

3. Select Promote To Primary Domain Controller.

4. Confirm the promotion.

 You should be certain that you want a server to be a domain controller, because if you want to demote it to be a member server later, you must reinstall Windows NT Server.

To allow workstations to log on to a domain, you must perform three steps:

1. Add the computer names of all domain Windows NT Workstations using Server Manager.

2. Add user accounts to the domain using User Manager.

3. On the workstation, go to Control Panel, Network applet, Identification tab and click Change and change the domain name.

It is possible (and sometimes desirable) to have multiple domains on a network. These domains can be segregated by geography or purpose.

In addition to PDCs and BDCs, Windows NT Servers can be member servers. This means that the server just provides resources upon request to clients and does not participate in the authentication of users.

PDCs and BDCs control access to resources on a particular domain, but what if a user needs access to a resource on another domain? Then, you must establish a trust relationship between domains.

By establishing a trust relationship, secure access between domains is allowed. But users in one domain are not required to be defined in another domain. Trusted domains make Windows NT a more scaleable network scheme, especially in enterprise-wide networks. If it weren't for the use of trusted domains, large Windows NT-based networks would not be workable because of the huge amount of administration involved. With the trusted domain concept, for example, the Sales department can have its own little part of the network, separate from the rest of the network. If it's necessary for the Sales domain to share information and resources with the

Marketing department domain, Windows NT can easily provide the cross-access needed via domain trusts.

To establish trusts between domains, perform the following steps:

1. Launch the User Manager For Domains.
2. Select the Policies menu.
3. Select Trust Relationships.
4. In the Trust Relationships dialog box, select the domains that you want to be trusted or trusting domains.

It is important to note that trusts are one-way by default. This means that although the Production domain (the trusting domain) grants a trust to the Engineering domain (the trusted domain) to access the Design share, Production does not have any additional rights to the Engineering domain unless this is defined in the Trust Relationships dialog box. Two-way trusts are simply two one-way trusts between domains.

Managing Local And Global Groups

Managing users would be difficult if it weren't for group administration. The group concept is to assign access rights only to groups, and then control access by adding and deleting users from the various groups as needed. By taking this approach, you rarely should have to adjust access rights for individual users to a resource. The user accounts by themselves have almost no rights assigned; all of these rights are inherited from the groups in which they are placed.

A good method for approaching user security in Windows NT is to create groups for each resource on the network so that each resource has a group that manages access for that particular resource. After establishing this setup of resource groups, you will spend most of your time managing the groups and their members, not the resources.

Windows NT has two types of groups: local and global. Local groups only are available on the local computer; global groups are available across domain lines. This distinction is very important to understand. Another important difference is that local groups can contain both users and global groups, whereas global groups only can contain users. No local or global groups can be members of another global group.

So, if you want the Engineering domain to access the color printer in the Marketing domain, a global group (for example, EngnrPrint) should be created, with access rights to the color printer in Marketing. Note again that just because the Marketing domain trusts the EngnrPrint global group to access the color printer, it does not mean that either domain has any additional rights to other domain resources, unless explicitly defined.

As mentioned earlier, Windows NT comes with some built-in local and global groups, which have default users and access privileges assigned. Table 5.1 lists these groups, whether they are local or global, the default members assigned, and their description.

Table 5.1   Windows NT's built-in groups.

Group Name	Default Members	Local/ Global	Description
Account Operators	None	Local	Members can administer domain user and group accounts
Administrators	Domain Admins, Administrator	Local	Members can administer fully the computer/domain
Backup Operators	None	Local	Members can bypass file security to back up files
Domain Admins	Administrator	Global	Designated administrators of the domain
Domain Guests	Guest	Global	All domain guests
Domain Users	Administrator	Global	All domain users
Everyone	All	Global/Local	All users
Guests	Guest	Local	Users granted access to the computer/domain
Print Operators	None	Local	Members can administer domain printers
Replicators	None	Local	Supports file replication in a domain
Server Operators	None Administrator	Local	Members can administer domain servers
Users	Domain Users	Local	Ordinary users

Each group can have a certain type of access at the directory level:

> **Full Control** Users can add files, read and change files, change directory permissions, delete and take ownership of directories and files.

> **List** Users can list the files and subdirectories within that directory.

> **Read** Users are able to read files and run applications within the directory.

> **Add** Users can add files to the directory, but cannot read or change them.

> **Add & Read** Users can add and read files in the directory, but cannot change them.

> **Change** Users can add, read, delete, and change the contents of files in the directory.

> **No Access** Users cannot access the directory (even if the user is a member of a group that has been granted access).

 When a user belongs to multiple groups in a domain, the least restrictive rights take precedence. For example, if a user has Full Control of a resource via group membership, and Read via another group membership, that user has Full Control of that resource.

Of Policies, Profiles, And Logon Scripts

There are a number of methods you can use to specify settings for network users. This type of customization is handled through Windows NT policies, profiles, and logon scripts, described in the following subsections.

System Policies

System policies control user environments and actions. System policies are created and administered via the System Policy Editor (Start|Programs| Administrative Tools (Common)|System Policy Editor).

The System Policy Editor allows you to specify what programs are available in users' Control Panels, customize users' desktops, specify network settings, control network logon and access, and customize users' Start menu options.

You can define a default system policy for all domain users, or you can apply different policies for users, computers, or groups. By setting up system policies, you modify Registry settings for computers or users—specifically, the current user and local machine Registry values.

To define a system policy as the default policy, perform the following: Save the policy in the path \WinNT\System32\Repl\Export\Scripts, with a file name of NTCONFIG.POL. Files stored in this directory are duplicated to other Windows NT Servers and Workstations that are participating in Replication. The copied files are stored in \WinNT\System32\Repl\ Import\Scripts, which is shared as the NETLOGON share.

If you define a system policy in the System Policy Editor, you must choose between two modes: Registry mode and Policy File mode. To do this:

1. Select the File menu in the System Policy Editor.
2. Select either Open Policy or Open Registry.
   Open Policy lets you edit an existing policy. Open
   Registry leads you to the Registry areas for Local
   Computer and Local User. Make changes to the policy
   directly in the Registry, then save the changes.

> Whenever you change the Registry, you run the risk of reducing the Registry to ruins. Depending on what portion of the Registry is damaged, Windows NT may not boot anymore. *Always back up the Registry* before *making changes, and take care when modifying the Registry.* Use the **RDISK.EXE** command with the /s switch to make an Emergency Repair Disk for emergency Registry recovery.

Profiles

You can set and manage individual users' desktop configuration information with user profiles. Settings such as screen savers, network connections, customized desktops, mouse settings, and program groups can be specified with a user profile. Profiles can be created for both users and groups. User profiles are located in the Winnt\Profiles\<*username*> directory.

User profiles protect your network resources from your users and your users from themselves. Establishing user profiles can help you when network users remove or relocate program items and groups. By forcing users to maintain settings with user profiles, you produce a nonmodifiable, consistent user interface, reducing your support costs as well as the users' frustration levels.

You can force a user to use a certain profile by creating a mandatory user profile that cannot be changed or saved by the user. These are produced by establishing a roaming profile for a user, copying that profile to a shared directory, assigning the appropriate users to the profile, changing the name of the NTUSER.DAT file to NTUSER.MAN, and entering the profile UNC path into the User Profile Path dialog box, located in the User Environment Profile screen of User Manager for each user.

Incidentally, in the event of a PDC failure, the user will not receive the mandatory profile at logon. When this happens, Windows NT accesses the user's last locally cached profile or the default profile assigned to the user's workstation. The locally cached profile is used if the user has logged on to the domain successfully in the past. The default profile is used if the user never has logged on to the domain successfully.

Use the following steps to create a roaming profile:

1. Copy the user's profile from the workstation to a shared network path.

2. Open Control Panel, and double-click System.

3. Select the user's profile entry, select Copy To, and type in the full UNC path name to the server where the profile will reside.

4. In the User Profile dialog box, enter the full UNC path name for the profile in the User Profile path field.

You also can set the user's home directory settings in the user's profile. To do this for an existing account that currently has a local home directory, you must perform the following steps:

1. Select the Connect option in the User Environment Profile dialog box in User Manager for Domains.

2. Select a shared drive letter, and then enter the full UNC path name of the user's new home directory. The full UNC path name contains the server name on which the home directory resides (the domain name is not required). The variable %HOMEPATH% contains the user's home directory UNC path name only after the new home directory has been established.

If you have users who change settings constantly and/or inappropriately, it's a good idea to establish profiles and force users to stick to these settings. Although this can upset users, it's the best way to protect everyone.

Logon Scripts

When you consider all of the user configuration utilities and capabilities that come with Windows NT Server, it seems strange to include logon scripts. However, to maintain backward compatibility, you must provide for the use of logon scripts—for several reasons. First, because user profiles only work with Windows NT-based computers, DOS-based clients require logon scripts to provide consistent network connections. Also, if you still have an old LAN Manager server on your network, logon scripts preserve backward compatibility to those servers for all clients.

In addition, you can specify a user's network connections or network printer connections without developing a sophisticated user profile plan. In the event that you only have defined personal profiles but you want to define persistent network connections, logon scripts can do that too. Finally, if you don't want to spend an extensive amount of time developing a complex and coherent user profile strategy, logon scripts are a quick and easy alternative.

Utilizing logon scripts is beneficial in custom-building a user's environment without managing all aspects of it. For backup purposes, you should export logon scripts from the PDC to all BDCs on the network. That way, should the PDC go down, the BDCs maintain copies of the logon scripts and make them available to users at logon. Logon scripts do not need to be exported to every workstation. Always place files that are to be exported into subdirectories of the Winnt\System32\Repl\Export directory. The default export directory for logon scripts on the PDC is Winnt\System32 \Repl\Export\Scripts.

Replication

Windows NT has provided a quick and efficient way to set up mirrored directory structures among servers through a process called "directory replication." A major boon of system file replication is logon and authentication load balancing between PDCs and BDCs. Replication of such files maintains current versions of logon scripts, system policy files, and user profiles.

The Directory Replicator Service is composed of an export server that serves as the master directory. The servers selected for importing receive the replicated master directory in their import directories.

By replicating logon scripts, system policy files, and user profiles to all domain controllers, true load balancing can be achieved. Therefore, when users log on to the domain, authentication of that user is handled by the first domain controller to respond to the authentication request. By having the replicated system files on that domain controller, the controller is able to authenticate the user and log him or her on to the network without having to contact another server. If the system files are located only on the PDC, the BDC must send for and receive copies of all applicable system files from the PDC. This increases the load on the network.

Note that only Windows NT Server computers are able to be configured to export files for replication. Machines that run Windows NT Server and Workstation can be configured to import files during replication. MS-DOS clients and Windows 95 and 98 clients do not support replication. Also, it's important to understand that a special account for the Directory Replicator Service must be created on the export server. You should configure this account with a password that never expires, and the account must be able to log on during all hours. Replication export servers have replication-specific entries in the Registry that control the timing of directory export notices. Windows NT Workstations, Windows 95 and 98 clients, and MS-DOS clients cannot be configured as export servers.

Finally, only domain controllers should receive logon scripts. Because these are the only servers that can authenticate users, unnecessary network traffic is created when you replicate logon scripts to machines that don't authenticate users.

Managing Shared Resources

The customary method for sharing files, directories, and resources on Windows NT Server is by creating a share. The process is simple; use the following steps to share a resource or directory:

1. Select the directory or resource you wish to share in Windows NT Explorer or via the My Computer icon.

2. Right-click the directory or resource, and select Sharing from the drop-down menu (the default is Not Shared).

3. Click the Shared As button. When you do this, Windows NT displays a default share name (this is usually the first eight characters of the selected directory name). You can change the share name if desired. It is important to note, however, that share names that are greater than eight characters long cannot be accessed from DOS-based clients.

You also can limit access to the share to a maximum number of users on the Sharing tab. It's a good idea to limit the number of users, to prevent users from overloading a slow computer or to ensure that other server processes can run unimpeded. Select the Maximum Allowed option if you do not want to impose this limitation. To set the number of allowed users, select the Allow button and a number appears in the Users box. You may use the up and down arrows to set this number, or type a number directly in the Users box.

Subdirectories inherit the permissions of the parent directories as their default share permissions.

After creating the share, you can assign permissions to the share. To do this, select the Permissions button or click the Security tab. Note that the default setting for newly created shares is Full Control for Everyone. You have four levels of security available for the purpose of restricting access to server shares: No Access, Read, Change, and Full Control. Note that you must always set explicit directory permissions on new shares. The default permissions grant Full Control to group Everyone!

You also can manage access to shares via the Server Manager utility by performing the following steps:

1. Launch Server Manager (Start|Programs|Administrative Tools (Common)|Server Manager).

2. Highlight the desired machine and choose Properties from the Computer menu.

3. Select one of the following buttons:

   ➤ **Users** Shows you the number of users connected to the resource.

   ➤ **Shares** Shows you all of the shares on the domain, the number of users accessing shared resources, and the local name of the resource being shared.

   ➤ **In Use** Shows all the open resources on the domain, the users who have the resources open, the type of operation taking place on the resources, the number of locks on the resource, and the path for the open resource.

   ➤ **Replication** Shows you the control interface used to manage replication (see the Replication section earlier in this chapter).

   ➤ **Alerts** Allows you to build a list of all Windows NT-based computers that are to receive administrative alerts.

To create a share in Server Manager, perform the following steps:

1. Launch Server Manager.

2. Highlight the computer name on which you want to create a new share.

3. Select Shared Directories from the Computer menu.

4. Click the New Share button, enter the share name and path of the share, and click OK.

 If you want to manage shares from a remote location, they must be managed from Server Manager, not Windows NT Explorer.

There are a number of administrative shares that are hidden from users but are accessible to the Administrator. These shares all have a dollar sign ($) appended to them to keep them hidden. Table 5.2 lists these shares and their purposes.

 Windows NT's built-in administrative shares cannot be deleted or renamed.

Table 5.2   Windows NT's hidden administrative shares.

Share Name	Description
Admin$	The directory where Windows NT Server (or Workstation) is installed, and used for remote administration of Windows NT.
Driveletter$	The letter of the drive on which a storage device is installed. This can be accessed remotely by members of the following groups: Administrators, Backup Operators, and Server Operators.
IPC$	IPC stands for Interprocess Communications, the resource used to share the named pipes interface, which is required by communications programs.
NETLOGON$	The share used by the logon server, set by default to Winnt\system32\Repl\ImportScripts. This share is utilized by the NETLOGON service for processing domain requests on Windows NT Server.
Print$	Used for management and support of shared printers.
Repl$	The shared export directory, which is used for replication. It is set by default to the Winnt\System32\Repl\Export directory.

Setting Priorities

Windows NT's multiprocessing environment requires that some processes have a higher execution priority than others. The kernel handles the setting of priorities for each process and has the ability to increase or decrease the priority of a process to improve or alter how it executes. There are 32 priority levels (0 through 31); the higher-numbered priorities are executed before the lower-numbered priorities. Although the system has the ability to use all 32 levels directly, you have only a limited ability to set priorities. By default, all user- and administrator-launched applications are assigned a base priority of 8 (/normal). However, users can launch applications with 4 (/low) or 13 (/high) priority, and an administrator can launch applications with 24 (/realtime) priority. To launch an application with an alternate priority level, use the following syntax at a command prompt:

```
start [/low|/normal|/high|/realtime] application
```

Windows NT offers two other priority controls to alter the levels of running processes. The first is a slide bar that controls the performance boost for foreground applications. (A "foreground application" is the process operating in the active window on your screen—usually indicated by a colored title bar.) This slide bar control is located on the Performance tab in the System applet in the Control Panel. By default, foreground applications have a priority of 10 (maximum). Move the slider to the right to increase the priority for foreground applications, and to the left to decrease priority (left=8, middle=9, right=10).

The second control is accessed via the Task Manager. By selecting any of the listed processes on the Process tab, you can change the priority to low, normal, high, or realtime via the Set Priority menu accessed through the right-click pop-up menu. However, only administrators have the ability to set a process' priority to realtime.

Client-Based Windows NT Management

Windows NT Server comes with a tool called the "Network Client Administrator," which helps you install the programs and tools that come with Windows NT Server. It is located in the Winnt\system32 directory, and is accessible from the Start menu (Start|Programs|Administrative Tools (Common)|Network Client Administrator).

The Network Client Administrator comes with installation files for clients running Windows 95, the Microsoft Network Client for MS-DOS 3.0, LAN Manager for MS-DOS 2.2c, LAN Manager for OS/2 2.2c, Remote Access Client for MS-DOS 1.1a, and TCP/IP-32 for Windows For Workgroups.

You can use the Network Client Administrator to share installation files contained on the Windows NT Server CD and copy the directories and files on the Windows NT Server CD to a network server. The Client Administrator lets you install network client software by creating an installation disk set or a network installation startup disk. Depending on the kind of software you want to install, you can determine the type of disk you need to create with the Client Administrator (see also Table 5.3).

Use the Network Client Administrator to copy the files and directories in the \CLIENTS directory of the Windows NT Server CD. To avoid using up too much hard disk space, you can delete the directories you don't need. However, do not delete \CLIENTS\MSCLIENT\NETSETUP. Those files are required for the creation of network installation startup disks for Windows 95, Windows 98, Windows For Workgroups, and the Microsoft Client for MS-DOS.

To use a network installation startup disk to install Windows NT Server, Windows NT Workstation, or Windows For Workgroups, you have to create the necessary subdirectories in the Clients directory and then copy the needed files. For specific instructions on copying the files, see the README.TXT file in the Clients\Support directory on the Windows NT Server installation CD.

Network installation startup disks are usable only on x86 or Pentium computers; they can't be used for Alpha, MIPS, or Power PC computers.

Table 5.3 Determining the type of installation disk set or network installation disk you need.*		
Client Type	**Installation Disk Set**	**Installation Startup Disk**
Windows NT Server	—	X
Windows NT Workstation	—	X
Windows 95	—	X
Windows For Workgroups	—	X
TCP/IP-32 for Windows For Workgroups	X	—
Network Client for MS-DOS	X	X
LAN Manager for MS-DOS	X	—
LAN Manager for MS OS/2	X	—
RAS for MS-DOS	X	—

*__Note__: X = is available or is supported
—= is not available or is not supported

Practice Questions

Question 1

What is the difference between local and global groups?

- ○   a. It is possible for local groups to contain global groups, but global groups cannot contain local groups.

- ○   b. Only user accounts from the local domain can be contained within a local group, whereas user accounts from both the local and trusted domains can be contained in global groups.

- ○   c. It is not possible to create a local group on the domain controllers, whereas global groups are created only on the domain controllers.

- ○   d. Local groups can only contain global groups, and global groups can only contain user accounts.

The correct answer is a. Global groups help organize domain users into logical units, whereas local groups provide users with permissions or rights to domain resources. The domain controllers of the domain are the only ones that can create global groups, whereas local groups can be created on any workstation or server within the domain. Global groups are limited to containing only user accounts for the domain.

Question 2

> Mary is leaving the company and David is her replacement. What is the best way to give David the same access to all of the resources previously used by Mary?
>
> O a. Create an account for David in Server Manager using Mary's account as a template. Then delete Mary's account.
>
> O b. Rename Mary's account in User Manager For Domains. Tell David to change the account password when he logs on for the first time.
>
> O c. Rename Mary's account in Server Manager. Tell David to change the account password when he logs on for the first time.
>
> O d. Create an account for David in the User Manager For Domains using Mary's account as a template, then delete Mary's account.

Answer b is correct. Renaming Mary's account through User Manager For Domains and instructing David to change the password is the best way to give David the same access as Mary. Server Manager is not used to manage user accounts; therefore, answers, a and c are incorrect. Although creating a new account by copying the existing account is a possible method, it is not Microsoft's current position that this is the best course of action. The text for answer d states the account is deleted once the copy is completed. If this action is followed, there is no need to copy the account in the first place; it would be much simpler to rename it. An alternative not listed here is to retain the old account for the possible return of that user or for security audit purposes. Because answer d is more work than necessary and does not recommend changing the account's password, answer d is incorrect.

Question 3

Which of the following built-in groups, other than Administrators, have the default right to log on locally to a Windows NT Server?

- ○ a. Server Operators and Account Operators only
- ○ b. Server Operators only
- ○ c. Server Operators, Account Operators, Backup Operators, and Print Operators
- ○ d. Server Operators, Account Operators, and Backup Operators only

Answer c is correct. All of the following built-in groups have the right by default to log on locally to a Windows NT Server: Server Operators, Account Operators, Backup Operators, and Print Operators.

Question 4

How do you demote a BDC to a file server?

- ○ a. Choose the Network option in Control Panel, select the BDC, and click Demote.
- ○ b. Highlight the BDC in the Server Manager, and select Demote on the Computer menu.
- ○ c. Reinstall Windows NT Server.
- ○ d. Restart the BDC, and choose Member Server at the startup screen.

Answer c is correct. Although you promote a BDC to a PDC by using Server Manager, you need to reinstall Windows NT Server to change the role of the server from a domain controller to a member server. The converse also is true. For this particular scenario, you must reinstall Windows NT Server and select Stand-Alone or Member Server when the system asks for a role for the server.

Question 5

> Bill used to belong to the Production group. Now he has been reassigned to Engineering. Because of this change, he must be able to access program source files in the \Source directory on the file server. The Engineering and Administrators groups have Full Control permissions to the \Source directory. The Production group has No Access permission. After logging on as a member of the Engineering group, Bill notices that he still cannot access the files in the \Source directory on the file server. What is the best way for Bill's domain administrator to grant him the required access to the \Source directory?
>
> ○   a. Remove Bill's user account from the Administrators group.
>
> ○   b. Remove Bill's user account from the Production group.
>
> ○   c. Grant all permissions for the \Source directory to Bill's user account.
>
> ○   d. Add Bill's user account to the Administrators group.

Answer b is correct. If a user belongs to a group that has No Access permissions for a directory, then he or she will be denied access to that NTFS directory, because No Access always wins. Even if Bill was added to the Administrators group, he still would not be able to access files in the \Source directory. The only way to grant Bill full access to the \Source directory is to remove his user account from the Production group.

Question 6

You want to modify user logon scripts to ensure that users have access to the latest shared resources. What is the best way to do this?

○ a. Save the logon scripts in a subdirectory of \Winnt\ System32\Repl\Export on the PDC and configure Windows NT to replicate these scripts to other domain controllers.

○ b. Put the scripts in the \Winnt\System32\Repl\Export directory on the PDC and have Windows NT replicate these scripts to each domain workstation.

○ c. Place the logon scripts in a subdirectory of \Winnt\ System32\Repl\Export on the PDC and replicate these scripts to each domain workstation.

○ d. Store the logon scripts in the \Winnt\System32\Repl\ Export directory on the PDC and configure Windows NT to replicate these scripts to each domain controller.

Answer a is correct. Logon scripts should be exported from the PDC to all BDCs responsible for authenticating logons on the network. The default export directory for logon scripts on the PDC is the C:\Winnt\System32\ Repl\Export\Scripts directory; therefore, answer a is correct. The Replicator Service only grabs files that appear in subdirectories beneath the …\Export\Scripts directory. It's the presence of the subdirectory in answer a that makes it absolutely correct.

Question 7

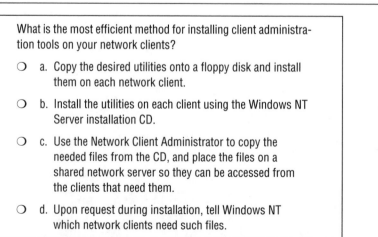

What is the most efficient method for installing client administration tools on your network clients?

○ a. Copy the desired utilities onto a floppy disk and install them on each network client.

○ b. Install the utilities on each client using the Windows NT Server installation CD.

○ c. Use the Network Client Administrator to copy the needed files from the CD, and place the files on a shared network server so they can be accessed from the clients that need them.

○ d. Upon request during installation, tell Windows NT which network clients need such files.

Answer c is correct. The Network Client Administrator is the best method for sharing installation files contained on the Windows NT Server CD. The Client Administrator lets you efficiently install network client software by creating an installation disk set or a network installation startup disk for network clients.

Question 8

> Which of the following is the best application to use to create a new shared directory on a domain server from your Windows NT Workstation computer?
>
> O a. User Manager
>
> O b. Server Manager
>
> O c. Windows Explorer
>
> O d. Network Client Administrator

Answer b is correct. Server Manager allows users to create new shares on remote computers. None of the other utilities will do the job, so answers a, c, and d are all incorrect. Server Manager is not a Windows NT Workstation utility; it is a Windows NT Server utility. However, it can be added to Windows NT Workstation by installing it from the administrative tools from the Windows NT Workstation distribution CD.

Question 9

> Which of the following types of computers can be configured to export files during replication? [Check all correct answers]
>
> ❏ a. Windows NT Servers that are configured as domain controllers
>
> ❏ b. Windows NT member servers
>
> ❏ c. Windows NT Workstations
>
> ❏ d. Windows 95 clients

Answers a and b are correct. Only those computers running Windows NT Server (member servers and Primary and Backup Domain Controllers) can be configured to export files during replication.

Question 10

> You want to force John to use the same user profile on any workstation; how do you do this?
>
> ○ a. Create a network profile on the PDC in the \Winnt\ Profiles directory named for John's account, followed by the .dat suffix. Remove any local profiles from John's workstation.
>
> ○ b. Rename John's current profile from NTUSER.DAT to NTUSER.MAN.
>
> ○ c. Using the Copy Profile To box from the System option in Control Panel, copy John's current profile from his workstation to a shared network path. Delete the current profile from his workstation.
>
> ○ d. Copy John's workstation profile to a shared network path using the Copy Profile To box. Then, type the network path in the User Profile Path box on John's machine.

Answer d is correct. A user's profile first must be copied from his or her workstation to a shared network path to create a roaming user profile. This is accomplished by choosing the Profile entry on a user's machine from the User Profiles tab in the System option in Control Panel, selecting Copy To, and providing the UNC name to the server where the profile will be located. The User Profile Path field on the User Environment Profile dialog box should then be set to the full UNC path name of the copied user profile.

Need To Know More?

 Heywood, Drew: *Inside Windows NT Server, 2nd Edition*. New Riders, Indianapolis, IN, 1998. ISBN 1-56205-860-6. Chapter 11, entitled "Sharing Drives, Directories, and Files," deals very nicely with issues relating to shares and NTFS permissions and access information.

 Siyan, Karanjit S.: *Windows NT Server 4 Professional Reference, 2nd Edition*. New Riders, Indianapolis, IN, 1997. ISBN 1-56205-805-3. A nice discussion of using Server Manager to manage shared resources is located in Chapter 6: "Implementing Windows NT Server Domains."

 Strebe, Matthew, Charles Perkins, and James Chellis: *MCSE: NT Server 4 Study Guide, 2nd Edition*. Sybex Network Press, San Francisco, CA, 1998. ISBN 0-7821-2222-1. Chapter 9 contains useful information about creating and maintaining your user environment.

Search the TechNet CD (or its online version through **www.microsoft.com/technet**) using the keywords "user management," "replication," "domain controllers," and "groups."

 The *Windows NT Server Resource Kit* contains lots of useful information about shares and share permissions. You can search the TechNet CD or the CD accompanying the *Resource Kit*, using keywords like "shares," "resource management," and "user management."

6

Windows NT Networking

· ·

Terms you'll need to understand:

√ Protocol

√ NetBIOS

√ NetBEUI

√ TCP/IP

√ IPX/SPX

√ DLC

√ AppleTalk

√ SNMP

√ DHCP

√ WINS

√ DNS

√ CSNW

√ GSNW

√ Frame type

√ SLIP

√ PPP

√ PPTP

√ FTP

√ Gopher

√ HTTP

√ Protocol binding

Techniques you'll need to master:

√ Installing and configuring network protocols

√ Implementing services that complement certain protocols

√ Understanding and configuring protocol bindings

√ Adjusting frame type settings

To enable communications on a computer network, you must tell Windows NT how it's supposed to "talk" to other computers and peripheral devices. In the networking world, this is established through the use of protocols. Basically, a protocol is an agreed-upon set of standards that define how computers communicate. In this chapter, we explain what protocols are available with Windows NT Server and when to use which protocol, as well as the properties of each protocol. In addition, pointers are provided to additional resources for this topic.

Built-In Windows NT Protocols

Windows NT Server comes with a number of protocols that can be enabled for communications purposes:

➤ Network Basic Input/Output System (NetBIOS)

➤ NetBIOS Extended User Interface (NetBEUI)

➤ Transmission Control Protocol/Internet Protocol (TCP/IP)

➤ NWLink Internetwork Packet Exchange/Sequenced Packet Exchange (IPX/SPX)

➤ Data Link Control (DLC)

➤ AppleTalk

We define and explain all of these protocols and their uses in the following sections.

NetBIOS

NetBIOS is installed automatically when Windows NT is installed. NetBIOS was originally developed in the 1980s by IBM. NetBIOS is an extremely fast protocol that requires very little communications overhead, which is why it's used by Windows NT for basic operations (for example, browsing and interprocess communications between network servers). Unfortunately, however, it is not a routable protocol; therefore, it is unusable in networks that have routing capabilities.

NetBEUI

NetBEUI is a simple Network layer transport protocol that was developed to support NetBIOS networks. NetBEUI, like NetBIOS, is not routable, so it really has no place on an enterprise network. NetBEUI is the fastest transport protocol available to Windows NT. Benefits of NetBEUI include its speed as well as good error protection, and it is easy to implement, with small memory overhead. The disadvantages of NetBEUI include the fact that it's not routable, there is very little support for cross-platform applications, and there are very few troubleshooting tools.

TCP/IP

TCP/IP is the most widely used protocol in networking today, due in part to the vast growth of the global Internet, which is a TCP/IP-based network. TCP/IP is the most flexible of the transport protocols, and is able to span wide areas. In addition, it has excellent cross-platform support, excellent routing capabilities, and support for the Simple Network Management Protocol (SNMP), the Dynamic Host Configuration Protocol (DHCP), the Windows Internet Name Service (WINS), the Domain Name Service (DNS), as well as a host of other useful protocols discussed in "TCP/IP Connectivity Issues," later in this chapter.

NWLink (IPX/SPX)

NWLink is Microsoft's "clean room" implementation of Novell's IPX/SPX protocol suite for NetWare networks. This protocol was included with Windows NT to enable communication with NetWare servers. With NWLink, Windows NT clients can access resources located on a NetWare server, and vice versa.

Put simply, Windows NT Server requires that NWLink be installed to enable communications with NetWare clients and servers. In addition, the File and Print Services for NetWare is also required for NetWare clients and servers to access Windows NT files and printers. The Client Service For NetWare (CSNW) is designed for Windows NT Workstations that require a direct link to NetWare servers. The Gateway Service For NetWare (GSNW) lets Windows NT Servers map a drive to a NetWare server, which provides access to NetWare server resources for Windows NT Workstations (via a gateway). Additional information about NWLink can be found in "NWLink Connectivity Issues," later in this chapter.

DLC

Windows NT uses the Data Link Control (DLC) protocol primarily for connectivity to Systems Network Architecture (SNA) gateways, and more importantly, for connecting to network-attached printers, such as the Hewlett-Packard JetDirect. The use of DLC for network printing is detailed further in Chapter 8.

AppleTalk

It should come as no surprise that the AppleTalk protocol is used for communication with Macintosh computers. By enabling AppleTalk, you allow Mac clients to store and access files located on a Windows NT Server, print to Windows NT printers, and vice versa. (Note that you must install the Windows NT Services for Macintosh before you can install AppleTalk; and remember, Mac support is available only from an NTFS partition.)

NWLink Connectivity Issues

Put simply, NWLink is IPX for Windows NT: IPX is the protocol, and NWLink is the networking component that provides the protocol. NWLink is provided for connectivity to NetWare networks—both to allow NetWare clients to access Windows NT Servers and to allow Windows NT clients to access NetWare servers. It is important to note, however, that NWLink by itself does not enable this type of communication; you must first install Gateway Service for NetWare and Client Service for NetWare. Basically, CSNW is a redirector, whereas GSNW is what makes file and print sharing on NetWare servers available to Microsoft clients.

IPX has a number of benefits: It supports routing between networks, it's faster than TCP/IP, and it's easy to install and maintain. Unfortunately, IPX doesn't have a sufficient central addressing scheme to prohibit multiple networks from using identical addresses, and it doesn't support the Simple Network Management Protocol (SNMP).

Installing NWLink

Installing the NWLink protocol is much like installing other protocols in Windows NT. There are, however, some special issues. To install NWLink, perform the following steps:

1. Open the Control Panel (Start|Settings|Control Panel).

2. Double-click the Network icon.

3. Click the Protocols tab in the Network dialog box.

4. Click the Add button.

5. Select NWLink IPX/SPX Compatible Transport from the list of available protocols.

6. Enter the path to the Windows NT Server installation CD in the path field of the setup dialog box, and then click Continue.

   If you have installed Windows NT's Remote Access Service (RAS), Windows NT asks if you want to bind NWLink to RAS. Either click OK to enable binding, or click Cancel.

7. Click the Close button, and then click Yes when Windows NT asks whether to restart the computer.

 Although in most cases it's fine to leave the default frame type (auto) as is, some Ethernet adapters don't work well with this setting. For new installations, the Ethernet 802.2 setting is recommended.

To change the Ethernet frame type and IPX network number, perform the following steps:

1. Open the Control Panel.

2. Double-click the Network icon.

3. Click the Protocols tab in the Network dialog box.

4. Double-click NWLink IPX/SPX Compatible Transport from the list of available protocols.

5. Click the Manual Frame Type Detection button.

6. Click the Add button.

7. Select your preferred frame type.

8. Type the IPX network number for the adapter in the Network Number field.

9. Click the Add button.

10. Repeat the previous three steps for each frame type.

11. Click OK, and then click the Close button.

12. Click Yes when asked to restart the computer.

There are more issues to consider when establishing communications between Windows NT and NetWare networks. We cover these details in Chapter 7.

TCP/IP Connectivity Issues

TCP/IP currently is the most used networking protocol, as well as the standard protocol of the Internet. The beauty of the TCP/IP protocol suite lies in its ability to link many disparate kinds of computers and peripheral devices. Using this protocol stack, you enable most TCP/IP clients to access Windows NT-based resources and vice versa.

Windows NT provides for a number of useful TCP/IP services:

➤ **Dynamic Host Configuration Protocol (DHCP)** This service enables the assignment of dynamic TCP/IP network addresses, based on a specified pool of available addresses. When a network client configured for DHCP logs on to the network, the DHCP service assigns the next available TCP/IP address for that network session. This really simplifies address administration.

➤ **Windows Internet Name Service (WINS)** This service enables the resolution of NetBIOS network names to IP addresses (similar to DNS). This way, you don't have to remember the IP address of the client with whom you are trying to communicate—you can enter the computer name and Windows NT does the rest. Also, if a TCP/IP-based network does not have a WINS server, each time one computer tries to access another, it must send a b-node broadcast, which creates unnecessary network traffic and can slow a busy network to a crawl. WINS servers provide computer-name-to-IP address resolution, reducing these broadcast messages and improving network performance.

➤ **Domain Name System (DNS)** This service allows for fully qualified domain names (FQDNs), such as **www.lanw.com,** to be resolved to IP addresses.

➤ **Serial Line Internet Protocol (SLIP)** SLIP was originally developed for the Unix environment and is still widely used among Internet providers. Although SLIP provides good performance with little system overhead requirements, it does not support error checking, flow control, or security features. SLIP is good for connecting to Unix hosts or Internet providers. This protocol is quickly being replaced by PPP.

➤ **Point-to-Point Protocol (PPP)** PPP addresses many of the insufficiencies of SLIP, such as providing the ability to encrypt logons, as well as support for additional transport protocols, error checking, and recovery. In addition, PPP is optimized for low-bandwidth connections and, in general, is a more efficient protocol than SLIP.

➤ **Point-to-Point Tunneling Protocol (PPTP)** PPTP creates secure connections between private networks over the Internet. Benefits of PPTP include lower administrative, transmission, and hardware costs than other solutions for this type of connectivity.

➤ **World Wide Web (WWW)** This service comes as a part of Windows NT Server 4. WWW makes it possible to publish Web pages, whether for an Internet-based Web site or for an internal intranet.

➤ **File Transfer Protocol (FTP)** This protocol is great for the fast transfers of files to and from a local hard drive to an FTP server located elsewhere on another TCP/IP-based network (such as the Internet).

➤ **Gopher** This service serves text and links to other Gopher sites. This service predates HTTP (the Web protocol). Although Gopher sites are still out there, Gopher's use has been lessened because HTTP handles information transfer better than this outdated method. Gopher is no longer supported in IIS 4.

> **Hypertext Transfer Protocol (HTTP)** This World Wide Web protocol allows for the transfer of HTML documents over the Internet or an intranet, and responds to actions like a user clicking on a hypertext link.

Installing And Configuring TCP/IP

There are a few items that you need to have on hand when you install TCP/IP. The following list describes these items:

> **Any DHCP and WINS information about your network** If you already have these services configured, the process of configuring TCP/IP is greatly eased. If the computer is not a DHCP client, configure your server's IP address.

> **Your server's IP address** This is the unique address that identifies a particular computer on a TCP/IP network. This number consists of four numbers, separated by periods (i.e., 125.115.125.48). The first one to three numbers identify the network on which the computer is located, and the remaining numbers identify the computer on that network.

> **Your network's subnet masks for each network adapter on the network** The subnet mask is a number mathematically applied to the IP address. This number determines which IP addresses are a part of the same subnetwork as the computer applying the subnet mask.

> **Your server's default gateway** The gateway is the computer that serves as a router, a format translator, or a security filter for a network.

> **The domain name server for the network** This is a computer that serves as an Internet host and performs translation of fully qualified domain names into IP addresses.

If you did not install TCP/IP when you first installed Windows NT Server, you must perform the following steps to install and configure this protocol suite:

1. Open the Control Panel or right-click Network Neighborhood and select Properties.
2. Double-click the Network icon.
3. In the Networks window, click the Protocols tab.

4. Click the Add button.

5. Select TCP/IP from the list of available protocols. Windows NT may request the installation CD or the location of the installation files.

6. In the Network window, click the Close button.

7. Either enter the TCP/IP address of the computer or select Obtain An IP Address From A DHCP Server, whichever is appropriate for this installation. Then, specify the subnet mask and default gateway.

8. If your network has a DNS server or a constant Internet connection, click the DNS tab and enter the DNS address.

9. If your network has a WINS server, click the WINS tab and enter the WINS address.

10. Click OK to close the TCP/IP Properties dialog box. If you did not specify a primary WINS address, Windows NT gives a warning.

11. Click the Close button.

12. Click Yes when Windows NT asks to restart the computer.

NetBEUI Connectivity Issues

NetBEUI is by far the easiest protocol to install and configure on a Windows NT network. To install this protocol, perform the following steps:

1. Open the Control Panel.

2. Double-click the Network icon.

3. In the Networks window, click the Protocols tab.

4. Click the Add button.

5. Select NetBEUI from the list of available protocols and click OK.

6. Enter the path to the installation CD, or the location of the installation files.

7. If you have RAS installed, Windows NT asks if you want to support it with this protocol. Click Cancel to leave it unsupported.

8. In the Network window, click the Close button.

9. Select Yes when Windows NT asks to restart the computer.

Protocol Bindings

Protocol binding is the process Windows NT uses to link network components from various levels of the network architecture to enable communication between those components. To set the binding order for network protocols, double-click the Network icon in Control Panel and click the Binding tab. This is where the bindings of installed network components are listed in order of upper-layer services and protocols to lower-layer network adapter drivers.

Binding should be ordered to enhance the system's use of the network. For example, if your network has both TCP/IP and NetBEUI installed—and most network devices use TCP/IP—workstation bindings should be set to bind TCP/IP first and NetBEUI second. In other words, the most frequently used protocol should be bound first. This speeds network connections. Because servers use whatever protocol is sent to them by each workstation, the binding order needs to be changed on the workstations only. Network speed is affected by the binding order on the workstations but not on the servers.

Practice Questions

Question 1

> Your TCP/IP-based network is experiencing drastic increases in broadcast traffic. What is the best way to decrease the amount of broadcast traffic on your network?
>
> ○   a. Divide your network into two physical subnets, and install a bridge.
>
> ○   b. Divide your network into two logical subnets, and install a gateway.
>
> ○   c. Install a DHCP server.
>
> ○   d. Install a WINS server.

Answer d is correct. If a TCP/IP network does not have a WINS server, each computer on the network has to send a broadcast message to other computers on the network, which increases network traffic. By making use of a WINS server, you provide computer-name-to-IP address resolution that reduces the number of broadcast messages.

Question 2

> Of the following, which are required for access to a NetWare server from a Windows NT Workstation running Client Service for NetWare? [Check all correct answers]
>
> ❑   a. A group on the NetWare server called NTGATEWAY containing the Windows NT Workstation's user account
>
> ❑   b. Gateway Service For NetWare
>
> ❑   c. A user account on the NetWare server
>
> ❑   d. The NWLink protocol

Answers c and d are correct. Any user accessing a NetWare server directly will need a user account on that NetWare server; therefore, answer c is correct. A Windows NT Workstation running the Client Service for NetWare can access a NetWare server directly by using the NWLink protocol; therefore, answer d also is correct. It is necessary to place user accounts in the NTGATEWAY group on the NetWare server only if workstations are accessing the NetWare server via a gateway. That is not the case in this example; therefore, answer a is incorrect. If a Windows NT Server is to act as a gateway to a NetWare server, the Gateway Service For NetWare must be loaded onto a Windows NT Server. Because this scenario discusses a Windows NT client accessing a NetWare server, answer b also is incorrect.

Question 3

Your network uses multiple protocols. Where in Windows NT is the binding order of the protocols changed to increase network speed?

- ○ a. On the domain controllers only
- ○ b. On the workstations only
- ○ c. On the servers only
- ○ d. On both the workstations and servers (including the domain controllers)

Answer b is correct. Because Windows NT Servers use the protocol sent to them by workstations, the binding order needs only to be changed on the workstations. Network speed is affected by the binding order on the workstations but not on the servers; therefore, answers a, c, and d all are incorrect.

Question 4

What is an advantage of SLIP over PPP?

- ○ a. SLIP supports security, whereas PPP does not support security.
- ○ b. SLIP supports error checking, whereas PPP does not support error checking.
- ○ c. SLIP supports flow control, whereas PPP does not support flow control.
- ○ d. SLIP requires less system overhead than PPP.

Answer d is correct. SLIP requires less system overhead than PPP. SLIP does not support error checking, flow control, or security—these are features of PPP. Therefore, answers a, b, and c are incorrect.

Question 5

> You want to install TCP/IP on a member server in a nonrouted
> network. You have already assigned an IP address manually to
> the server. What other parameter must you specify to install TCP/
> IP on the server?
>
> ○ a. The subnet mask
>
> ○ b. The default gateway
>
> ○ c. The DHCP server IP address
>
> ○ d. The WINS server IP address

Answer a is correct. When installing TCP/IP on a nonrouted network, the IP address and subnet mask parameters must be specified.

Question 6

> Your Ethernet network consists of a Windows NT 4 Server, sev-
> eral Windows NT Workstation clients, a NetWare 3.11 client, and
> one NetWare 4.1 client. NWLink is running on the network. Each
> of the NetWare clients is using different frame types. How would
> you configure the NWLink IPX/SPX Properties dialog box on the
> Windows NT 4 Server to enable the server to recognize both
> NetWare clients?
>
> ○ a. By enabling Auto Frame Type Detection
>
> ○ b. By selecting the Manual Frame Type Detection option
>   and adding a NetWare client's network number and
>   frame type to the frame type configuration list
>
> ○ c. By selecting the Auto Frame Type Detection option and
>   adding both NetWare clients' network numbers and
>   frame types to the frame type configuration list
>
> ○ d. By selecting the Manual Frame Type Detection option
>   and adding each of the NetWare clients' network
>   numbers and frame types to the frame type
>   configuration list

Answer d is correct. If frame types other than 802.2 are being used on a network, Manual Frame Type Detection must be enabled. Frame types belonging to each client must be added to the frame type configuration list on the NWLink IPX/SPX Properties dialog box.

Question 7

Your network users need to access your network resources across the Internet. How can you allow Internet-based user access while still providing security?

- ○ a. Implement the SLIP protocol
- ○ b. Implement the FTP protocol
- ○ c. Implement the Point-to-Point Protocol
- ○ d. Implement the Point-to-Point Tunneling Protocol

Answer d is correct. The Point-to-Point Tunneling Protocol (PPTP) uses the Internet as a connection medium while still maintaining network security.

Question 8

To end the process of maintaining user accounts on two different types of servers, you have decided to migrate users from the NetWare server to a Windows NT 4 Server. What must be installed on the Windows NT Server to provide those clients with access to NetWare? [Check all correct answers]

- ❑ a. Gateway Service for NetWare
- ❑ b. The NWLink protocol
- ❑ c. Client Service for NetWare
- ❑ d. SAP Agent

Answers a and b are correct. GSNW must be installed on the Windows server; therefore, answer a is correct. For the Windows NT Server to communicate with the NetWare server, the NWLink protocol must be installed on the Windows NT Server; therefore, answer b is also correct. When GSNW is installed, NWLink will be automatically installed if it is not already present.

Need To Know More?

Heywood, Drew: *Inside Windows NT Server, 2nd Edition.* New Riders, Indianapolis, IN, 1998. ISBN 1-56205-860-6. Chapter 9, "Using TCP/IP," discusses detailed issues relating to installing and configuring the TCP/IP protocol suite.

Siyan, Karanjit S.: *Windows NT Server 4 Professional Reference, 2nd Edition.* New Riders, Indianapolis, IN, 1997. ISBN 1-56205-805-3. Chapters 13 through 16 all discuss various aspects of protocol management.

Strebe, Matthew, Charles Perkins, and James Chellis: *MCSE: NT Server 4 Study Guide, 2nd Edition.* Sybex Network Press, San Francisco, CA, 1998. ISBN 0-7821-2222-1. Chapter 6, "Networking and Network Protocols," and Chapter 8, "Windows NT Networking Services," both cover a lot of useful information about managing network protocols.

Search the TechNet CD (or its online version through **www.microsoft.com/technet**) using the keywords "protocol management," "TCP/IP," "NWLink," and "internetworking."

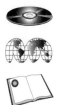

The *Windows NT Server Resource Kit* contains lots of useful information about shares and share permissions. You can search the TechNet CD or the CD accompanying the *Resource Kit*, using keywords like "protocols," "binding," and "networking services."

The Windows NT/NetWare Relationship

7

Terms you'll need to understand:

√ NetWare

√ NWLink Internetwork Packet Exchange/Sequenced Packet Exchange (IPX/SPX)

√ Client Service for NetWare (CSNW)

√ Gateway Service for NetWare (GSNW)

√ File And Print Services For NetWare (FPNW)

√ Frame type

Techniques you'll need to master:

√ Adjusting frame type settings

√ Installing, configuring, and enabling GSNW

√ Installing, configuring, and enabling CSNW

√ Implementing FPNW

√ Using Microsoft's NetWare Migration Tool

By making NetWare connectivity part and parcel of Windows NT Server, Microsoft has made it possible to integrate its products directly and easily with existing networks all over the world. Considering its built-in NetWare access capabilities, and the add-ins available at low cost from Microsoft for Windows NT Server to enhance these capabilities, it's clear that NetWare interoperability is an important concern in Redmond.

Even if you don't have any NetWare servers on your Windows NT network, you must still understand what Microsoft offers by way of NetWare compatibility and access. Although much of this material will be old hat to those who work in hybrid NetWare–Windows NT environments, those who don't have the benefit of direct exposure should study this chapter carefully.

Protocols And Compatibility Issues

To avoid paying royalties to Novell, Microsoft built its own implementation of the Internetwork Packet Exchange/Sequenced Packet Exchange (IPX/SPX) protocols, called "NWLink" (to avoid infringing on Novell trade names). Surprisingly, some comparisons between Novell's IPX/SPX client implementations and Microsoft's NWLink have shown the latter implementation to be slightly faster than the former. In other words, these guys are serious about their NetWare compatibility, and have done a pretty good job.

Although NetWare does support multiple protocols—primarily IPX/SPX and TCP/IP—it's most common to find IPX/SPX used to communicate between NetWare's clients and its servers. In fact, Novell itself does not support any protocols other than IPX/SPX for versions of NetWare older than 3.x (which usually means version 2.2). Thus, it's safe to assume that IPX/SPX is the protocol used to communicate between the NetWare server and its clients.

When it implemented IPX/SPX, Novell also elected to use a special frame format for the protocol, on Ethernet and other network types. Even though the emerging standard at the time (which has since become the official standard) was to use 802.2 frame formats for networked communications, Novell elected to use what's often called a "raw 802.3" frame format for its implementation of IPX/SPX on Ethernet.

To make a long and complex story as short as possible, the upshot of Novell's initial decision, and its subsequent divergence from industry standard frame types, introduced the possibility of a frame type mismatch when using IPX/SPX (or NWLink). You must be aware of these problems when communicating on a network, and understand NWLink's ability to automatically detect 802.2 IPX frame types on a Windows NT Server machine.

Here's what you need to know to set frame types properly:

1. Although NWLink is provided primarily for NetWare access and interoperability, Windows NT-based networks can use only NWLink, where no NetWare is present.

2. Until NetWare 3.12 shipped, NetWare's default frame type was raw 802.3, which Microsoft calls simply "802.3 frame type."

3. For NetWare 3.12 and all 4.x versions (including IntranetWare), the default frame type uses 802.2 headers atop the native frame type for the network technology in use. Microsoft calls this the "802.2 frame type," without regard to technology.

4. The total battery of frame types you're most likely to encounter is:

    a. 802.2 frame type (industry standard, default for NetWare 3.12 and higher-numbered versions)

    b. 802.3 frame type (so-called "raw 802.3 header" format, developed by Novell, default for older, pre-3.12 versions of NetWare)

c. 802.3 with SNAP header (sometimes called "Ethernet_SNAP frame type" in Microsoft terminology)

d. 802.5 frame type (the native format for Token Ring networks)

e. 802.5 frame type with SNAP header (sometimes called "Token_Ring_SNAP" in Microsoft terminology)

(*Note:* SNAP stands for SubNetwork Access Protocol, and provides a mechanism that permits nonstandard higher-level protocols to appear within a standard IEEE Logical Link Control frame like the frame types previously mentioned. It's often used to transport AppleTalk or SNA in IP network environments.

5. If any workstation (or server) is configured for an incorrect IPX frame type (that doesn't match the rest of the population), an improperly configured machine will not be able to interact with the network. This can occur even though the network may otherwise work properly, and all other machines may communicate successfully.

6. NWLink's default auto detect type setting is 802.2. If the initiation broadcast does not receive an 802.2 response, but does get some other frame type, then Windows NT will attempt to use 802.3, Ethernet II, then SNAP in an attempt to detect the correct frame type in use. If a match is found, the default auto detect setting is set to the determined type. However, auto detect only functions in an environment with a single frame type.

7. For client/server applications like SQL Server database access, or NetBIOS-based applications, native NetWare clients using IPX/SPX can communicate directly with a Windows NT Server running such an application without requiring anything other than NWLink and the server side of the application to be installed on that machine. In essence, the client side of the client/server application supplies everything the clients and server need to communicate, as long as they have a protocol in common. Because the assumption is that native NetWare clients use IPX/SPX, a Windows NT Server must install NWLink to communicate with such clients across the network.

Gateway Service For NetWare

Microsoft often refers to this software component by its acronym, GSNW. But there's more to GSNW than meets the eye, and this can lead to some confusion. If you examine the listing in Figure 7.1 carefully, notice that the complete name of the software component as it appears in the Select Network Service dialog box, generated from the Services tab, Network applet, Control Panel is "Gateway (and Client) Services for NetWare."

Unless you've actually looked at this on screen at some point, or been warned of this subtlety, you may be surprised to learn that GSNW includes Client Service For NetWare (CSNW; discussed in the next section) in its capabilities and functionality. In English, this means that any Windows NT Server with GSNW installed also can function as a client to a NetWare server. This explains why you must remove existing NetWare client software—especially Novell's NetWare Client for Windows NT—from any Windows NT Server before installing GSNW on that machine.

Understanding GSNW

It's important to understand what GSNW does, and what's involved in installing it. Generically speaking, the term "gateway" refers to a software component permitting computers that do not share a common set of protocols

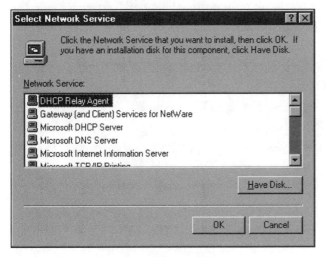

Figure 7.1   The unabridged expansion for GSNW is actually Gateway (and Client) Services for NetWare.

and services to communicate with one another. In other words, the gateway translates from one protocol and service world to another, and vice versa.

GSNW is no exception: What GSNW does is make it possible for ordinary Microsoft Network clients (PCs running Windows 3.x, Windows 95 or 98, or even Windows NT Workstation or Server) to access resources on a NetWare server by translating requests from those clients stated in Microsoft Network terms into NetWare terms and then translating the concomitant responses from the NetWare server from NetWare terms back into Microsoft Network terms. The gateway is in the middle of these communications.

 This is the "trick" that makes this work: The Windows NT Server where GSNW runs exports a logical volume from the NetWare server through the gateway that Microsoft Network clients can access as if it were any other Windows NT-based network share. The gateway also can create a similar function for NetWare-based printers, and make NetWare-based print services available to Microsoft Network clients. The chief selling point for GSNW is that it provides access to NetWare resources for Microsoft Network clients without requiring any additional software, or software changes, for those clients.

Installing, Configuring, And Enabling GSNW

Gateway Services for NetWare is an optional network service included as part of Windows NT Server 4: This means it's included with the distribution media for the product, but not installed by default whenever you install the core operating system. To install GSNW, you must open the Network applet in Control Panel, select the Services tab, and then click the Add button in the resulting display. This produces the screen shown in Figure 7.1, where GSNW appears as the second choice in the list. To begin the process of installing GSNW, highlight its entry, then click the OK button at the bottom of the window. This will bring up a prompt for the Windows NT Server CD.

It's important to note that if you elect to install GSNW on a Windows NT Server that does not already have NWLink running, NWLink will be installed automatically as a part of the GSNW installation process. Thus, although NWLink is required for GSNW to run, it's not necessary to install it in advance, nor is it a problem if NWLink has already been installed.

Here's a high-level overview of the GSNW installation process, emphasizing those elements and information that must be supplied during installation:

1. Before installing and configuring GSNW you must create the following accounts on the NetWare server where the gateway will connect:

   a. A user account on the NetWare server with rights to the NetWare file system directories that gateway users from the Windows NT side will need.

   b. A group account named NTGATEWAY on the NetWare server with rights to all file and print resources that gateway users will need.

   [*Note:* All users who go through a single GSNW gateway have the same access and the same rights to the NetWare resources; the only way to create different collections of access and rights is to set up multiple gateways (only one instance of GSNW per individual Windows NT Server is permitted).]

2. To install GSNW, you must log in to the Windows NT Server as an Administrator. In the Network applet in Control Panel, select the Services tab, click the Add button, and select Gateway (and Client) Services For NetWare. Supply the Windows NT Server CD or point to a copy of the \i386 directory where the necessary source code files reside. The software will more or less install itself.

3. To configure GSNW, double-click on the GSNW icon in Control Panel. The Gateway Service For NetWare dialog box appears.

   a. Click on the Gateway button to elicit the Configure Gateway dialog box.

   b. Check the Enable Gateway box to enable the Gateway Service.

   c. In the Gateway Account field, enter the NetWare user name you created in Step 1a. Enter the Password into the Password field, then confirm that password in the Confirm Password field.

   d. Click the Add button to create a NetWare share for use by Microsoft networking clients. A New Share dialog box appears.

   e. In the Share Name field, enter a name through which the NetWare directory will be shared.

   f. In the Network Path field, enter a UNC name for the NetWare directory that's being shared. For the SYS:Public directory on a server named NETONE, the syntax is \\NETONE\SYS\ PUBLIC.

   g. In the Comment field, you can add an optional descriptive phrase that will appear in the Browse window for Microsoft clients on the network.

   h. In the Use Drive field, select a drive letter on the Windows NT Server to be assigned to the NetWare directory. This drive letter remains taken as long as GSNW runs on the Windows NT Server; by default, Z is the letter assigned to the first such share name.

i. The User Limit box permits administrators to limit the number of users who can access the NetWare share simultaneously. Because the gateway bogs down under increasing load, it's a good idea to limit the number of users to 10 or so (unless the server is extremely fast or only lightly loaded).

j. Click OK to save all changes. You'll return to the Configure Gateway dialog box. Click OK again to exit the Gateway Service for NetWare dialog box. All changes will take effect upon the next system boot.

4. The only way to create NetWare shares is through the interface described in Steps 3d through 3j (not through Explorer or My Computer, as is the case for normal Windows NT Server shares). Likewise, you must use the GSNW applet in Control Panel to set permissions for NetWare shares. Here's how:

a. From an administrative logon, launch the GSNW applet from Control Panel.

b. When the Gateway Services For NetWare dialog box appears, choose the Gateway button.

c. In the Configure Gateway dialog box that appears, highlight the NetWare share name and choose the Permissions button. Use this interface to set permissions for the NetWare share.

5. Using NetWare Print Resources through the Gateway requires none of the shenanigans needed to establish and set permissions for the NetWare shares. Instead, configure NetWare print queues through the Printers icon in Control Panel (as with any other Windows NT Server-attached printer). Here's what's involved:

a. From an administrative logon, launch the Printers applet. Select the Add Printer icon. This will display the Add Printer Wizard window (Start| Settings|Printers).

b. Select the Network Printer radio button, and then click the Next button. This brings up the Connect to Printer dialog box.

c. In this dialog box, you will see two icons—one labeled "NetWare Or Compatible Network" and the other labeled "Microsoft Windows Network." You can expand and navigate this directory tree the same way you would the Microsoft Windows Network tree: Double-click Network, select a server, and then double-click and select the printer you wish to manage.

Otherwise, the procedure is exactly the same as installing an ordinary Windows NT network printer (covered in Chapter 8 of this book).

 Remember that it is necessary to map a drive on the Windows NT Server for the NetWare share, and that NetWare shares and their permissions only can be managed through the GSNW applet, not through ordinary file management tools. NetWare printers, on the other hand, can be handled like any other network printers through the Printers applet, once GSNW has been installed on a Windows NT Server.

Client Service For NetWare

GSNW makes NetWare resources available to ordinary Microsoft Network clients, but CSNW works only with Windows NT machines in order to make them act as native clients to NetWare servers elsewhere on the network. This system component is called CSNW only on Windows NT Workstation 4, which ships without GSNW; however, CSNW is part and parcel of GSNW on Windows NT Server 4 machines. In either case, its job is to let Windows NT machines link up to and browse NetWare resources alongside Microsoft Windows Network resources.

File And Print Services For NetWare

FPNW, as it's usually called, is not included with Windows NT Server 4; it must be purchased separately (at the time of writing, it costs $149 in the U.S. market). What GSNW is to Microsoft Network clients, FPNW is to native NetWare clients: It makes resources from a Windows NT Server available to NetWare clients, without requiring any additional software or configuration changes to those clients. In other words, FPNW makes a Windows NT Server look like a NetWare 3.11 server to any native NetWare clients on a network.

Microsoft's (NetWare) Migration Tool

The program, which ships as an optional element in the Windows NT Server 4 distribution media, is called NWCONV.EXE. It can take user and group definitions from a NetWare server, along with most of the associated rights and permissions that pertain to them, and re-create that information on a Windows NT Server 4 machine.

Likewise, NWCONV.EXE also can grab volumes, directories, and files from a NetWare server and copy them to a Windows NT Server, translating and preserving most of the file system permissions involved at the same time. This program is fairly sophisticated and offers lots of bells and whistles for dealing with duplicate accounts and for converting information from its NetWare server incarnation to a reasonable Windows NT Server facsimile. For more details about this utility, consult Karanjit Siyan's book (see "Need To Know More?" at the end of this chapter).

Chapter 7

Practice Questions

Unless you work in a mixed NetWare/NT environment, you'll want to review the basics about GSNW, CSNW, FPNW, and NWLink. If these sound like gibberish, check the Glossary first, then reread this chapter (and at least one of the references in the "Need To Know More?" section).

Question 1

> At XYZ Corp., a handful of NetWare 3.11 clients remain in use. These machines need access to files on a newly installed Windows NT Server. To support such access without changes to the existing clients, which of the following services and/or protocols must be available on the Windows NT Server? [Check all correct answers]
>
> ❑   a. Gateway Service for NetWare (GSNW)
>
> ❑   b. Client Service for NetWare (CSNW)
>
> ❑   c. File and Print Services for NetWare (FPNW)
>
> ❑   d. The NWLink protocol
>
> ❑   e. The Migration Tool for NetWare

The correct answers are c and d. File and Print Services for NetWare make a Windows NT Server look like a NetWare server to NetWare network clients, so it's what provides file access; this means that answer c must be checked. But native NetWare 3.x clients need IPX/SPX to access real NetWare servers, or Windows NT Servers running FPNW; because NWLink is Microsoft's implementation of IPX/SPX, answer d must be checked as well. GSNW provides mediated access to NetWare services for Microsoft Network clients, so it's not required, meaning answer a should be left unchecked. Likewise, CSNW makes it possible for Windows NT Workstations and servers to obtain direct access to a NetWare server; thus, answer b should remain unchecked as well.

Finally, the Migration Tool may be used to copy account and group information, security settings, and files from a NetWare server to a Windows NT Server. It does NetWare 3.x clients no good whatsoever, meaning that answer e must be unchecked.

Question 2

The Palmer Food Cooperative struggles by with donated equipment for its network. The keystone of its network is Windows NT Server 4. Because of a recent gift of a NetWare server, the coop's Windows For Workgroups machines now need access to resources on that machine. How can these client machines access the new server without adding any additional software?

○　a. Install Gateway Service for NetWare on the Windows NT Server, and make those users members of an NTGATEWAY group on that server.

○　b. Install NWLink and File and Print Services for NetWare on the Windows NT Server.

○　c. Install Gateway Service for NetWare on the Windows NT Server, and create a group that has permission to access the NTGATEWAY group on the NetWare server.

○　d. Install Gateway Service for NetWare on the NetWare server, and NWLink on the Windows NT Server.

Answer c is correct. The key to answering this question is to understand GSNW and what must happen on the NetWare side of a connection that uses GSNW. In essence, GSNW provides a way to "translate" ordinary Microsoft Network client traffic bound for a Windows NT Server into a usable kind of NetWare equivalent. This prevents administrators from having to add software to network clients that need access to NetWare resources, which is especially useful on older machines (like those running Windows For Workgroups at the coop) where memory and system resources are already at a premium. The correct answer to this question requires you to recognize that GSNW does the job, but also requires you to know that it's necessary to set up a group account on the NetWare server to handle GSNW requests from the Windows NT Server.

Answer a is incorrect because it places the NetWare group on the Windows NT Server. Answer b is incorrect because it provides a way to make Windows NT services available to NetWare clients, not vice versa. Finally, answer d is incorrect because it puts the gateway on the NetWare server (a highly unlikely place to run a Windows NT service, in fact).

Question 3

> QXR Co. has a NetWare 4.11 network, but it's adding a Windows NT Server, to provide access to a SQL Server client/server application for its NetWare clients. What elements and/or protocols must be available on the Windows NT Server so that NetWare clients can use the SQL Server application?
>
> ○   a. NWLink IPX/SPX Compatible Transport
> ○   b. Gateway Service for NetWare
> ○   c. Client Service for NetWare
> ○   d. Migration Tool for NetWare
> ○   e. File and Print Services for NetWare

Answer a is correct. The presence of a client/server application means that the application's clients already have whatever software is necessary to communicate with the server, assuming clients and the server share a common protocol. Given that QXR has a predominantly NetWare network, the protocol that's necessary is IPX/SPX, known on the Windows NT Server as NWLink. Answer b is incorrect because it makes NetWare resources available to Microsoft Network clients (and QXR wants to go in the other direction). Answer c is incorrect because it makes NetWare resources available to Windows NT Server and Workstation clients (and QXR still wants to go in the other direction). Answer d is incorrect because nobody said anything about migrating from NetWare to Windows NT. And finally, answer e is incorrect because the client/server application supplies its own client-side intelligence, and no need for additional file and print services was requested from the Windows NT Server.

Question 4

One of the PCs on a network is unable to establish a working connection, but all other computers are working correctly. The only protocol in use on the network is NWLink. Of the following possibilities, which is the most likely cause of this problem?

- ○ a. Faulty network interface devices
- ○ b. A protocol mismatch
- ○ c. A PC memory conflict
- ○ d. An incorrect IPX frame type

Answer d is correct. The clue to answering the question correctly lies in the statement that "the only protocol in use on the network is NWLink." Because IPX does not require a fixed frame type, but works with multiple frame types, a frame type mismatch easily can render a machine unable to communicate successfully with the network, even though the hardware is working correctly. The key to answering this question correctly is careful reading. Anyone who knows anything about networks knows that a "loose connection" is the most common cause of problems, but that appears nowhere in this list of choices. Because the problem statement includes an indication that only *one* PC is having problems, and gives "faulty network interface *devices*" as a possibility, this knocks out what typically might be the next most obvious cause, namely a faulty network interface card, thereby eliminating answer a from further consideration. Answer b is patently false because the only protocol in use is NWLink (or IPX/SPX, if you prefer). Answer c is possible, but unlikely, because most memory conflicts will cause a machine to crash rather than simply rendering network access inoperative.

Question 5

> On a network that contains multiple versions of NetWare, some clients are configured for NetWare 2.2, while others are configured for NetWare 4.11. Among other protocols, NWLink is in use on this network. The NetWare 2.2 clients use an 802.3 raw frame type, whereas the NetWare 4.11 clients use the 802.2 frame type. What kinds of information must be supplied in the NWLink IPX/SPX Properties dialog box to allow the same Windows NT Server to recognize both flavors of NetWare clients on this network?
>
> ○ a. Select Auto Frame Type Detection, and add the clients' IPX network numbers and frame types to the frame type configuration list.
>
> ○ b. Select Manual Frame Type Detection, and add the network numbers and frame types for both 2.2 and 4.11 clients to the frame type configuration list.
>
> ○ c. Select only Auto Frame Type Detection; the rest is automatic.
>
> ○ d. Select Manual Frame Type Detection, and add the 2.2 clients' network numbers and frame types to the frame type configuration list.

Answer b is correct. The secret to answering this question is to understand how automatic frame type detection works in Windows NT Server. As long as the only frame type in use is 802.2, automatic detection works fine. But because older NetWare clients—especially NetWare 2.2 clients—use only 802.3 frames, Manual Frame Type Detection must be selected during the configuration process. This eliminates answers a and c from consideration. Answer d is incorrect, because Manual Frame Type Detection requires entry of all frame types and network numbers in use.

Question 6

XYZ Corp. seeks to make its Windows NT Workstation and Windows 95 clients able to access a NetWare server without installing NetWare client software on those machines. How can this objective be met most effectively?

○ a. Install Gateway Services for NetWare on a Windows NT Server on the same network.

○ b. Install NWLink on the Windows NT Workstation and Windows 95 computers.

○ c. Install Gateway Services for NetWare on the NetWare server.

○ d. Install File and Print Services for NetWare on a Windows NT Server on the same network.

Answer a is correct. The whole point of a gateway is to permit clients to access services that their current configurations would otherwise make inaccessible. For that reason, answer a is the only correct answer, because it opens a gateway for the Windows NT and Windows 95 workstations to access NetWare resources with no change to their current configurations. Answer b is incorrect, because by adding NWLink to the workstations, it not only violates the requirement that no NetWare client software be added to those machines, it does not do the complete job (additional software would be necessary to make it possible for these machines to communicate with a NetWare server). Answer c is incorrect because it mentions the right software product, but puts it on a NetWare server rather than on a Windows NT Server, where it was designed to be run. And finally, answer d is incorrect because File and Print Services for NetWare let native NetWare clients access Windows NT, not native Microsoft Networking clients access NetWare (thus completely missing the point of the question).

Question 7

QXR Corp. operates a NetWare 4.11 network, but wants to add a Windows NT Server to provide access to a NetBIOS application for NetWare clients to use. What protocols and/or software elements must be available on the Windows NT Server to enable successful access to this application?

- ○ a. IPX routing (RIP for NWLink)
- ○ b. Client Service for NetWare
- ○ c. File and Print Service for NetWare
- ○ d. NWLink
- ○ e. Gateway Services for NetWare

Answer d is the only correct choice. Like client/server applications, NetBIOS applications include their own client-side capabilities. This eliminates higher-level services from consideration, disqualifying answers b, c, and e. Answer a is incorrect because the question doesn't mention the need to manage IPX traffic flow across multiple network segments (the only reason to use RIP for NWLink). This leaves only the transport protocol on top of which NetBIOS will run between the Windows NT Server and the NetWare clients—namely, IPX/SPX, known to Windows NT Server as NWLink, as specified in answer d.

Question 8

On a mixed network that includes both Windows NT Server and NetWare server machines, the Windows NT Servers are configured to autodetect the IPX frame types in use. What kinds of frame types will the Windows NT Server be able to identify successfully? [Check all correct answers]

- ❏ a. 802.2 frame type
- ❏ b. 802.3 frame type
- ❏ c. 802.3 frame type with SNAP header
- ❏ d. 802.5 frame type
- ❏ e. 802.5 frame type with SNAP header

Answers a, b, c, d, and e are all correct. The AutoDetect capabilities of Windows NT Server only function in a single frame type environment. If this is the case, then all of the frame types listed are corrrect.

Question 9

Once you've successfully enabled the Windows NT Gateway Services for NetWare, what additional steps are necessary to actually use the gateway?

- ○   a. Choose Bindery Emulation on the Windows NT Server.
- ○   b. Map a shared drive letter on the Windows NT Server for the NetWare volume available through the gateway.
- ○   c. Create user accounts that can access the gateway through the NTGATEWAY group on the NetWare server.
- ○   d. Create an NTGATEWAY group on the NetWare server.

Answer b is correct. The necessary follow-up step to gateway installation that lets users with access to the NetWare server obtain files through a drive mapped through the Windows NT Server side of the gateway is contained in answer b. As it happens, enabling the Gateway Service for NetWare handles many of the elements in the preceding list of items. Answer a is correct because it refers to the method of directory information access chosen for the Windows NT Server, and also is selected during installation of the Gateway itself. Part of the installation process requires creating the necessary user accounts in the NTGATEWAY group on the NetWare server, thereby eliminating answer c from consideration. In the same vein, the NTGATEWAY group itself also must be defined for the gateway to be enabled, so answer d also is incorrect.

Question 10

Which of the following software elements and/or protocols are required for a Windows NT Workstation running Client Service for NetWare to successfully access NetWare-based resources? [Choose all correct answers]

- ❑ a. Gateway Service for NetWare

- ❑ b. File and Print Service for NetWare

- ❑ c. NWLink

- ❑ d. A valid account on a NetWare server

- ❑ e. Membership in the NTGATEWAY group on the NetWare server to which Gateway Service for NetWare is connected

---

Answers c and d are correct. Answer c supplies the necessary protocol to communicate from client to server; answer d provides the necessary permission to access the NetWare server once communication commences. The complete name for the gateway appears as Gateway (and Client) Service for NetWare in the Services applet in Control Panel under Windows NT Server. This means that CSNW is a subset of GSNW, strictly for use by the server where GSNW is installed. Whether explicitly supplied on a Windows NT Workstation or implied in the contents of GSNW on a Windows NT Server, the answers to this question are the same: None of the gateway or access services is required to use CSNW capabilities. This automatically eliminates answers a, b, and e.

Need To Know More?

 Gaskin, James E.: *The Complete Guide to NetWare 4.11/ IntraNetWare, 2nd Edition.* Sybex Network Press, Alameda, CA, 1997. ISBN 0-7821-1931-X. For a comprehensive look at NetWare networking, there's no better reference than this one. Use it to deal with NetWare specifics and the NetWare side of any NetWare-to-Windows NT connection.

 Heywood, Drew: *Inside Windows NT Server, 2nd Edition.* New Riders, Indianapolis, IN, 1998. ISBN 1-56205-860-6. Chapter 16, "Windows NT Server and NetWare," explains salient software, communications issues, and connectivity concerns.

Minasi, Mark, Christa Anderson, and Elizabeth Creegan: *Mastering Windows NT Server 4, 4th Edition.* Sybex Network Press, Alameda, CA, 1997. ISBN 0-7821-2067-9. Minasi's been a Windows NT guru ever since the product appeared; his experience and practical orientation show in Chapter 13, "Novell NetWare in an NT Server Environment." Worthwhile because of the tips and tricks it provides, and a good overview as well.

 Siyan, Karanjit S.: *Windows NT Server 4 Professional Reference, 2nd Edition.* New Riders, Indianapolis, IN, 1997. ISBN 1-56205-805-3. Chapter 12, "Integrating NetWare with Windows NT Server," brings Siyan's usual depth of coverage and details to this topic; this is the best available preparation material for NetWare topics.

Strebe, Matthew, Charles Perkins, and James Chellis: *MCSE: NT Server 4 Study Guide, 2nd Edition.* Sybex Network Press, San Francisco, CA, 1998. ISBN 0-7821-2222-1. Chapter 13, "Interoperating with NetWare," covers this ground well (only Siyan offers more depth and details).

Search the TechNet CD (or its online version through **www.microsoft.com.technet**) using the keywords "NetWare," "NWLink," "Gateway Services," and related product names. The Windows NT *Concepts and Planning Manual* also includes useful information on making NT to NetWare connections, and vice versa.

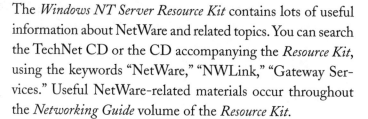

The *Windows NT Server Resource Kit* contains lots of useful information about NetWare and related topics. You can search the TechNet CD or the CD accompanying the *Resource Kit*, using the keywords "NetWare," "NWLink," "Gateway Services." Useful NetWare-related materials occur throughout the *Networking Guide* volume of the *Resource Kit*.

Windows NT Printing

Terms you'll need to understand:

- √ Client application
- √ Connecting to a printer
- √ Creating a printer
- √ Network interface printer
- √ Print client
- √ Print device
- √ Print job
- √ Print resolution
- √ Print server
- √ Print server services
- √ Print spooler
- √ Printer driver
- √ Printer/Logical printer
- √ Queue/Print queue
- √ Rendering

Techniques you'll need to master:

- √ Installing and configuring a printer
- √ Managing printing clients
- √ Managing the print spooler
- √ Setting up print priorities
- √ Establishing logical printers and printing pools

It is the job of the network administrator to make sure that users have access to needed resources—and the printer is one of the most often-used resources. One of the biggest complaints about other network operating systems has been the inability to handle printers effectively and efficiently. Microsoft has developed an intuitive and simple way to manage these much-used resources. This chapter focuses on the Microsoft approach to printing and defines a few Microsoft-specific printing terms.

The Windows NT Print Lexicon

The following list contains Microsoft-specific printing terminology that must be mastered. It is very important that you know and fully understand all of these terms and concepts.

➤ **Client application** A network program that originates print jobs (this can be located on a print server or client computer on the network).

➤ **Connecting to a printer** The process of attaching to a network share that resides on the computer on which the logical printer was created (performed through the Add Printer Wizard, accessed from the Start menu, Settings, Printers option. It is also available via the My Computer, Printers folder).

➤ **Creating a printer** The process of naming, defining settings for, installing drivers for, and linking a printing device to the network. In Windows NT, this process is performed through the Add Printer Wizard.

➤ **Network interface printer** Built-in network interface cards for print devices that are directly attached to the network (for example, the Hewlett-Packard JetDirect). (Note that it's wise to assume that the DLC protocol must be installed to communicate with directly attached print devices.)

➤ **Print client** A computer on a network (called a "client computer") that transmits the print jobs to be produced by the physical printing device.

➤ **Print device** The print device is commonly referred to as the printer—in other words, the print device is the physical hardware device that produces printed material. This is very confusing to most people. Just remember that the print device is the piece of hardware that actually spits out paper with your material printed on it.

➤ **Print job** The code that defines the print processing commands as well as the actual file to be printed. Windows NT defines print jobs by data type, depending upon what adjustments must be made to the file for it to print accurately (i.e., one data type can be printable as-is, whereas another may need a form feed to conclude the data stream for the print job to be executed properly).

➤ **Print resolution** The measurement of pixel density that is responsible for the smoothness of any image or text being printed. This is measured in dots per inch (DPI)—the higher the DPI, the better the quality of the printed material.

➤ **Print server** The server computer that links physical print devices to the network, and manages sharing those devices with computers on the network.

➤ **Print server services** Software components located on the print server that accept print jobs and send them to the print spooler for execution. These components, such as Services For Macintosh, enable a variety of client computers to communicate with the print server to process print jobs.

➤ **Print spooler** The collection of dynamic link libraries (DLLs) that acquires, processes, catalogues, and disburses print jobs. A print job will be saved to disk in a spool file. Print despooling is the process of reading what is contained in the spool file and transmitting it to the physical printing device.

➤ **Printer driver** Programs that enable communications between applications and a specific print device. Most hardware peripherals, such as printers, require the use of a driver to process commands.

➤ **Printer/logical printer** The logical printer (Microsoft calls this "the printer") is the software interface that communicates between the operating system and the physical printing device. The logical printer handles the printing process from the time the print command is issued. Its settings determine the physical printing device that renders the file to be printed, as well as how the file to be printed is sent to the printing device (e.g., via a remote print share or local port).

➤ **Queue/print queue** In printing terms, a queue is a series of files waiting to be produced by the printing device.

➤ **Rendering** The rendering process in Windows NT is as follows: A client application sends file information to the Graphics Device Interface (GDI), which receives the data, communicates that data to the physical printing device driver, and produces the print job in the language of the physical printing device. The printing device then interprets this information and creates a file (bitmap) for each page to be printed.

Printing With Windows NT Server

Windows NT print settings are managed through the Printers folder, which is accessible from the Control Panel or the Start menu (Start|Settings|Printers), it's also accessed via My Computer. (*Note:* The Printers folder replaces the old Windows NT 3.51 Print Manager.) This approach is extremely straightforward when compared to earlier versions of Windows NT and other network operating systems.

Windows NT takes a modular approach to printing, as shown in Figure 8.1; each component has a specific use and interfaces with the other components in the print architecture.

The following list defines each component of the Windows NT printing architecture:

➤ **Graphics Device Interface (GDI)** The component that provides network applications with a system for presenting graphical information. The GDI works as a translator between the application's print requests and the device driver interface (DDI) to make sure a job is rendered accurately.

➤ **Print device** The physical hardware device that produces printed output.

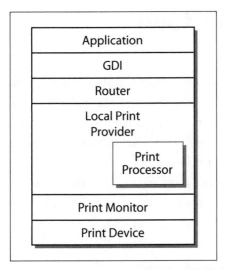

Figure 8.1   The Windows NT print architecture components work together to render print jobs for the user.

➤ **Print driver** The software component that enables communication between the operating system and the physical printing device.

➤ **Print monitor** The component that passes the print job, which has been translated to the print device's language, to the physical printing device.

➤ **Print processor** The component that makes any necessary modifications to the print job before passing the job to the print monitor. Windows NT actually has two print processors, one for the Windows platform and one for the Macintosh.

➤ **Print router** The component that directs the print job to the appropriate printing device.

➤ **Print spooler** (also called the **print provider**) The component that accepts print jobs from the router, calls the processor to make any needed changes to the print job, and transfers the jobs one at a time to the print monitor.

Printing From Windows NT Clients

This is where Windows NT's approach to printing really shines. Client computers need access to print devices, so they must add the printer via the Add Printer Wizard. Previously, all client computers required that the print driver be installed on each client machine that needed access to a print device. No more! All that is needed for printing from a Windows NT client is that the driver be installed on the print server. This simplifies the printing process, because if an updated print driver is released, it just needs to be installed on the server, not on every client machine.

Printing From Windows 95 And 98 Clients

This process is the same as for Windows NT clients. All that is needed is a connection between the client computer and the print device, and that the print driver is installed on the server.

Printing From MS-DOS And Windows 3.x Clients

Unfortunately, the simplicity of printing from Windows NT, 95, and 98 clients does not extend to other client machines, such as DOS, Windows 3.x, and Macintosh clients. It is best to create a central repository for print drivers for these computers. You may then use this central repository for these types of clients.

Spooling

When a user sends out a print job, it goes to the print spooler, which is responsible for tracking the print job through the printing process, routing jobs to the correct ports, and assigning priorities to print jobs.

Print Priorities

By default, the spooler prints jobs in the order in which they are received. It is possible, however, to ensure that print jobs from certain users are printed before any other job. To adjust priority levels for individual users or groups, you must create a different logical printer to a particular printing device (this is discussed in detail in the "Logical Printers And Printing Pools" section, later in the chapter). To assign higher priority to print jobs from certain users, these steps must be performed on a logical printer:

1. Go to the Printers Folder (Start|Settings|Printers).

2. Select the logical printer you wish to alter, then select Properties (not Server Properties) from the File menu.

3. Select the Scheduling tab.

4. Adjust the slide bar to assign a higher priority (this can be set anywhere from 1 to 99, with 1 being the lowest—as well as the default setting).

Separate Spool Files

If the printers on your network are hit pretty hard with many print jobs at a time, the print spooler can get fairly large. It is important to make sure that the spooler file is big enough to handle all of the jobs that are sent to it. It may become necessary, therefore, to create individual spool files for each printer on the network. This is performed through the Registry by creating files under the following Registry key:

```
HKEY_LOCAL_MACHINE\SYSTEM\CurrentControlSet\Control\Print\Printers
```

Stopping And Restarting The Spooler Service

It is possible for print jobs to get stuck in the spooler. To remedy this, stop and restart the spooler service by performing the following steps:

1. Go to the Control Panel.

2. Double-click the Services icon.

3. Highlight the entry labeled "Spooler" in the list of services.

4. Click the Stop button, and confirm that you want to stop the service.

5. Click the Start button.

6. Click Close on the Services dialog box.

Changing The Spool Location

The default directory for the print spooler is \Winnt\System32\Spool. Here are the steps for changing the location of the spooler directory:

1. Go to the Printers Folder.

2. Select Server Properties from the File menu.

3. Select the Advanced tab.

4. Enter the path to the new spool directory in the Spool Folder text box.

The reason why you may want to change this setting is that the drive for the default path has limited space for storing print jobs. (*Note:* You must restart the print server before these changes take effect.)

Logical Printers And Printing Pools

A logical printer is the software interface that enables communication between Windows NT and the physical printing device. You can create multiple logical printers that send print jobs to a single print device (and, conversely, a single logical printer that sends jobs to multiple print devices).

It is necessary to create different logical printers (with different share names) to assign priorities to print jobs from various groups and users to a single print device. All of this is defined through the Add Printer Wizard in the Printers folder. You simply provide different settings (such as access rights, access times, and priorities) for different shares that attach to the same physical print device.

When a printer services multiple printing devices, it creates what is called a "printer pool." Put simply, a single logical printer spools out jobs to the next available printing device in the printer pool. It is necessary for all of the print devices in a printer pool to use the same print driver. With this setup, the printer assigns files to be printed to whichever print device is free in the printer pool.

Practice Questions

Question 1

Several users are trying to print to a print server. You receive many complaints from the users that they have sent several jobs to the print server, but the jobs have not printed and cannot be deleted. How do you resolve this problem?

○ a. Verify that the Pause printing option is not checked on the print server.

○ b. Delete the stalled printer from the print server, create a new printer, and tell your users to resend their jobs to the new printer.

○ c. Delete all files from the spool folder on the print server, and tell your users to resend them.

○ d. Stop the spooler service, and then restart it.

Answer d is correct. This scenario is a quintessential example of a stalled print spooler. To fix the problem, select Services in Control Panel, stop the spooler service, and then restart it. The Pause printing command will prevent print jobs from printing, but it will not prevent jobs from being deleted, so this is not the problem. Therefore, answer a is incorrect. There's no need to re-create the printer from scratch, so answer b is also incorrect. You should never have to involve users in the problem-solving process (other than to gather information from them); therefore, answer c is also incorrect.

Question 2

You have a Windows NT Server that provides print services to 20 Windows NT computers on your network. You have an HP LaserJet attached to the Windows NT print server. Hewlett-Packard has just released an updated printer driver. What must be done to distribute the updated driver to all the computers that print to this print server?

○ a. Install the updated driver on all client computers; there is no need to update the server.

○ b. Install the updated driver on the print server, and do nothing more.

○ c. Install the updated driver on the print server and on all client computers.

○ d. Create a separate logical printer with the updated driver on the print server, and tell all your users to print to the new printer.

○ e. Install the updated driver on the print server, and instruct all client computers to download the updated driver from the server.

Answer b is correct. The best way to update a printer driver for Windows NT clients is to update the driver on the print server. There is no need to update the driver manually on each client computer that is running Windows NT; therefore, answer a is incorrect. When a client computer sends a print job to the print server, the updated driver is automatically copied to the client; therefore, answers c, d, and e are also incorrect.

Question 3

> You run a network for a small consulting firm. You have only a single printer on the network. The company executives have asked that you configure printing so that all documents from the executives print before other documents. How is this performed?
>
> ○ a. Create a separate logical printer, assign rights to the executive group, and set the printer priority to 1.
>
> ○ b. Create a separate logical printer, assign rights to the executive group, and set the printer priority to 99.
>
> ○ c. Create a separate logical printer for the executive group, and configure the printer to start printing immediately.
>
> ○ d. Create a separate logical printer for the executive group, and configure the printer to print directly to the physical print device.

Answer b is correct. It is possible to set priorities between groups of documents by creating different logical printers for the same physical print device and setting different priority levels on the printers. To set printer priority, select the Scheduling tab in Printer Properties. The highest priority is 99; therefore, b is the correct answer. The lowest priority is 1; therefore, answer a is incorrect. The "start printing immediately" setting will not give the executives print priority over others. It simply instructs the print server to print without waiting for the entire print job to be saved to the spooler; therefore, answer c is incorrect. Printing directly to the printer will not offer print priority. It just instructs the print server to print without storing the print job to the spooler at all; therefore, answer d is incorrect.

Question 4

> You have just installed a new printer on your print server. You send a print job to the printer, but it comes out as pages of nonsense. What is the most likely cause of the problem?
>
> ○ a. The DLC protocol is not installed.
>
> ○ b. The print spooler is corrupt.
>
> ○ c. An incorrect printer driver has been installed.
>
> ○ d. There is not enough hard disk space for spooling.

Answer c is correct. If an incorrect printer driver has been installed, documents may print illegibly. A print job won't print at all if the wrong protocol is in use, so answer a is incorrect. Likewise, nothing will print without the spooler; therefore, answer b is incorrect. As in answer b, a print job won't print without proper spooling; therefore, answer d is incorrect.

Question 5

You want to create a printer pool with five print devices. Which condition must be present for you to create this printer pool?

○   a. All print devices must use the same protocol.

○   b. All physical print devices must be connected to the same logical printer.

○   c. All print devices must use the same printer port.

○   d. All print devices must be located in the same room.

Answer b is correct. To create a printer pool, all print devices must be connected to the same print server. It is not necessary that all print devices use the same protocol; therefore, answer a is incorrect. All print devices also should be identical. Answers c and d are both incorrect because you don't have to use the same port for multiple printer devices, and printers don't have to be in the same room.

Question 6

You have a printer pool that consists of Printer 1 and Printer 2. Printer 1 is printing a job and Printer 2 is idle. A paper jam occurs on Printer 1's print device. What will happen to the rest of the job that was being printed?

○   a. The print job will be completed on Printer 2.

○   b. The print job will be canceled.

○   c. The print job will be completed on Printer 2 because Printer 2 has a higher priority level.

○   d. The print job is held for completion by Printer 1 until the device is fixed.

Answer d is correct. If a physical print device in a printer pool fails in the middle of a print job, the print job is retained at that physical print device until the device is fixed. Any other print jobs sent to the printer pool will print to other physical print devices in the printer pool. The print job will not be sent to Printer 2; therefore, answer a is incorrect. The print job will not be canceled if the device fails; therefore, answer b is also incorrect. Priority levels have nothing to so with failed devices; therefore, answer c is incorrect as well.

Question 7

> You want to configure a Windows NT computer to be the print server for an HP network interface print device. However, you are unable to locate the option to install a port for the printer. Why is this?
>
> ○ a. PostScript printing is enabled on the print device and must be disabled.
>
> ○ b. You didn't install the print driver on the print server.
>
> ○ c. The print processor is corrupt and must be fixed.
>
> ○ d. The DLC protocol is not installed on the print server.

Answer d is correct. For Windows NT to provide support for HP network interface print devices, you must install the DLC (Data Link Control) protocol. You can't install a printer driver if Windows NT cannot recognize the print device. PostScript printing has nothing to do with print device installation; therefore, answer a is incorrect. You can't install a print driver if Windows NT can't recognize the print device; therefore, answer b is incorrect. The print processor is not involved in the installation of printers; therefore, answer c is also incorrect.

Need To Know More?

 Heywood, Drew: *Inside Windows NT Server, 2nd Edition*. New Riders, Indianapolis, IN, 1998. ISBN 1-56205-860-6. Chapter 6, "Managing Print Services," details the issues relating to printing and printer permissions and management.

 Siyan, Karanjit S.: *Windows NT Server 4 Professional Reference, 2nd Edition*. New Riders, Indianapolis, IN, 1997. ISBN 1-56205-805-3. A nice discussion of using Windows NT print services is located in Chapter 17, "Windows NT Printing."

Strebe, Matthew, Charles Perkins, and James Chellis: *MCSE: NT Server 4 Study Guide, 2nd Edition*. Sybex Network Press, San Francisco, CA, 1998. ISBN 0-7821-2222-1. Chapter 14 contains detailed information about creating and maintaining your printing environment.

Search the TechNet CD (or its online version through **www.microsoft.com/technet**) using the keywords "printing," "logical printers," "print management," and "print devices."

 The *Windows NT Server Resource Kit* contains a lot of useful information about printers and printer management. You can search the TechNet CD or the CD accompanying the *Resource Kit*, using keywords like "shares," "resource management," and "user management."

9

Windows NTBACKUP

. . . .

Terms you'll need to understand:

√ Backup

√ Restoration

√ Tape drive

√ Differential backup

√ Incremental backup

√ Backup marker

√ Backup log

Techniques you'll need to master:

√ Installing, configuring, and implementing NTBACKUP.EXE

√ Assigning the right to back up the system

√ Establishing a backup plan

√ Scheduling backups

√ Using AT.EXE to perform scheduled backups

Backing up critical data is an important task for any network administrator. Windows NT Server 4 ships with a program called NTBACKUP.EXE. Although it is automatically installed with Windows NT Server, you must install drivers for your tape backup and have a good understanding of how the backup process works to successfully back up and restore important data.

NTBACKUP Facts

NTBACKUP's advantages include:

> ➤ The program is free; you do not have to purchase a third-party back-up utility.

> ➤ Because it is a native Windows NT program, the chances of the server running into stability problems are slim to none.

> ➤ It can back up from the two supported file systems, FAT and NTFS. It also can restore just as easily to either file system.

It also has disadvantages:

> ➤ The only acceptable media that NTBACKUP supports is a tape drive; you cannot back up to another hard drive, floppy, or even across the network to a network drive.

> ➤ There is no built-in scheduler program included with NTBACKUP; to accomplish an unattended backup, you must write a batch file (discussed later in this chapter).

> ➤ You cannot back up a remote Registry with NTBACKUP. (This task must be done locally. To back up the Registry of all the domain controllers, you must attach a tape drive physically to each one. You can, however, back up files both locally and remotely.)

> ➤ NTBACKUP only does a "file-by-file" backup and not a disk-image backup.

> ➤ NTBACKUP cannot backup open files.

> ➤ NTBACKUP has no support for tape drive autoloaders.

Who Has The Right?

Just like everything else in Windows NT Server, a user must have the right to perform backups and restorations. All users can back up any files and folders with the read permission assigned to that user. This right must be granted to the user by selecting User Rights from the Policies menu in the User Manager For Domains tool. To restore files and folders, a user must have the Restore Files And Directories right, which is also granted in the User Manager For Domains. By default, members of the Backup Operators and Server Operators have these rights. Note that throughout this book, we reference the backup utility with the term NTBACKUP; however, once the application is launched, it is only named Backup on the desktop.

Backup Types

Table 9.1 lists the different backup types in NTBACKUP.

Backup Markers

A backup marker, or mark, is an attribute of a file or folder set on certain types of backup to indicate that the file or folder has been backed up before by Windows NT.

Examples Of Different Backup Types

Example 1: Monday is a normal backup and Tuesday through Friday are differential backups that do not set markers. Each differential backup backs up all the changes since Monday. If

Table 9.1	NTBACKUP's backup types.	
Type Of Backup	**Backs Up**	**Marked?**
Daily Copy	Files and folders that have changed during that day	No
Copy	All selected files and folders	No
Differential	Selected files and folders if they have changed since the last backup	No
Incremental	Selected files and folders if they have changed since the last backup	Yes
Normal	All selected files and folders	Yes

data is corrupted or bad on Friday, you only need to restore the Monday and Thursday backups. This strategy takes more time to back up, but less time to restore.

Example 2: Monday is a normal backup and Tuesday through Friday are incremental backups that do set markers. Each incremental backup only backs up changes since the previous day. If data becomes corrupted on Friday, you would need to restore all backups beginning with Monday. This strategy takes less time to back up, but more time to restore.

NTBACKUP.EXE

You launch NTBACKUP from Start|Programs|AdministrativeTools |Backup. When you start the program, you will see the screen shown in Figure 9.1.

If you have a blank tape in the tape drive, in the left pane you would see a tape icon with the words "blank tape" next to it. If there is something on tape, like in Figure 9.1, there is a tape icon and specific information about the tape itself. In the right pane is a list of the tape's contents.

The next step in NTBACKUP is to choose what drive, files, or folders are to be backed up. To accomplish this, choose Drives from the Window menu.

A list of available drives appears. If you want to back up an entire drive, place an X in the box next to the drive letter itself (see Figure 9.2). If

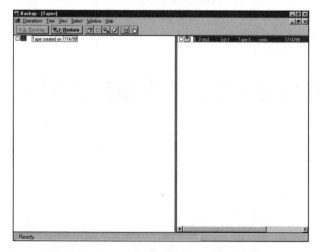

Figure 9.1   Windows NTBACKUP tape selection.

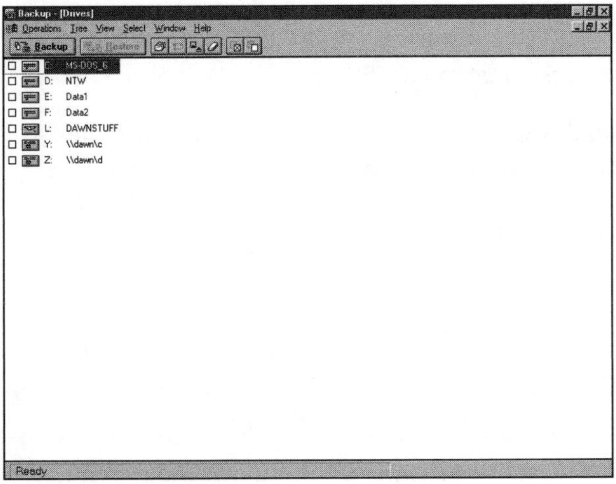

Figure 9.2   Select the drive to be backed up by placing an X next to it.

there are certain directories that you would like to back up, double-click the drive in the pane. If you decide to select certain directories, the screen will split into two panes. The left pane contains the drives, and the right pane contains the files in the directories written on the left pane, as shown in Figure 9.3.

Alternatively, you can select individual files by double-clicking the folders to show all files and placing an X next to the file. You have now selected the files that need to be backed up.

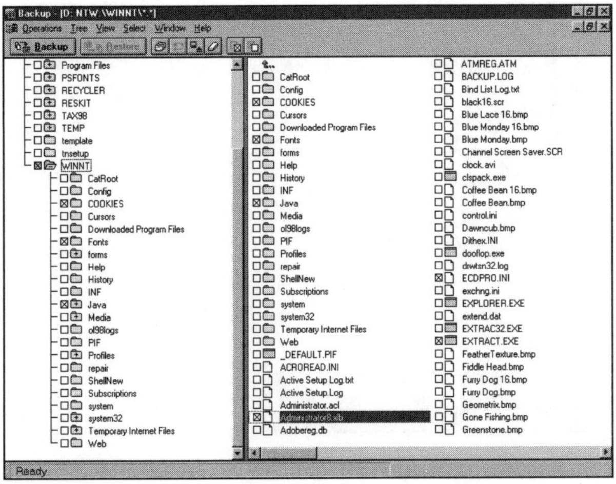

Figure 9.3   You can select files to be backed up along with other directories.

Here are a few items to remember about NTBACKUP:

➤ Do not back up temporary files.

➤ Back up the Registry on both the PDC and all BDCs. The Registry contains the directory databases. Backing up on all domain controllers prevents the loss of all user accounts and security information.

Backup Options

After you have selected which items to back up, select different NTBACKUP options from the Backup Information dialog box (shown in Figure 9.4). These options include Tape Name, Verify After Backup, Backup Registry, and Restrict Access To Owner Or Administrator. To find the Options dialog box, click Backup in the Backup dialog box. Table 9.2 describes each option, along with the tape name.

After you select the options, type a meaningful description of the backup in the description box (for example, download server; drive C:). Finally, choose the backup type to be performed.

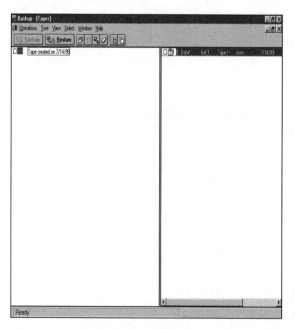

Figure 9.4 NTBACKUP's Backup Information dialog box.

Table 9.2 Vital statistics about NTBACKUP's tape options.	
Option	**Description**
Operation: Append	Adds new backup set after the last backup set on the tape.
Operation: Replace	Overwrites all data on the tape.
Verify After Backup	Confirms files/folders were backed up.
Backup Registry	This option is available only if you have selected at least one other file. You *cannot* back up only the Registry.
Restrict Access To	Limits access to users with the correct permissions. When the Owner/Administrator is backing up the Registry, you always should choose this option.
Hardware Compression	If your tape drive supports data compression, select this option.

The last set of options to set is the Log Information. If you would like to create a backup log, simply put a path in the log file line of the backup information dialog box. The default is BACKUP.LOG in the \Winnt folder. The three options under Log Information are shown in Table 9.3. After the backup completes, you'll see a dialog box that provides details on the tape that was created, as shown in Figure 9.5.

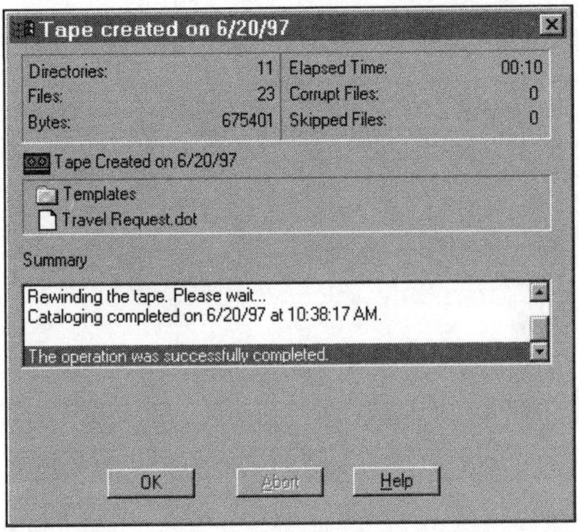

Figure 9.5 Details on a successful backup.

Table 9.3   Vital statistics about Log Information options.

Option	Description
Full Detail	Logs all backup information, including the names of all of the files and folders backed up and skipped.
Summary Only	Logs only the major backup operations, such as loading and unloading the tape and starting backup.
Do Not Log	No log is created.

Scheduled Backup

There is not a scheduler inside the NTBACKUP program, but you can write a batch file to start the NTBACKUP process. The syntax follows:

```
NTBACKUP.EXE BACKUP [pathname[options]]
```

Table 9.4 shows the options or switches that you can use with this command line process.

Table 9.4   Vital statistics about NTBACKUP options.

Option/Switch	Description
/a	This is not available for a blank tape. This appends the backup set to any existing backup set.
/b	Backs up the local Registry.
/d text or description	Allows for a backup description.
/e	Logs exceptions; similar to a summary log.
/l file name	Assigns a log file name.
/r	Limits the rights of the backup operation to Administrators, Backup Operators, or Owners.
/t{normal|copy |incremental| differential|daily}	Allows you to specify which type of backup to perform.
/v	Confirmation of backup.
/hc: {on|off}	Enables or disables hardware compression (if your tape drive will support it). The default is off.
Cmd /c net use x:	Connects to a remote share. Use this to connect to a remote machine.
Cmd /c net use x: /delete	Disconnects from remote shares.

You *cannot* back up a remote Registry using NTBACKUP!

Using The AT Command

Once you have a batch file with the NTBACKUP link included, you can use AT.EXE to schedule the batch file to run at a specific time (see Table 9.5). AT.EXE schedules commands to be run by the scheduling service in Windows NT. The scheduling service must be running on the machine that will run the scheduled task. The syntax for the AT command follows:

```
AT [\\computername] [id] [/delete] time [interactive] [/every:
date[,...]| next; date[,...] "command"
```

Restoring With NTBACKUP

Restoring data with the NTBACKUP program is quite simple. You can restore data to the same system or a completely different system, which is a great advantage. (Note that a Registry cannot be restored remotely.)

 There are several steps to the restoration procedure:

1. Start NTBACKUP.EXE.

2. Load the tape to view the catalog, to see which files and folders are available for restoring. A catalog contains the

Table 9.5	Vital statistics about AT.EXE options.
Option	**Description**
computername	Specifies a remote machine.
Id	Assigns an ID number to a scheduled command.
/delete	Cancels a scheduled command. If the ID is omitted, all the scheduled commands are omitted.
Time	Expresses time in time:minute mode; runs from 00:00 through 23:59.
/interactive	Allows user to see network activity in real time.
/every: date[,...]	Specifies the days for the command to run.
/next:date[,...]	Specifies the next day of the month the command is to run.
"command"	Specifies the actual command to be run, e.g., NTBACKUP.

information on each backup set. This is useful if you have more than one backup set per tape. To create a catalog, simply view the Backup dialog box, and select Catalog under the Operations menu. This will create a catalog set (see Figure 9.6).

3. After the cataloging is complete, select the files and folders to be restored.

   The dialog box shown in Figure 9.6 looks very similar to the Backup selection screen. You have the option to restore the entire backup set or individual files and folders. To select the files or folders to be restored, place an X in the checkbox next to the item you wish to restore. (You can select more than one object at a time by holding down the Shift key.)

4. After you have selected the files or folders to be restored, set the options for the restore procedure. You will see that the Restore Information dialog box (shown in Figure 9.7) looks very similar to the Backup Information dialog box.

   In the Restore Information dialog box, you will find useful information, including Tape Name, Backup Set, Creation Date, Owner, a number of Restore options (detailed next), and Log Information. The Restore To Drive line provides the location where the program restores the data. Or, you may select an alternate location. If you are unsure of the alternate path, select the ... button to browse for your preferred restore location.

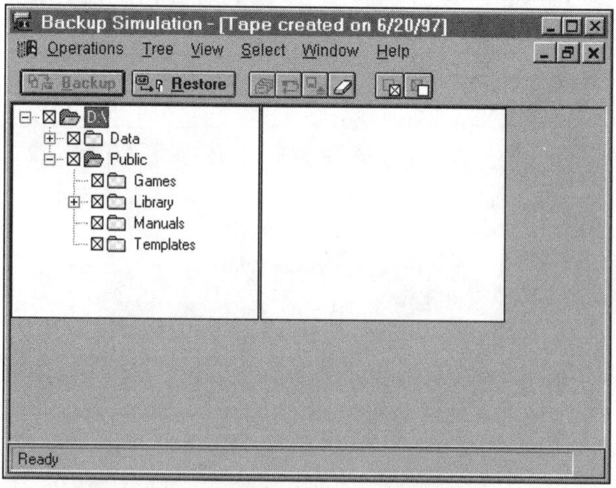

Figure 9.6   Select the files to be restored.

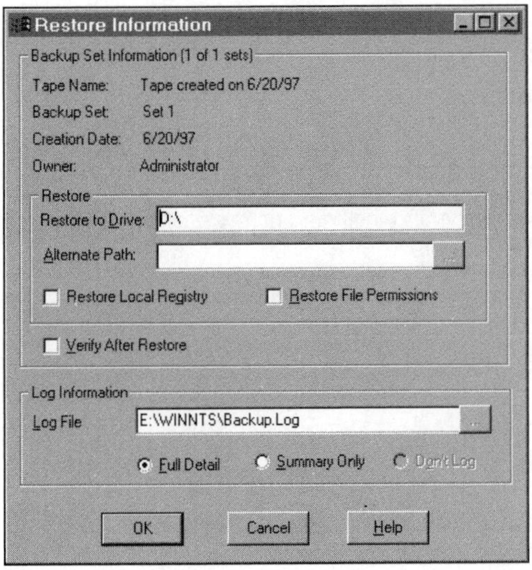

Figure 9.7   NTBACKUP's Restore Information dialog box.

5. Once the restore location is selected, you can choose additional options, as listed in Table 9.6.

6. After you have set restore options, set the Backup Log options. See Table 9.7 for an explanation of each option.

7. Once you select the options, click OK to start the restore process.

Next, you will see the Restore Status dialog box, shown in Figure 9.8. When the restore process is complete, you will see the following message: The operation was successfully completed.

Table 9.6   Vital statistics about restoration options and their descriptions.

Option	Description
Restore Local Registry	If you backed up the Registry, this option will restore the local Registry.
Restore File Permissions	Restores NTFS permissions. If this is not selected, the files and folders will follow the general rule of inheriting the new parent directory permissions.
Verify After Restore	Does a check of the tape against the files on the hard drive.

Table 9.7	Backup Log options and their descriptions.
Option	**Description**
Log File	The location of the restore text file. You can browse for the location.
Log Information: Full Detail	Logs everything, including names of all files and folders restored.
Log Information: Summary Only	Logs failures and major operations, such as the loading of the tape.
Log Information: Don't Log	No log is created.

Backup Tips

Here are a few items to keep in mind when backing up your Windows NT system:

➤ Always back up the Registry on all domain controllers (PDCs and BDCs).

➤ Keep at least three copies of backup tapes. One should be located off site for safety.

➤ Create a backup log for each backup process.

➤ Have a weekly routine for performing a trial restore.

➤ Grant the appropriate rights to users who will perform the backup and restore procedure.

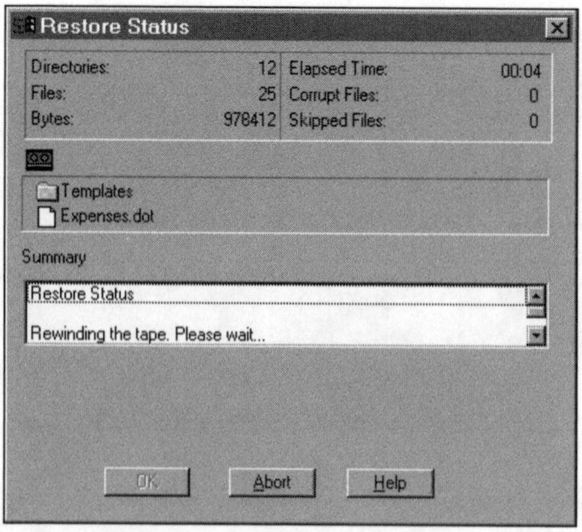

Figure 9.8 NTBACKUP Restore Status dialog box.

Practice Questions

Question 1

> You want to use NTBACKUP.EXE to back up some local files. What type of media can the NTBACKUP program use?
>
> O   a. Floppy
>
> O   b. Tape
>
> O   c. Writable CDs
>
> O   d. Across the network to another hard drive

Answer b is correct. The only backup media type that NTBACKUP.EXE supports is a tape drive.

Question 2

> Where should you check to see if NTBACKUP ran successfully?
>
> O   a. User Manager For Domains
>
> O   b. Server Manager
>
> O   c. Backup Log
>
> O   d. The Registry

Answer c is correct. To find out whether a backup was successful, you must check the Backup Log in NTBACKUP. The User Manager For Domains is where most administration takes place for Windows NT, such as adding users and changing their passwords. Backup is not affected directly by User Manager; therefore, answer a is incorrect. (You do, however, assign backup rights in User Manager.) Server Manager is for server administration as well. You can verify the remote users with Server Manager, but you cannot check if the backup was successful; therefore, answer b is incorrect. Although *everything* in Windows NT lives in the Registry, you wouldn't look there for successful backup information; therefore, answer d is incorrect.

Question 3

What files always should be backed up? [Check all correct answers]

❑ a. Temporary files

❑ b. Mission-critical data

❑ c. Registries on all domain controllers

❑ d. The Winnt directory

Answers b, c, and d are correct. In case of a disaster, you always should have a copy of your data; therefore, answer b is correct. The Registry always should be backed up as well, so answer c also is correct. The Winnt directory should be backed up to provide you with a source to restore corrupted files and prevent you from having to re-install the entire OS. Therefore, answer d is correct. Remember, do not waste your time on temp files. They simply take up space; therefore, answer a is incorrect.

Question 4

You have 10 machines in one domain. Of these machines, one is a PDC, one is a BDC, and the rest are workstations. Your boss says he needs a backup of all the domain's files and folders, including the Registry of the domain controllers. You notice that there is one tape drive in the domain and it is installed on the BDC. What should you do to back up everything the boss wants on the PDC?

Trick! question

○ a. Nothing. You can do a remote backup of everything on the PDC.

○ b. Install a tape drive on the PDC to back up everything requested on the PDC, and use the tape drive on the BDC to back up everything requested on the BDC.

○ c. Nothing. You cannot back up your domain controllers.

Answer b is correct. You must install a tape drive on each domain controller to back up the Registry. The Registry cannot be backed up remotely; therefore, answer a is incorrect. You should always back up your domain controllers; therefore, answer c is incorrect.

Question 5

When you installed Windows NT Server, you noticed that the backup utility was installed automatically. When you try to use your tape drive, nothing happens. What could be the cause of this?

○ a. Even though Windows NT installs the NTBACKUP program, you still must install the drivers for the tape drive.

○ b. You have to shut down your server before you can run NTBACKUP.

○ c. You must have the RAS service running.

○ d. You must have CSNW installed.

Answer a is correct. When Windows NT is installed, NTBACKUP is installed automatically. However, you must still install the drivers for the tape backup. A server can be up during backup; therefore, answer b is incorrect. Windows NT's Remote Access Service is a communications program and has nothing to do with backups; therefore, answer c is incorrect. The CSNW is required for individual Windows NT clients to communicate with NetWare servers; therefore, answer d is incorrect.

Question 6

Sheila is a member of the local group called Sales. She can back up files that she reads on a daily basis, but she cannot restore any files. What is the problem?

○ a. Sheila is not a member of Domain Admins, so she cannot see any files.

○ b. Sheila is not a member of the Backup Operators, Server Operators, or the Replicator group.

○ c. Sheila is not a member of the Backup Operators, Server Operators, or Administrator group.

Answer c is correct. You must be granted a right to restore data. Backup Operators, Server Operators, and the Administrator group all have the right to do this; therefore, answer c is the only correct answer. Remember, if users can read a file, they can back up the file, but to restore the file, they must have the Restore Files and Directories right.

Need To Know More?

 Donald, Lisa, and James, Chellis: *MCSE: NT Server 4 in the Enterprise Study Guide, 2nd Edition*. Sybex Network Press, San Francisco, CA, 1998. ISBN 0-7821-2221-3. Chapter 5, "Storage," contains an insightful discussion of the NTBACKUP program.

Heywood, Drew: *Inside Windows NT Server, 2nd Edition*. New Riders, Indianapolis, IN, 1998. ISBN 1-56205-860-6. Chapter 11, "Backing Up Files," has a great discussion of backup and disaster recovery issues.

Siyan, Karanjit S.: *Windows NT Server 4 Professional Reference, 2nd Edition*. New Riders, Indianapolis, IN, 1997. ISBN 1-56205-805-3. Chapter 20, "Data Protection in Windows NT Servers," contains a lengthy discussion of data protection.

Search the TechNet CD (or its online version through **www.microsoft.com/technet**) using the keywords "backup," "restore," "disaster recovery," and "tape backup devices."

 The *Windows NT Server Resource Kit* contains a lot of useful information about backing up your system. You can search the TechNet CD or the CD accompanying the *Resource Kit*, using keywords like "backup," "NTBACKUP," and "restore."

Windows NT Remote Access Service (RAS)

Terms you'll need to understand:

√ Remote Access Service (RAS)

√ RAS clients

√ Telephony Application Programming Interface (TAPI)

√ RAS Phonebook

√ Encryption

√ Autodial

√ Logging

√ Null modem

√ Name resolution

Techniques you'll need to master:

√ Installing and configuring RAS

√ Configuring the RAS Phonebook

√ Implementing RAS security measures

RAS (Remote Access Service) is a secure and reliable method of extending a network across communication links to remote computers. Modems and other communication devices act just like a network interface card (NIC) over a RAS connection. A remote client via RAS can access and operate everything a standard network-attached client can. In this chapter, we provide the details you need to know about RAS.

Windows NT RAS

RAS in Windows NT 4 is a significant improvement over the communications capabilities of version 3.51. Many of its advances were borrowed from Windows 95, including the ease of installation, process of configuration, and the look and feel. RAS is able to support 256 simultaneous connections; act as a firewall, a gateway, or a router; and maintain tight security.

The communication links through which RAS can connect include:

➤ Public Switched Telephone Network (PSTN)

➤ Integrated Services Digital Network (ISDN)

➤ X.25 packet switching network

Standard LAN protocols are used over the RAS connection. Thus, TCP/IP, IPX/SPX, or NetBEUI can be used for network communication over the link established by RAS. Because the actual network protocol is used, the remote client connection acts just as if it were connected to the network locally. The only difference is that the speed of data transfer is slower over the RAS connection than it would be if the computer accessing the server were physically attached to the network. Always remember that a client is a client is a client, whether locally connected or using RAS.

RAS Clients

A RAS client is any machine that is able to dial in or connect to a RAS server and establish an authorized connection. Although optimized for the integration of Microsoft-based operating systems, other system types can gain access with the proper software, protocols, and configuration.

The links established between a client and a server using RAS are called wide area network (WAN) links. Because RAS is most often used to connect a computer (or an entire LAN) to a centrally located network over a long distance, it is treated as a WAN link. The communication protocols used to establish a RAS connection are called WAN protocols. Windows NT supports two WAN protocols:

➤ **SLIP** The Serial Line Internet Protocol connection supports TCP/IP, but does not support IPX/SPX or NetBEUI. SLIP does not support DHCP; thus, every client must have an assigned IP address. SLIP does not support encrypted passwords, either. This protocol is provided only as a means for a Windows NT Server to act as a client when dialing into a Unix server; it cannot be used to accept inbound connections on Windows NT.

➤ **PPP** The Point-to-Point Protocol supports several additional protocols, including AppleTalk, TCP/IP, IPX/SPX, and NetBEUI, and was designed as an improvement to SLIP. PPP supports DHCP and encrypted passwords. PPP is the most common and widely supported WAN protocol.

Windows NT Server can act as a RAS client whenever it dials out over a modem (or other communication link device) to establish a connection with another server or computer system. The most common situation in which Windows NT is a client is when a LAN connects to the Internet.

RAS Servers

Windows NT Server can support up to 256 simultaneous incoming RAS connections. Important points to remember about Windows NT as a RAS server include:

➤ It only supports PPP clients—SLIP is not supported for dialup.

➤ A NetBIOS gateway is established between the server and PPP-attached RAS client to sustain standard Windows NT network operations.

➤ RAS supports both IP and IPX routing.

> ➤ RAS supports NetBIOS and Windows Sockets applications.

> ➤ It supports Point-to-Point Tunneling Protocol (PPTP) connections, which makes it possible for Windows NT computers to communicate securely over the Internet. In addition, it also supports Multilink PPP (MP), where numerous connections can be aggregated.

Point-To-Point Tunneling Protocol (PPTP)

PPTP enables "tunneling" of IPX, NetBEUI, or TCP/IP inside PPP packets in such a way as to establish a secure link between a client and server over the Internet. PPTP connections are useful for establishing virtual private networks (VPNs) in small companies that cannot afford expensive leased lines for network communications over long distances. PPTP enables users anywhere in the world to connect back to the home office's network. PPTP uses a powerful encryption security scheme that is more secure than standard communications over the network itself. Thus, all traffic over the Internet using PPTP is safe.

Like all other network protocols, PPTP must be installed through the Protocols tab of the Network applet in the Control Panel.

Multilink PPP (MP)

Windows NT has the capability to combine the bandwidth of multiple physical links, which increases the total bandwidth that could be used for a RAS connection. This aggregation of multiple communication links can be used as an inexpensive way to increase the overall bandwidth with the least amount of cost. MP must be supported by both the client and server systems. MP cannot be used with the callback security feature (discussed in detail later in this chapter).

The checkbox to enable MP is located on the Network Protocol Configuration dialog box (see Figure 10.1).

Telephony API (TAPI) Properties And Phone Books

In Windows NT, the Telephony Application Programming Interface (TAPI) provides a standard method of controlling communications over voice, data, or fax. Although the hardware is not provided with Windows NT, TAPI can be used to control many PBX systems and communications devices for automated activity.

When you install a modem or the RAS components of Windows NT, TAPI automatically is installed. It is required to control any communications device. Each time a dial-out connection is attempted, TAPI controls the modem and moderates the connection. Once the connection is established, TAPI continues to oversee the operation of the communications link.

The Dialing Properties dialog box (reached through the Modems applet) controls how TAPI uses your modem to place calls. You can control long-distance dialing, calling card use, prefix numbers, and tone/pulse dialing. You can also define multiple configurations based on physical location. If you travel with a Windows NT Server notebook, you can define a dialing property profile for each of the cities you visit regularly.

TAPI is also the controlling entity for the phonebook entries used to establish RAS connections. All of the functions and features of the modem and the communication types established over a modem are configured through a TAPI-controlled interface.

Installing RAS

RAS is installed through the Services tab of the Network applet. Installing RAS correctly does take some preparation and know-how. When performing the installation, you must remember the following:

1. Physically install or attach the modem first. During installation, if a modem has not been installed, you will be forced to install one.

2. Install RAS through the Services tab of the Network applet.

3. Select the communications port.

4. Add an installed modem as a RAS device.

5. Configure the port for one of the following:

   ➤ Dial out only

➤ Receive calls only

➤ Dial out and receive calls

6. Select the LAN network protocols (see Figure 10.1).

➤ If Dial out was selected, only the outbound protocols can be chosen.

➤ If Receive calls was selected, only the inbound protocols can be configured.

➤ If Dial out and receive calls was selected, then both outbound and inbound protocols can be configured.

7. Select protocol-specific configuration for each inbound protocol (see Figures 10.2 and 10.3).

Once RAS itself is installed, you need to check your port and modem configuration through the Ports and Modems applets of the Control Panel.

If RAS is configured to receive calls, that port and modem cannot be used by any other application. RAS locks the port to maintain control to monitor for inbound calls.

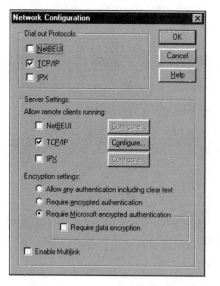

Figure 10.1   The Network Configuration dialog box for RAS.

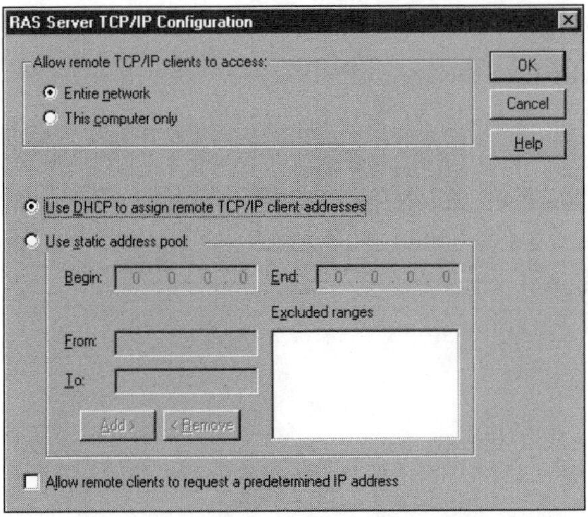

Figure 10.2   The RAS Server TCP/IP Configuration dialog box.

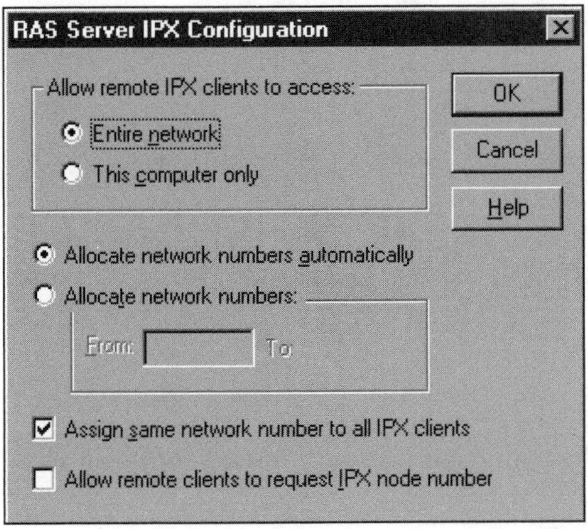

Figure 10.3   The RAS Server IPX Configuration dialog box.

RAS Routing, Gateway, Firewall

You can select whether to let RAS clients using network protocols access just the RAS server or the entire network. When you limit RAS clients to the RAS server, you are using RAS as a firewall; no network access of any kind through the RAS server is permitted. If you allow RAS clients to access the entire network, you are using RAS as a router. When NetBEUI is the only protocol in use, RAS acts as a gateway to enable the nonroutable protocol, NetBEUI, to access the network.

RAS Phonebook

The dial-out capabilities of RAS are controlled and accessed through the RAS Phonebook. This utility, Dial-Up Networking (DUN), is found in the Programs|Accessories folder of the Start menu or via My Computer. The first time DUN is launched, the RAS Wizard appears to help you create your first phonebook entry. Every time after that, the Phonebook dialog box appears. Through this interface, you can create and modify dial-up parameters for every RAS connection.

Phonebook entries consist of:

➤ Name, phone number, modem to use

➤ Server type and protocol settings

➤ Connection scripts

➤ Security settings

➤ X.25 settings (if applicable)

RAS Security

RAS has numerous levels and types of security that protect your network from unauthorized remote access. The following sections highlight these security features.

RAS Encryption

Windows NT can be configured to increase or decrease connection security through:

➤ The Security tab of a phonebook entry for outbound RAS links

➤ The Network Protocol Configuration dialog box for inbound RAS links (as shown in Figure 10.1)

The three settings available for RAS data encryption are:

1. **Accept any authentication, including clear text** This is the most permissive setting. It should be used when the user is not concerned about passwords. This option allows a connection using any authentication provided

by the server; therefore, it is useful when connecting to a non-Microsoft server.

2. **Accept only encrypted authentication** This option is beneficial when the transmission of clear text passwords is not desired and when you are connecting to a non-Microsoft server.

3. **Accept only Microsoft encrypted authentication** For this setting, the Microsoft Challenge Handshake Authentication Protocol (MS-CHAP) must be used; therefore, it is useful when calling a Microsoft server. If the Require Data Encryption box is checked, all the data sent over the wire is encrypted. Data encryption is provided by Windows NT using the Rivest-Shamir-Adleman (RSA) Data Security Incorporated RC4 algorithm. If the data fails to encrypt correctly, the connection is terminated automatically.

RAS Callback

Callback is a security feature in which a RAS connection is established only after the server has disconnected the inbound call and then called the user back. Setting callback is performed via the User|Properties option in User Manager For Domains or the User|Properties command of the Remote Access Manger, by selecting from the following:

➤ **No Call Back** This is the default setting. It means that when a user is establishing a RAS connection, he or she will not be called back.

➤ **Set By Caller**   Callback can be set by the user. This is a good way to save on long-distance charges, because the server calls the client back at the number set by the caller.

➤ **Preset To:** You can configure the callback for a preset number. This heightens security because the user must call from a predetermined phone number.

The RAS Logon Process

With Windows NT 4, you can log on to a domain via RAS at the Logon prompt by selecting the Connect Via Dial-In option and providing the proper domain. This allows you to establish a RAS connection to the remote network without requiring you to log on locally first.

When you are using TCP/IP via a slow RAS connection, an LMHOSTS file might speed up network access and name resolution. Place an LMHOSTS file on the RAS client. Ensure that LMHOSTS entries have the #PRE tag so that the IP addresses will be cached.

Additional RAS Features

There is much more to RAS than what's covered in this chapter. You'll need to review the reference materials listed at the end of this chapter for more RAS information. However, we have included a short list of important RAS features and options.

AutoDial

AutoDial is the ability of Windows NT to remember the location of resources accessed over a RAS connection. This is done by maintaining a map that correlates a network address to a phonebook entry. When that resource is referenced, RAS reestablishes the WAN connection to regain access to that resource without additional user interaction. AutoDial is enabled by default. AutoDial does not function over IPX/SPX, but it works with TCP/IP and NetBEUI.

Logging

Troubleshooting RAS difficulties is much simpler when the logging capabilities are employed. There are two logging features of Windows NT that record RAS-related activities. The first is the MODEMLOG.TXT file that records the activities of the modem. This is enabled through a modem's properties in the Modems applet in the Advanced Connections Settings area. This file is placed in the Windows NT root directory.

The second log file is DEVICE.LOG. This file only can be enabled through the Registry. The "Logging" value located in \HKEY_LOCAL_MACHINE \SYSTEM\CurrentControlSet\Services\RasMan\Parameters should be set to 1. The DEVICE.LOG file will be stored in the \Winnt\system32\ras directory.

The Event Viewer captures some RAS information that may be useful for troubleshooting and deciphering RAS. By default, all server errors, user connect attempts, disconnects, and so on, are logged in the System Log.

An additional tool for RAS troubleshooting is the PPP.log. To enable PPP logging, change the Registry parameter value to 1 in:

```
HKEY_LOCAL_MACHINE\SYSTEM\CurrentControlSet\Services\RasMan\PPP\Logging
```

Null Modem

A null modem is a serial cable that enables two computers to connect without the need for a modem. These special cables are common peer-to-peer attachment devices, but they can be used by Windows NT RAS to establish a standard Windows NT network connection. A null modem can be installed through the Modems applet by selecting it from the standard modems. A cable is not actually required for the setup, and this offers you a way out when installing RAS if you don't already have the modem at hand. Once installed, a null-modem cable can be used just like a modem, which is itself used by RAS just as if it were a NIC—that is, a workstation attached via a null-modem cable can fully participate in a domain, but at a slower data transfer rate.

Name Resolution

In situations where static lookups occur, the configuration with optimal resolution speed and WAN link traffic is to store the HOSTS (DNS) and the LMHOSTS (WINS) files on the local hard drives of the RAS clients. This configuration makes it somewhat difficult to maintain the newest version of the files on multiple remote clients.

Practice Questions

Question 1

If no standards are in place for the operating system, protocol, or the method of access for your remote clients, what is the highest level of security you can implement and still allow your users to connect via RAS?

○ a. Allow Any Authentication Including Clear Text

○ b. Microsoft Encrypted Authentication

○ c. PGP Encryption

○ d. Require Encrypted Authentication

Answer a is correct. With nonstandardized configurations implementing any encryption security other than Allow Any Authentication Including Clear Text, some clients are restricted from accessing the network via RAS. Microsoft Encrypted Authentication and Require Encrypted Authentication are encryption security schemes that require special configuration or operating systems; therefore, answers b and d are incorrect. PGP Encryption is not a native Windows NT option; therefore, answer c is incorrect.

Question 2

Which of the following statements about PPP and SLIP are true? [Check all correct answers]

❑ a. PPP supports encrypted passwords; SLIP does not.

❑ b. SLIP supports NetBEUI, IPX/SPX, and TCP/IP; PPP only supports TCP/IP.

❑ c. PPP supports DHCP; SLIP does not.

❑ d. SLIP is used to access Unix servers.

❑ e. PPP is the most commonly used WAN protocol.

Answers a, c, d, and e are correct. PPP supports encrypted passwords; SLIP does not. Therefore, answer a is correct. PPP supports DHCP; SLIP does not. Therefore, answer c is correct. SLIP is used to access Unix servers; therefore, answer d is correct. PPP is the most commonly used WAN protocol; therefore, answer e is also correct. PPP supports NetBEUI, IPX/SPX, and TCP/IP, but SLIP only supports TCP/IP; therefore, answer b is incorrect.

Question 3

Which of the following Windows NT networking activities are supported by a PPP RAS connection? [Check all correct answers]

❑   a. Printer share access

❑   b. Named pipes

❑   c. WinSOCK API applications over TCP/IP

❑   d. Interprocess Communications (IPC)

❑   e. User logon authentication

All five answers are correct. Because a RAS connected client is no different from a direct connected client (other than in its speed of data transfer), all standard network activities still occur over the WAN link.

Question 4

While connected to the office LAN, you create a shortcut on your desktop that points to a documents folder located on the LAN's file server. After working with a few files from this folder, you close your RAS session. Later, you attempt to reopen the files you edited earlier. What happens?

○   a. Access is denied because no link to the LAN exists.

○   b. The file is pulled from the network cache.

○   c. A file with a similar name on your local hard drive is accessed instead.

○   d. RAS AutoDial attempts to reconnect to the office LAN.

Only answer d is correct. RAS maintains a map list of the resources accessed over WAN links. When one of these resources is referenced, it will attempt to AutoDial to regain a connection to the server hosting the resource. Answer a would be the result if AutoDial was not enabled, but you always should assume the default configuration for computers. Therefore, answer a is incorrect. Answers b and c are fictitious activities that do not occur; therefore, they are incorrect.

Question 5

Where can you find information related to RAS problems to aid in troubleshooting? [Check all correct answers]

- ❏ a. Event Viewer
- ❏ b. DEVICE.LOG
- ❏ c. Dr. Watson
- ❏ d. MODEMLOG.TXT
- ❏ e. Windows NT Diagnostics

Answers a, b, and d are correct. The Event Viewer, DEVICE.LOG, and MODEMLOG.TXT can be useful troubleshooting tools for RAS problems. Dr. Watson does not track RAS events; it focuses on applications. Therefore, answer c is incorrect. Windows NT Diagnostics will not provide useful information related to RAS; therefore, answer e is incorrect.

Question 6

What is the best method for offering reliable and secure access to your network over the Internet for your remote users?

- ○ a. Internet Information Server
- ○ b. Serial Line Interface Protocol
- ○ c. Point-to-Point Tunneling Protocol
- ○ d. Require Encrypted Authentication

Answer c is correct. PPTP offers a reliable and secure network connection over the Internet. Internet Information Server will offer only WWW, FTP, and Gopher services—not access to the entire network, and without additional security. Therefore, answer a is incorrect. SLIP doesn't offer access over the Internet, it cannot be used to dial into a Windows NT Server, and it does not support encryption; therefore, answer b is incorrect. Require Encrypted Authentication is a mid-level security setting, but it does not directly offer connection over the Internet nor will it imply access to the network. Therefore, answer d is incorrect.

Question 7

You have a field technician who travels extensively around the country. Her schedule changes often, and she rarely visits the same place twice. It is important that she is able to connect to the office LAN periodically, but your organization's security policy requires callback security on all RAS connections. How can you configure her account so that she is able to gain access, while also supporting your organization's security?

○　a. Set the callback security to No Call Back only for her account.

○　b. Enable callback security with Set By Caller selected.

○　c. Set the callback security to Preset To with her home phone number.

○　d. Set the callback security to Roaming, and give her the page number to configure the callback number remotely.

○　e. Turn on the callback Caller ID capture.

Answer b is correct. Setting the Set By Caller option will allow her to input the callback number each time she needs to connect. Setting the No Call Back option will violate the organization's security policy; therefore, answer a is incorrect. Setting the Preset To number will not allow her to gain access to the network because she never calls from the same location more than once; therefore, answer c is incorrect. There is not a Roaming callback setting; therefore, answer d is incorrect. Windows NT does not have a Caller ID capture setting, but this can be obtained through third-party software; however, it is not required for this situation, so answer e is incorrect.

Question 8

> Which protocols can be used over a RAS connection?
>
> ○   a. TCP/IP, NetBEUI, but not NWLink
>
> ○   b. TCP/IP, NWLink, but not NetBEUI
>
> ○   c. Only TCP/IP
>
> ○   d. TCP/IP, NetBEUI, and NWLink

Answer d is correct. TCP/IP, NetBEUI, and NWLink can all be used over RAS. TCP/IP, NetBEUI, but not NWLink, is the restriction for the AutoDial feature but not a limitation of RAS as a whole. Therefore, answer a is incorrect. TCP/IP, NWLink, but not NetBEUI, are the protocols that can be routed over RAS but not a limitation as to which protocols can be used. Therefore, answer b is also incorrect. Only TCP/IP can be used over SLIP, but RAS is not limited to SLIP. Therefore, answer c is incorrect.

Question 9

> What are the possible uses of a null-modem cable?
> [Check all correct answers]
>
> ❑   a. Attach a workstation to a domain.
>
> ❑   b. Enable subnet routing.
>
> ❑   c. Test a RAS server locally.
>
> ❑   d. Establish a VPN over the Internet.
>
> ❑   e. Temporarily connect two LANs.

Answers a, c, and e are correct. Attaching a workstation to a domain is a use for a null-modem cable; therefore, answer a is correct. A RAS server can be tested using a null-modem cable to simulate a remote client; therefore, answer c is correct. Two closely adjacent LANs can be connected over a null-modem cable; therefore, answer e is correct. Subnet routing can be implemented only when two NICs are installed on the same machine; therefore, answer b is incorrect. A VPN over the Internet can be established only with PPTP and a connection to the Internet, requiring a modem. There-fore, answer d is incorrect.

Question 10

> Which of the following represent possible uses for a null-modem cable? [Check all correct answers]
>
> ❑   a. Attach a workstation to domain
> ❑   b. Establish a PPTP connection across the Internet
> ❑   c. Test a RAS server with a local client
> ❑   d. Interconnect two LANs temporarily

Answers a, c, and d are correct. By definition, a null-modem cable uses a serial port that usually limits bandwidth to 115 Kbps. Within these limita-tions, a null-modem cable may be used to attach a workstation to a RAS server, and thus to a domain. Therefore, answer a is correct. A null-modem cable is an excellent way to test a RAS server with a local client. Therefore, answer c is correct. Two adjacent networks can be interconnected, albeit slowly, using a null-modem cable. Therefore, answer d is correct. A PPTP connection across the Internet requires real Internet access, which means using a modem or some other, higher-speed communications device. A null-modem cable won't work here. Therefore, answer b is incorrect.

Question 11

> If static name resolution is used, what is the proper location of the HOSTS and LMHOSTS files to optimize the lookup time?
>
> ○   a. Both HOSTS and LMHOSTS should be stored on the RAS clients.
> ○   b. HOSTS should be stored on the RAS server, and LMHOSTS should be stored on the RAS clients.
> ○   c. Both HOSTS and LMHOSTS should be stored on the RAS server.
> ○   d. HOSTS should be stored on the RAS clients, and LMHOSTS should be stored on the RAS server.

Answer a is correct. The fastest lookup time will occur when the HOSTS and LMHOSTS files are stored on the local hard drive of each RAS client, because no WAN traffic need occur to resolve a resource location. All other answers are incorrect because they discuss storing these files somewhere other than on the client, which increases the lookup time.

Need To Know More?

 Heywood, Drew: *Inside Windows NT Server, 2nd Edition*. New Riders, Indianapolis, IN, 1998. ISBN 1-56205-860-6. The installation, configuration, and use of RAS are discussed in Chapter 14.

 Siyan, Karanjit S.: *Windows NT Server 4 Professional Reference, 2nd Edition*. New Riders, Indianapolis, IN, 1997. ISBN 1-56205-805-3. Chapter 18 covers RAS in great detail.

 Strebe, Matthew, Charles Perkins, and James Chellis: *MCSE: NT Server 4 Study Guide, 2nd Edition*. Sybex Network Press, San Francisco, CA, 1998. ISBN 0-7821-2222-1. RAS is examined in Chapter 11.

 Search the TechNet CD (or its online version through **www.microsoft.com/technet**) using the keywords "RAS," "Remote Access," "PPP," and "modems."

 The *Windows NT Server Resource Kit* contains some discussion of RAS—for example, Appendix E, "RAS Reference," in the *Networking Guide*.

Performance Monitor

Terms you'll need to understand:

√ Performance Monitor

√ Server optimization

√ Objects

√ Counters

√ Baselining

√ Update interval

Techniques you'll need to master:

√ Using Performance Monitor

√ Key characteristics to monitor

√ Viewing network data in Chart, Alert, Log, and Report views

√ Logging network statistics

√ Establishing a baseline

√ Setting administrative alerts

It's important to understand server optimization to properly maintain Windows NT Server. Even though Windows NT Server installs quickly and easily, fine-tuning your system can be quite a task. There are many factors for administrators to consider when "tweaking" the server to achieve optimal performance.

Luckily, Microsoft has thrown in a wonderful tool called Performance Monitor (PerfMon). This server optimization tool comes with both Windows NT Server and Windows NT Workstation. Performance Monitor allows an administrator to observe almost every component within a Windows NT Server—both locally and remotely. In this chapter, we examine the details of Performance Monitor to assist you in maintaining optimal server performance.

How Performance Monitor Works

Performance Monitor treats system components as objects. This allows the system to track network performance trends to help establish a baseline against which you can make certain decisions regarding network optimization. Performance Monitor lets you examine important server characteristics, such as pages per second, processor usage, and even the number of available bytes. All of the data gathered can be viewed in different forms, including a Chart view, Alert view, Log view, and Report view. Figure 11.1 shows the Performance Monitor interface.

Performance Monitor records the behavior of objects in the system by using counters. Windows NT provides a specific set of counters for each server object. As in programming, these objects usually consist of code containing different properties and behavior patterns. The counters provide information on each object type. Some examples of objects in Performance Monitor include Processor, Server, System, and Thread. Figure 11.2 shows a list of these objects. Table 11.1 lists some of the most important objects, counters for those objects, and their significance.

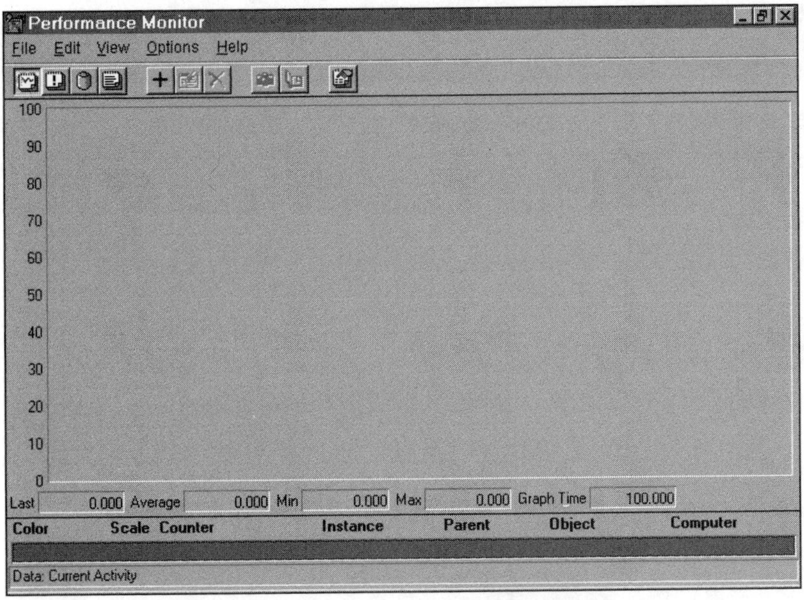

Figure 11.1   The Performance Monitor interface, with nothing set to monitor.

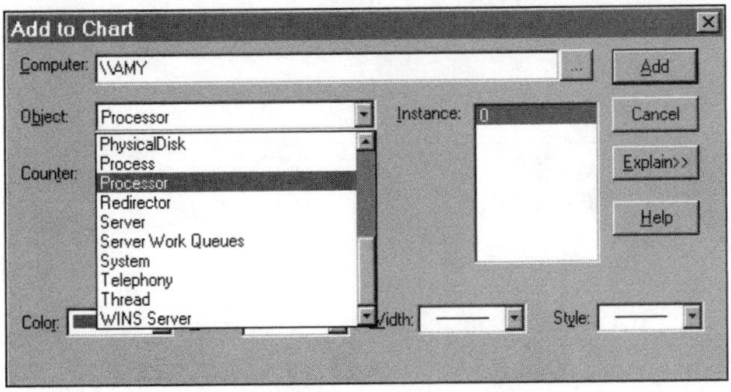

Figure 11.2   Server objects that can be added to a chart for monitoring
through Performance Monitor.

Table 11.1 **Performance Monitor's objects and counters, and their definitions and uses.**

Objects And Counters	Description	Significance
MEMORY:		
Available Bytes	The amount of virtual memory now available.	When the value falls below a threshold, Windows NT takes memory from running applications to maintain a minimum amount of virtual memory.
Pages/Second	The number of pages that had to be written to or read from the disk and placed in physical memory.	This indicates if you need more RAM. A value greater than 5 could indicate a bottleneck in your system.
Page Faults/Second	Number of times/second that a required virtual memory page was not in the working set in main memory.	This indicates that the data was not set in memory.
PAGING FILE:		
% Usage	Amount of the actual paging file that is in use by the system.	If this value is close to 100% you should increase your paging file size.
PHYSICAL DISK:		
Average Disk Sec/ Transfer	The amount of time a disk takes to fulfill requests.	A value greater than .3 can indicate that the disk controller is retrying the disk continuously, due to writing failures.
% Disk Time	The percentage of time that the disk is in use.	If this value is above 85%, consider upgrading the disk drive or controller.
SYSTEM:		
Processor Queue Length	The number of threads shown is an indicator of the system performance, because each thread requires a certain number of processor cycles.	If this value is greater than 2, you should consider a new processor.

(continued)

Table 11.1	Performance Monitor's objects and counters, and their definitions and uses *(continued)*.	
Objects And Counters	**Description**	**Significance**
PROCESSOR:		
Interrupts/Second	Measures the rate of requests from I/O devices.	If there is a dramatic increase in this number with an increase in system activity, check your hardware.
% Processor Time	Shows how busy a processor is.	Anything over 80% means the processor might be the problem.

Which View Do I Want?

Performance Monitor has several views available. Once Performance Monitor is open, you can determine which is best suited for your needs. To choose a view, select the View menu. Your options include Chart, Alert, Log, and Report. Table 11.2 lists all the views and their individual purposes.

Creating A Chart

The Chart view displays counter information in the form of a graph or histogram. Each counter is represented by a separate, different-colored line for every entry, along with a legend at the bottom of the graph that explains each counter's purpose.

Once you have decided on the view, you must then decide what to monitor.

Table 11.2	Performance Monitor's views and their purposes.
View	**Purpose**
Chart	Displays collected data as a line graph or histogram.
Alert	Defines and monitors alert conditions based on criteria set by the Administrator (for example, notifying the administrator if disk space is low).
Log	Allows you to save performance data in a log file on disk.
Report	Lists counters and their current values.

What Gets Monitored?

The first decision is to determine on which computer Performance Monitor will be run. Remember that Performance Monitor is run locally by default, but you also can select a computer on the network to be monitored. To select a remote machine, simply type the computer name in the dialog box or click on the ellipsis (...) button to get a browse list of the systems available on the network.

Which Object Should I Select?

Once you have determined which computer needs monitoring, you must select the objects to be monitored. Depending on your hardware and software, you may encounter objects that other machines might not have. For instance, if you have NWLink installed, you might see a counter called NWLink IPX for monitoring IPX traffic on the network.

Which Counter Should I Select?

Each object in Performance Monitor has specific counters associated with it; for example, the Server object's counters include Bytes Total/Second, Files Open, and Errors Logon. To add a counter to the chart window, click the plus sign (+) on the toolbar or select Add To Chart from the Edit menu. If you are unsure about what a counter does, hit the Explain button to get a detailed description of the counter (see Figure 11.3).

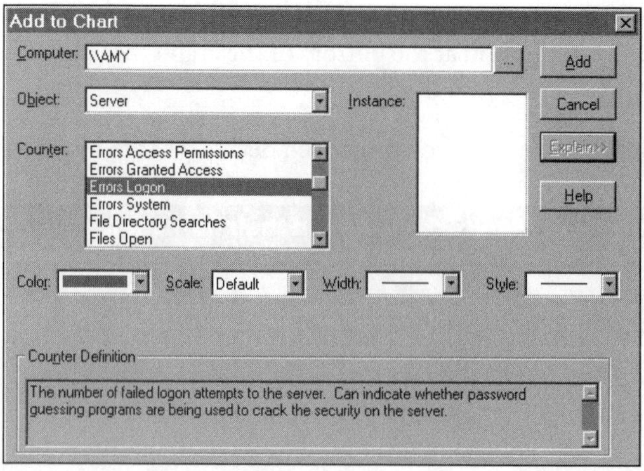

Figure 11.3 Performance Monitor with counter definitions enabled.

What If I Have More Than One Object?

If you want to monitor more than one object, you can select an instance to determine which object to monitor. For example, if you have more than one processor and you want to monitor all of them, the first processor would be instance zero, the second processor would be instance one, and so on. Once you have selected all of the necessary data, select Add, and the Chart will display lines for each selected processor.

Setting Chart Options

All four views in Performance Monitor have options that will affect only that particular view. The chart options allow you to change general preferences, such as the minimum and maximum value for the vertical axis and the type of chart you want to see. To choose the options, go to the Options menu and select Chart. When you need to monitor trends over time, you should use the line chart (see Figure 11.4). When you want to compare counters to other counters, you should consider the histogram. Figure 11.5

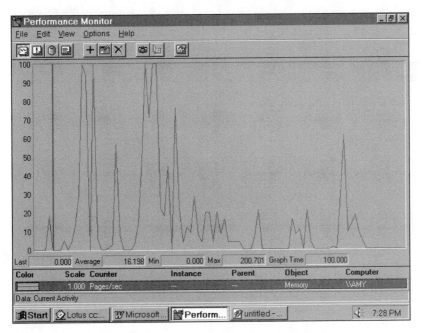

Figure 11.4   Performance Monitor charting memory usage.

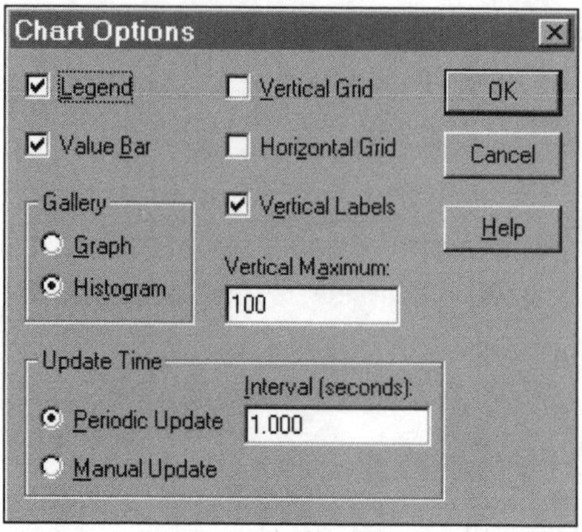

Figure 11.5 The Chart Options dialog box in Performance Monitor.

shows the Chart Options dialog box. All of the chart options and their descriptions are listed in Table 11.3.

Adjusting The Update Interval

Adjusting the update interval is the most important item in the Options dialog box. It is very important that you select the correct interval for your

Table 11.3 **Performance Monitor's chart options.**	
Chart Option	**Description**
Legend	If this option is selected, the legend for each chart line appears at the bottom of Performance Monitor.
Value Bar	The value bar shows the values of Last, Average, Min, Max, and Graph Time.
Gallery	This allows you to choose what type of graph you want displayed.
Update Time	There are two options: Periodic Update (most commonly used) and Manual Update.
Vertical Grid	This displays gridlines on the vertical axis.
Horizontal Grid	This displays gridlines on the horizontal axis.
Vertical Labels	This displays a label for the y-axis.
Vertical Maximum	This sets the maximum value for the vertical axis.

data retrieval. If you sample too frequently, you could cause your system overhead to soar and slow the network; if you do not sample often enough, you could lose important data.

Starting A Performance Monitor Chart

To create a chart in Performance Monitor, follow these steps:

1. From the Start menu, select Programs|Administrative Tools (Common)|Performance Monitor.

2. From the View menu, select Chart.

3. From the Edit menu, select Add To Chart.

4. In the Add To Chart dialog box, select the computer to be monitored, the object (or objects) on that computer to be monitored, and which counters are to be observed.

5. Set different counter options, such as frequency, alert interval, etc.

6. Save your configuration in a file.

7. Analyze the data you have collected.

Creating A Report

The Report view in Performance Monitor displays a simple list of counters and their values. The values are updated at each set interval. (*Note:* There is no chart associated with the Report view.) Start Performance Monitor and select Report on the View menu. In Chart view, the more counters you add, the harder it becomes to read the data, so Report view is a definite plus. In Figure 11.6, there are so many counters added to the report that Chart view would be very hard to read.

Choosing Counters

Each view has its own set of counters, and these counters will not appear in any other window. To add counters, click on the plus sign (+) on the toolbar

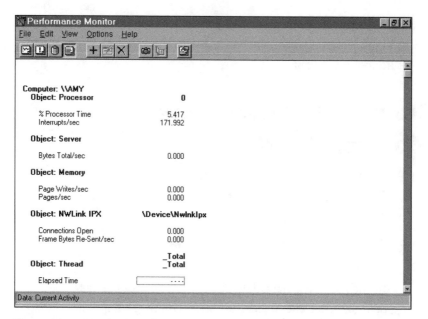

Figure 11.6 Monitoring objects through the Report view in Performance
Monitor.

or select Add To Report from the Edit menu. The only real difference
between adding chart counters and adding report counters is that report
counters show up as numeric values rather than as a line on a chart.

Report Options

The Report view has only one useful option (unlike the Chart view, which
has several): the update interval value. The default value is to update every
five seconds. To change this interval, select Report from the Options menu,
as shown in Figure 11.7.

So You Want To Save This Data
For Later?

When you add a counter to the Report or Chart view, you will soon notice
that data is displayed based on the current activity. There is no way to save
the data being collected in the chart or report for later use. The Log view
allows you to do that; you can specify the objects that you want to observe

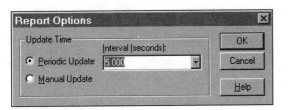

Figure 11.7   Selecting the interval update time on the Report Options dialog box in Performance Monitor.

and the interval at which to record the data. You even have the option of recording data from both local and remote machines in one log file. After the data is captured to a specific location, you can view this data in any other view. Figure 11.8 illustrates a log file that has been set to monitor three objects.

Setting Log Options

Once you have selected the counters to be monitored, you must select where you want Performance Monitor to place the log file. Select Log from the Options menu. This brings up the Log Options dialog box (see Figure

Figure 11.8   The Performance Monitor Log view, set to capture information on the Browser, Gateway Service For NetWare, and Paging File.

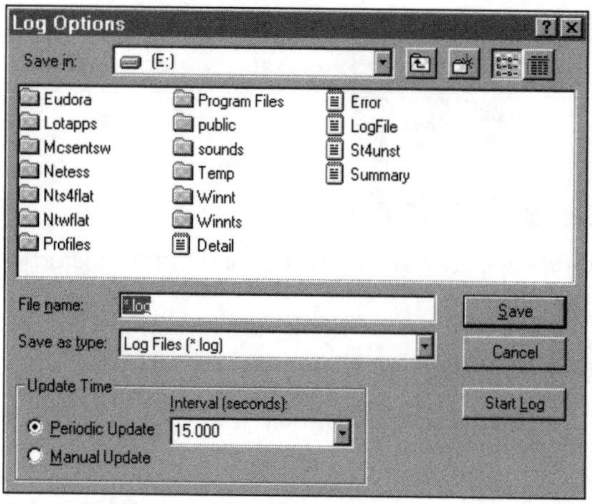

Figure 11.9 Selecting the location for the log to be stored in Performance Monitor.

11.9). Browse through the directories in the Save In window until you locate the directory where you want the log files to be stored. There is also an Update Time section in the Log Options dialog box.

Here are the steps to follow to log data to a file:

1. From the Add To Log window, highlight the objects you want to monitor, and click the Add button for each.

2. When you have selected all of the objects to be monitored, click the Done button.

3. From the Options menu, choose Log. At this point, the Log Options dialog box should appear. This is where you should specify a file name, location, and update interval for the log.

4. Once you have selected all the important information in the Log Options dialog box, click on Start Log. The log will start building, and you will notice the size of the file growing in the File Size field.

5. After you have collected enough data, choose Stop Log from the Options|Log menu.

Viewing Logged Data

Following are the steps to follow to view logged data. This process is the same for every view you choose:

1. Open Performance Monitor in the window or view of your choice.

2. From the Options menu, choose Data From.

3. Select the Log File bullet box, and type the path and name of the log file to view, or click the ellipsis (...) button to browse for the file (see Figure 11.10).

4. Click OK to close the Data From dialog box.

Setting Alerts In Performance Monitor

The Alert view usually is the favorite view among administrators. If you need to monitor many servers at a time, the last thing you want to do is sit in front of the monitor and wait for something to happen. With the Alert view, you do not have to be strapped to one machine all day; the alert will monitor any counter and will carry out a specific task when the counter exceeds or falls below a predetermined threshold. You can have Performance Monitor notify you when an event occurs. You can even specify a command line that you want to run after the alert is sent out. In Table 11.4, the common threshold values for alert counters are defined.

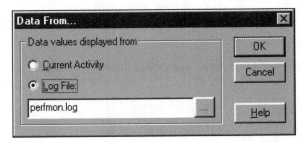

Figure 11.10   Selecting the location from which to view saved data in Performance Monitor.

Table 11.4 Performance Monitor's counters and their threshold values.	
Object: Counter	**Threshold**
Processor: % Processor Time	>90
System: Processor Queue Length	>2
Physical Disk: % Disk Time	>70
Logical Disk: Free Space	<10
Memory: Pages/Second	>30
Memory: Available Bytes	<4 MB

You can use the Alert view to monitor a critical resource such as free disk space: You will be notified when the system falls below a certain level.

Getting Started In Alert View

To add a new alert, follow these steps:

1. Start Performance Monitor.

2. Select Alert from the View menu.

3. Select Add To Alert from the Edit menu, or click the plus sign (+) on the toolbar. The Add To Alert dialog box will appear (see Figure 11.11).

4. Select the computer you wish to monitor. Remember, the local machine is the default.

5. In the Object field, select from the drop-down list the object you wish to monitor.

6. Next, select the counters that fall in line with the object. Do not forget about the Explain button; it provides a brief explanation of each counter.

7. Select the instance you wish to monitor. The counting of the physical hardware begins with zero.

8. Select the color of the alert. This is very helpful if you have set more than one instance of an alert.

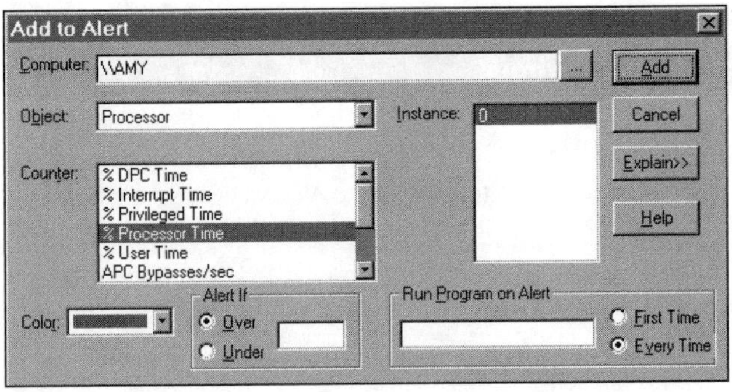

Figure 11.11   Adding alerts in Performance Monitor.

9. Enter a number in the Alert If Over/Under box (refer to Table 11.4 for important values).

10. If an application is supposed to run when something triggers an alert, specify in the Run Program On Alert dialog box both the application name and whether the program is to run every time the alert is triggered or only the first time the alert is triggered.

Setting Alert Options

As with charts, alerts can be customized with a variety of options. To set alert options, select Alert from the Options menu. The Alert Options dialog box will appear (see Figure 11.12). The options provided in the Alert Options dialog box, along with their descriptions, are listed in Table 11.5.

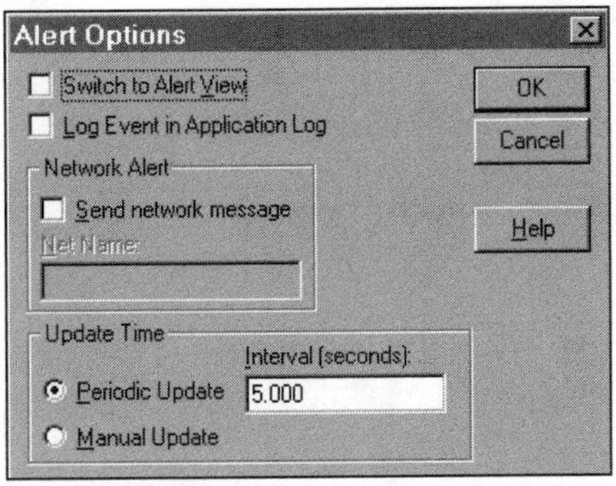

Figure 11.12   The Alert Options dialog box in Performance Monitor.

Table 11.5	Performance Monitor's alert options and their descriptions.
Alert Option	**Description**
Switch To Alert View	Performance Monitor switches to Alert view when an alert is triggered.
Log Event In Application Log	You can view an event in the Application Log in Event Viewer.
Send Network Message	Performance Monitor sends a message to the machine specified in the text box.
Update Time	Two options are available here: Periodic Update, which tells Performance Monitor when to read new data; and Manual Update, in which the user must tell Performance Monitor to update the data.

It is highly recommended that you add at least one computer name to the Send Network Message box in the Alert Options dialog box. This ensures that someone will be notified in case of emergency.

Practice Questions

Question 1

When you are running a graphics-intensive program, you notice your hard drive is very active. You do not know what to do next. What object and counter can you monitor to see if you need to add more RAM to your machine?

○   a. Memory: Pages/Thread

○   b. Memory: Pages/Second

○   c. Processor: % Processor Time

○   d. None of the above

Answer b is correct. To find out how overloaded your system memory is, you would look at Memory: Pages/Second to decide whether you need more RAM. There is no such thing as Pages/Thread; therefore, answer a is incorrect. If you want to find out the percentage of elapsed time that a processor is busy, you would look at % Processor Time; therefore, answer c is incorrect. Because b is the correct answer, d is incorrect.

Question 2

You decide that Alert view is the best option for your group. When you are monitoring resources, you notice that just running Performance Monitor itself causes a performance hit. What can you do to fix this problem?

○   a. Increase the interval of time that Performance Monitor will obtain data.

○   b. Turn off Performance Monitor, because it does nothing useful anyway.

○   c. Decrease the interval of time that Performance Monitor will obtain data.

○   d. Use User Manager For Domains to monitor your resources.

Answer a is correct. Increasing the interval gives the server more time be-tween data gathering sessions, rather than retrieving data every five sec-onds. Performance Monitor is a useful tool that should be used regularly. Therefore, answer b is incorrect. Decreasing the interval only makes the server work much harder; therefore, answer c is incorrect. User Manager For Domains doesn't allow you to monitor server resources—it's where ac-counts are created and maintained. Therefore, answer d is incorrect.

Question 3

Your boss called you and said he was confused about certain counters in Performance Monitor. Where can you tell him to look for information? [Check all correct answers]

- ❑   a. Tell him to look in the Registry.
- ❑   b. Tell him to click on the counter itself and click the Explain button.
- ❑   c. Tell him to select Search For Help On from the Help menu.
- ❑   d. Tell him to change the view to Report.

Answers b and c are correct. In Performance Monitor, you can click on the counter itself and click the Explain button to get a better explanation of the objects and counters; therefore, answer b is correct. Although it would be more difficult, you can search for help on this topic from the Help menu; therefore, answer c is also correct. You should *never* go to the Registry to "look up" information; therefore, answer a is incorrect. Unless you know what each counter does, the report view won't clarify things; therefore, an-swer d is incorrect.

Question 4

Which feature of Performance Monitor can you use to have the system notify you when a certain threshold is reached?

- ○   a. The Log view
- ○   b. The Registry view
- ○   c. The Chart view
- ○   d. The Alert option

The correct answer is d. The Alert option notifies you if a threshold is reached. The Log view allows you to save data for perusal at a later date; therefore, answer a is incorrect. There is no such thing as the Registry view; therefore, answer b is also incorrect. The Chart view allows you to view current activity; therefore, answer c is incorrect.

Question 5

> What counter and object would you look at if you wanted to see how busy your processor was?
>
> ○ a. System: Interrupts/Second
>
> ○ b. Memory: Pages/Second
>
> ○ c. Processor: % Processor Time
>
> ○ d. None of the above

Answer c is correct. Processor: % Processor Time is used to see how busy the processor is. Anything over 80% might mean you need to replace the processor or add additional ones. System: Interrupts/Second doesn't provide information about the CPU; therefore, answer a is incorrect. Checking Memory: Pages/Second allows you to verify if the amount of RAM in your system is adequate; therefore, answer b is incorrect. Because answer c is correct, answer d is incorrect.

Question 6

> Which option allows you to save the server data for later viewing?
>
> ○ a. Log
>
> ○ b. Alert
>
> ○ c. Chart
>
> ○ d. Disk

Answer a is correct. The Log option allows you to collect data to a file to be viewed later. The Alert option notifies administrators when certain system thresholds are reached; therefore, answer b is incorrect. The Chart option allows you to view current system data; therefore, answer c is incorrect. There is no Disk option in Performance Monitor; therefore, answer d is also incorrect.

Question 7

In the past, you have only monitored one object at a time. You realize that you should monitor at least ten objects at any given time. You really like the Chart view, but realize it looks messy. What can you do to solve your problem?

○   a. Switch the Performance Monitor to Report view.

○   b. Do nothing. You cannot monitor ten objects at a time.

○   c. Switch to Alert view.

○   d. Use Windows NT Diagnostics to view the data.

Answer a is correct. Report view is much easier to look at when you are monitoring many objects at a time. You cannot get a graph from Report view, but you can see more things on the screen at one time. It is possible to view many more than ten objects at a time; therefore, answer b is incorrect. Because the Alert view sends network messages to the Administrators when something goes wrong, answer c also is incorrect. Windows NT Diagnostics will not allow you to view counters and objects; therefore, answer d is incorrect.

Need To Know More?

 Donald, Lisa, and James Chellis: *MCSE: NT Server 4 in the Enterprise Study Guide, 2nd Edition*. Sybex Network Press, San Francisco, CA, 1998. ISBN 0-7821-2221-3. Chapter 15 contains information on Performance Monitor, Task Manager, and Server service optimizations.

 Heywood, Drew: *Inside Windows NT Server, 2nd Edition*. New Riders, Indianapolis, IN, 1998. ISBN 1-56205-860-6. The Performance Monitor is discussed in Chapter 13, on pages 561-576.

Siyan, Karanjit S.: *Windows NT Server 4 Professional Reference, 2nd Edition*. New Riders, Indianapolis, IN, 1997. ISBN 1-56205-805-3. Chapter 21 contains a lengthy discussion of the Performance Monitor, Task Manager, process priority settings, and Server service optimizations.

The Windows NT Server 4 manuals cover planning, configuration, and installation issues quite well. The *Concepts and Planning Manual* contains useful documentation on the Performance Monitor in Chapter 8, "Monitoring Performance."

 The *Windows NT Server Resource Kit Supplement #1* contains many discussions on using Performance Monitor to investigate all aspects of a network.

The Windows NT Boot Process

12

. . . .

Terms you'll need to understand:

√ Boot, boot up, bootstrap, bootstrap loader

√ ARC names, ARC pathnames

√ MBR (Master Boot Record)

√ BOOT.INI, NTLDR, NTDETECT.COM, NTBOOTDD.SYS

√ Boot partition or boot drive

√ System partition or system drive

Techniques you'll need to master:

√ How to edit the BOOT.INI file

√ How to interpret and construct Advanced RISC Computer (ARC) device names and pathnames

√ How to troubleshoot the Windows NT boot sequence

Starting up a computer from scratch involves a lot more work, and many more pieces and parts, than might immediately meet the eye. Because a computer that won't boot is essentially a dead computer, it's important to understand the Windows NT boot process, and where that process can go awry.

In this chapter, we walk you through the Windows NT boot process, explain the important pieces and parts, and explore some of the things that can derail this process. Along the way, you'll get to know more about how computers work in general, and what's involved in fully understanding Windows NT's intricate boot process.

Bootstrapping A Computer

When you boot a computer that has Windows NT installed as one of its operating systems, the machine goes through a number of steps before an operating system (OS) can be selected. Then, if Windows NT is selected as the OS to boot, a number of additional steps follow before the login prompt dialog box ever appears.

The initial phase, called the bootstrap process, covers the steps necessary to turn a computer from a lump of inert metal and plastic into a device that is ready to accept and react to input. For ordinary PCs, this consists of the following steps:

1. **Power on the computer, or initiate startup**
    This one's easy—it requires only that the computer be plugged in and that you turn the power switch to On. For Windows NT, the startup process also may be initiated when you click Restart The Computer in the Shut Down Windows dialog box (Start|Shut Down), or when you select the Shut Down button, followed by Shutdown and Restart, through the Windows NT Security Dialog box that's always available by entering Ctrl+Alt+Del at any time while Windows NT is running.

2. **Power-on self-test (POST) processing**

   Once the computer begins its startup process, it performs a number of built-in diagnostics and hardware
   tests to make sure all of its components are working
   properly. This is driven by firmware on the motherboard through the BIOS, and may involve other
   BIOSs (like those typically found on graphics adapters)
   once the onboard BIOS completes its checks. This
   activity produces all the messages and status information that flashes by on your screen while the computer
   is going through the hardware check stages of startup.
   POST also determines how much RAM is available on
   the machine, and checks to make sure essential peripherals (like keyboard, mouse, and so on) are present and
   connected.

3. **Initial startup process**

   Once the hardware has been checked out, this exhausts
   the onboard diagnostics and self-check capabilities of
   most computers. At this point, it's time to read some
   real software from disk to continue the boot process,
   which requires that an operating system to establish a
   runtime environment for the computer be loaded.
   If booting from a floppy, the first sector on the disk
   contains the Partition Boot sector; if booting from a
   hard disk, the first sector contains the Master Boot
   Record (MBR) and the Partition Table. These records
   contain the information that points the computer in
   the right direction to obtain boot information; they
   also provide a map for how the disk (or floppy) is
   physically arranged. The MBR is probably the most
   important record on any hard disk; it contains the
   partition table that describes a disk's physical layout
   and arrangement, and includes a small program whose
   job is to examine the partition table and identify the
   system partition. The program then locates the system

partition's starting address on disk (sector 0), and loads a copy of the Partition Boot Sector into memory. Once this step is complete, the program transfers execution to another program, usually an operating system loader from code included in the Partition Boot Sector just loaded. This Partition is identified in the partition table by being marked as the "active partition," which indicates that it is the partition to which control should next be passed during the boot process.

Warning! For reasons too arcane to explain fully here, it's essential to recognize that the files that reside in the system partition on a drive are the files needed to boot a computer and some operating system, whereas the files that reside in what Microsoft calls the boot partition on a drive are those files needed to run Windows NT itself. Thus, the boot files—that is, NTLDR, BOOT.INI, NTDETECT.COM, and so on—reside in the system partition, whereas the Windows NT OS files—including NTOSKRNL.EXE, the Windows NT kernel—reside on the boot partition. It's backwards. Get it?

4. **Boot loader process**

   When the Partition Boot Sector code is loaded, a program designed to bring up a designated operating system—or, as with Windows NT's NTLDR program, to provide a menu of load choices—runs. This starts an execution sequence for full-blown programs from files on disk (as opposed to code embedded in the MBR or a Partition Boot Sector), ultimately resulting in complete loading of an operating system, after which the computer will be ready to run applications or services on demand.

Windows NT Server also runs on RISC CPUs, as well as on generic PCs. The boot process differs for RISC machines to some degree. We'll point out these differences in Tips as we step through the rest of this process. The primary difference as far as the bootstrap process is concerned is that once a RISC computer completes its POST routines, built-in firmware selects a startup disk by reading a boot precedence table from nonvolatile RAM on the machine. This identifies the system partition (where the boot files reside) and indicates if a floppy may be used as an alternate boot selection. The information in nonvolatile RAM also indicates where the OSLOADER.EXE program resides and names the folder that contains the OS to be booted.

At this point, the bootstrap process is complete, and the activities specific to the operating system to be booted begin. Once NTLDR is loaded into memory, it becomes possible to choose an operating system (or one of multiple versions of the same operating system), one of which is definitely Windows NT. The steps that follow next assume that Windows NT is selected as the operating system to boot.

5. **Selecting the OS**

   When NTLDR executes, it reads another important Windows NT boot file, BOOT.INI, which we discuss in detail later in this chapter. BOOT.INI provides information about what choices of operating system to offer, defines their locations on disk, and assigns some important default characteristics for the load process. These make it possible to boot a Windows NT machine without requiring human intervention, so that keyboard input is not strictly required to start up a Windows NT machine. We now will choose a version of Windows NT in the loader menu, to begin the process of loading Windows NT itself.

At this point in the process for RISC machines, the program that loads is called OSLOADER.EXE. It performs all of the functions that are supplied for PCs by NTLDR, NTDETECT.COM, and BOOTSECT.DOS.

6. **Detecting hardware**

   Now the Windows NT program named
   NTDETECT.COM executes. This is a hardware
   recognition program that collects a list of currently
   installed components and returns the information to
   NTLDR. NTDETECT will not run, however, unless
   you select a version of Windows NT on the boot loader
   screen (or the default selection is Windows NT, and
   the timer times out). During this phase, the following
   message appears on screen:

   ```
   NTDETECT V1.0 Checking Hardware . . .
   ```

7. **Choosing a load configuration**

   Once NTDETECT finishes its job, the boot loader
   resumes control, and the following message appears:

   ```
   OS Loader V4.0

   Press spacebar now to invoke Hardware Profile/Last
   Known Good menu.
   ```

   The boot loader waits several seconds to give you time
   to press the spacebar. If it isn't pressed and there's only
   one hardware profile defined for the computer (which
   is completely typical, except for laptops), the boot
   loader loads Windows NT's default configuration.
   Otherwise, you can elect to use an alternate hardware
   profile here (for laptops, this usually means selected
   Networked or Detached hardware profiles), or switch
   to the Last Known Good Configuration menu, which
   permits you to boot Windows NT using the Registry
   values defined the last time the machine booted
   successfully.

8. **Loading the Windows NT kernel**

   The next phase, once the configuration or Registry
   versions have been identified (or chosen by default as is
   most often the case), is to load the operating system

kernel for Windows NT. At this point, a sequence of periods appears on screen, as the boot loader loads NTOSKRNL.EXE and the Hardware Abstraction Layer (HAL.DLL) into memory.

> On RISC machines, OSLOADER.EXE handles everything through this step. It concludes its job by loading the appropriate version of NTOSKRNL.EXE and HAL.DLL for the CPU in use.

The remaining steps are identical whether the machine is a PC clone or a RISC computer.

9. **Initializing the kernel**

When the PC's screen turns blue and displays a message like the following

```
Microsoft (R) Windows NT (TM) Version 4.0 (Build 1381)
1 System Processor (64 MB Memory)
```

this indicates that the kernel has initialized properly and that it has taken control; at this point, Windows NT may be said to be running the computer. During kernel initialization, the following tasks are completed:

➤ Initializing low-level device drivers loaded along with the kernel in the preceding step

➤ Loading and initializing other device drivers, as needed

➤ Running diagnostic or setup programs, such as CHKDSK, before loading services

➤ Loading and initializing all services identified with automatic startup in the OS configuration

➤ Creating the paging file for temporary storage and swap space

➤ Starting all subsystems needed for Windows NT (such as the Win32 subsystem, security subsystem, and possibly the OS/2 or POSIX subsystems)

10. **Logging on**
    When kernel initialization is complete, the Begin
    Logon dialog box appears (this contains the message
    "Press Ctrl+Alt+Delete to log on"). Once a successful
    logon occurs, Windows writes the values in the Regis-
    try to a special backup file that will provide the data
    needed to invoke the Last Known Good Configuration
    boot option the next time the machine starts up (a
    successful login is required to make this change,
    because numerous Registry values will not be updated
    until the first actual logon occurs).

The Windows NT Boot Components

The most important components of the Windows NT boot process are
worth memorizing:

➤ **BOOT.INI** This is the PC information file that describes Windows
  NT boot defaults, plus operating system locations, settings, and menu
  selections. This file resides in the root directory of the system partition.

➤ **BOOTSECT.DOS** This MS-DOS boot sector file is used if NTLDR
  offers the option to boot to some other Microsoft (or near-equivalent)
  operating system such as DOS, Windows 95, or Windows 98. This
  file resides in the root directory of the system partition.

➤ **NTDETECT.COM** This is the PC hardware detection program
  that gathers equipment and configuration information prior to booting Windows NT (to make sure the stored configuration agrees with
  the detected one). This file resides in the root directory of the system
  partition.

➤ **NTLDR** This is the PC operating system loader program, which can
  load Windows NT, or another designated operating system, and then
  relinquish control once the loading is complete. This file resides in the
  root directory of the system partition.

➤ **NTOSKRNL.EXE** This is the executable file for the Windows NT operating system that includes all the basic capabilities and components necessary to establish a working runtime environment. This file resides in the \Winnt\System32 directory on the boot partition.

➤ **OSLOADER.EXE** This is the OS loader program for RISC computers, which provides all of the services and information provided by BOOTSECT.DOS, NTDETECT.COM, and NTLDR on PCs. This file resides in a nonvolatile memory area that's always available when the machine boots.

There's one other PC-based Windows NT boot file that is worth noting. It is named NTBOOTDD.SYS, and must be present when a SCSI drive, with its onboard BIOS disabled, is used either as the system partition or the boot partition on a Windows NT system. This file replaces the functions that the onboard BIOS would normally provide with a software-based driver. Like the other boot files, NTBOOTDD.SYS resides in the root directory of the system partition.

ARC Names And Attached Hard Drives

To fully understand the ins and outs of the BOOT.INI file that drives much of NTLDR's behavior during the Windows NT boot process, it is essential to understand what Microsoft calls Advanced RISC Computer (ARC) names (and sometimes, ARC pathnames). ARC represents a common naming convention used within disk controller software to specify the unique combination of disk controller, disk drive, and disk partition that identifies the boot partition for Windows NT. These names appear in the BOOT.INI file and must sometimes be edited by hand, particularly when recovering from failure of the primary member of a mirrored or duplexed drive pair.

ARC names not only provide a method to specify the type and location of the disk controllers, drives, and partitions in use, but also include pointers to files and directories. Such names typically take one of two forms:

```
scsi(0)disk(0)rdisk(0)partition(1)\path
multi(0)disk(0)rdisk(0)partition(1)\path
```

Here's a breakdown of the terms involved:

> **scsi(*) or multi(*)** Normally, most ARC names will begin with multi(*); scsi(*) appears only when a SCSI controller with its onboard BIOS disabled is in use. Multi(*) is used for other hard disks of all kinds, including IDE, EIDE, ESDI, and SCSI (where the onboard BIOS is enabled, as is most often the case). The (*) indicates the address of the hardware adapter from which to boot, numbered ordinally, beginning with zero. Controller number is determined by the BIOS loading order: the first controller installed is (0), next is (1) and so on. Controller BIOS loading order is determined during installation. The first controller found is loaded first, unless mass storage detection is interupted and a different controller is manually installed first. When an ARC name starts with SCSI, RDISK always takes a zero value.

> **disk(*)** If the first parameter in the ARC name is SCSI, then disk (*) is the next meaningful parameter. The number following disk represents the physical SCSI ID of the disk drive. If Multi is the first parameter, then disk (*) is ignored and will be set to zero.

> **rdisk(*)** If first parameter is multi, then rdisk (*) is the next meaningful parameter. The first drive in the chain is (0), next is (1), and so on. Unless the drives are SCSI, then the (*) is the actual SCSI ID assigned to the disk. If SCSI is the first parameter, rdisk (*) is ignored and will be set to zero.

> **partition(*)** This portion of the name indicates the disk partition that contains the designated files. Unlike the other numbering schemes in ARC names, partition numbers begin with one, so that the first partition is partition(1), the second partition(2), and so on.

 Please note that for PCs, a maximum of four partitions per drive is allowed. But one of those partitions can be something called an *extended partition*, which simply means that more than one logical drive can be created within that partition. The other three (or four, if no extended partition exists) are called primary partitions and can have only one logical drive per partition.

Here are two important things to remember about primary and extended partitions: (1) only a primary partition can be a system partition (where boot files reside and initial boot phases occur), but Windows NT system files (the boot partition) can reside on a logical drive within an extended partition; and (2) on a drive with primary and extended partitions, the extended partition is always numbered the highest. If Windows NT files reside on an extended partition and a new primary has been defined, this means the partition number for the extended partition increases by one as a result of that new definition.

➤ **\path** Indicates the directory (or subdirectory) on the partition where the operating system files may be found. The default path for Windows NT is \Winnt.

> Working with ARC names requires understanding the rules by which they're to be applied or interpreted. Remember that scsi(*) appears only for SCSI controllers with their onboard BIOSs disabled, and that numbering for scsi(*), multi(*), disk(*), and rdisk(*) starts with zero, but that numbering for partition(*) starts with one. Remember also that when multi(*) appears, disk(0) is the only valid value, and that when scsi(*) appears, rdisk(0) is likewise the only valid value. These three rules, properly applied, will help you understand ARC.

Managing The BOOT.INI File

You can make changes to BOOT.INI from the Control Panel, System Applet, Startup/Shutdown tab, or by using a text editor such as Notepad. In case problems occur as a result of these changes, always make a backup copy of the file to a floppy to keep around. Here's an exhibit of a typical BOOT.INI file (without most of the many possible bells and whistles):

```
[boot loader]
timeout=30
default=multi(0)disk(0)rdisk(0)partition(3)\WINNT
[operating systems]
multi(0)disk(0)rdisk(0)partition(3)\WINNT="Windows
NT Server Version 4.00"
multi(0)disk(0)rdisk(0)partition(3)\WINNT="Windows
NT Server Version 4.00 [VGA mode]" /basevideo /sos
C:\ = "MS-DOS"
```

Note that this file is divided into two sections, labeled [boot loader] and [operating systems]. The [boot loader] section supplies the timeout interval after which the default operating system to load (defined in the following default= line) will load automatically. The [operating systems] section supplies the complete menu of operating system choices that NTLDR displays right after the program loads. You can disable the timer before it elapses by striking any arrow or letter key on the keyboard or by setting the timer to -1 in boot.ini, which permanently disables it. Then, you can wait as long as you like to make your menu selection.

Using The Control Panel

Using the System applet found in Control Panel to change BOOT.INI is definitely the safest method, but it doesn't expose everything you may sometimes need to access. The System applet includes a Startup/Shutdown tab that permits you to choose a default boot selection, and to set the interval for the delay before the default boot selection is automatically invoked. This delay time corresponds to the timeout value in the [boot loader] section of the file shown previously. Also, the value assigned to the default= statement in that section defines the ARC name for the default OS to be loaded.

Using A Text Editor

BOOT.INI is a plain, pure-ASCII file that should be edited with a plain text editor like Notepad or some other equivalent program. As with any initialization file, be careful when editing. Anything between quotation marks in the [operating systems] section of the file is fair game, but it is vital to be careful if you must edit an ARC name by hand. If you configure the BOOT.INI file incorrectly, Windows NT may not boot. That's why you should always create an Emergency Repair Disk before making any changes to BOOT.INI, and be sure to have a set of Windows NT boot disks on hand.

BOOT.INI has the following DOS attributes: read-only, system, and hidden. You will need to turn off the read-only attribute to make changes to the file, and you'll probably want to turn off the hidden attribute as well. It's necessary to restore the file to read-only after editing, so be sure to remember this step before you try to reboot.

Troubleshooting The Windows NT Boot Process

There are lots of ways that things can break down and interfere with the Windows NT Boot process. Here, we recount those problems—and their fixes—that you're most likely to encounter when dealing with boot problems. While you're troubleshooting, remember that hardware problems are always possible (if vexing and unpleasant), and that sometimes the computer won't boot because a component has failed, not because of the kinds of software and configuration difficulties we recount here.

That's why our first step with a PC that won't boot Windows NT is to insert a DOS boot disk. If the machine will boot DOS, it's pretty easy to run DOS-based diagnostics to check out the hardware. This eliminates many of the potential avenues for problems from further consideration. Our next step is to boot the system from a set of Windows NT boot floppies—if that works, it illustrates that the machine itself will still boot Windows NT, no matter how badly the current configuration may be mangled or disturbed.

The next step is to try to boot using the Last Known Good Configuration boot option. If this works, it indicates the problem lies in changes made to the system since the last time it booted successfully. This should narrow the field considerably, and let you focus on the most likely causes of problems. If you can't get to this point, you'll have to get the hardware working before you can proceed any further.

Common Boot-Related Problems, Causes, And Fixes

Here's a litany of potential woes, with possible causes, and definite fixes.

I/O Error Accessing Boot Sector File

These types of errors can occur when a power failure or fluctuation interrupts file system activity or software installation. Sometimes, these errors occur when installing another operating system over an existing Windows NT installation. The symptom will be some kind of BIOS-level error message from the computer that indicates that the boot sectors are damaged or that the drive is unavailable. The only way to repair this problem is to boot the PC from a DOS floppy, and run the FDISK/MBR command to rebuild the MBR.

Corrupted Partition Tables

This generally won't happen unless you attempt to use some operating system other than Windows NT, or other operating systems incompatible with the IBM/Microsoft partitioning scheme, to create or manipulate partitions on a drive. For obvious reasons, Unix can be a culprit here. If this happens, a backup is your best bet—you'll have to reformat the drive, reestablish the partitions, and then restore the data. If no data was written to the drives following their partition changes, it may be possible to restore the partition table to its prior state and attempt to carry on from there. But this can be an unbelievable exercise in frustration.

BOOT: Couldn't Find NTLDR

When this error message appears, it indicates that NTLDR is corrupt or missing. This may sometimes pop up if the wrong partition has been made active in Disk Administrator, but is usually remedied by copying a good copy of NTLDR onto the root of the errant drive.

NTDETECT V1.0 Checking Hardware...

If this message appears repeatedly on your PC, it means that NTDETECT.COM is corrupted or missing. In most cases, a fresh copy of the program onto the root of the errant system partition will do the trick.

Windows NT Could Not Start Because The Following File Is Missing Or Corrupt: \Winnt\System32\ntoskrnl.exe

This may indicate any number of problems, but it generally means that NTLDR couldn't find the Windows NT operating system kernel file needed to complete the OS load. The most frequent cause of this problem is that allocation of free space on a Windows NT drive results in a change to the partition number for the boot partition where the Windows NT system files reside. Proper assignment of the partition number for the boot partition will usually fix this problem.

Could Not Read From The Selected Boot Disk...

This is your clue that something is amiss with the boot partition. It could be that there is a missing or malfunctioning drive (unlikely, but possible). Otherwise, it might be that the disk partition specified in an ARC name does not contain a file system that's recognizable to the NTLDR program. In that case, you'll want to check to see if partition allocations have changed lately, or if someone has been tinkering with BOOT.INI. Restoring the malfunctioning drive or correcting the ARC name should fix the problem.

STOP: 0x000007E: Inaccessible Boot Device

A STOP error is as fatal as it gets; Windows NT won't go any further until you fix the problem. This error occurs most frequently when a SCSI controller that fails to adhere completely to the SCSI standard is installed in a Windows NT machine. It can also occur if you add a SCSI controller to a Windows NT machine that boots from an IDE hard disk: In that case, make sure that no SCSI device is set to SCSI ID 0 (or otherwise disable booting from the SCSI drive(s)). This prevents the SCSI controller from attempting to boot the disk, and will also stop NTDETECT.COM from assigning the SCSI adapter a bus number equal to zero, which may cause BOOT.INI to point to the wrong partition.

Practice Questions

Question 1

> A Windows NT Server PC is configured with two 2.2 GB EIDE hard drives, with both drives attached to a controller built into the motherboard. Each disk contains a single primary partition; the Windows NT system files reside on Disk 1, and the boot files reside on Disk 2. Which of the following ARC names correctly identifies the system disk?
>
> ○ a. multi(1)disk(1)rdisk(0)partition(0)
>
> ○ b. multi(0)disk(1)rdisk(0)partition(1)
>
> ○ c. multi(0)disk(0)rdisk(0)partition(0)
>
> ○ d. multi(1)disk(0)rdisk(0)partition(0)
>
> ○ e. multi(0)disk(0)rdisk(1)partition(1)

Trick! question

Answer e is correct. The options for the first element in an ARC name are either scsi or multi, but scsi applies only to a genuine SCSI drive whose onboard BIOS has been disabled. Because multi(*) appears at the start of all five choices, all of them are correct to that point. The number that follows multi within the parentheses is the ordinal number of the disk controller to which the drive (or drives) is attached. Ordinal numbers start with 0. There is only one controller mentioned in the question, which immediately rules out answers a and d because they allude to a second controller (as denoted by multi(1)) to which neither drive in the preceding question is attached.

The disk(*) element in an ARC name designates the SCSI bus number for a SCSI drive with its BIOS disabled, and is always zero for a non-SCSI disk. This eliminates answer b from further consideration.

The rdisk(*) element in an ARC name indicates the SCSI logical unit number (LUN) or the drive that contains the operating system. rdisk(*) is always set to zero when an ARC name starts with "scsi". Because this one starts with "multi", it indicates the position in the order in which drives are attached to the controller. Further, the question indicates that the Windows NT system files are on the first disk, and boot files on the second disk. Knowing that rdisk numbers begin with zero, this means that the Windows NT system files live on the drive named multi(0)disk(0)rdisk(0) partition(1), and that the boot files live on the drive named multi(0)disk(0)rdisk(1)partition(1).

One small trick to ARC names is that although scsi, multi, disk, and rdisk all number ordinally, starting with 0, partition numbers start with 1. Thus, any valid ARC name will not ever have zero as a value for partition(*). Because each of the partitions mentioned in this question is the one and only on its drive, it must be partition(1). Partitions are numbered cardinally, starting with 1.

Here's the real trick in this question: Boot files reside on the system partition on a Windows NT Server. This means that the correct answer is the ARC name for the drive that contains the boot files, or answer e. Note that the correct ARC name for the first disk, where the Windows NT system files reside, does not appear as an option in the list of answers on the question.

Question 2

Jane has just installed a new device driver for her UPS on her Windows NT Server, and now the machine will not boot properly. What is the easiest way to get the system to boot, so that the driver problem can be fixed?

○ a. Add the /NoSerialMice option to the BOOT.INI file.

○ b. Run the emergency repair process to restore the Windows NT Registry.

○ c. Boot Windows NT from the Emergency Repair Disk (ERD).

○ d. Select the Last Known Good Configuration option when it appears during the next reboot.

Answer d is correct. Answer d is the only option that really makes sense, because it reverts the Windows NT Server to the working configuration that held the last time it booted successfully. Because this cheerfully ignores anything changed since then—such as the errant UPS driver that may (or may not) be causing the problem—it brings the Server back up so that Jane can try again from a relatively pristine state.

Answer a has nothing to do with getting an unbootable Windows NT machine running for troubleshooting purposes (even if it may be the fix that's finally enacted for a UPS that resets a PC when its serial port is probed). And because it's impossible to boot from the ERD, answer c is incorrect. Answer b sounds tempting, but it raises interesting questions about how the emergency repair process knows what to fix in the Registry and how it can change the behavior of possibly damaged or mismatched driver software. Therefore, answer b is incorrect.

Question 3

Which ARC name listed below correctly identifies that Windows NT boot files reside on the fourth partition on a SCSI disk drive whose onboard BIOS is disabled, with a SCSI Bus ID of 1 on the first SCSI controller on the Server machine?

○ a. scsi(0)disk(0)rdisk(0)partition(3)

○ b. scsi(0)disk(1)rdisk(0)partition(4)

○ c. scsi(0)disk(1)rdisk(1)partition(4)

○ d. multi(0)disk(0)rdisk(0)partition(4)

Answer b is correct. The secret to answering this question lies in knowing how to "unpack" its contents, and what values to assign based on the information it contains. Partitions are numbered cardinally, starting from one, so any correct answer must end in partition(4). This automatically disqualifies answer a.

Any SCSI hard disk with its onboard BIOS disabled must begin with the string scsi(*). This automatically disqualifies answer d. Likewise, if the scsi keyword begins an ARC name, the value for rdisk will always be zero; this disqualifies answer c.

By process of elimination, this means that b must be the right answer. By unpacking the question, we discover that:

➤ The first SCSI controller with BIOS disabled translates into scsi(0).

➤ The SCSI Bus ID provides the value for disk(*), whenever the BIOS is disabled, which translates into disk(1).

➤ Because the BIOS is disabled, rdisk(*) is always rdisk(0).

➤ The value for partition equals its number on the drive, so partition(*) translates into partition(4).

Once again, only b matches the entire string.

Question 4

> XYZ Corp.'s newest Windows NT Server uses disk mirroring for its system partition. What is the best way to create an emergency boot disk that points to the mirror partition to permit the server to boot should the primary partition fail?
>
> ○ a. Choose Emergency Repair Disk from the Fault Tolerance menu in Disk Administrator.
>
> ○ b. Format a blank floppy using the server. Copy NTLDR, NTDETECT.COM, and BOOT.INI from the system partition to the floppy. Manually edit BOOT.INI to specify the ARC pathname for the mirror partition.
>
> ○ c. Choose Emergency Repair Disk from the Tools menu in Disk Administrator.
>
> ○ d. In the System applet in Control Panel, choose the Recovery tab, and check the Create Emergency Repair Disk option.

Answer b is correct. A strong working foundation with Windows NT makes this question trivial. The only way to boot from the mirror partition on a Windows NT Server is for the boot process to point at the controller, drive, and partition where the boot files reside. This only can be done by hand, because none of the administrative utilities mentioned in the preceding answers know how to construct such an emergency boot disk automatically. This means that answers a, c, and d are completely fanciful (and reflect nonexistent options in all three cases).

Question 5

> Both system and boot partitions are not working on the PDC, but
> disk mirroring means that the mirror may still be intact. How should
> you modify the BOOT.INI file on an emergency boot floppy to boot
> the system from the mirrored copy? [Check all correct answers]
>
> ❑   a.   Do nothing; the BOOT.INI file will handle this
> automatically.
>
> ❑   b.   Modify the ARC name specifications in the [operating
> systems] section of the file.
>
> ❑   c.   Modify the ARC name specification in the default= line
> of the [boot loader] section of the file.
>
> ❑   d.   Add an /m switch to the appropriate lines in the
> [operating systems] section of the file.

Answers b and c are correct. Windows NT boots from the ARC name
specified in the [operating systems] section of the BOOT.INI file if a deliberate OS selection is made, but most commonly, it boots from the default line in the [boot loader] section. Therefore, changes to the ARC names
in both parts of BOOT.INI will be required; as we've already explained,
these changes must be entered by hand to point to the mirror copy in a
mirrored set of drives. Answer a is incorrect because BOOT.INI does not
handle mirrored sets automatically. Answer d is incorrect because there is
no /m switch defined among the available Windows NT boot options.

Question 6

> When the System Administrator at XYZ Corp. tries to boot into DOS on a dual-boot Windows NT machine, she gets an error message that reads:
>
> ```
> I/O Error accessing boot sector file
> multi(0)disk(0)rdisk(0)partition(2):
> \bootsect.dos
> ```
>
> What is the most expedient way to fix this problem?
>
> ○ a. Boot from the Last Known Good Configuration.
>
> ○ b. Start the computer from the Windows NT boot disks and copy BOOTSECT.DOS from another server.
>
> ○ c. Boot the computer from the Emergency Repair Disk and follow the prompts.
>
> ○ d. Start the computer from the Windows NT boot disks and insert the Emergency Repair Disk when prompted.

The correct answer is d; the Windows NT boot disks permit the system to boot completely and the ERD then can regenerate a new BOOTSECT.DOS. Here, full-blown repair is needed, because BOOTSECT.DOS stores partition information entirely specific to the computer where it is generated. Any copy of this file from another machine is useless; this disqualifies answer b. Because the machine won't boot completely, the Last Known Good Configuration option never appears; this eliminates answer a. Because the ERD is not bootable, answer c is incorrect.

Question 7

> On a Windows NT Server computer, there are two duplexed SCSI drives. The boot partition is on the drive that is connected to the primary SCSI controller, the mirror on the drive connected to the secondary SCSI controller. If the primary controller fails, how must you modify the BOOT.INI file so that the system will now boot from the mirror? (The SCSI BIOS is enabled on the controller.)
>
> ○ a. Change scsi(0) to scsi(1) on the appropriate lines.
>
> ○ b. Change scsi(1) to scsi(2) on the appropriate lines.
>
> ○ c. Change multi(0) to multi(1) on the appropriate lines.
>
> ○ d. Change multi(1) to multi(2) on the appropriate lines.

Answer c is correct because the primary must therefore be multi(0), this must change to multi(1). Therefore, answer d is incorrect. As with Question 3, the key is knowing how to "unpack" ARC names. Unless the BIOS is disabled on a SCSI controller, the initial keyword in an ARC name is always multi. Because there's no mention of BIOS in the question, this eliminates answers a and b immediately. The rest of the answer hinges on understanding that SCSI controllers are numbered ordinally, starting with zero.

Question 8

XYZ Corp. has just added a new IDE hard drive and controller to a Windows NT Server. The machine continues to boot from its SCSI drive, which has its BIOS disabled. Each drive has only a single primary partition. Of the following options, which is the correct ARC name for the machine's system partition?

○ a. scsi(0)disk(0)rdisk(0)partition(1)

○ b. scsi(0)disk(1)rdisk(0)partition(0)

○ c. scsi(1)disk(0)rdisk(0)partition(1)

○ d. scsi(1)disk(1)rdisk(0)partition(1)

○ e. scsi(0)disk(0)rdisk(1)partition(1)

Answer a is correct. Once again, a working knowledge of ARC name construction comes in handy. Because the drive in question is SCSI, but its onboard BIOS is disabled, the ARC name must begin with scsi(*). Because there is only one SCSI controller, and numbering begins with zero, it must begin with scsi(0); this disqualifies answers c and d immediately.

For ARC names that begin with scsi(*), only the disk(*) keyword is significant; in such cases rdisk(*) is always rdisk(0); this disqualifies answer e. Here again, disks are numbered by their SCSI bus number, starting with zero. By default, disk(0) is the correct value (because no replacement bus number was specified); this disqualifies answer b (and d).

By process of elimination, this leaves answer a, which may be constructed as follows:

➤ scsi(*) becomes scsi(0) because the BIOS is disabled, and it is the first and only SCSI controller.

➤ disk(*) becomes disk(0) because that's the default assignment and no overriding values were supplied.

➤ rdisk(*) must be rdisk(0) because the BIOS is disabled on a SCSI controller, and this value is therefore ignored.

➤ partition(*) becomes partition (1) because it is the first and only partition on the drive, and partition numbering begins with 1.

Question 9

> After modifying the Registry, a Windows NT Server machine will not fully boot; it hangs on the blue screen. What is the easiest way to get the machine to boot?
>
> ○ a. Start the computer from the Windows NT boot disks and restore the Registry from a backup.
>
> ○ b. Start the computer from the Windows NT boot disks and select the Emergency Repair option.
>
> ○ c. Start the computer from the Emergency Repair Disk and follow the prompts.
>
> ○ d. Choose the Last Known Good Configuration option when it appears during bootup.

Answer d is correct. The easiest approach to this kind of problem, be it caused by untoward edits to the Registry or installation of drivers or new system components, is to choose the Last Known Good Configuration option during bootup. Answers a and b may produce the same results eventually, but they're nowhere near as easy (and perhaps not as up-to-date as the Last Known Good Configuration). Answer c is flat wrong, because you can't boot from the ERD.

Question 10

> While booting a Windows NT Server, the following error message
> appears right after the Last Known Good Configuration prompt:
>
> ```
> Windows NT could not start because the follow-
> ing file is missing or corrupt:
>   \Winnt\System32\ntoskrnl.exe.
> Please reinstall a copy of the above file.
> ```
>
> You're certain that this file is present, even though the boot pro-
> cess cannot locate it. What's the most likely cause of this error
> message?
>
> ○ a. Missing NTLDR
>
> ○ b. Missing BOOTSECT.DOS
>
> ○ c. Missing NTDETECT.COM
>
> ○ d. Missing BOOT.INI

Answer d is correct. The most common cause of this error is setting an invalid partition as active in Disk Administrator—that is, one that does not include any of the requisite Windows NT boot files. When this happens, none of these files is actually present on the designated boot partition, but it's really the absence of BOOT.INI that makes the difference, because it's the file that indicates where the other files are located. This message also will appear if the ARC name for the NTOSKRNL.EXE file is incorrect in BOOT.INI (which is sometimes specified as the default= entry in the [boot loader] section, and always in at least two entries in the [operating systems] section).

Question 11

> Which of the following files must appear in the system partition of
> an Intel PC-based Windows NT machine, if that machine uses one
> or more SCSI drives with their onboard BIOSs disabled?
> [Choose all correct answers]
>
> ❑   a.   BOOT.INI
>
> ❑   b.   NTLDR
>
> ❑   c.   NTOSKRNL.EXE
>
> ❑   d.   NTBOOTDD.SYS
>
> ❑   e.   OSLOADER.EXE
>
> ❑   f.   BOOTSECT.DOS

Answers a, b, and d are correct. The files that always appear in the
system partition on a PC running Windows NT are: BOOT.INI,
NTDETECT.COM, and NTLDR. When a drive with its onboard BIOS
disabled is used as the boot or system partition, an additional file,
NTBOOTDD.SYS, also is required. Answer e applies only to RISC machines
(that is, non-Intel CPUs) running Windows NT; answer c names a file that
appears in the default directory where the Windows NT system files reside
(usually specified as Winnt\System32). Answer f applies only to a multiboot
machine with DOS or Windows 95 as a bootable OS. Because it's not required
for Windows NT per se, it's not a correct answer to this question.

Question 12

> Of the choices listed below, what is the most likely cause of the
> following Windows NT error message at boot time?
>
> `Boot: Couldn't find NTLDR`
> `Please insert another disk`
>
> ○   a.   An incorrect hard disk partition is set active.
>
> ○   b.   NTLDR is missing or corrupt.
>
> ○   c.   A floppy was left in the A: drive.
>
> ○   d.   The designated system disk is damaged or inaccessible.

Answer c is correct. The most common cause of this error message, by far, is powering down a Windows NT machine with a floppy in the floppy drive. Because many PCs' BIOSs try to boot from any floppy inserted during bootup, this error occurs whenever you forget to remove a floppy before the machine is powered back up. Thus, answer c is by far the most likely. Answers a, b, and d are possible, but nowhere near as likely to provoke this error message. When you see it, look for (and remove) a floppy and try again.

Need To Know More?

 Heywood, Drew: *Inside Windows NT Server, 2nd Edition.* New Riders, Indianapolis, IN, 1998. ISBN 1-56205-860-6. Chapter 1 includes a useful overview section entitled, "Customizing the Boot Process" (pp. 66 through 72), covering most of the high points of this subject.

 Strebe, Matthew, Charles Perkins, and James Chellis: *MCSE: NT Server 4 Study Guide, 2nd Edition.* Sybex Network Press, San Francisco, CA, 1998. ISBN 0-7821-2222-1. The section of Chapter 17 that deals with boot issues, "Troubleshooting the Windows NT Boot Process" (pp. 634 through 638), provides some useful "if you get this error message, here's the likely cause" examples and fixes.

 Search the TechNet CD (or its online version through **www.microsoft.com/technet**) using the keywords "Windows NT boot," "BOOT.INI" (or other important boot file names), and related topics. The Knowledge Base, in particular, contains lots of good troubleshooting tips and configuration details.

The *Windows NT Server Resource Kit* is the most detailed of all available resources on boot-related topics. You can search the TechNet CD or the CD accompanying the *Resource Kit,* using the same keywords mentioned in the preceding paragraph. Useful boot-related information appears in the *Resource Guide* volume, especially on pages 83 through 113.

Troubleshooting

Terms you'll need to understand:

√ Troubleshooting

√ Boot failures

√ NTLDR

√ NTOSKRNL

√ BOOT.INI

√ BOOTSECT.DOS

√ NTDETECT.COM

√ Event Viewer

√ Last Known Good Configuration (LKGC)

√ Registry

√ Emergency Repair Disk (ERD)

√ Dr. Watson

√ Kernel debugger

Techniques you'll need to master:

√ Understanding the trouble-shooting process

√ Troubleshooting media errors, domain controller communication difficulties, stop message errors or halt on blue screen, hardware problems, and dependency failures

√ Recognizing installation failures

√ Troubleshooting boot failures

√ Using Windows NT's built-in repair tools

Troubleshooting a Windows NT-based network can be both extensive and difficult. There is much more troubleshooting material than we could ever sift down into a single chapter. So, we've focused on the troubleshooting issues that are most relevant to Windows NT Server.

The Troubleshooting Process

Troubleshooting is more often an art than a science. Thus, there is rarely a single action that will fix the same problem each time it occurs. However, you can streamline your problem-solving techniques with a few simple rules:

➤ Have patience.

➤ Understand your system.

➤ Attempt to isolate and repeat the fault.

➤ Suspect the most recent change or addition.

➤ Inspect the most common points of failure.

➤ Peruse your problem's history.

➤ Attempt easy fixes first.

➤ Let the problem guide your solution.

➤ Make a single alteration or fix at a time.

➤ Dissect a multisided problem into numerous single issues.

➤ Maintain a log of problems, correction attempts, and solutions.

Keep these troubleshooting principles in mind as you read the sections that follow.

Installation Failures

Five common types of errors can occur during the initial installation of Windows NT:

➤ Media errors

➤ Domain controller communication difficulties

➤ Stop message errors or halt on blue screen

➤ Hardware problems

➤ Dependency failures

Media errors are problems with the distribution CD-ROM itself, the copy of the CD-ROM hosted on a network drive, or the communication between the installation and the distribution files. The only ways to resolve media errors are to attempt to switch media, such as from one server's CD-ROM to another, or to copy the CD-ROM files to a network drive. If media errors are encountered, always start the installation process over from the beginning.

Not being able to communicate with the existing domain controller prevents the current installation from joining the domain. This is especially a problem when installing a BDC. This is often due to a mistyped name, a network failure, or the domain controller being offline. Verify the viability of the domain controller directly and with other workstations (if present).

Stop messages and halting on the blue screen during installation are usually caused by the wrong driver for a controller card. If any information is presented to you about the error, try to determine if the proper driver is installed. If not or if you can't tell, double-check your hardware and the drivers required to operate them under Windows NT.

Hardware problems should occur only if you failed to comply with the Hardware Compatibility List (HCL) or a physical defect has surfaced in previously operational devices. In such cases, replacing the device is the only solution. However, it is not uncommon for a device to be improperly configured or installed. Always double-check the setup of your hardware before purchasing a replacement. One common error is the failure of the Windows NT setup to recognize a second SCSI drive during initial setup. In such cases, select the S option when prompted to identify additional devices before continuing with the installation, or use the Devices applet to add them after the installation is complete.

 Dependency failures occur when one or more dependent services fail due to the absence of an underlying service, hardware, or driver. An example of a dependency failure is when Windows NT Server and Workstation services fail because the NIC fails to initialize properly. If Windows NT boots with such errors, check the Event Log.

Boot Failures

Boot failures are problems during the startup of Windows NT.

NTLDR Error Message

If NTLDR is missing, the following error occurs:

```
BOOT: Couldn't find NTLDR. Please insert another disk.
```

Resolve using the ERD to repair or replace.

Boot Error Due To Floppy In Drive A:

If a Windows NT bootable floppy with a defective BOOT.INI is in Drive A:, the following error occurs:

```
BOOT: Couldn't find NTLDR. Please insert another disk.
```

If the floppy is not bootable, the following error occurs:

```
Invalid system disk. Replace the disk, and then press any key.
```

In either case, eject the floppy and then reboot or press any key.

NTOSKRNL Missing Error Message

If NTOSKRNL is corrupt, missing, or the BOOT.INI points to the wrong partition, the following error occurs:

```
Windows NT could not start because the following file is missing
or corrupt:
\winnt\System32\ntoskrnl.exe
Please re-install a copy of the above file.
```

Repair the NTOSKRNL file using the ERD repair process or edit or correct the BOOT.INI.

BOOT.INI Missing Error Message

If no BOOT.INI is present, NTLDR will launch Windows NT from \winnt of the current partition. If this fails, the following error occurs:

```
BOOT: Couldn't find NTLDR. Please insert another disk.
```

To alleviate this problem, replace the BOOT.INI file from a backup or use the ERD to repair.

BOOTSECT.DOS Missing Error Message

If the BOOTSECT.DOS file is not present to boot to MS-DOS or another operating system (not Windows NT), an error message appears:

```
I/O Error accessing boot sector file
multi(0)disk(0)rdisk(0)partition(1):\bootsect.dos
```

This indicates that the BOOT.INI file has been changed, the partition numbering has changed, or the partition is missing, inactive, or inaccessible. To attempt repair/replace of the BOOTSECT.DOS file, use the ERD repair procedure.

NTDETECT.COM Missing Error Message

If the NTDETECT.COM file is not present, an error message appears:

```
NTDETECT V1.0 Checking Hardware...
NTDETECT failed
```

This error must be repaired with the ERD repair process.

Repair Tools

Fortunately, Windows NT does not leave you high and dry when you encounter errors. A handful of tools can be used to repair and correct operational difficulties. These tools are examined in the sections that follow.

Event Viewer

The Event Viewer, located in Start|Programs|Administrative Tools (Common), is used to inspect the three logs automatically created by Windows NT. These logs are:

> ➤ **System** Records information and alerts about Windows NT's internal processes.

> ➤ **Security** Records security-related events.

➤ **Application** Records Windows NT application events, alerts, and system messages.

Each log records a different type of information, but all collect the same information about each event: date, time, source, category, event, user ID, and computer. Plus, each event recorded has at worst an error code number or at best a detailed description with a memory HEX buffer capture.

Most system errors, including stop errors that result in the blue screen, are recorded in the System log. This allows you to review the time and circumstances around a system failure.

Last Known Good Configuration

The Last Known Good Configuration (LKGC) is a recording made by Windows NT of all the Registry settings that existed the last time a user successfully logged in to the server. Every time a login completes, Windows NT records a new LKGC. If a system error occurs or the Registry becomes corrupted so that booting or logging in is not possible, the LKGC can be used to return to a previously operational state. The LKGC is accessed during bootup when this message displays: "Press the spacebar now to boot with the Last Known Good Configuration." A menu then appears where you can select to load using the LKGC (by pressing L) or other stored configurations.

The Registry

Editing the Registry by hand should be the last resort, only to be attempted when all other possible avenues of repair have been exhausted. A single, improperly configured Registry entry can render an installation of Windows NT DOA. There are two Registry editing utilities—REGEDIT and REGEDT32. Both of these must be launched from the Run command or a command prompt. REGEDIT displays all five hives of the Registry in a single display window, and the entire Registry can be searched at one time. REGEDT32 displays each of the five hives in a separate display window, but it offers more security and control related functions.

It is a good idea to back up your Registry regularly. This can be done using:

➤ NTBACKUP

➤ Disk Administrator (SYSTEM key only)

➤ Either of the Registry editing tools (REGEDIT or REGEDT32)

➤ The REGBACK utility from the Resource Kit CD-ROM

The best times to make a backup are before and after any significant change to your system, such as hardware installation, software installation, or service pack application. If Windows NT fails to operate properly but does boot, you can attempt a repair by restoring the Registry from a backup.

There are a few things you should note about working with the Registry. When you edit the Registry, you are working with it in memory, so changes will go into effect as soon as they are made. However, in some cases a reboot is required to correct memory settings and launched applications to fully comply with the changes. It is always a good idea to reboot after editing the Registry. Also, when a key of the Registry is saved (or backed up), you capture all of the subcontents of that key. This is important to remember when restoring portions of the Registry from backup. All of the subkeys below the point at which restoration occurs also will be overwritten by the saved version. Any and all changes made since the backup will be lost in the restored sections.

Emergency Repair Disk

The ERD is the miniature first aid kit for Windows NT. This single floppy contains all the files needed to repair the system partition and many boot partition-related problems. The ERD is most often used to repair or re-place files that are critical to the boot process of Windows NT. An ERD usually is created during the installation of Windows NT, but additional and updated ERDs can be created using the RDISK.EXE utility. At the Run command, RDISK /S forces Windows NT to save to disk all current Registry settings in memory to \Winnt\System32 \Config, followed by a prompt for a preformatted disk. The ERD contains the following files:

➤ SYSTEM. _HKEY_LOCAL_MACHINE\SYSTEM compressed

➤ SOFTWARE._HKEY_LOCAL_MACHINE\SOFTWARE compressed

➤ SECURITY._HKEY_LOCAL_MACHINE\SECURITY compressed

➤ SAM. _HKEY_LOCAL_MACHINE\SAM compressed

➤ NTUSER.DA_Default profile, compressed

➤ AUTOEXEC.NT Winnt\System32\autoexec.nt

➤ CONFIG.NT Winnt\System32\config.nt

➤ SETUP.LOG a list of installed files and their checksums

➤ DEFAULT. _KHEY_USERS\DEFAULT compressed

The ERD does not contain the entire Registry, but just enough to fix the most common errors.

To use the ERD to make repairs, you need the three setup floppies that are used to install Windows NT. The repair process is as follows:

1. Reboot the computer using Windows NT Setup disks 1 and 2 or boot the Windows NT CD and specify repair instead of install.

2. Select R for Repair. A menu appears containing the following options:

   ➤ Inspect Registry files

   ➤ Inspect startup environment

   ➤ Verify Windows NT system files

   ➤ Inspect boot sector

3. Deselect any items you do not wish to perform, then press Continue.

4. Insert disk 3 and the ERD when prompted.

Reinstalling Windows NT

If you have tried every troubleshooting path you can think of, consider reinstalling Windows NT. Multiple configuration problems can be corrected at once by reinstallation. However, reinstallation can cause new problems. All existing applications may need to be reinstalled and reconfigured. Most configuration and setup changes made to Windows NT will be lost, including installation of specialized drivers, additional services, and protocols.

There are two types of reinstallation possible with Windows NT: full and upgrade. A full reinstallation overwrites everything, just as if Windows NT was installed on a new system for the first time. No data from the previous configuration is saved, not even the Security ID (SID). Thus, a full reinstall causes the computer to have a new identity within the domain.

An upgrade reinstall retains most of the configuration of the current installation, while repairing and restoring areas of Windows NT that are damaged. An upgrade reinstall also retains the SID so the machine will not change identities. It is recommended to use an upgrade install to repair a PDC or BDC before attempting a full reinstall.

Remember, no matter what type of reinstall is performed, always protect mission-critical files by performing a backup before reinstalling the NOS. The reinstallation process does not guarantee the integrity of any data residing on the system.

Printing Solutions

When working with printers, there seem to be an infinite number of issues to resolve before normal operation is restored. Many printer problems are either simple or obvious, so take these measures before moving on to the more complicated solutions:

➤ Always check the physical aspects of the printer—cable, power, paper, toner, etc.

➤ Check the logical printer on both the client and server.

➤ Check the print queue for stalled jobs.

➤ Make sure the printer driver has not become corrupted by reinstalling it.

➤ Attempt to print from a different application or a different client.

➤ Print using Administrator access.

➤ Stop and restart the spooler using the Services applet.

➤ Check the status and CPU usage of the SPOOLSS.EXE using the Task Manager.

➤ Check the free space on the drive hosting the spooler file, and change its destination.

For additional information on print troubleshooting, see Chapter 8.

Remote Access Service

There are many things that can go wrong with RAS—everything from the configuration of the computers on both ends, to the modem settings, to the condition of the communications line. There is no ultimate RAS trouble-shooting guide, but here are some solid steps in the right direction:

➤ Check all physical connections.

➤ Check the communication line itself, with a phone if appropriate.

➤ Verify the RAS installation, the port configurations, and the modem setup.

➤ Check that both the client and the server dialup configurations match—including speed, protocol, and security.

➤ Verify that the user account has RAS privileges.

➤ Inspect the RAS-related logs—DEVICE.LOG and MODEMLOG. TXT (see Chapter 10).

The key to troubleshooting RAS is knowing the possible configuration options available to you. Most RAS problems are related to configuration (unless there is damage to the communication line)—either something was set incorrectly or someone made an alteration.

Miscellaneous

The following sections cover a handful of great troubleshooting topics that just don't fit well into any of the other sections.

Permissions Problems

If a permissions problem is suspected, perform the action using the Administrator account or temporarily add the user account to the Admin-istrators group. Double-check group memberships for conflicting access levels, especially No Access. Check the Access Control List (ACL) on the object in question for group and No Access assignments. Check the permissions on the share if appropriate. Check user, group, or computer policies for access restrictions. You may also attempt to take ownership to see if that changes the account's ability to access resources. Permission problems almost always are linked to multiple group memberships that include a No Access setting.

You should also remember that any changes made to a user's access permissions, especially those of group members, will not have an effect on that user until the next time they log on to the network. The Access Token used by the security system of Windows NT is created at the time of logon and is not altered during a session. The only way to take advantage of new settings is to log off and log back on so the Access Token is re-created using the new data.

A related issue to permissions is that of logging in after an account has expired. Accounts expire after 11:59 P.M. on their expiration date. After an account expires, that user is unable to establish any new network connections; however, he or she can continue to use any existing connections. Watch out for the time a login failure occurs—local or over RAS—even when everything else about the situation seems to indicate the problem should not be occurring.

UPS

An uninterruptible power supply (UPS) can be configured to use a serial port to communicate with Windows NT. This enables the UPS to inform Windows NT when a power failure occurs and when to power down. There are numerous configurations possible for a UPS; most are dependent on the manufacturer, but all are controlled through the UPS applet.

Some of the most common problems with UPSs are:

> ➤ Failure to add the /NOSERIALMICE parameter to the BOOT.INI file to prevent Windows NT from polling the UPS port for a mouse. This often causes the computer to power off, and thus, it can never boot.

➤ Failure to properly define the interface voltages for the control features. If the UPS sends a positive signal when Windows NT expects a negative signal, Windows NT will not respond. Once the battery in the UPS is drained, the computer will lose power and data in memory will be lost.

➤ Improper time settings for battery life and recharge time. Conservative numbers should be used to give a margin of error.

➤ Missing or wrong cable. UPS interfaces require a special UPS cable, not a standard RS-232 serial cable.

A UPS functions well if, and only if, Windows NT is properly configured to understand its communications.

Re-Creating The Setup Disks

If you need a new set of installation floppies, run the WINNT.EXE (or WINNT32.EXE) program from the installation CD with the /OX parameter. This creates the three floppies without initializing the actual installation process. However, you must preformat the disks beforehand.

Master Boot Record

If the Master Boot Record (MBR) fails on the system partition—the section of the disk that contains BOOT.INI, NTLOADER, and NTDETECT—the ERD will not help with its restoration. Instead, you'll need to use the first disk from DOS 6.0 (or higher), or create a W95/W98 startup disk (Start|Settings|Control Panel|Add/Remove Programs|Startup tab, click the Create Disk button), which creates a bootable disk with FDISK and other utilities on it. Executing FDISK /MBR re-creates the MBR and allows the system to boot.

Dr. Watson

Dr. Watson is Windows NT's application error debugger. It detects application errors, diagnoses the errors, and logs the diagnostic information. Most of the information gathered by Dr. Watson is useful only when working with a Microsoft technical professional to diagnose an application error. Data captured by Dr. Watson is stored in the DRWTSN32.LOG log file. Dr. Watson also can be used to create a binary crash dump file of the memory where the failing application operates.

Dr. Watson launches itself automatically whenever an application error occurs. However, to configure Dr. Watson, you can launch it by executing DRWTSN32 at the command prompt or in the Run dialog box. The configuration options of Dr. Watson are fairly obvious. The only two that may cause some confusion are:

> ➤ **Dump Symbol Table** Adds the corresponding symbol data to the dump file, greatly increasing its size.

> ➤ **Dump All Thread Contexts** Forces a dump file to be created for all active threads, not just those owned by the failed application.

BOOT.INI Switches

To improve the troubleshooting abilities of the bootup, you can use one of the following switches after each OS line in the BOOT.INI file (remember, those are the ones with the ARC name followed by the displayable name in quotes):

> ➤ **/BASEVIDEO** Boots using the standard VGA video driver.

> ➤ **/BAUDRATE=**n Sets the debugging communication baud rate when using the Kernel Debugger. The default is 9600 for a modem and 19200 for a null-modem cable.

> ➤ **/CRASHDEBUG** Loads the debugger into memory. It remains inactive unless a Kernel error occurs.

> ➤ **/DEBUG** Loads the debugger into memory to be activated by a host debugger connected to the computer (see Kernel Debugger, under Advanced Troubleshooting later in this chapter.)

> ➤ **/DEBUGPORT= COM**x Sets the debugging COM port.

> ➤ **/MAXMEM:n** Sets the maximum amount of RAM that Windows NT can use.

> ➤ **/NODEBUG** No debugging information is being used.

> ➤ **/NOSERIALMICE=[COM**x **| COM**x,y,z**...]** Disables serial mouse detection of the specified COM port(s).

> ➤ **/SOS** Each driver name is displayed when it is loaded.

VGA Mode

If you set your video driver to something that prevents a readable display, you can select VGA Mode from the boot menu to boot with the standard VGA driver loaded. Then, you can modify the display drivers to correct the problem.

NTDETECT Debugged

If NTDETECT fails to detect the proper hardware, it may be corrupted or damaged, or your hardware may not be functioning properly. A debugged or checked version of NTDETECT is stored on the CD in the Support\Debug\I386 directory. First, rename NTDETECT.COM to NTDETECT.BAK, then copy the file named NTDETECT.CHK to the system partition and rename it to NTDETECT.COM. Then you can reboot; this version of NTDETECT will give a verbose display of all detection activities to help isolate the problem. NTDETECT.COM has the attributes of Hidden, System, and Read Only set. You need to deselect these attributes before renaming the file, and reset them after. Once you've solved the hardware detection problem, return the original NTDETECT from NTDETECT.BAK or an ERD.

ESDI Hard Drives

Some ESDI hard drives are not supported by Windows NT. ESDI are pre-IDE type storage devices that have the ability of being low-level formatted with varying numbers of sectors per track. Due to special formatting geometry and drive controllers, Windows NT may be able to access cylinders beyond 1,024. If Windows NT has direct access to the cylinders above 1,024, only Windows NT—not DOS—can access these areas. If the controller can handle the translation so that it is transparent, both Windows NT and DOS can access cylinder areas above 1,023.

The determination of whether Windows NT can even use an ESDI disk cannot be made until an installation is attempted. If Windows NT fails to install properly on an ESDI disk, after NTLDR starts, a Fatal System Error:0x0000006b message will be displayed. When this occurs, you can deduce that the ESDI drive is not supported by Windows NT.

Advanced Troubleshooting

In addition to the tools and utilities listed previously in this chapter, there are three more troubleshooting mechanisms that require a professional support engineer to interpret. We list them here only for your general understanding.

Blue Screen

No matter what "they" tell you, Windows NT has general protection faults (GPFs), but they aren't called that. When a GPF occurs under Windows NT, the "blue screen of death" appears. This is a test display of the stop message error. There are lots of details included on this screen, such as the location of the error, type of error, and whether or not a memory dump is created. Unfortunately, most of the data is in hex or a strange acronym shorthand that you won't be able to read. Stop codes can be decoded somewhat with the help of TechNet.

Kernel Debugger

The Kernel Debugger records the activity of Windows NT during bootup and when a stop error occurs. To employ the Kernel Debugger, two computers with the same version of Windows NT connected by a null-modem cable or RAS must be used. One is designated as the host, the other the target. The host machine must have the symbol files installed from the Windows NT CD-ROM (or the version associated with the installed service pack). The debugging software is located on the CD in the \support\debug\platform directory. This must be copied onto the host machine as well.

Memory Dump

A memory dump is the act of writing the entire contents of memory to a file when a stop error occurs. The contents of this file can be inspected to determine the cause of the failure. Memory dumps are configured on the Startup/Shutdown tab of the System applet. The options are:

➤ Write the error event to the System log

➤ Send an Administrative alert

➤ Write a dump file

➤ Automatically reboot

The default location and name of the memory dump file on a Windows NT Server is Winnt\Memory.dmp. The DUMPEXAM.EXE utility can be used to view the contents of a memory dump file; however, most of the contents require a Microsoft technical professional to interpret.

Practice Questions

Question 1

Which of the following can be corrected by the repair process using the three installation disks and a recent Emergency Repair Disk? [Check all correct answers]

☐   a. Boot sector corruption

☐   b. Inability to locate Master Boot Record

☐   c. NTLDR not found

☐   d. Corrupt NTOSKRNL

Answers a, c, and d are correct. The ERD repair process often can correct boot sector problems, replace the NTLDR, and repair the NTOSKRNL. The MBR cannot be repaired with the ERD or the installation floppies—that requires a Fdisk.exe. Therefore, answer b is incorrect.

Question 2

A UPS is attached to your Windows NT Server. You have configured Windows NT's UPS utility to wait five seconds before sending an initial warning message after a power failure. The UPS is fully charged and has five minutes of battery life. You are using the correct UPS cable to attach the device to the serial port of the Windows NT machine. To test your setup, you unplug the device from the wall. No warning message ever appears and the computer loses power after five minutes. Why?

○   a. The Expected Battery Life setting is less than the actual battery life of the UPS.

○   b. The UPS Interface Voltage for the power failure signal is set incorrectly.

○   c. The UPS service was not installed through the Network applet.

○   d. The Delay Between Warning Message setting is greater than 300 seconds (five minutes).

Answer b is correct. The UPS Interface Voltage for the power failure signal is set incorrectly: If the UPS sends a positive signal when Windows NT is expecting a negative signal, Windows NT will not respond, because it won't understand the communication from the UPS. If the Expected Battery Life setting was less than the actual battery life of the UPS, the computer would power down before the UPS ran out of juice. In this situation, the computer never understood the communications from the UPS; therefore, answer a is incorrect. There is no UPS service to install: The UPS applet is a default utility of Windows NT, so answer c is incorrect. The Delay Between Warning Message setting cannot be greater than 300 seconds (five minutes), because the situation stated it was set to five seconds. Therefore, answer d is incorrect.

Question 3

Which two parameter switches are present by default on the VGA Mode selection ARC name line in the BOOT.INI file? [Check all answers]

❑   a. /NODEBUG

❑   b. /BASEVIDEO

❑   c. /NOSERIALMICE

❑   d. /SOS

❑   e. /VGAVIDEO

Answers b and d are correct. /BASEVIDEO and /SOS are present on the VGA Mode line by default. /NODEBUG and /NOSERIALMICE are not present on the VGA Mode line by default; therefore, answers a and c are incorrect. /VGAVIDEO is not a valid parameter; therefore, answer e is incorrect.

Question 4

The SYSTEM Registry key contains errors. You do not have a recent ERD, but you do have a floppy copy of the SYSTEM key itself. Which of the following programs should you use to restore the SYSTEM key from the floppy?

○   a. Disk Administrator

○   b. System applet

○   c. Network Client Administrator

○   d. Server Manager

Answer a is correct. The Disk Administrator is the correct utility to use to restore the SYSTEM key if you have a stored copy. The other three utilities do not offer Registry restoration options; therefore, answers b, c, and d are incorrect.

Question 5

Your Windows NT Server has been experiencing numerous stop errors recently. Where should you configure Windows NT so that a memory dump will occur before the system reboots to help pinpoint the problem?

○   a. The server properties within Server Manager

○   b. The recovery option in Dr. Watson

○   c. The tracking tab of the Task Manager

○   d. On the Startup/Shutdown tab of the System applet

Answer d is correct. The Startup/Shutdown tab of the System applet is the location of the memory dump options for Windows NT. The Server Manager does not offer memory dump configuration options, so answer a is incorrect. Dr. Watson is used to perform memory dumps on application faults, not for Windows NT Server itself; therefore, answer b is incorrect. The Task Manager does not have a tracking tab nor does it offer memory dump options; this means that answer c is also incorrect.

Question 6

> After installing a new SCSI driver, Windows NT will not boot suc-
> cessfully. No other changes have been made to the system. What
> is the easiest way to return the system to a state where it will
> boot properly?
>
> ○ a. Use the repair process with the ERD.
>
> ○ b. Use the Last Known Good Configuration.
>
> ○ c. Launch the Kernel Debugger.
>
> ○ d. Boot to DOS and run the setup utility to change the
> installed drivers.

Answer b is correct. The LKGC is the fastest way to return to a bootable configuration, especially because only a single change was made to the system. The ERD repair process will restore the system so it can boot; however, this requires a recent ERD and all three installation diskettes, and this process can take upwards of 30 minutes. Therefore, answer a is incorrect. The Kernel Debugger will not help this situation, especially because it was not preconfigured to watch the boot process before the new driver was installed; therefore, answer c is incorrect. There is no DOS setup utility—that only was available for Windows 3.1; therefore, answer d is incorrect.

Question 7

> During the boot process, you receive an error message after the
> Last Known Good Configuration prompt:
>
> ```
> Windows NT could not start because the
> following file is missing or corrupt: \winnt
> \system32\ntoskrnl.exe. Please reinstall
> a copy of the above file.
> ```
>
> What are the possible explanations for this error?
> [Check all correct answers]
>
> ❏ a. The NTOSKRNL.EXE file is missing.
>
> ❏ b. The BOOT.INI file points to the wrong partition.
>
> ❏ c. The NTOSKRNL.EXE file is corrupt.
>
> ❏ d. The BOOT.INI file is missing.

Answers a, b, c, and d, are correct. All of these explanations can result in the given error message. When the boot process cannot find NTOSKRNL.EXE, it does not indicate if the problem is with the file itself, its location, or the pointers to it.

Question 8

Which of the files on the ERD lists the files installed during setup and the checksums of each of these files?

- ○ a. INSTALLED.DAT
- ○ b. CONFIG.NT
- ○ c. DEFAULT._
- ○ d. SOFTWARE._
- ○ e. SETUP.LOG

Answer e is correct. SETUP.LOG is the only file on the ERD that lists the files installed during setup and their corresponding checksums. INSTALLED.DAT is not a file present on an ERD; therefore, answer a is incorrect. CONFIG.NT, DEFAULT._, and SOFTWARE._ are all files on an ERD, but they do not contain installed file and checksum information; therefore, answers b, c, and d are incorrect.

Question 9

Your Windows NT Server experiences yet another stop error. Fortunately you enabled the memory dump option through the System applet. What utility can you use to view the contents of the .DMP file?

- ○ a. Event Viewer
- ○ b. Debug Inspector
- ○ c. DUMPEXAM.EXE
- ○ d. Windows NT Diagnostics

Answer c is correct. Only DUMPEXAM.EXE can be used to view the contents of .DMP files. The Event Viewer and Windows NT Diagnostics are not able to view the contents of a memory dump file, so answers a and d are incorrect. There is not a Debug Inspector, so answer b is incorrect.

Question 10

> Which of the following are valid ways to make full or partial back-ups of the Registry? [Check all correct answers]
>
> ❑ a. Create an ERD using the RDISK /S command.
>
> ❑ b. Use NTBACKUP.
>
> ❑ c. Copy all of the contents of the \Winnt\System32\Config directory.
>
> ❑ d. Use the Disk Administrator.
>
> ❑ e. Use REGEDT32.

Answers a, b, c, d, and e are correct. All of these methods are valid ways to create full or partial backups of the Windows NT Registry. However, it should be noted that the files stored in \Winnt\System32\Config (answer c) are only as current as the last reboot or execution of RDISK /S.

Question 11

> Bob, one of your users, tries to access a new project data file stored in the shared Account directory. Bob is not currently a member of the Accounts group, which has exclusive access to this directory. You add Bob to the Accounts group. Bob still is unable to access the directory, but he can access other resources. Why?
>
> ○ a. Bob did not use the Network Neighborhood to access the share.
>
> ○ b. Bob did not log off and log back in.
>
> ○ c. Bob is logged in remotely.
>
> ○ d. Bob typed in the wrong password.

Answer b is correct. By not relogging in to the system, Bob's access token was not rebuilt using the new group membership, so he effectively was not a member of the Account group. The Network Neighborhood does not have to be used to access a share; a mapped drive or a UNC name can be used to access a share; therefore, answer a is incorrect. The method of Bob's access is not relevant—a local and a remote logon have the same abilities under Windows NT. Therefore, answer c is incorrect. If Bob failed to use the correct password, he would not be logged in and thus would be unable to access any resources; therefore, answer d is incorrect.

Need To Know More?

 Heywood, Drew: *Inside Windows NT Server, 2nd Edition.* New Riders, Indianapolis, IN, 1998. ISBN 1-56205-860-6. This book does not have a chapter focused on troubleshooting; however, tips and tricks about resolving problems are scattered throughout the text.

 Siyan, Karanjit S.: *Windows NT Server 4 Professional Reference, 2nd Edition.* New Riders, Indianapolis, IN, 1997. ISBN 1-56205-805-3. This book also fails to include a focused chapter on resolving problems, but troubleshooting information is present in some chapters.

 Strebe, Matthew, Charles Perkins, and James Chellis: *MCSE: NT Server 4 Study Guide, 2nd Edition.* Sybex Network Press, San Francisco, CA, 1998. ISBN 0-7821-2222-1. Chapter 17 contains lots of great troubleshooting information. Other tips and tricks are scattered through the rest of the text as well.

 Searching the TechNet CD (or its online version through **www.microsoft.com/technet**) and the *Windows NT Server Resource Kit* using the keyword "troubleshooting" will result in numerous hits on relevant materials. However, for more focused searching, use keywords associated with the topic or subject in question, such as "boot," "installation," "printing," "Emergency Repair Disk," or "Registry."

Sample Test #1

In this chapter, we provide pointers to help you develop a successful test-taking strategy, including how to choose proper answers, how to decode ambiguity, how to work within the Microsoft testing framework, how to decide what you need to memorize, and how to prepare for the test. At the end of the chapter, we include 60 questions on subject matter pertinent to Microsoft Exam 70-067:"Implementing and Supporting Microsoft Windows NT Server 4.0." After this chapter, you'll find the answer key to this test; after that, you'll find yet another sample test, followed by another answer key. In addition, we provide you with some practice scenario questions in the Scenarios section following Chapter 17. This gives you three opportunities to prepare!

Also, remember that you can take adaptive practice exams on Windows NT Server 4.0 online at **www.coriolis.com/cip/c ore4rev/** to help you prepare even more. Good luck!

Questions, Questions, Questions

There should be no doubt in your mind that you are facing a test full of specific and pointed questions. If the version of the Windows NT Server 4.0 exam that you take is fixed-length, it will include 30 questions; and you will be allotted 60 minutes to complete the exam. If it is an adaptive test (and the software should tell you this as you begin the exam), it will consist of somewhere between 15 and 35 questions (on average) and take somewhere between 20 and 30 minutes.

Whichever type of test you take, for this exam, questions belong to one of five basic types:

➤ Multiple-choice with a single answer

➤ Multiple-choice with multiple answers

➤ Multipart with a single answer

➤ Multipart with multiple answers

➤ Pick one or more points on a graphic

Always take the time to read a question at least twice before selecting an answer, and always look for an Exhibit button as you examine each question. Exhibits include graphics information related to a question. An exhibit is usually a screen capture of program output or GUI information that you must examine to analyze the question's contents and formulate an answer. Thus, the Exhibit button brings up graphics and charts used to help explain a question, provide additional data, or illustrate page layout or program behavior.

Not every question has only one answer; many questions require multiple answers. Therefore, it's important to read each question carefully, to determine how many answers are necessary or possible, and to look for additional hints or instructions when selecting answers. Such instructions often occur in brackets, immediately following the question itself (as they do for all multiple-choice, multiple-answer questions).

Picking Proper Answers

Obviously, the only way to pass any exam is to select enough of the right answers to obtain a passing score. However, Microsoft's exams are not standardized like the SAT and GRE exams; they are far more diabolical and convoluted. In some cases, questions are strangely worded, and deciphering them can be a real challenge. In those cases, you may need to rely on answer-elimination skills. Almost always, at least one answer out of the possible choices for a question can be eliminated immediately because it matches one of these conditions:

➤ The answer does not apply to the situation.

➤ The answer describes a nonexistent issue, an invalid option, or an imaginary state.

➤ The answer may be eliminated because of the question itself.

After you eliminate all answers that are obviously wrong, you can apply your retained knowledge to eliminate further answers. Look for items that sound correct but refer to actions, commands, or features that are not present or not available in the situation that the question describes.

If you're still faced with a blind guess among two or more potentially correct answers, reread the question. Try to picture how each of the possible remaining answers would alter the situation. Be especially sensitive to terminology; sometimes, the choice of words ("remove" instead of "disable") can make the difference between a right answer and a wrong one.

Only when you've exhausted your ability to eliminate answers, but remain unclear about which of the remaining possibilities is correct, should you guess at an answer. An unanswered question offers you no points, but guessing gives you at least some chance of getting a question right; just don't be too hasty when making a blind guess.

 If you're taking a fixed-length test, you can wait until the last round of reviewing marked questions (just as you're about to run out of time, or out of unanswered questions) before you start making guesses. If you're taking an adaptive test, you'll have to guess to move on to the next question if you can't figure out an answer some other way. Either way, guessing should be your technique of last resort!

Decoding Ambiguity

Microsoft exams have a reputation for including questions that can be difficult to interpret, confusing, or ambiguous. In our experience with numerous exams, we consider this reputation to be completely justified. The Microsoft exams are tough, and deliberately made that way.

The only way to beat Microsoft at its own game is to be prepared. You'll discover that many exam questions test your knowledge of things that are not directly related to the issue raised by a question. This means that the answers you must choose from, even incorrect ones, are just as much a part of the skill assessment as the question itself. If you don't know something about most aspects of Windows NT Server 4.0, you may not be able to eliminate obviously wrong answers because they relate to a different area of Windows NT Server than the one that's addressed by the question at hand. In other words, the more you know about the software, the easier it will be for you to tell right from wrong.

Questions often give away their answers, but you have to be Sherlock Holmes to see the clues. Often, subtle hints appear in the question text in such a way that they seem almost irrelevant to the situation. You must realize that each question is a test unto itself and that you need to inspect and successfully navigate each question to pass the exam. Look for small clues, such as the mention of times, group permissions and names, and configuration settings. Little things like these can point at the right answer if properly understood; if missed, they can leave you facing a blind guess.

Working Within The Framework

The test questions appear in random order, and many elements or issues that receive mention in one question may also crop up in other questions. It's not uncommon to find that an incorrect answer to one question is the correct answer to another question, or vice-versa. Take the time to read every answer to each question, even if you recognize the correct answer to a question immediately. That extra reading may spark a memory, or remind you about a Windows NT Server feature or function, that helps you on another question elsewhere in the exam.

If you're taking a fixed-length test, you can revisit any question as many times as you like. If you're uncertain of the answer to a question, check the box that's provided to mark it for easy return later on. You should also mark questions you think may offer information that you can use to answer other questions. On fixed-length tests, we usually mark somewhere between 25 and 50 percent of the questions on exams we've taken. The testing software is designed to let you mark every question if you choose; use this framework to your advantage. Everything you will want to see again should be marked; the testing software can then help you return to marked questions quickly and easily.

For fixed-length tests, we strongly recommend that you first read through the entire test quickly, before getting caught up in answering individual questions. This will help to jog your memory as you review the potential answers and can help identify questions that you want to mark for easy access to their contents. It will also let you identify and mark the real tricky questions for easy return as well. The key is to make a quick pass over the territory to begin with, so that you know what you're up against; and then to survey that territory more thoroughly on a second pass, when you can begin to answer all questions systematically and consistently.

If you're taking an adaptive test, and you see something in a question or one of the answers that jogs your memory on a topic, or that you feel you should record if the topic appears in another question, write it down on your piece of paper. Just because you can't go back to a question in an adaptive test doesn't mean you can't take notes on what you see early in the test, in hopes that it might help you later in the test.

For adaptive tests, don't be afraid to take notes on what you see in various questions. Sometimes, what you record from one question, especially if it's not as familiar as it should be or reminds you of the name or use of some utility or interface details, can help you on other questions later on.

Finally, some Microsoft tests combine 15 to 25 adaptive questions with 10 fixed-length questions. In that case, use our recommended adaptive strategy for the adaptive part, and the recommended fixed-length or short-form strategy for the fixed-length part.

Deciding What To Memorize

The amount of memorization you must undertake for an exam depends on how well you remember what you've read, and how well you know the software by heart. If you are a visual thinker, and you can see the drop-down menus and dialog boxes in your head, you won't need to memorize as much as someone who's less visually oriented. The tests will stretch your recollection of commands and functions of Windows NT Server.

At a minimum, you'll want to memorize the following kinds of information:

➤ Windows NT installation switches and options

➤ Windows NT disk organizations, including disk mirroring, disk duplexing, stripe sets (with and without parity), and volume sets

➤ The Windows NT boot process and how to troubleshoot boot problems

➤ How to set up and manage users and groups within workgroups and domains

If you work your way through this book while sitting at a machine with Windows NT Server installed, and try to manipulate this environment's features and functions as they're discussed throughout, you should have little or no difficulty mastering this material. Also, don't forget that The Cram Sheet at the front of the book is designed to capture the material that is most important to memorize; use this to guide your studies as well.

Preparing For The Test

The best way to prepare for the test—after you've studied—is to take at least one practice exam. We've included one here in this chapter for that reason; the test questions are located in the pages that follow (and unlike the preceding chapters in this book, the answers don't follow the questions immediately; you'll have to flip to Chapter 15 to review the answers separately [see Chapter 17 for the answers to Chapter 16's sample test]).

Give yourself 90 minutes to take the exam, keep yourself on the honor system, and don't look at earlier text in the book or jump ahead to the answer key. When your time is up, or you've finished the questions, you can check your work by consulting Chapter 15 or 17. Pay special attention to the explanations for the incorrect answers; these can also help to reinforce your knowledge of the material. Knowing how to recognize correct answers is good, but understanding why incorrect answers are wrong can be equally valuable.

Taking The Test

Relax. Once you're sitting in front of the testing computer, there's nothing more you can do to increase your knowledge or preparation. Take a deep breath, stretch, and start reading that first question.

There's no need to rush, either. You have plenty of time to complete each question and to return to those questions that you skip or mark for return (if you are taking a fixed-length test). If you read a question twice and remain clueless, you can mark it if you're taking a fixed-length test; if you're taking an adaptive test, you'll have to guess and move on. Both easy and difficult questions are intermixed throughout the test in random order. If you're taking a fixed-length test, don't cheat yourself by spending too much time on a hard question early on in the test, and thereby depriving yourself of the time you need to answer the questions at the end of the test. If you're taking an adaptive test, don't spend more than five minutes on any single question—if it takes you that long to get nowhere, it's time to guess and move on.

On a fixed-length test, you can read through the entire test, and before returning to marked questions for a second visit, figure out how much time you've got per question. As you answer each question, remove its mark. Continue to review the remaining marked questions until you run out of time, or you complete the test.

On an adaptive test, set a maximum time limit for questions, and watch your time on long or complex questions. If you hit your limit, it's time to guess and move on. Don't deprive yourself of the opportunity to see more questions by taking too long to puzzle over questions, unless you think you can figure out the answer. Otherwise, you're limiting your opportunities to pass.

That's it for pointers. Here are some questions for you to practice on!

Sample Test #1

Question 1

A Windows NT Server PC is configured with two 1 GB SCSI hard drives. Both drives are attached to the same SCSI drive controller with an operating onboard BIOS. Each disk contains a single primary partition; the Windows NT system files reside on Disk 1, and the boot files reside on Disk 2. Which of the following ARC names correctly identifies the boot partition that appears in the BOOT.INI?

- ○ a. multi(0)disk(0)rdisk(0)partition(1)
- ○ b. multi(0)disk(1)rdisk(0)partition(1)
- ○ c. multi(0)disk(0)rdisk(0)partition(0)
- ○ d. multi(1)disk(0)rdisk(0)partition(0)
- ○ e. multi(0)disk(0)rdisk(1)partition(1)

Question 2

You perform a daily backup on all the files you have access to, but you are unable to restore these files from the backup tape. You are a member only of the Marketing group. What is preventing the restoration?

- ○ a. You are not a member of the Administrators group, so you should not even be able to make backups.
- ○ b. You are not a member of the Domain Users, Print Operators, or Replicator group.
- ○ c. You are not a member of the Backup Operators, Server Operators, or Administrator group.
- ○ d. You failed to check the Enable Restore option when you performed the backups.

Question 3

> Which of the following statements are true about PPP and SLIP?
> [Check all correct answers]
>
> ☐ a.   PPP supports DHCP; SLIP does not.
>
> ☐ b.   SLIP supports NetBEUI, IPX/SPX, and TCP/IP; PPP
>   supports only TCP/IP.
>
> ☐ c.   SLIP is the most commonly used WAN protocol.
>
> ☐ d.   SLIP is used to access Unix servers.
>
> ☐ e.   SLIP supports encrypted passwords; PPP does not.

Question 4

> After failed attempts to print several documents, you inspect the
> print queue. You discover that all of your print jobs are listed in
> the display window and that you are unable to delete any of them.
> What is the best course of action to resolve this problem?
>
> ○ a.   Turn off the Pause Printing command from the Printer
>   window.
>
> ○ b.   Delete the printer from the print server, and create a
>   new printer.
>
> ○ c.   Delete all files from the spool folder on the print server.
>
> ○ d.   Stop the spooler service, and then restart it.

Question 5

> You add four new drives to your Windows NT Server computer,
> sized 900 MB, 700 MB, 500 MB, and 350 MB. You wish to estab-
> lish a disk stripe set with parity. What is the total size of the larg-
> est set you can create using any or all of these drives?
>
> ○ a.   1200 MB
>
> ○ b.   1000 MB
>
> ○ c.   900 MB
>
> ○ d.   1500 MB

Question 6

Your BDC experiences a power surge that results in the destruction of the primary drive. The primary drive was comprised of two partitions—one used for the boot files and the other for the system files. Fortunately, you implemented a disk mirror on both partitions using a duplicate drive. How should you modify the BOOT.INI file on an emergency boot floppy to boot the system from the mirrored copy? [Check all correct answers]

❑   a.   Add an /m switch to the appropriate lines in the [operating systems] section of the file.

❑   b.   Modify the ARC name specification in the default= line of the [boot loader] section of the file.

❑   c.   Modify the ARC name specifications in the [operating systems] section of the file.

❑   d.   Do nothing; the BOOT.INI file will handle this automatically.

Question 7

Where should updated logon scripts be placed, and how should the replication service be configured so they will be distributed throughout the network automatically?

○   a.   In the Scripts subdirectory of \Winnt\System32\Repl\Export on the PDC, replicate to all other domain controllers.

○   b.   In the \Winnt\System32\Repl\Export directory on the PDC, replicate to each domain workstation.

○   c.   In the Scripts subdirectory of \Winnt\System32\Repl\ Export on the PDC, replicate to each domain workstation.

○   d.   In the \Winnt\System32\Repl\Export directory on the PDC, replicate to all other domain controllers.

Question 8

If you performed a directory listing on your Intel-based Windows NT Server machine, the one with a SCSI controller card without an onboard BIOS, which of the following files would appear in the system partition? [Check all correct answers]

❑ a. BOOT.INI

❑ b. NTLDR

❑ c. NTOSKRNL.EXE

❑ d. NTBOOTDD.SYS

❑ e. OSLOADER.EXE

❑ f. BOOTSECT.DOS

Question 9

While performing normal daily activities, you notice that your server's hard drive is extremely active. You suspect your physical RAM needs to be increased. Which one Performance Monitor object and counter could you monitor to determine if the drive thrashing is due to a memory shortage?

○ a. Memory: Pages/Thread

○ b. Memory: Pages/Second

○ c. Processor: % Processor Time

○ d. LogicalDisk: Avg. Disk Bytes/Transfer

Question 10

Within a single domain, you have two Windows NT Server machines—a PDC and a BDC—plus fourteen Windows NT Workstation machines. You need to perform a backup of the domain data and the Registry for both of the domain controllers. You have a tape backup installed only on the BDC machine. Using NTBACKUP as your backup software, what should you do to ensure you capture all of the data necessary?

- ○ a. Nothing. You can do a remote backup of everything on the PDC.
- ○ b. Install a second tape drive on the PDC.
- ○ c. Nothing. You cannot back up your domain controllers.
- ○ d. Create an ERD for the PDC.

Question 11

While connected to the office LAN remotely, you interact with numerous documents stored on a machine hosted by the LAN via a shortcut added to your desktop. After closing your RAS connection, you attempt to access another document through your desktop shortcut. What happens?

- ○ a. Access is denied because no link to the LAN exists.
- ○ b. The file is pulled from the network cache.
- ○ c. A file with a similar name on your local hard drive will be accessed instead.
- ○ d. RAS AutoDial attempts to reconnect to the office LAN.

Question 12

Which items below describe disk striping without parity? [Check all correct answers]

- ❏ a. Requires three physical drives
- ❏ b. Can be implemented with FAT
- ❏ c. Provides fault tolerance
- ❏ d. Has faster read-write performance than disk mirroring
- ❏ e. Cannot recover data if a single drive within the set fails

Question 13

What is the best method for offering full network capabilities to remote users without compromising security over the Internet?

○ a. TCP/IP

○ b. Serial Line Internet Protocol

○ c. Point-to-Point Tunneling Protocol

○ d. Require Encrypted Authentication

Question 14

A network is comprised entirely of Windows NT Servers and Windows NT Workstations, except for a single NetWare server. What is the best way to provide the Workstation systems with access to the NetWare server's resources that are rarely used?

○ a. On each Windows NT Server, install CSNW

○ b. On each Windows NT Workstation, install CSNW

○ c. On a Windows NT Server, install GSNW

○ d. On a Windows NT Workstation, install GSNW

Question 15

How do you demote a BDC to a file server without domain controller capabilities?

○ a. Choose the Network option in Control Panel, select the BDC, and click Demote.

○ b. Highlight the BDC in the Server Manager, and select Demote on the Computer menu.

○ c. Reinstall Windows NT Server.

○ d. Restart the BDC, and choose Member Server at the startup screen.

Question 16

Which of the following is the best application to use to create a new shared directory on a domain server from your Windows NT Workstation computer? (Assume you have remote tools installed on the workstation from the Windows NT Server CD.)

○ a. User Manager

○ b. Server Manager

○ c. Windows Explorer

○ d. Network Client Administrator

Question 17

On an NWLink-based network using a star topology, one of the workstations is not able to establish a network connection. None of the other clients on the system is having communication difficulties. Of the following possibilities, which is the most likely to be the cause of this problem?

○ a. Faulty NIC on the server

○ b. A protocol mismatch

○ c. A PC memory conflict

○ d. An incorrect IPX frame type

Question 18

You have two SCSI hard drives on a single drive controller in your Windows NT Server computer. There is only one partition on each of the two drives. The first drive's partition is formatted with FAT, and the second drive's partition is formatted with NTFS. The drive controller has onboard BIOS. The boot files are located on the second drive. What is the ARC name for the system partition?

○ a. multi(0)disk(1)rdisk(0)partition(1)

○ b. multi(0)disk(0)rdisk(1)partition(1)

○ c. multi(1)disk(0)rdisk(1)partition(1)

○ d. multi(0)disk(0)rdisk(1)partition(0)

○ e. multi(1)disk(0)rdisk(0)partition(1)

Question 19

A Windows NT Server is added to a NetWare network. The NetWare-based network is comprised of various versions of NetWare—from very old to the latest release. The Windows NT Server is configured to autodetect the IPX frame types in use. If all of the following frame types are present, which kinds of frame types will a Windows NT Server detect successfully? [Check all correct answers]

❏ a.   802.2 frame type

❏ b.   802.3 frame type

❏ c.   802.3 frame type with SNAP header

❏ d.   802.5 frame type

❏ e.   802.5 frame type with SNAP header

Question 20

To track the level of processor use, what Performance Monitor object and counter should you watch?

○ a.   System: Interrupts/Second

○ b.   Memory: Pages/Second

○ c.   Processor: % Processor Time

○ d.   Processor: Interrupts/Second

Question 21

A user is a member of the following groups with the indicated access privileges to a share named ProjectA:

- Sales: Change

- Department12: Full Control

- DomainUsers: Read

The user is the leader of the team responsible for the data in Project A, so his user account has been assigned Change permissions on the directory hosted on an NTFS volume pointed to by this share. What is the resultant access privilege for this share for this user?

- O a. No Access
- O b. Read
- O c. Change
- O d. Full Control

Question 22

The Springfield Homeless Shelter operates its network on donated equipment. The network is based on a Windows NT Server 4 computer. Recently, a NetWare server was donated. The existing Windows For Workgroups machines now need access to resources on the NetWare server. How can these client machines access the new server without adding any additional software?

- O a. Install Gateway Service For NetWare on the Windows NT Server, and configure access for the NTGATEWAY group.
- O b. Install NWLink and File And Print Services For NetWare on the Windows NT Server.
- O c. Install Gateway Services for NetWare on the Windows NT Server, and create a group that has permission to access the NTGATEWAY group on the NetWare server.
- O d. Install Gateway Service For NetWare on the NetWare server, and NWLink on the Windows NT Server.

Question 23

In an attempt to customize the activity of Windows NT, you modify numerous entries in the Registry. You perform a reboot to force your changes to take effect; however, the Windows NT Server machine will not fully boot; it hangs on the blue screen. What is the easiest way to return the machine to an operating configuration?

- ○ a. Start the computer from the Windows NT boot disks, and restore the Registry from a backup.
- ○ b. Start the computer from the Windows NT boot disks, and select the Emergency Repair option.
- ○ c. Start the computer from the Emergency Repair Disk, and follow the prompts.
- ○ d. Choose the Last Known Good Configuration option when it appears during bootup.

Question 24

What component of Windows NT can be used to verify that NTBACKUP completed a batch file automated backup successfully?

- ○ a. User Manager For Domains
- ○ b. Server Manager
- ○ c. Backup log
- ○ d. The Registry

Question 25

The NTFS file system must be used to achieve, employ, or use which of the following under Windows NT 4.0? [Check all correct answers]

- ❏ a. Partitions larger than 250 MB
- ❏ b. File-level security
- ❏ c. Disk striping with parity
- ❏ d. Updating the ERD
- ❏ e. Long file names
- ❏ f. File-level compression

Question 26

Which of the following components are required for a Windows NT Workstation running Client Service For NetWare to access NetWare-based resources successfully? [Check all correct answers]

❑ a. Gateway Service For NetWare

❑ b. File And Print Services For NetWare

❑ c. NWLink

❑ d. A valid account on a NetWare server

❑ e. Membership in the NTGATEWAY group on the NetWare server to which Gateway Service For NetWare is connected

Question 27

To improve the printing speed of your office, you decide to establish a printer pool using five printers. Which of the following conditions are required to create a printer pool? [Check all correct answers]

❑ a. All print devices must use the same print driver.

❑ b. All physical print devices must be connected to the same logical printer.

❑ c. All print devices must use the same printer port.

❑ d. All print devices must be located in the same room.

Question 28

Your Ethernet network consists of a Windows NT 4 Server, several Windows NT Workstation clients, a NetWare 3.11 client, and one NetWare 4.1 client. NWLink is running on the network. Each of the NetWare clients is using different frame types. How would you configure the NWLink IPX/SPX Properties dialog box on the Windows NT 4 Server to enable the server to recognize both NetWare clients?

○ a. By enabling Auto Frame Type Detection

○ b. By selecting the Manual Frame Type Detection option and adding a NetWare client's network number and frame type to the frame type configuration list

○ c. By selecting the Auto Frame Type Detection option and adding both NetWare clients' network numbers and frame types to the frame type configuration list

○ d. By selecting the Manual Frame Type Detection option and adding each of the NetWare clients' network numbers and frame types to the frame type configuration list

Question 29

Your programmer has been hired away by a competitor. You hire a replacement. What is the best way (according to Microsoft) to give the new user the same access to network resources as the previous programmer?

○ a. Create a new account, and manually duplicate all of the settings and group memberships of the old account. Then delete the old account.

○ b. Rename the old account, and change the password in User Manager For Domains.

○ c. Rename the old account, and change the password in Server Manager.

○ d. Copy the old account, make any needed alterations to the copy, and disable the old account.

Question 30

You purchase a new HP network interface device for your printer. You want to attach the printer to the network directly instead of through a parallel cable to a server. During the installation, you are unable to locate the option to install a new port. Why?

○ a. PostScript printing is enabled on the print device and must be disabled.

○ b. You didn't install the print driver on the print server.

○ c. The print processor is corrupt and must be fixed.

○ d. The DLC protocol is not installed on the print server.

Question 31

Due to a change in your organization, users must now move from one computer station to another depending on the project in which they are currently involved. What must you do so that users can maintain the look and feel of their desktops no matter what machine they log in to?

○ a. Create a single network profile on the PDC in the \Winnt\Profiles directory, followed by the .DAT suffix. Have all user accounts load this profile.

○ b. Rename all current profiles from NTUSER.DAT to NTUSER.MAN.

○ c. Using the Copy Profile To box from the System option in Control Panel, copy all current profiles from the workstations to a shared network path. Delete the current profile from the workstations.

○ d. Copy each user's workstation profile to a shared network path using the Copy Profile To box. Change the type of profile to roaming. Then, type the network path in the User Profile Path box for each user account.

Question 32

You want to enable your Windows NT Workstation and Windows 95 clients to access a NetWare server without installing NetWare client software on those machines. How can this objective be met most effectively?

- O a. Install Gateway Services For NetWare on a Windows NT Server on the same network.
- O b. Install NWLink on the Windows NT Workstation and Windows 95 computers.
- O c. Install Gateway Services For NetWare on the NetWare server.
- O d. Install File And Print Services For NetWare on a Windows NT Server on the same network.

Question 33

Your company employs numerous independent consultants who operate throughout the United States. They regularly dial into the central Windows NT Server-based LAN to upload new orders and download the latest product descriptions. Each user purchased his or her own equipment and operating system. In this situation, what is the highest level of native Windows NT security you can implement and still allow your users to connect via RAS?

- O a. Allow Any Authentication Including Clear Text
- O b. Require Microsoft Encrypted Authentication
- O c. Enable PGP Encryption
- O d. Require Encrypted Authentication

Question 34

After upgrading a Windows NT 3.51 Server to version 4, you discover one of the storage drives is formatted with HPFS. You can convert this to NTFS using the CONVERT utility bundled with Windows NT 4.

- O a. True
- O b. False

Question 35

Your Windows NT boot partition resides on the fourth partition of a SCSI disk drive, the onboard BIOS of which is disabled. It is attached to a drive controller with a Bus ID of 1. What is the ARC name listed in the BOOT.INI file that points to the system files?

- ○ a. scsi(0)disk(0)rdisk(0)partition(3)
- ○ b. scsi(0)disk(1)rdisk(0)partition(4)
- ○ c. scsi(0)disk(1)rdisk(1)partition(4)
- ○ d. multi(0)disk(0)rdisk(0)partition(4)

Question 36

What are the RAS restrictions for protocols used over a remote connection?

- ○ a. TCP/IP, NetBEUI, but not NWLink
- ○ b. TCP/IP, NWLink, but not NetBEUI
- ○ c. Only TCP/IP
- ○ d. TCP/IP, NetBEUI, and NWLink

Question 37

Your organization wants to migrate users from a NetWare server to a Windows NT 4 Server to terminate the process of maintaining user accounts on two different types of servers. What must be installed on the Windows NT Server to provide clients with access to the NetWare resources after this migration is complete? [Check all correct answers]

- ❏ a. Gateway Service For NetWare
- ❏ b. The NWLink protocol
- ❏ c. Client Service For NetWare
- ❏ d. SAP agent

Question 38

The Sales department of your organization has asked that its print jobs be handled in priority over those from the Research department. Because you only have a single printer on your network, and this will improve overall work performance, you agree to make this change. How is it performed?

O a. Create a separate logical printer, assign rights to the Sales group, and set the printer priority to 1.

O b. Create a separate logical printer, assign rights to the Sales group, and set the printer priority to 99.

O c. Create a separate logical printer for the Sales group, and configure the printer to start printing immediately.

O d. Create a separate logical printer for the Sales group, and configure the printer to print directly to the physical print device.

Question 39

The system and boot partitions can participate in which of the following drive sets supported by Windows NT Server? [Check all correct answers]

❑ a. Disk mirroring

❑ b. Disk striping without parity

❑ c. Volume set

❑ d. Disk duplexing

Question 40

On a Windows NT Server, a disk mirror is implemented. During a thunderstorm, the primary disk of the mirror fails. The mirror did not contain the system or boot partitions. What are the steps required to restore the mirror set?

- ○ a. Replace the failed disk, reformat both drives, re-create a mirror set, and restore the data from a backup tape.

- ○ b. Replace the failed disk; Windows NT Server will automatically restore the mirror set.

- ○ c. Break the mirror set, replace the failed drive, and re-create the mirrored drive.

- ○ d. Replace the failed disk, select the mirror set and the replaced drive, and select Regenerate from the Fault Tolerance menu.

Question 41

There are 25 Windows 95 machines on your network. You want to upgrade them to Windows NT Workstation with a minimum of effort. The installation files reside in a shared directory named \\Server5\Wks4. What is the best way to handle the installation across the network?

- ○ a. Attach to the shared directory and run WINNT.EXE /b across the network.

- ○ b. Attach to the shared directory and run SETUP.EXE across the network.

- ○ c. Install the Windows NT Workstation client using Network Client Administrator.

- ○ d. Use Network Client Administrator to create a DOS Installation Startup Disk, attach to the shared directory, and run SETUP.EXE across the network.

Question 42

You want to install Windows NT Server 4 on an old Pentium machine. The machine was purchased in November 1995. What tools can be used to determine if the system can support the operation of Windows NT? [Check all correct answers]

- ❑ a.   Microsoft Windows NT Diagnostics
- ❑ b.   System Sleuth
- ❑ c.   NTHQ disk
- ❑ d.   A current copy of the Hardware Compatibility List

Question 43

You have a machine with an IDE CD-ROM drive. You had no difficulty installing Windows 95 on the machine, but the CD-ROM is not supported by Windows NT Server 4. How can you install Windows NT Server 4 on that machine anyway? [Check all correct answers]

- ❑ a.   Create a set of installation disks from another Windows NT Server machine, and use the disks to perform the install.
- ❑ b.   Use the XCOPY command to copy the files from the \i386 directory onto the Windows 95 machine's hard disk, and run WINNT.EXE from there.
- ❑ c.   While running Windows 95, change to the \i386 directory on the Windows NT CD, and run WINNT32.EXE.
- ❑ d.   Copy the installation files from \i386 to a server, map a drive from the Windows 95 machine to that directory, and run WINNT.EXE from there.

Question 44

After recent data loss due to hardware failures and a power brown-out, you want to protect your data. You decide to use Windows NT Server's built-in fault tolerance schemes to offer you the protection you need. Which of the following techniques will provide you with some type of fault tolerance? [Check all correct answers]

- ❑ a. RAID 1
- ❑ b. Disk duplexing
- ❑ c. Volume set
- ❑ d. Disk striping without parity
- ❑ e. RAID 5

Question 45

If static name resolution is used, what is the proper location of HOSTS and LMHOSTS to optimize the lookup time?

- ○ a. Both HOSTS and LMHOSTS should be stored on the RAS clients.
- ○ b. HOSTS should be stored on the RAS server, and LMHOSTS should be stored on the RAS clients.
- ○ c. Both HOSTS and LMHOSTS should be stored on the RAS server.
- ○ d. HOSTS should be stored on the RAS clients, and LMHOSTS should be stored on the RAS server.

Question 46

You have a 50 MB partition you wish to use as a share for users to store noncritical document files. What is the best file system type to format this partition with?

- ○ a. FAT
- ○ b. CDFS
- ○ c. NTFS
- ○ d. HPFS

Question 47

If you need to maximize the storage space on a Windows NT Server without care for fault tolerance, what is the best drive configuration to use?

- ○ a.   Disk mirroring
- ○ b.   Disk striping with parity
- ○ c.   Volume set
- ○ d.   Disk stacking

Question 48

You need to install Windows NT Server across a network onto a computer that currently runs Windows 95. Which of the following procedures will perform this activity?

- ○ a.   Connect to the network directory that contains the Windows NT installation files, and run WINNT32.EXE /b.
- ○ b.   Connect to the network directory that contains the Windows NT installation files, and run WINNT.EXE /b.
- ○ c.   Connect to the network directory that contains the Windows NT installation files, and run SETUP.EXE.
- ○ d.   Create a client installation disk using Network Client Administrator, boot the machine with that disk, and run NETWORK.EXE.

Question 49

The primary SCSI drive controller fails on your Windows NT Server computer. That controller hosted the drive containing the system files. Fortunately, you had a second drive controller that hosted the duplexed hard drive. Your system partition is hosted on an IDE drive. How should you modify the BOOT.INI file so the system can start up using the duplexed drive? The controller BIOS is enabled.

- ○ a.   Change scsi(0) to scsi(1) on the appropriate lines.
- ○ b.   Change scsi(1) to scsi(2) on the appropriate lines.
- ○ c.   Change multi(0) to multi(1) on the appropriate lines.
- ○ d.   Change multi(1) to multi(2) on the appropriate lines.

Question 50

You wish to upgrade a Windows For Workgroups computer to a Windows NT Server 4 machine. Which of the following steps should be performed to retain as much of the original configuration as possible?

○ a. Install Windows NT in a separate directory, and reinstall all applications.

○ b. Install Windows NT in a separate directory, and import WIN.INI and SYSTEM.INI into the Registry.

○ c. Run WINNT32.EXE and install Windows NT into WFW's home directory, c:\windows.

○ d. Run WINNT.EXE and install Windows NT into WFW's home directory, c:\windows.

Question 51

If you place data on a FAT formatted partition, users can access that data provided that: [Check all correct answers]

❑ a. users can log on across the network to the machine hosting the partition.

❑ b. a share is defined for the partition.

❑ c. users have READ or better permission to the share.

❑ d. users have READ or better file permissions.

Question 52

When operating over a PPP RAS connection, which of the following Windows NT networking activities can occur? [Check all correct answers]

❑ a. Printer share access

❑ b. Named pipes

❑ c. WinSOCK API applications over TCP/IP

❑ d. Interprocess Communications (IPC)

❑ e. User logon authentication

Question 53

In addition to Services for Macintosh, which other item must be present on a Windows NT Server computer to grant access to Macintosh clients?

- ○ a.   File and Print Services for NetWare
- ○ b.   An NTFS partition
- ○ c.   An HPFS partition
- ○ d.   TCP/IP

Question 54

You want to implement directory replication to distribute security files across the network. Which of the following computer types can be used as export servers? [Check all correct answers]

- ❑ a.   Windows NT Servers that are configured as domain controllers
- ❑ b.   Windows NT member servers
- ❑ c.   Windows NT Workstations
- ❑ d.   Windows 95 clients

Question 55

You print a document using your normal word processor. When you get to the printer to retrieve your work, you find pages of nonsensical lines of seemingly random characters. You remember that this printer was recently added. What is likely to be the cause of the print problem?

- ○ a.   The DLC protocol is not installed.
- ○ b.   The print spooler is corrupt.
- ○ c.   An incorrect printer driver has been installed.
- ○ d.   There is not enough hard disk space for spooling.

Question 56

When you press the Ctrl+Alt+Del key sequence to log onto a Windows NT Server PDC, which of the following names can appear in the From pull-down list? [Check all correct answers]

❏ a. Username

❏ b. Domain name

❏ c. Trusted domain name

❏ d. Computer name

❏ e. Hardware profile name

Question 57

You have a pure IPX/SPX NetWare network in which all Windows 98 clients use NetWare client software. You've recently added a Windows NT Server machine with SQL Server. How can you grant access to SQL Server without altering the current configuration of the Windows 98 clients?

○ a. Install GSNW on the Windows NT Server.

○ b. Install NWLink on the Windows NT Server.

○ c. Install FPNW on the Windows NT Server.

○ d. Install Services for NetWare on the Windows NT Server.

Question 58

The Guest account on a Windows NT Server is enabled by default?

○ a. True

○ b. False

Question 59

Which of the following statements are true about domain controllers? [Check all correct answers]

- ❏ a. A PDC is the central authority for a single domain.
- ❏ b. A BDC can maintain SAM databases for several domains.
- ❏ c. A PDC can only have three BDCs.
- ❏ d. Only a single PDC can exist on a network.
- ❏ e. A BDC can be promoted to a PDC.

Question 60

Because of a merger, you've been ordered to change the name of your Windows NT Server-based domain. After making the name change on the Identification tab of the Network applet on the PDC and rebooting, what other action must you take to complete the name change over?

- ○ a. Force domain synchronization via the Server Manager.
- ○ b. Use IPCONFIG to push domain updates to all clients.
- ○ c. Change the domain name setting on all clients.
- ○ d. Nothing. The entire network will update itself to the PDC automatically.

Answer Key #1

1.	a	21.	c	41.	a
2.	c	22.	c	42.	c, d
3.	a, d	23.	d	43.	b, d
4.	d	24.	c	44.	a, b, e
5.	d	25.	b, f	45.	a
6.	b, c	26.	c, d	46.	a
7.	a	27.	a, b	47.	c
8.	a, b, d	28.	d	48.	b
9.	b	29.	b	49.	c
10.	b	30.	d	50.	d
11.	d	31.	d	51.	a, b, c
12.	b, d, e	32.	a	52.	a, b, c, d, e
13.	c	33.	a	53.	b
14.	c	34.	b	54.	a, b
15.	c	35.	b	55.	c
16.	b	36.	d	56.	b, c
17.	d	37.	a, b	57.	b
18.	b	38.	b	58.	b
19.	a, b, c, d, e	39.	a, d	59.	a, e
20.	c	40.	c	60.	c

Here are the answers to the questions presented in the sample test in Chapter 14.

Question 1

Answer a is correct. The options for the first element in an ARC name are either scsi or multi, but scsi applies only to a genuine SCSI drive whose onboard BIOS has been disabled. Because multi(*) appears at the start of all five choices, all of them are correct to that point. The number that follows multi within the parentheses is the ordinal number of the disk controller to which the drive (or drives) is attached. Ordinal numbers start with 0; because there's only one controller mentioned in the question, that immediately rules out answer d, because it alludes to a second controller (as denoted by multi(1)) to which neither drive in the preceding question is attached.

The disk(*) element in an ARC name designates the SCSI bus number for a SCSI drive with its BIOS disabled, and is always zero for a non-SCSI disk. This eliminates answer b from further consideration.

The rdisk(*) element in an ARC name indicates the SCSI logical unit number (LUN) or the drive that contains the operating system. RDISK(*) always is set to zero when an ARC name starts with "scsi"—because this one starts with "multi", it indicates the position in the order in which drives are attached to the controller. Further, the question indicates that the Windows NT system files are on the first disk, and boot files on the second disk. Knowing that rdisk numbers ordinally (beginning with zero) and partition numbers cardinally (beginning with one), we know that the Windows NT system files live on the drive named multi(0)disk(0)rdisk(0)partition(1), and that the boot files live on the drive named multi(0)disk(0)rdisk(1)partition(1). Therefore, answer a is correct.

One small trick to remembering about ARC names is that whereas scsi, multi, disk, and rdisk all number ordinally, starting with 0, partitions number cardinally, starting with 1. Thus, no valid ARC name will ever have zero as a value for partition(*). Therefore, answer c is incorrect. Because each of the partitions mentioned in this question is the only one on its drive, it must be partition(1).

Here's the real trick in this question: System files reside on the boot partition on a Windows NT Server. This means that the correct answer is the ARC name for the drive that contains the system files, or answer a.

Question 2

Answer c is correct. You must be granted the Restore Files And Directories user right to restore data. By default, the Backup Operators, Server Operators, and Administrator groups all have the right to do this. Any user can back up a file if he or she can read it. The Administrators group has the user right, but it's not the only group with this user right by default. Because answer a mentions both of these issues, it's incorrect for being wrong and incomplete. These groups do not have settings that affect the ability of their members to operate NTBACKUP, making answer b incorrect. There is no such option as Enable Restore for a backup; restoration is a right granted to select groups and specific users, so answer d is incorrect.

Question 3

Answers a and d are correct. PPP supports DHCP; SLIP does not. Therefore, answer a is correct. SLIP is used to access Unix servers. Therefore, answer d is correct. PPP supports NetBEUI, IPX/SPX, and TCP/IP; SLIP only supports TCP/IP. Therefore, answer b is incorrect. PPP is the most commonly used WAN protocol. Therefore, answer c is incorrect. PPP supports encrypted passwords; SLIP does not. Therefore, answer e is incorrect.

Question 4

Answer d is correct. The spooler service is most likely the cause of the problem. By restarting the spooler service, it will pull all print jobs from the spool and print them. Even if the printer is paused, that would not prevent you from deleting print jobs. Therefore, answer a is incorrect. Deleting and re-creating the logical printer will force you to resend your documents; in addition, this is not the best solution. Therefore, answer b is incorrect. Deleting all the files from the print spool folder will remove the print jobs from the queue, but it does not address why the printer is not printing and it does not restore the printer to proper activity. Therefore, answer c is incorrect.

Question 5

Answer d is correct. 1500 MB is the total size of the largest set created from these drives, using only the 900, 700, and 500 MB drives. 1200 MB would be the size of the set if you used all four drives and 300 MB on each drive. This is not the largest possible configuration using this set of drives, so answer a is incorrect. 1000 MB is the amount of data that could be stored on the largest set created from these drives, but the question asked for the total size of the set, so answer b is incorrect. 900 MB is the size of the largest individual drive; you must use three devices to create a disk stripe set with parity. 900 MB is also the size of a stripe set with parity created, with 225 MB from each drive or 300 MB from three of the drives. Therefore, answer c is incorrect.

Question 6

Answers b and c are correct. Windows NT boots from the ARC name specified in the [operating systems] section of the BOOT.INI file if a deliberate OS selection is made, but most commonly, it boots from the default line in the [boot loader] section. Therefore, changes to the ARC names in both parts of BOOT.INI will be required; these changes must be entered by hand to point to the mirror copy in a mirrored set of drives. Answer a is incorrect because there is no /m switch defined among the available Windows NT boot options. Answer d is incorrect because BOOT.INI does not handle mirrored sets automatically.

Question 7

Answer a is correct. Logon scripts should be exported from the PDC to all BDCs responsible for authenticating logons on the network. The NETLOGON share is where all user accounts pull logon scripts. This share corresponds to the SCRIPTS subdirectory of \Winnt\System32\Repl\Export, making answers b and d incorrect. Replication of logon scripts should not occur with workstations but should remain on domain controllers, so answer c is incorrect. The replicator service only grabs files that appear in subdirectories beneath the ...\Export\Scripts directory; it's the presence of the subdirectory in answer a that makes it correct.

Question 8

Answers a, b, and d are correct. The files that appear in a PC system partition running Windows NT are BOOT.INI, NTDETECT.COM, and NTLDR. When a BIOS-disabled SCSI drive is used as the boot or system partition, an additional file, NTBOOTDD.SYS, is also required. Answer c names a file that appears in the default Windows NT system 32 directory (Winnt\system32\). Therefore, answer c is incorrect. Answer e applies only to RISC machines (that is, non-Intel CPUs) running Windows NT. Therefore, answer e is incorrect. Answer f names the file that appears in the system partition only on a multi-boot machine that numbers DOS, Windows, Windows 95, or some other near DOS-equivalent among the list of boot options in BOOT.INI. Therefore, answer f is incorrect.

Question 9

Answer b is correct. The Memory: Pages/Second counter can be watched to decide whether you need more RAM. There is no counter named Pages/Thread. Therefore, answer a is incorrect. If you want to find out the percentage of elapsed time that a processor is busy, you would look at % Processor time. Therefore, answer c is incorrect. The LogicalDisk: Avg. Disk Bytes/Transfer counter indicates the amount of bytes transferred to and from a disk, but does not relate to memory. Therefore, answer d is incorrect.

Question 10

Answer b is correct. Adding a second tape drive to your network is the only solution for capturing the Registry on the PDC without switching backup software products. The Registry cannot be backed up remotely using NTBACKUP. Therefore, answer a is incorrect. A domain controller can be protected by a backup, and all of its files can be backed up remotely, but the Registry can only be backed up locally using NTBACKUP, so answer c is incorrect. An ERD does not contain an entire copy of the Registry, so answer d is incorrect.

Question 11

Only answer d is correct. RAS maintains a map list of the resources accessed over WAN links. When one of these resources is referenced, it will attempt to AutoDial to regain a connection to the server hosting the resource. Answer a would be the result if AutoDial was not enabled, but you always should assume the default configuration for computers unless indicated otherwise. Therefore, answer a is incorrect. Answers b and c are fictitious activities that do not occur, so they are incorrect.

Question 12

Answers b, d, and e are correct. Disk striping without parity can host either NTFS or FAT, so answer b is correct. Disk striping without parity does have better performance than disk mirroring, so answer d is correct. Disk striping without parity cannot be recovered without a full backup, so answer e is correct. Disk striping without parity requires only two physical drives to be implemented. Therefore, answer a is incorrect. Disk striping without parity is not a fault tolerant storage method, so answer c is incorrect.

Question 13

Answer c is correct. PPTP offers a reliable and secure network connection over the Internet. TCP/IP can be used to offer complete access to the entire network, but without any security. Therefore, answer a is incorrect. SLIP will not offer access over the Internet, it cannot be used to dial into a Windows NT Server, and it does not support encryption. Therefore, answer b is incorrect. Require Encrypted Authentication is a mid-level security setting, but it does not directly relate to establishing a connection over the Internet, nor does it imply access to the network, so answer d is incorrect.

Question 14

Answer c is correct. The installation of GSNW on a single Windows NT Server is the best solution because it involves the least work and continued administration. Installing CSNW on all Windows NT Servers and Windows NT Workstations are both valid options, but each involves too much work. Therefore, answers a and b are incorrect. GSNW cannot be installed onto Windows NT Workstation. Therefore, answer d is incorrect.

Question 15

Answer c is correct. Although you promote a BDC to a PDC by using Server Manager, you need to reinstall Windows NT Server to change the role of the server from a domain controller to a member server, and vice versa. For this particular scenario, you must reinstall Windows NT Server and select Stand-Alone or Member Server when the system asks for a role for the server. The Network applet is not used in any way to work with domain controller status, so answer a is incorrect. The Demote command in the Server Manager menu will appear only when two PDCs are booted into the same domain, and the second PDC will remain inactive in security support until it is demoted to BDC status. Therefore, answer b is incorrect. There is no such selection as Member Server on a BDC's startup screen or boot menu, so answer d is incorrect.

Question 16

Answer b is correct. Server Manager allows users to create new shares on remote computers. The User Manager does not have the ability to modify shares, so answer a is incorrect. Windows Explorer cannot be used to create shares on other computers over the network; it is able only to access existing shares. Therefore, answer c is incorrect. NCA does not modify shares—it is used to create boot disks for installing new client machines. Therefore, answer d is incorrect. Server Manager is not a Windows NT Workstation utility; it is a Windows NT Server utility. However, it can be added to Windows NT Workstation by installing it from the administrative tools from the Windows NT Server distribution CD.

Question 17

Answer d is correct. Because NWLink can use various frame types, the workstation easily could be misconfigured to use a different frame type than the rest of the network. If the other machines on the network were experiencing problems, the server's NIC could be suspect, but because the problem is limited to a single workstation, the server NIC probably is not the culprit. Therefore, answer a is incorrect. Because the only protocol in use is NWLink (or IPX/SPX, if you prefer), there is no possibility of protocol mismatch, so answer b is incorrect. Most memory conflicts will cause a machine to crash rather than simply rendering network access inoperative. Therefore, answer c is incorrect.

Question 18

Answer b is correct. Answer b indicates the first partition of the second hard drive on the first multi type drive controller. This is the location of the system partition (the location of the boot files) for this question. Note that the question asks about the system partition. Remember that the boot partition is the ARC name found in the BOOT.INI file. This question asked about the "wrong" partition to focus on ARC name conventions rather than BOOT.INI contents. Answer a displays an improperly formatted ARC name: When multi is used, the disk(0) number must be zero, so answer a is incorrect. Answer c points to a second drive controller that doesn't exist for this example. Therefore, answer c is incorrect. Answer d uses an incorrect number for the partition element—this number never can be zero, as the first partition is defined by using the number one. Therefore, answer d is wrong. Answer e indicates a second drive controller that doesn't exist—the first drive on that controller, the system partition in this example, is on the first and only existing controller and on the second hard drive, so answer e is incorrect.

Question 19

Answers a, b, c, d, and e are correct. The Auto Detect capabilities of Windows NT Server only function in a single frame-type environment. If this is the case, then all of the frame types listed are correct.

Question 20

Answer c is correct. Processor: % Processor Time is used to see how busy the processor is. Anything over 80% might mean you need to replace the processor and add additional ones. System: Interrupts/Second doesn't provide information about the CPU. Therefore, answer a is incorrect. Checking the pages per second allows you to verify if the amount of RAM in your system is adequate. Therefore, answer b is incorrect. The Processor: Interrupts/Second indicates the level of hardware interrupts occurring, not the use level of the CPU. Therefore, answer d is incorrect.

Question 21

Answer c is correct. Of the three share permissions that pertain to the Project A share, Full Control is the most permissive, so that becomes his share permission. The NTFS permission is Change. The less permissive of Change and Full Control is Change, so the effective permission is Change. To calculate share and NTFS permissions combined, take the most permissive of each kind and then the least permissive of the remaining share and NTFS permissions. If No Access appears anywhere, the resulting permission always will be No Access.

Question 22

Answer c is correct. The key to answering this question is to understand GSNW and what must happen on the NetWare side of a connection that uses GSNW. In essence, GSNW provides a way to "translate" ordinary Microsoft Network client traffic bound for a Windows NT Server into a usable kind of NetWare equivalent. This prevents administrators from having to add software to network clients that need access to NetWare resources, which is especially useful on older machines (for example, those running Windows For Workgroups at the shelter) where memory and system resources already are at a premium. The correct answer to this question requires you to recognize that GSNW does the job, but it also requires you to know that it is necessary to set up a group account on the NetWare server to handle GSNW requests from the Windows NT Server.

Answer a is incorrect because it places the NetWare group on the Windows NT Server. Answer b is incorrect because it provides a way to make Windows NT services available to NetWare clients, not vice versa. Finally, answer d is incorrect because it puts the gateway on the NetWare server (a highly unlikely place to run a Windows NT service).

Question 23

Answer d is correct. The easiest approach to this kind of problem, be it caused by untoward edits to the Registry or installation of drivers or new system components, is to choose the LKGC (Last Known Good Configuration) option during bootup. Answers a and b may produce the same results eventually, but they're nowhere near as easy (and perhaps not as up-to-date as the LKGC). Answer c is flat wrong, because you can't boot from the ERD.

Question 24

Answer c is correct. To find out whether a backup was successful, you must check the Backup log in NTBACKUP. The User Manager For Domains is where most administration—such as adding users and changing their passwords—takes place for Windows NT. Backup is not affected directly by User Manager. Therefore, answer a is incorrect. Server Manager is for server administration, but you cannot check if a backup was successful. Therefore, answer b is incorrect. Configuration information for Windows NT lives in the Registry, but you wouldn't look there for successful backup information. Therefore, answer d is incorrect.

Question 25

Answers b and f are correct. The features from this list that require NTFS are file-level security and file-level compression. Both FAT and NTFS can be used on partitions larger than 250 MB, can be used in disk striping with parity configurations, and support long file names. Therefore, answers a, c, and e are incorrect. Updating the ERD is completely independent of file system type. Therefore, answer d is incorrect.

Question 26

Answers c and d are correct. In addition to CSNW, NWLink and a valid access account on the NetWare system are the only other requirements to interact with NetWare resources from a Windows NT Workstation system. GSNW could be used on a Windows NT Server to provide access to NetWare, but this was not within the parameters of the situation described in this question. Therefore, answer a is incorrect. File and Print Services for NetWare is used to grant NetWare clients access to Windows NT-hosted resources; however, this was not a requirement of the situation in this question. Therefore, answer b is incorrect. The NTGATEWAY group is only used in conjunction with GSNW, which was not part of the situation in this question. Therefore, answer e is incorrect.

Question 27

Answers a and b are correct. All print devices must use the same driver. Therefore, answer a is correct. To create a printer pool, all print devices must be connected to the same print server. Therefore, answer b also is correct. Answers c and d are both incorrect—you don't have to use the same port for multiple printer devices, and printers don't have to be in the same room.

Question 28

Answer d is correct. If frame types other than 802.2 are being used on a network, Manual Frame Type Detection must be enabled. Frame types belonging to each client must be added to the frame type configuration list on the NWLink IPX/SPX Properties dialog box.

Question 29

Answer b is correct. Answer b makes the switch with the simple change of a name and a password; it's fast and simple, which is why Microsoft recommends this approach. Creating a new account manually is both time-consuming and tedious. Because answer a is inefficient, it's clearly not the best way to do this. Answer c is a nice try, but you must use User Manager For Domains, not Server Manager, to make this change. Answer d will work and leaves the old account around in case the old programmer ever comes back. Although this process leaves the old account around for security auditing, it's Microsoft's current position that it is best to rename the account instead of keeping it around.

Question 30

Answer d is correct. For Windows NT to provide support for HP network interface print devices, you must install the DLC protocol to create a network attached port. PostScript printing has nothing to do with print device installation. Therefore, answer a is incorrect. You can't install a print driver if Windows NT can't recognize the print device. Therefore, answer b is incorrect. The print processor is not involved in the installation of printers. Therefore, answer c is also incorrect.

Question 31

Answer d is correct. By moving the profiles to a server, changing them to roaming, and configuring the user accounts to access the new storage location, the goal with be accomplished. A single network profile that retains the .DAT suffix will not give each user a familiar desktop setting; instead, it will cause desktop chaos because each user's changes will be saved. Therefore, answer a is incorrect. Changing all profiles from custom to mandatory will not establish roaming profiles and will prevent users from making any future changes to their profiles. Therefore, answer b is incorrect. Moving the profiles from the workstations to a server without changing them to roaming or editing the user accounts will not accomplish the goal, because accounts will not be pulled from the server and they will not be present on the workstations. Therefore, answer c is incorrect.

Question 32

Answer a is correct. The whole point of a gateway is to permit clients to access services that their current configurations otherwise would make inaccessible. For that reason, answer a is the only correct answer because it opens a gateway for the Windows NT and Windows 95 workstations to access NetWare resources with no change to their current configurations.

Answer b is incorrect. Adding NWLink to the workstations does not complete the task of connecting to the NetWare server. (Additional software would be necessary to make it possible for these machines to communicate with a NetWare server.) Answer c mentions the right software product, but puts it on a NetWare server rather than on a Windows NT Server, where it was designed to be run. And finally, File and Print Services For NetWare let native NetWare clients access Windows NT, not native Microsoft Networking clients access NetWare (thus completely missing the point of the question). Therefore, answer d is incorrect.

Question 33

Answer a is correct. With nonstandardized configurations implementing any encryption security other than Allow Any Authentication Including Clear Text, some clients are restricted from accessing the network via RAS. Microsoft Encrypted Authentication and Require Encrypted Authentication are encryption security schemes that require special configuration or operating systems. Therefore, answers b and d are incorrect. PGP Encryption is not a native option of Windows NT. Therefore, answer c is incorrect.

Question 34

Answer b is correct; this is a false statement. Because Windows NT 4 no longer supports HPFS, you'll have to obtain the ACLCONV utility from Microsoft to convert the HPFS partition into NTFS. For Windows NT 4, you can convert only FAT partitions into NTFS partitions. Because NT 3.51 will switch HPFS to NTFS, it might be even better to convert HPFS to NTFS before installing the upgrade to 4.

Question 35

Answer b is correct. The secret to answering this question lies in knowing how to "unpack" its contents and what values to assign based on the information it contains. Partitions are numbered cardinally, starting from one, so any correct answer must end in partition(4). This automatically disqualifies answer a.

Any SCSI hard disk with its onboard BIOS disabled must begin with the string scsi(*). This automatically disqualifies answer d. Likewise, if the scsi keyword begins an ARC name, the value for rdisk will always be zero; this disqualifies answer c.

By process of elimination, this means that b must be the right answer. When we unpack the question, we see that:

➤ The first SCSI controller with BIOS disabled translates into scsi(0).

➤ The SCSI Bus ID provides the value for disk(*) whenever the BIOS is disabled, which translates into disk(1).

➤ Because the BIOS is disabled, rdisk(*) is always rdisk(0).

➤ The value for partition equals its number on the drive, so partition(*) translates into partition(4).

Only answer b matches the entire string. Note that Bus IDs are numbered ordinally (starting with zero), but even without this piece of information the other selections were ruled out already.

Question 36

Answer d is correct. TCP/IP, NetBEUI, and NWLink can all be used over RAS. TCP/IP and NetBEUI, but not NWLink, is the restriction for the AutoDial feature, but not a limitation of RAS as a whole. Therefore, answer a is incorrect. TCP/IP and NWLink, but not NetBEUI, are the protocols that can be routed over RAS, but not a limitation as to which protocols can be used. Therefore, answer b is incorrect. Only TCP/IP can be used over SLIP, but RAS is not limited to SLIP. Therefore, answer c is incorrect.

Question 37

Answers a and b are correct. Gateway Services For NetWare must be installed on the Windows NT Server. For the Windows NT Server to communicate with the NetWare server, the NWLink protocol must be installed on the Windows NT Server. Therefore, answer b also is correct. When GSNW is installed, NWLink is automatically installed if it's not already present. CSNW is not used because there are no longer individual user accounts on the NetWare server. Therefore, answer c is incorrect. The SAP agent is not used when providing clients access to NetWare resources through Windows NT. Therefore, answer d is incorrect.

Question 38

Answer b is correct. The highest priority is 99. It is possible to set priorities for different groups of users by creating multiple logical printers for the same physical print device and setting different priority levels on each logical printer. To set printer priority, select the Scheduling tab in the Printer Properties dialog box. The lowest priority is 1. Therefore, answer a is incorrect. The start printing immediately setting will not give the executives print priority over others. It simply instructs the print server to print without waiting for the entire print job to be saved to the spooler. Therefore, answer c is incorrect. Printing directly to the printer will not offer print priority. It just instructs the print server to print without storing the print job to the spooler at all. Therefore, answer d is incorrect.

Question 39

Answers a and d are correct. Disk mirroring can contain the same system and/or boot partitions as the original disk. Disk duplexing can contain the system and/or boot partitions as the original disk. Disk striping without parity cannot contain the system or boot partitions, so answer b is incorrect. A volume set cannot contain the system or boot partitions, so answer c is incorrect.

Question 40

Answer c is correct. The steps in answer c will restore the mirror set properly, with the roles of the drives reversed. The steps in answer a cause you to perform many long and unnecessary steps—neither formatting the two drives nor restoring from tape backup is required, so answer a is incorrect.

Windows NT will not restore a mirror set automatically. Therefore, answer b is incorrect. The steps in answer d are used to repair a stripe set with parity. Therefore, answer d is incorrect.

Question 41

Answer a is correct. To perform a network installation of Windows NT on a computer running Windows 95, it's necessary to obtain access to and run the WINNT.EXE program with the /b switch. Both answers b and d refer to SETUP.EXE, which is the install program for Windows 3.x and Windows 95, not Windows NT (you must choose WINNT.EXE because it's the only version of the Windows NT installation program that works on non-Windows NT systems). Answer c is incorrect because it assumes that NCA includes support for installing Windows NT Workstation, which is not the case. Strictly speaking, using NCA to create a startup disk requires more effort to install Windows NT Workstation over Windows 95 than to launch WINNT.EXE from a share.

Question 42

Answers c and d are correct. The Windows NT Hardware Qualifier (NTHQ) disk may be constructed by running the MAKEDISK.BAT program in the \Support\Hqtool directory on the Windows NT CD-ROM. Because NTHQ checks the machine against a built-in version of the HCL, it will do the job (except on machines with hardware newer than August 1996, which the software may not recognize). But because the machine is older than NTHQ, NTHQ should work correctly. This makes answer c correct. The HCL is indeed the source of the latest information on what works with Windows NT, even though checking by hand is more work than using NTHQ. This will produce a correct assessment of the machine, making answer d correct as well. Windows NT Diagnostics aren't available until Windows NT is installed successfully on a machine, nor does the program perform hardware checking on its own; rather, it reports the contents of the Registry written by the NTDETECT.EXE program that runs at bootup. This means answer a is incorrect. System Sleuth is an old PC diagnostics program that doesn't perform Windows NT hardware compatibility checks of any kind, which makes answer b incorrect as well.

Question 43

Answers b and d are correct. Because the machine can recognize and use the CD-ROM while it's still running Windows 95, the easiest approach is to copy the files from the \i386 directory to a directory on the machine's hard disk. But this will work only if the drive is formatted to permit creation of another partition for NTFS or if the FAT partition where the files are deposited may be converted to NTFS later (see Chapter 3 for a discussion of FAT and NTFS). That's why b is correct. Answer d also is correct, because if the drives on the machine need to be reformatted completely—as often will be the case when upgrading from Windows 95 to Windows NT—it might be smarter to copy the installation files to a server and perform a network install. This leaves the drives on the machine free to be reformatted completely but will require a boot disk (that you might build using the Network Client Administrator).

Answer a is incorrect because the installation disks alone don't convey all the Windows NT installation files; there's still a need to gain access to the CD-ROM or a copy of its contents. Answer c is incorrect because the 16-bit installation program, WINNT.EXE, works with Windows 95; WINNT32.EXE works only with versions of Windows NT 3.5 and higher.

Question 44

Answers a, b, and e are correct. RAID 1 is disk mirroring that provides some fault tolerance. Therefore, answer a is correct. Disk duplexing is a fault-tolerant storage method. Therefore, answer b also is correct. RAID 5 is disk striping with parity that provides fault tolerance. Therefore, answer e is also correct. A volume set is not fault tolerant. Therefore, answer c is incorrect. Disk striping without parity is not fault tolerant, so answer d is incorrect.

Question 45

Answer a is correct. The fastest lookup time occurs when the HOSTS and LMHOSTS files are stored on the local hard drive of each RAS client because no WAN traffic needs to occur to resolve a resource location. The other options do not result in optimized lookup time. Therefore, answers b, c, and d are incorrect.

Question 46

Answer a is correct. FAT is the best choice because it requires much less overhead than NTFS, and Microsoft does not recommend NTFS on partitions smaller than 400 MB. CDFS is not a file system type that can be used to format a hard drive; it's the format of a CD-ROM. Therefore, answer b is incorrect. NTFS has too much overhead for a partition of this size. Therefore, answer c is incorrect. HPFS is not supported by Windows NT 4.0. Therefore, answer d is incorrect.

Question 47

Answer c is correct. A volume set will maximize your storage capacity and allow you to add additional space as needed. Disk mirroring will cut your storage capacity in half to implement fault tolerance, so answer a is incorrect. Disk striping with parity will reduce your storage capacity by one full drive to implement fault tolerance. Therefore, answer b is incorrect. Disk stacking is not a valid storage method for Windows NT, so answer d is incorrect.

Question 48

Answer b is correct. It accurately describes a network install scenario and cites the correct version of the install program, so it is correct. WINNT32.EXE works only with Windows NT, not with Windows 95; this disqualifies answer a. SETUP.EXE is not the name of a program used to install Windows NT, so answer c is incorrect. Likewise, answer d is incorrect because NETWORK.EXE will not perform a networked Windows NT installation.

Question 49

Answer c is correct. As with Question 35, the key is knowing how to "unpack" ARC names. Unless the BIOS is disabled on a SCSI controller, the initial keyword in an ARC name always is multi. Because there's no mention of BIOS in the question, this eliminates answers a and b immediately. The rest of the answer hinges on understanding that SCSI controllers are numbered ordinally, starting with zero. Because the primary must therefore be multi(0), this must change to multi(1); this makes c the only correct answer.

Question 50

Answer d is correct. Strictly speaking, upgrading from Windows For Workgroups (WFW) to Windows NT Server is not an installation option. But by installing Windows NT Server into the same directory in which WFW resides, the install program is smart enough to grab what information it can carry into the Windows NT environment by detecting and reading the WIN.INI and SYSTEM.INI files and converting program and group information into corresponding Windows NT Registry entries.

Answer a does not give the install program the implicit directive to convert the WFW .INI files and fails the "upgrade" requirement. Answer b apparently assumes that some magic import function for .INI files is available; because there isn't, this answer is incorrect. Finally, answer c provides the correct directory placement but calls the 32-bit version of the install program, which works only with Windows NT, not with WFW.

Question 51

The correct answers are a, b, and c. If users cannot log on to the machine across the network, they can't get to any partitions on that machine, whether FAT or NTFS. If a share is not defined where the confidential data resides, no user can obtain access to the data across the network. Finally, the user's share permissions must permit them at least to Read the data in that share, or they still won't be able to access it. The final element, d, is irrelevant because FAT partitions do not support file-level security—hence, they have no associated permissions.

Question 52

All answers—a, b, c, d, and e—are correct. Because a RAS-connected client is no different from a direct-connected client, other than speed of data transfer, all standard network activities still occur over the WAN link.

Question 53

Answer b is correct. Services for Macintosh requires an NTFS partition. FPNW is not required for Macintosh access. Therefore, answer a is incorrect. HPFS is not even supported by Windows NT 4.0. Therefore, answer c is incorrect. TCP/IP is not a required protocol for Macintosh clients; however, it is the protocol used most often in addition to AppleTalk. Therefore, answer d is incorrect.

Question 54

Answers a and b are correct. Only those computers running Windows NT Server (member servers and primary and backup domain controllers) can be configured to export files during replication. Windows NT Workstations and Windows 95 cannot be export servers. Therefore, answers c and d are incorrect.

Question 55

Answer c is correct. If an incorrect printer driver has been installed, then documents may print illegibly. A print job won't print at all if the wrong protocol is in use, so answer a is incorrect. Likewise, nothing will print without the spooler. Therefore, answer b is incorrect. As in answer b, a print job won't print without proper spooling. Therefore, answer d is incorrect.

Question 56

Answers b and c are correct. On a PDC, only the local domain name and any trusted domain names appear in the From pull-down box of the WinLogon dialog box. The username appears in the Username field by default, but this is not in the From pull-down list. Therefore, answer a is incorrect. The local computer name does not appear on a PDC as it does on a Windows NT Workstation. Therefore, answer d is incorrect. Hardware profile names appear at the beginning of bootup, not at the logon prompt. Therefore, answer e is incorrect.

Question 57

Answer b is correct. To grant NetWare clients access to SQL server hosted on a Windows NT Server system only requires that a common protocol be present, namely NWLink (the IPX/SPX-compatible protocol). GSNW is used to grant Windows NT clients access to NetWare resources. Therefore, answer a is incorrect. FPNW is required only to grant Windows NT file and printer access to NetWare clients. This does not apply to SQL Server access. Therefore, answer c is incorrect. There is no such service as Services for NetWare. Therefore, answer d is incorrect.

Question 58

Answer b is correct. This is a false statement. The Guest account on Windows NT Server is disabled by default.

Question 59

Answers a and e are correct. A PDC is the central authority for a domain. A BDC can be promoted to a PDC, but only while the PDC is still online. A BDC can only host the SAM database for a single domain—it is tied to a single PDC. Therefore, answer b is incorrect. There are no limits to the number of BDCs that can exist in a domain. The limitation of three applies to backup browsers. Therefore, answer c is incorrect. Only a single PDC can exist in a domain, but a network can be comprised of many domains. Therefore, answer d is incorrect.

Question 60

Answer c is correct. All clients must be manually reconfigured for the new domain. Synchronization will not update clients to the new domain. Therefore, answer a is incorrect. The IPCONFIG tool cannot perform domain update pushes. Therefore, answer b is incorrect. The network will not automatically update itself to the PDC. Therefore, answer d is incorrect.

Sample Test #2

See Chapter 14 for Sample Test #1 and pointers to help you develop a successful test-taking strategy, including how to choose proper answers, how to decode ambiguity, how to work within the Microsoft testing framework, how to decide what you need to memorize, and how to prepare for the test. In this chapter, we include another test on subject matter pertinent to Microsoft Exam 70-067:"Implementing and Supporting Microsoft Windows NT Server 4.0." After this chapter, you'll find the answer key to this test.

Also, remember that you can take adaptive practice exams on Windows NT Server 4 online at **www.coriolis.com/cip/c ore4rev/** to help you prepare even more. Good luck!

Question 1

Users are complaining that even after they change their Windows NT passwords, they are not correctly authenticated. You determine the need to force a domain synchronization of the SAM. What must you do to force a synchronization? [Check all correct answers]

❏ a. From the Computer menu, select Synchronize Entire Domain.

❏ b. Open Server Manager.

❏ c. Select the PDC.

❏ d. Select the BDC.

Question 2

Your BDC and PDC synchronization schedule generates excessive WAN traffic when replication occurs. You set the ReplicationGovernor value to try to increase performance; now, replication never occurs. What did you do wrong?

○ a. You set the ReplicationGovernor value too high.

○ b. You set the ReplicationGovernor value too low.

○ c. You set the ReplicationGovernor value to 0.

○ d. You set the ReplicationGovernor value to 100.

Question 3

What type of share is depicted with a $ after the share name?

○ a. Ghost

○ b. Hidden

○ c. UNC

○ d. $ is not legal in a share

Question 4

Pagefile.sys on your server has gotten larger than initially defined. What will be the result? [Check all correct answers]

❑ a.   Slower applications

❑ b.   Slower network I/O

❑ c.   Fragmented paging file

❑ d.   Increased performance

Question 5

If a RAID disk fails that is a member of a stripe set with parity, what will happen as a result? [Check all correct answers]

❑ a.   The system will crash.

❑ b.   As data is requested, it is regenerated in RAM.

❑ c.   As data is requested, requests are rejected if the data is on the failed drive.

❑ d.   System performance will slow.

Question 6

Which of the following would be considered a valid reason for using FAT instead of NTFS? [Check all correct answers]

❑ a.   Faster (lower overhead requirements) for smaller partitions

❑ b.   Ability to boot to DOS

❑ c.   Recoverability is of primary importance

❑ d.   Supports partitions over 4 GB

Question 7

In the event of a power failure, what UPS option would be checked if a set of instructions are to be completed before the system is shut down?

○ a. Execute Command File

○ b. Shut Down Command

○ c. Remote Execute File

○ d. Remote UPS Shutdown

Question 8

The Windows NT Server default print spooler runs at what priority?

○ a. 1

○ b. 9

○ c. 15

○ d. 31

Question 9

When a non-HCL CD-ROM drive is present on a computer, how can Windows NT Server be installed? [Check all correct answers]

❑ a. Boot to another OS with supported CD-ROM drivers. Copy the entire CD to the hard drive. Launch WINNT from the hard drive copy of the CD.

❑ b. Use the three boot floppies, and then use the S command to add drivers for the CD-ROM during the storage detection phase of setup.

❑ c. Boot to another OS with supported CD-ROM drivers. Launch WINNT from the CD.

❑ d. It cannot be accomplished without replacing the CD-ROM device.

Question 10

You have several clients who would like to dial into your RAS server. Some are running PPP and some are running SLIP and would rather not change to PPP. How can your Windows NT Server be configured for SLIP?

○ a. SLIP services are provided by the Resource Kit only and therefore must be purchased.

○ b. From the Network applet in the Control Panel, add the SLIP service.

○ c. Windows NT Server does not support inbound SLIP.

○ d. Windows NT Server will support SLIP or PPP for any connection; users should not have any problem connecting.

Question 11

Over time, your system seems to have become sluggish. To improve performance on your Windows NT Server, which of the following should be considered? [Check all correct answers]

❑ a. Use disk striping.

❑ b. Install faster hard disks.

❑ c. Install another disk controller.

❑ d. Rearrange file to balance disk access.

❑ e. Implement disk mirroring.

Question 12

Which of the following RAID levels are supported by Windows NT? [Check all correct answers]

❑ a. RAID 0

❑ b. RAID 1

❑ c. RAID 4

❑ d. RAID 5

Question 13

> The Power Users group appears on which installations of Windows NT? [Check all correct answers]
>
> ❑ a. Windows NT Server PDC
>
> ❑ b. Windows NT Server BDC
>
> ❑ c. Windows NT Server member server
>
> ❑ d. Windows NT Workstation

Question 14

> When implementing fault tolerance, which Windows NT methods can contain the boot partition? [Check all correct answers]
>
> ❑ a. Mirroring
>
> ❑ b. Stripe set
>
> ❑ c. Stripe set with parity
>
> ❑ d. Duplexing

Question 15

> Which of the following statements are true? [Check all correct answers]
>
> ❑ a. A PDC must be demoted to a BDC before the BDC is promoted.
>
> ❑ b. Promoting a BDC causes the existing PDC to be demoted.
>
> ❑ c. After a PDC goes offline, a BDC can be promoted.
>
> ❑ d. Two PDCs can function on the same network.

Question 16

What are the minimum hardware requirements for disk mirroring?

- ○ a.   2 hard drives and 2 disk controllers
- ○ b.   1 hard drive and 2 disk controllers
- ○ c.   2 hard drives and 1 disk controller
- ○ d.   1 hard drive and 1 disk controller

Question 17

You are installing a Windows NT Server in a NetWare environment using both 802.2 and 802.3 frame types. Which setting would be the best way to configure the NWLink protocol to ensure network functionality?

- ○ a.   Manually add both 802.2 and 802.3 frame types.
- ○ b.   Select Automatic Frame Type Detection.
- ○ c.   The 802.3 is backward compatible with 802.2, so manually install 802.3.
- ○ d.   The 802.3 is backward compatible with 802.2, so let the system automatically install 802.3.

Question 18

Which top-level Registry key houses the details for hardware profiles?

- ○ a.   HKEY_CLASSES_ROOT
- ○ b.   HKEY_USER
- ○ c.   HKEY_LOCAL_MACHINE
- ○ d.   HKEY_CURRENT_USER

Question 19

When copying files from an NTFS partition to a FAT partition on a Windows NT Server system, which of the following occur? [Check all correct answers]

❑ a. Long file names stay.

❑ b. Long file names are lost.

❑ c. Permissions are kept.

❑ d. Permissions are lost.

Question 20

You are using Performance Monitor to determine whether the sluggish system performance is due to a processor overload. Which of the following would indicate a processor bottleneck?

○ a. Processor: % Processor Time average over time is greater than 80%

○ b. Processor: % Processor Time peaks to over 80% randomly

○ c. Processor: % Processor Time drops below 80% randomly

○ d. Processor: % Processor Time is never over 80%

Question 21

Your Windows NT Server system has been locking up randomly. You are trying to determine whether the problem is caused by hardware failures such as I/O devices, disk controllers, and NICs. When using Performance Monitor, which counter should be monitored for these types of failures?

○ a. An increase in % Processor Time

○ b. A decrease in Interrupts/Second

○ c. An increase in network card Total Bytes/Sec

○ d. An increase in Interrupts/Second

Question 22

To install Windows NT onto a RISC system, which of the following must be present on that computer?

○ a. 4 GB of free space

○ b. A FAT partition

○ c. A 10BaseT NIC

○ d. Mouse

Question 23

Which of the following actions will result in a full backup of the Registry?

○ a. Stop the Server service.

○ b. Run a normal backup.

○ c. Run a differential backup.

○ d. Back up any part of the Registry.

Question 24

Which of the following client network startup disks are provided with the Windows NT Server 4.0 product CD-ROM? [Check all correct answers]

❏ a. Microsoft LAN Manager for OS/2

❏ b. Remote Access Service for DOS

❏ c. Microsoft TCP/IP 32 for Windows For Workgroups 3.11

❏ d. Microsoft Windows 95

❏ e. Microsoft Network Client 3.0 for MS-DOS and Windows

Question 25

> Your PDC experiences a drive failure and goes offline. You need to add three new user accounts to the network for visiting consultants. Which of the following processes will result in functioning network user accounts?
>
> ○ a. Promote the BDC, then add the user accounts using User Manager For Domains.
>
> ○ b. Install the administrative tools suite onto a client from the Windows NT Server 4.0 CD, and then use User Manager For Domains on that client to create the user accounts.
>
> ○ c. Create a logon script containing the appropriate NET USER commands to create the new accounts, add the script to the Administrator user account's configuration, and log in as Administrator to initiate the logon script.
>
> ○ d. Repair the PDC's failed drive, and then return the PDC to the domain. Add the user accounts using any copy of the User Manager For Domains in the domain.

Question 26

> You are trying to run a program on your Windows NT Workstation from a NetWare server over your RAS connection to a Windows NT Server on the same network. You have installed the NWLink compatible protocol at the remote computer, but still cannot connect to the NetWare Server. What is the problem? [Check all correct answers]
>
> ❑ a. You need to install FPNW on the RAS server.
>
> ❑ b. You need to install Gateway Services For NetWare on the RAS server.
>
> ❑ c. You need to install the Client Service for Netware on the remote Windows NT client.
>
> ❑ d. NetWare servers do not support NWLink over a RAS connection.

Question 27

> After you've installed Windows NT Server as a PDC, which user groups have the Logon Locally right? [Check all correct answers]
>
> ❏ a. Administrators
>
> ❏ b. Power Users
>
> ❏ c. Backup Operators
>
> ❏ d. Domain Users

Question 28

> You are running a network that has 50 NetWare clients communicating with a NetWare 3.12 server. You install a new Windows NT Server and would like to have your NetWare clients use the new Windows NT Server for printing and file storage services. Which product satisfies the requirement?
>
> ○ a. FPNW (File and Printer Services For NetWare) add-on product
>
> ○ b. GSNW (Gateway Service For NetWare)
>
> ○ c. CSNW (Client Service For NetWare)
>
> ○ d. NWLink (IPX/SPX compatible protocol)

Question 29

> Which methods can be implemented to install Windows NT Server on a computer that already has DOS installed? [Check all correct answers]
>
> ❏ a. Network
>
> ❏ b. Setup disks
>
> ❏ c. CD-ROM
>
> ❏ d. Tape
>
> ❏ e. Internet download

Question 30

You place an HP JetDirect print server on your network. When you go into Windows NT and try to configure the port for the JetDirect you do not see it on the list. What is the most likely problem?

- ○ a. The DLC protocol is not loaded.
- ○ b. NWLink is not loaded.
- ○ c. TCP/IP printing services is not installed.
- ○ d. The HP JetDirect is on the wrong side of the bridge.

Question 31

Which of the following statements are true regarding the process of a Windows NT system joining a domain?

- ○ a. An administrator's name and password are always required by the computer's user.
- ○ b. A domain account for the computer must be created.
- ○ c. Domain Services must be added on the Services tab of the Network applet.
- ○ d. Only providing the domain name on the Identification tab of the Network applet is required.

Question 32

Your network is configured as a single domain that has three domain controllers and 50 Windows NT Workstations. For security reasons, you assign roaming user mandatory profiles to all user accounts in the domain. The server on which the profiles are stored fails. What will happen when users attempt to log on to the domain while the server is shut down?

- ○ a. Users will log on successfully and will receive their profiles, but any changes made to the computer will be lost.
- ○ b. Users will not be able to log on to the domain.
- ○ c. Users can choose to log on to the domain and select a profile that is stored on a separate server.
- ○ d. Users will log on successfully and will receive the default user profile.

Question 33

You are administering a Windows NT Server with remote clients coming in through RAS. You are concerned about security but need to allow access to DOS clients using third-party PPP software. When configuring RAS, which option should be selected for authentication?

○ a. Allow Any Authentication Including Clear Text

○ b. Require Microsoft Encrypted Authentication

○ c. Allow Anonymous Authentication

○ d. Require MS-CHAP

Question 34

What command should be entered to convert your D: drive FAT partition to NTFS?

○ a. ntfs d:

○ b. convert d: /fs:ntfs

○ c. ntconv d: /fs:ntfs

○ d. convrt d: /fs:ntfs

Question 35

Which of the following are valid ARC names? [Check all correct answers]

❏ a. scsi(0)disk(1)rdisk(0)partition(1)\WINNT

❏ b. scsi(0)disk(1)rdisk(2)partition(1)\WINNT

❏ c. multi(0)disk(0)rdisk(2)partition(0)\WINNT

❏ d. multi(0)disk(0)rdisk(1)partition(1)\WINNT

Question 36

A user calls and says he is trying to connect to the network via the corporate Windows NT RAS server using NWLink. He says he has no problem connecting to the server but is unable to access any resources on the network. What could be the problem?

○ a. He is trying to connect to the network with a user ID that is only valid on the local machine.

○ b. NWLink does not support the RAS gateway.

○ c. The protocol he is using is configured for the local computer only and not the entire network.

○ d. The NIC used on the RAS server does not support ODI.

Question 37

You would like to use the Windows NT Migration Tool for NetWare to migrate your NetWare server to a Windows NT Server environment. You install NWLink and Gateway Service For NetWare on the Windows NT Server. You then create the NTGATEWAY account group and a migration user account on the NetWare server. Finally, you prepare an NTFS partition on the Windows NT Server. Which of the following items can be migrated by the Migration Tool with the above configuration? [Check all correct answers]

❑ a. NetWare files and directories

❑ b. NetWare volumes

❑ c. User and group accounts

❑ d. NetWare user passwords

Question 38

When you configure the Replicator service, you're asked to specify a logon account for the service. Why?

○ a. All services require a logon account to function under Windows NT.

○ b. The logon account establishes the security context for the service.

○ c. It allows you to audit the activity of the service.

○ d. It prevents the service from running at a priority higher than 13.

Question 39

Files are being systematically deleted from a BDC in the domain. As administrator, where would you go to set up event auditing?

○ a.   Start|Settings|Control Panel|Network|Audit

○ b.   Start|Administrative Tools (Common)|User Manager|Policies|Audit

○ c.   Start|Administrative Tools (Common)|User Manager|Policies|User Rights

○ d.   Start|Windows Explorer|Security|Auditing

○ e.   Start|Windows Explorer|Security|Permissions

Question 40

The spooler service performs which function in the Windows NT environment?

○ a.   It formats print jobs according to the installed printer drivers.

○ b.   It manages the distribution of printer drivers to network clients.

○ c.   It receives print jobs from the network, stores them to disk, and manages the output of print jobs to the physical print devices.

○ d.   There is not a spooler service in Windows NT.

Question 41

Which of the following items of information are preserved during a Windows NT 3.51 Server upgrade to Windows NT 4.0 Server? [Check all correct answers]

❏ a.   Local security accounts

❏ b.   Domain security accounts

❏ c.   Network settings

❏ d.   Custom Registry settings

Question 42

Your manager has changed the display adapter configuration on your Windows NT Server in order to play pinball in higher resolution. Unfortunately, he failed to do this correctly and now your display is misconfigured and the screen is garbled. What can you do to restore it with the least work? [Check all correct answers]

❑ a. Boot to VGA mode and reinstall display adapter driver.

❑ b. Reboot the server.

❑ c. Press Shift+Alt+D and select the correct display configuration from the list.

❑ d. As the computer reboots, select Last Known Good Configuration.

Question 43

Which of the following processors require a SCSI CD-ROM drive for installation?

○ a. RISC

○ b. Next

○ c. Intel

○ d. 80386

Question 44

Your Windows NT Server is configured with three logical drives: 800 MB, 900 MB, and 200 MB. You want to create a stripe set with parity. What is the largest RAID 5 array you can configure?

○ a. 600 MB

○ b. 400 MB

○ c. 1600 MB

○ d. You can't configure RAID 5 on logical drives

Question 45

Data transmitted between RAS clients must be encrypted according to your company's security policy. Which connection method can RAS clients use given this stipulation? [Check all correct answers]

❑ a. PPP

❑ b. SLIP

❑ c. PPTP

❑ d. X.25

❑ e. ISDN

Question 46

On a multi-boot computer, the C:\="MS-DOS" line in the BOOT.INI is used to boot the system; however, the system fails and an error stating "I/O Error accessing boot sector file" is displayed. Which of the following files is the most likely cause of the error?

○ a. NTLDR

○ b. BOOTSECT.DOS

○ c. BOOT.INI

○ d. NTDETECT.COM

Question 47

Which Performance Monitor feature can you use to have the system notify you when a certain threshold is reached?

○ a. Log view

○ b. Registry view

○ c. Chart view

○ d. Alert view

Question 48

Your director is taking an eight-week leave of absence. What is the most appropriate way to secure her account during her absence?

- ○ a. Delete the account and create a new account when she returns.
- ○ b. Remove her account from all groups during her absence.
- ○ c. Change the account name and password during her absence.
- ○ d. Disable the account during her absence.

Question 49

A Server Operator is performing monthly monitoring and notices that the number of Available Bytes in the memory monitoring object is consistently less than 1. What type of problem does this indicate?

- ○ a. Processor failure
- ○ b. Disk failure
- ○ c. Memory error
- ○ d. Excessive paging

Question 50

You need to make sweeping changes to all of the files on a Windows NT Server file server system. The changes involve removing two out-of-use user groups from the file permissions and adding various permissions for three newly created user groups. Which of the following actions will result in the most efficient implementation of this process?

○ a. Use My Computer to make the necessary changes one folder at a time.

○ b. Use the Find tool to locate all files with the .doc, .dat, and .xls extensions in the folders you wish to edit, select them all, then change the permissions via the Properties dialog box by right-clicking over the selected files.

○ c. Use the CACLS command in a batch file.

○ d. Use Server Manager to manipulate the file permissions via their shares.

Question 51

Which of the following items can be performed by the Windows NT Migration Tool for NetWare? [Check all correct answers]

❏ a. Transfer file and directory information from NetWare to Windows NT

❏ b. Transfer user and group information from NetWare to Windows NT

❏ c. Transfer user IDs and passwords from NetWare to Windows NT

❏ d. Maintain security between users and data to NTFS partitions

❏ e. Maintain security between users and data to FAT partitions

Question 52

Which of the following Registry entry changes would reduce domain controller synchronization traffic on a congested network? [Check all correct answers]

- ❑ a. Increase PulseMaximum
- ❑ b. Decrease PulseTimeout1
- ❑ c. Decrease ReplicationGovernor
- ❑ d. Decrease PulseConcurrency

Question 53

SCSI BIOS is not enabled. Which Windows NT system file is required?

- ○ a. SCSIBOOT.SYS
- ○ b. NTBOOTDD.SYS
- ○ c. BOOT.SYS
- ○ d. NTLDR.SYS

Question 54

As the network administrator, you would like to monitor TCP/IP traffic on four Windows NT 4 Servers from a Windows NT Workstation. What must be done first?

- ○ a. Load the Network Monitor.
- ○ b. Load the Windows NT Server SNMP agent.
- ○ c. Load the TCP/IP printing services.
- ○ d. Load the simple TCP/IP services.

Question 55

Which of the following statements about profiles are true? [Check all correct answers]

- ❑ a.   Multiple users can share a single mandatory profile.
- ❑ b.   Roaming profiles cannot be mandatory.
- ❑ c.   Roaming profiles are stored on a network share.
- ❑ d.   Roaming profiles are cached locally by default.

Question 56

You need to connect two 10BaseT networks, so you deploy a router and connect them. One network uses a star-star configuration and the other is a star-bus configuration. Both networks house only 16 devices: 3 Windows NT Servers and 13 Windows NT Workstations on each. And both networks only use NetBEUI. After you establish the connection, you discover that communications from either network are not reaching the other network. Why?

- ○ a.   Routers cannot be connected using 10BaseT.
- ○ b.   The total number of devices in a single NetBEUI network is exceeded.
- ○ c.   The topologies of the original networks are too different.
- ○ d.   NetBEUI is non routable.

Question 57

Which of the following file permission details are required to move a file from one folder on an NTFS partition to another folder on the same NTFS partition? [Check all correct answers]

- ❑ a.   Read
- ❑ b.   Write
- ❑ c.   Delete
- ❑ d.   Take Ownership

Question 58

To launch Windows NT on a RISC computer, which of the following files is required?

○ a. NTBOOTDD.SYS

○ b. BOOT.INI

○ c. OSLOADER.EXE

○ d. NTDETECT.COM

Question 59

After installing a new video driver, you system fails to boot and just shows the STOP error blue screen soon after the Boot Menu. What is the best first option to restore the system to an operational state?

○ a. Reinstall Windows NT.

○ b. Use the LKCG.

○ c. Boot to Safe Mode.

○ d. Replace the bad video driver with a standard driver from the distribution CD.

Question 60

When Windows NT boots, it automatically attempts to detect the state of the hardware to select a hardware profile if more than one hardware profile is present.

○ a. True

○ b. False

Answer Key #2

1.	a, b, c	21.	d	41.	a, b, c, d
2.	c	22.	b	42.	b, d
3.	b	23.	b	43.	a
4.	a, c	24.	d, e	44.	d
5.	b, d	25.	d	45.	a, c, d, e
6.	a, b	26.	b, c	46.	b
7.	a	27.	a, c	47.	d
8.	b	28.	a	48.	d
9.	a, c	29.	a, b, c	49.	d
10.	c	30.	a	50.	c
11.	a, b, c, d	31.	b	51.	a, b, d
12.	a, b, d	32.	d	52.	a, c
13.	c, d	33.	a	53.	b
14.	a, d	34.	b	54.	b
15.	b, d	35.	a, d	55.	a, c, d
16.	c	36.	c	56.	d
17.	a	37.	a, b, c	57.	b, c
18.	c	38.	b	58.	c
19.	a, d	39.	b	59.	b
20.	a	40.	c	60.	a

Question 1

Answers a, b, and c are correct. In Server Manager on the PDC, first select the PDC, then select Computer from the File menu, and then select Synchronize Entire Domain. This forces the PDC to send an update to all BDCs in the domain and synchronize the SAM. Selecting the BDC will only force that BDC to be updated rather than the entire domain. Therefore, answer d is incorrect.

Question 2

Answer c is correct. Setting the value to 0 would cause replication to never occur. The Registry key for ReplicationGovernor is 100% by default, so answers a and d are not reasonable because ReplicationGovernor can't be set higher than 100. Setting the value too low would impact the replication speed because ReplicationGovernor's value is a percentage of available bandwidth. Therefore, answer b is incorrect.

Question 3

Answer b is correct. The $ symbol is used to create a hidden share. By default, logical drive names are administratively shared as in C$. There is no such creature as a Ghost share, so answer a is incorrect. UNC (Universal Naming Convention) is the standard naming method for connecting to a network resource as in \\server_name\share_name. Therefore, answer c is incorrect. Because answer b is correct, answer d is incorrect.

Question 4

Answers a and c are correct. When a pagefile gets out of control, applications slow and the pagefile begins to fragment. Answers b and d are incorrect because network I/O is not affected and performance fails to improve during abnormal pagefile conditions.

Question 5

Answers b and d are correct. The purpose of RAID 5 is to survive a single disk failure. As data is requested, it is regenerated in memory. Therefore, answer b is correct. Because data is regenerated in RAM as it is requested, system performance will slow. Therefore, answer d is correct. During a disk failure condition, a RAID 5 system will continue operating. Therefore, answer a is incorrect. RAID 5 writes redundant information to another disk allowing a failure of one disk without causing a loss of system availability, so answer c is incorrect.

Question 6

Answers a and b are correct. If a partition is less then 400 MB, or if it is necessary to boot to DOS, FAT should be used. NTFS cannot be read when booting to DOS, so b is also a reasonable answer. Answer c is not a valid reason for using the FAT system because it boasts no fault tolerant features. FAT supports partitions up to 4 GB, thus larger partitions cannot host FAT. Therefore, answer d is incorrect.

Question 7

Answer a is correct. Choosing the Execute Command File option executes a command immediately before the operating system is shut down. The executed command has 30 seconds to complete. Answer b is incorrect because the system is already being shut down. There is no option to remote execute a file, so answer c is incorrect. There is never a case for shutting down a UPS remotely. Therefore, answer d is incorrect.

Question 8

Answer b is correct. The default priority level for applications launched on Windows NT is 9, or normal. Because the default setting is 9, answers a, c, and d are incorrect.

Question 9

Answers a and c are correct. Booting to an alternate OS with supported CD-ROM drivers offers you the ability to either manually copy the CD to the hard drive before launching WINNT or launching WINNT from the CD itself. However, in the latter case, you may need to indicate to copy all files before rebooting. If the CD-ROM device is not listed on the HCL, it most likely will not function properly—even if drivers are installed during the setup initialization. Therefore, answer b is incorrect. Because it's possible to launch the installation with an alternate OS, answer d is incorrect.

Question 10

Answer c is correct. Windows NT Server does not support the SLIP protocol for inbound connections. Dial-Up Networking clients can utilize either PPP or SLIP on outbound connections. However, the protocol is determined by the type of server to which the client is connecting. Inbound support for SLIP is not available on the Resource Kit. Therefore, answer a is incorrect. The Network applet does not offer support for inbound SLIP. Therefore, answer b is incorrect. Windows NT supports SLIP for outbound connections only. Therefore, answer d is incorrect.

Question 11

Answers a, b, c, and d are correct. There are several ways to improve performance on a Windows NT Server: Use disk striping instead of disk mirroring; install an additional disk controller (disk duplexing); install faster hard disks; or rearrange files to balance disk access. Of the available answers, disk mirroring will slow the system because data must be simultaneously written to multiple disks. Therefore, answer e is incorrect.

Question 12

Answers a, b, and d are correct. Microsoft supports RAID 0 (stripe set without parity), RAID 1 (mirroring and duplexing), and RAID 5 (stripe sets with parity). RAID 4 is not supported. Therefore, answer c is incorrect.

Question 13

Answers c and d are correct. The Power Users group appears on Windows NT Server member servers and Windows NT Workstation systems. It does not appear on PDCs or BDCs. Therefore, answers a and b are incorrect.

Question 14

Answers a and d are correct. Both mirroring and duplexing can contain the boot partition. The boot and system partitions cannot be part of any type of stripe set. Therefore, answers b and c are incorrect.

Question 15

Answers b and d are correct. Promoting a BDC causes the existing PDC to be demoted. This is the proper procedure to take before taking the original PDC system offline for repairs. Because a network can host multiple domains, multiple PDCs can function on one network. However, only a single PDC can function in a domain. No option to demote a PDC exists unless two PDCs are somehow brought online in the same domain, thus it is not possible. Plus, promoting a BDC causes the existing PDC to be demoted. Therefore, answer a is incorrect. If a PDC is offline, a BDC cannot be promoted. Part of the promotion process involved a domain synchronization that requires the PDC. Therefore, answer c is incorrect.

Question 16

Answer c is correct. Mirroring hard disks is the process of simultaneously writing data to two hard disks from a single controller. Two hard drives and two controllers are considered duplexed, not mirrored. Therefore, answer a is incorrect. You cannot achieve disk mirroring from a single disk. Therefore, answers b and d are incorrect.

Question 17

Answer a is correct. The best way to handle this situation would be to add both frame types manually in NWLink. When a network environment has two frame types, you cannot use the Automatic Frame Type Detection setting. Therefore, answer b is incorrect. The 802.3 and 802.2 frame types are not compatible. Therefore, answers c and d are incorrect.

Question 18

Answer c is correct. The HKEY_LOCAL_MACHINE key contains the hardware profile details in the Registry. The other keys do not contain this information. Therefore, answers a, b, and d are incorrect.

Question 19

Answers a and d are correct. Long file names are dependent on the operating system rather than the format of the disks. FAT under Windows NT supports LFNs. Therefore, answer a is correct. File-level permissions are not supported by FAT volumes. Therefore, answer d is correct. Because answer a is correct, answer b is incorrect. FAT volumes do not have the level of security offered by NTFS. Therefore, answer c incorrect.

Question 20

Answer a is correct. If the Processor: % Processor Time counter is consistently over 80%, the processor is the bottleneck of the system and should be upgraded. Occasional peaks above 80% are normal and no cause for alarm, making answer b incorrect. Answer c is not a reasonable answer and therefore incorrect. Answer d is the most desirable condition, and consequently not the correct answer.

Question 21

Answer d is correct. The Processor: Interrupts/Sec measures the rate of service requests from I/O devices. A large increase in the counter without a corresponding increase in system activity indicates a hardware problem. An increase in % Processor Time can be attributed to many things and is not indicative of server lockups. Therefore, answer a is incorrect. A decrease in Interrupts/Sec is a good thing, making answer b incorrect. An increase in network Total Bytes/Sec without corresponding system activity increases is of little concern. Therefore, answer c is incorrect.

Question 22

Answer b is correct. A RISC system requires a FAT partition to host the system partition. 4 GB of free space, a 10BaseT NIC, and a mouse are not required to install Windows NT on a RISC system. Therefore, answers a, c, and d are incorrect.

Question 23

Answer b is correct. Backing up the Registry is done as part of a normal system backup. The easiest way to back up the Registry is to do a Normal Backup and select the Backup Local Registry checkbox. Stopping the Server service has no impact on backing up the Registry. Therefore, answer a is incorrect. Differential backups don't allow backing up the Registry. Therefore, answer c is incorrect. Backing up of part of the Registry doesn't back up the entire Registry, making answer d incorrect.

Question 24

Answers d and e are correct. The only two client network startup disks provided with Windows NT Server CD are Windows 95 and DOS as network installation startup disks. The other three options are add-on packages for OS/2, DOS, and Windows for Workgroups, which are not related to network startup. Therefore, answers a, b, and c are incorrect.

Question 25

Answer d is correct. Returning the PDC to the domain is the only way to enable changes or additions to the SAM database. Once the PDC is present, any User Manager For Domains utility can be used to create new user accounts. The BDC cannot be promoted if the PDC is offline. Therefore, answer a is incorrect. The administrative tools are useless without a PDC to accept changes to the SAM database. Therefore, answer c is incorrect. Without a PDC no changes can be made to the SAM database, including adding new logon scripts to a user's account (even the administrator account) and creating new accounts using a script. Under normal circumstances, a script can be used to create new user accounts. Therefore, answer c is incorrect.

Question 26

Answers b and c are correct. To access programs on a NetWare server, the Client Service For NetWare (CSNW) and NWLink must be installed on the workstation, or GSNW must be installed on the RAS server. File and Print Services for NetWare is used to grant NetWare clients access to Windows NT resources; it would not impact connections in this situation. Therefore, answer a is incorrect. NetWare servers don't see how a client is connected whether over a RAS connection, a satellite, or a direct connection. Therefore, answer d is incorrect.

Question 27

Answers a and c are correct. Administrators and Backup Operators, along with Server Operators, have the Logon Locally user right by default on Windows NT Server systems. The Power Users group only appears on Windows NT Server when it's a member server, not when it's a domain controller. Therefore, answer b is incorrect. Domain Users do not have the Logon Locally user right for Windows NT Servers by default. Therefore, answer d is incorrect.

Question 28

Answer a is correct. FPNW makes a Windows NT Server look like a Novell NetWare 3.12 server to NetWare clients allowing the clients to perform normal printing. Answers b, c, and d are all associated with connections rather than printing, making those answers incorrect.

Question 29

Answers a, b, and c are correct. Windows NT Server can be installed onto a computer with DOS present via the network (assuming a network connection exists or can be established), using the three setup floppies in combination with the CD, or by launching WINNT from the CD directly. Windows NT cannot be restored from tape to perform an install, nor can it be downloaded from the Internet (at least not legally). Therefore, answers d and e are incorrect.

Question 30

Answer a is correct. DLC is used as an interface for accessing printers directly connected to the network. NWLink is not associated with printer communication, so answer b is incorrect. TCP/IP printing services is a reasonable answer, but HP JetDirect print devices use DLC protocol, making c incorrect. A bridge is a connection device and would not prevent data from reaching its destination, so d is incorrect.

Question 31

Answer b is correct. A computer account must be created for the system to join the domain. This computer account can either be created by an administrator beforehand or it can be created by providing the username and password of an administrator when the joining process is attempted. The computer user only needs to know the administrator name and password if a computer account does not already exist for the system. Therefore, answer a is incorrect. There is no such item as Domain Services to be installed from the Services tab of the Network applet. Therefore, answer c is incorrect. Providing only the domain name on the Identification tab of the Network applet will only work if a computer account already exists in the domain; otherwise, a computer account will need to be created. Thus, just changing the domain name is not enough. A computer account must exist for the computer. Therefore, answer d is incorrect.

Question 32

Answer d is correct. Users will receive the default user profile for the work-station because their normal mandatory profiles are not available. The best idea is to replicate profiles, but that strategy was not in place. Mandatory profiles simply mean that a user cannot change his or her settings. Because the profiles are lost, the users will not receive them at logon. Therefore, answer a is incorrect. Users will still be able to log in, making answer b incorrect. Users cannot select a profile on login, making answer c incorrect. To prevent a user from logging on when his or her mandatory profile is not available, change the path of the user's profile from …\Profiles\<username> to …\Profiles\<username>.man. (Be sure to make the change via the User Manager as well.)

Question 33

Answer a is correct. Non-Microsoft clients can't use Microsoft Encrypted Authentication, so Allow Any Authentication Including Clear Text must be used. Answers b and d are the same and incorrect. (MS-CHAP is Microsoft Challenge Handshake Authentication Protocol, which is Microsoft Encrypted Authentication.) Answer c is incorrect because anony-mous access is in direct conflict with your requirement for security.

Question 34

Answer b is correct. To convert your D: drive FAT partition to NTFS, type convert d: /fs:ntfs and press Enter. NTFS D: will result in an error because NTFS is not a command. Therefore, answer a is incorrect. Answers b and d are close. Notice that answer d is convrt; that is incorrect. There is also no command called ntconv, making answer c incorrect.

Question 35

Answers a and d are correct. Answers a and d are valid ARC names. When ARC names start with scsi(0), rdisk will be set to 0; this eliminates answer b. Partition can never be 0; this eliminates answer c.

Question 36

Answer c is correct. When trying to access resources on the network, verify that Entire Network is selected in the RAS Server IPX Configuration dia-log box, which is the problem here. Once connected to the network, a single logon permits access to any available resource, making answer a incorrect. RAS supports TCP/IP and RAS, making answer b incorrect. The Network Configuration dialog box is used to configure protocols. ODI is not a protocol. Therefore, answer d is incorrect.

Question 37

Answers a, b, and c are correct. The Windows NT Migration Tool for NetWare supports all the listed answers with the exception of passwords. Passwords for users must be newly created in the new Windows NT environment. Therefore, answer d is incorrect.

Question 38

Answer b is correct. The logon account establishes the security context for the service. All services do not require a logon account. Therefore, answer a is incorrect. Auditing of service activity is not dictated by its logon account. Therefore, answer c is incorrect. A logon account does not restrict the execution priority of a service below 13. Therefore, answer d is incorrect.

Question 39

Answer b is correct. The auditing section permits setup of auditing success and failure events for logon/logoff, file and object access, user/group management, and others. There is no Audit tab on the Network applet in Control Panel, making answer a incorrect. User Rights does not permit setting auditing events. Therefore, answer c is incorrect. No Security item exists under Windows Explorer. Therefore, answers d and e are incorrect.

Question 40

Answer c is correct. The spooler receives print jobs from the network, stores them to disk, and manages the output of print jobs to the physical print devices. The spooler does not format print jobs. Therefore, answer a is incorrect. The spooler does not manage printer driver distribution. Therefore, answer b is incorrect. The spooler service is an integral part of the printing subsystem of Windows NT. Therefore, answer d is incorrect.

Question 41

Answers a, b, c, and d are all correct. Luckily, all of the listed settings are maintained during an upgrade of Windows NT.

Question 42

Answers b and d are correct. Rebooting and selecting Last Known Good Configuration restores the previous settings and corrects the display with the least effort. Although answer a may seem reasonable, reinstalling the video driver will not necessarily restore the previous screen resolution and is considerably more work that booting with the LKGC. Therefore, answer a is incorrect. There's no Shift+Alt+D keystroke used to select video display configurations. Therefore, answer c is incorrect.

Question 43

Answer a is correct. A CD-ROM drive is required when installing Windows NT Server on a RISC computer. Windows NT cannot be installed without it. There is no version of Windows NT for the Next computer, so answer b is incorrect. Intel processors allow installation from a CD, a local directory, or over a network, making answer c incorrect. Windows NT requires a 486 processor installation, making answer d incorrect.

Question 44

Answer d is correct. A stripe set can only be configured over physical drives, not logical drives. Logical drives live on the same hard disk. Therefore, answer d is the only correct answer.

Question 45

Answers a, c, d, and e are correct. PPP supports MS-CHAP, which can require data encryption. Therefore, answer a is correct. PPTP encrypts all data. Therefore, answer c is correct. X.25 and ISDN both support PPP and PPTP connections. Therefore, answers d and e are correct. SLIP does not support data encryption. Therefore, answer b is incorrect.

Question 46

Answer b is correct. The BOOTSECT.DOS file is required to boot to DOS on multi-boot systems with Windows NT. If this file is missing or corrupt, the "I/O Error accessing boot sector file" message is displayed. The other files, whether missing or corrupt, would not cause this error message. Therefore, answers a, c, and d are incorrect.

Question 47

Answer d is correct. The Alert view is used to inform when monitored counters cross a custom-defined threshold. The Log view allows you to save data for perusal at a later date. Therefore, answer a is incorrect. There is no such thing as the Registry view. Therefore, answer b is incorrect. The Chart view allows you to view current activity, but not to schedule notification at certain threshold levels. Therefore, answer c is incorrect.

Question 48

Answer d is correct. Disabling the account is the most secure and requires the least amount of work. Deleting and re-creating the account provides security, but generates unnecessary work in account re-creation. Re-creating the account does not use the same SID. The security identifier is unique and never reused. So, although the account would look the same, it is not. You would then be forced to go back and add her again to all the original groups of which she was a member. Therefore, answer a is incorrect. Answer b is incorrect because it still leaves the account open and forces you to add her back to groups. Answer c still leaves the account open to hacking and is incorrect.

Question 49

Answer d is correct. Available Bytes is the measure of virtual memory available. If this counter is consistently less than one, memory from other applications is used, causing excessive paging. Processor failure or overuse would not affect available bytes, making answer a incorrect. Disk failures prevent data from being read rather than impacting virtual memory, so answer b is incorrect. Although a memory error is possible, it is not the most likely candidate based on the choices, making answer c incorrect as well.

Question 50

Answer c is correct. The CACLS command in a batch file is the most efficient method to perform sweeping file permission changes. Using My Computer to change lots of file permissions is a time consuming process. Therefore, answer a is incorrect. Using the Find tool to create a list of files to alter permissions is a functional possibility, but is not the most efficient method to accomplish the desired task. Additionally, the .doc, .dat, and .xls are most likely not all of the file types that require file permission alterations and this does not include their container folders. Therefore, answer b is incorrect. The Server Manager cannot be used to manipulate file permissions, especially via shares. Therefore, answer d is incorrect.

Question 51

Answers a, b, and d are correct. The Windows NT Migration Tool for NetWare is launched by running nwconv.exe. This allows you to transfer file and directory information as well as user and group information from NetWare to Windows NT, making answers a and b correct. Although user accounts are transferred, passwords cannot be transferred, making answer c incorrect. Security is maintained if the destination partition is NTFS, making answer d correct and answer e incorrect.

Question 52

Answers a and c are correct. Increasing PulseMaximum lowers the number of mandatory database replications that must occur in a given time period. This helps reduce traffic levels. Therefore, answer a is correct. Decreasing ReplicationGovernor decreases both the size of the data blocks transferred and the frequency of data transferred. This value shouldn't be set too low, or replication can't complete; lowering it will lower replication-related traffic. Therefore, answer c is correct. Decreasing PulseTimeout1 lowers the threshold at which a BDC is treated as nonresponsive by the PDC, and makes the network subject to increased replication traffic. Therefore, answer b is incorrect. Decreasing PulseConcurrency decreases the number of BDCs that the PDC attempts to update in a single pulse interval. This, too, lowers replication related traffic. Therefore, answer d is correct.

Question 53

Answer b is correct. If a SCSI BIOS is not enabled, NTBOOTDD.SYS must be in the root folder of the system partition, making b the only correct answer.

Question 54

Answer b is correct. The Simple Network Management Protocol (SNMP) agent must be loaded to monitor TCP/IP traffic. SNMP must be installed on the four servers. Network Monitor provides monitoring of a single IP address at a time, making answer a incorrect. TCP/IP printing services furnishes TCP/IP printing, not monitoring, so answer c is incorrect. Simple TCP/IP does not provide monitoring. Therefore, answer d is also incorrect.

Question 55

Answers a, c, and d are correct. Roaming profiles can be made mandatory simply by renaming the NTUSER.DAT file to NTUSER.MAN file. Therefore, answer b is incorrect.

Question 56

Answer d is correct. NetBEUI is a nonroutable protocol. A bridge or a gateway would need to be used to connect these two networks. Routers are often connected to networks using 10BaseT. In fact, routers are designed with a specific cabling media in mind. The only problems with one media form over another may occur if a router is obtained that does not have the proper connection ports. Therefore, answer a is incorrect. A NetBEUI network can host 256 devices. With only 32 total devices on both networks in this scenario, the maximum device limit is not exceeded. Therefore, answer b is incorrect. The topologies of star-star and star-bus are not so dissimilar that any special accommodations must be made to connect them together with a router. Therefore, answer c is incorrect.

Question 57

Answers b and c are correct. To move a file from one folder to another requires the Add permission to create the new file and the Delete permission to remove the original file. In reality, a move within the same partition is effectively only a pointer change in the file mapping structure for the drive. However, to preserve security, both the Add and Delete permissions must be present for the operation to complete successfully. Read permission is not required to move a file. Therefore, answer a is incorrect. Take Ownership permission is not required to move a file. Therefore, answer d is incorrect.

Question 58

Answer c is correct. OSLOADER.EXE is required on RISC system to launch Windows NT. It takes on the responsibilities of many files typically found on Intel systems for launching Windows NT. The other files are not ever found on a RISC system. Therefore, answers a, b, and d are incorrect.

Question 59

Answer b is correct. The best first step is to use the LKCG to restore the system settings to the state of the last successful logon. Reinstalling Windows NT is not the best first step nor is it always required for video driver problems. Therefore, answer a is incorrect. There is not a Safe Mode boot option for Windows NT. Therefore, answer c is incorrect. Booting into VGA Mode may be a useful alternative, but that is not listed as a selection in this question. You will not be able to replace the bad video driver until you can boot into Windows NT, which requires some action such as using the LKGC or VGA Mode first. Therefore, answer d is incorrect.

Question 60

Answer a is correct. This is a true statement.

Scenarios

Scenario 1

Suppose the following situation exists:

Your network has three BDCs to help spread the workload and prevent the PDC from becoming overloaded. A power fluctuation causes the PDC to go offline.

Required result:

- Add four new user accounts to the domain.

Optional desired results:

- Define roaming profiles for the new accounts.
- Force the users to change their passwords on the next logon.

Proposed solution:

- Create the new user accounts with an instance of the User Manager For Domains.
- Define a profile path for each user while configuring the user accounts.
- Select the User Must Change Password At Next Logon checkbox on each account.

(continued)

Scenario 1 *(continued)*

Which results does the proposed solution produce?

○ a. The proposed solution produces the required result and produces both of the optional desired results.

○ b. The proposed solution produces the required result and produces only one of the optional desired results.

○ c. The proposed solution produces the required result but does not produce any of the optional desired results.

○ d. The proposed solution does not produce the required result.

The correct answer is d. Without a PDC, no changes to the SAM database of a domain can occur; thus, new user accounts cannot be created. The best solution for this situation would be to temporarily promote a BDC to a PDC while repairs are made to the original PDC and it is brought back online.

Scenario 2

Suppose the following situation exists:

The system administrator for your network has been hired by a competitor. You replaced her with an employee from hardware management who is capable enough to fulfill the responsibilities of a system administrator with only minor additional training.

Required result:

• Grant the new system administrator the same access privileges as the previous system administrator.

Optional desired results:

• Prevent the old system administrator from reusing her access privileges.

• Keep enough data around to support a system-wide security audit.

Proposed solution:

• Delete the original system administrator account.

• Create a new user account for the new system administrator. Configure the new account with the same group memberships as the previous system administrator account.

(continued)

Scenario 2 *(continued)*

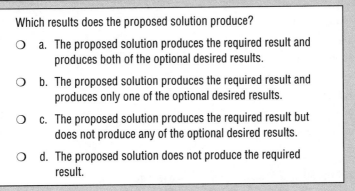

Which results does the proposed solution produce?

- ○   a.   The proposed solution produces the required result and produces both of the optional desired results.
- ○   b.   The proposed solution produces the required result and produces only one of the optional desired results.
- ○   c.   The proposed solution produces the required result but does not produce any of the optional desired results.
- ○   d.   The proposed solution does not produce the required result.

The correct answer is d. Deleting the original account prevents you from duplicating its settings for the new system administrator account; therefore, you're unable to grant the same access privileges. Disabling the original system administrator's account and using it as a template to create the new user account, or renaming the account and setting a new password, are both valid alternatives to deletion. Each option grants the new system administrator the exact same access privileges and prevents the old administrator from using the account to regain access. The only way to retain data for a security audit is to disable the account rather than delete or rename it.

Scenario 3

Suppose the following situation exists:

You need to install Windows NT Server onto three computers. One will become a BDC, and the other two will become member servers.

Required result:

- •   Automate the installation of all three servers.

Optional desired results:

- •   Ensure the names used on the new computers comply with the existing naming scheme.
- •   Create a drive mirror for the system partition on each system.

(continued)

Scenario 3 *(continued)*

Proposed solution:

- Install Windows NT Server onto each computer using the three boot floppies method, one at a time.

- Connect each system to the network after the installation is complete.

- Use Disk Administrator to create a mirror set using the system partition as the source drive.

Which results does the proposed solution produce?

○ a. The proposed solution produces the required result and produces both of the optional desired results.

○ b. The proposed solution produces the required result and produces only one of the optional desired results.

○ c. The proposed solution produces the required result but does not produce any of the optional desired results.

○ d. The proposed solution does not produce the required result.

The correct answer is d. The proposed solution does not automate the installation of Windows NT Server, plus a BDC cannot be installed without being attached to the network while the installation is being performed. A better solution for this situation would be to attach all the computers to the network, create a network boot disk to launch the installation from a network share, and employ unattend and udf files to automate the installation process.

Scenario 4

Suppose the following situation exists:

You've recently purchased a high-end computer with Windows 95 already installed. You've been using the system as your desktop for a few weeks, but now you need to transform this system into a Windows NT Server member server for your domain.

Required result:

- Perform the upgrade to a Windows NT Server member server.

Optional desired results:

- Retain the Start menu configuration.

- Retain the local user account.

Proposed solution:

- Install Windows NT Server into the same directory as Windows 95.

Which results does the proposed solution produce?

- ○   a. The proposed solution produces the required result and produces both of the optional desired results.

- ○   b. The proposed solution produces the required result and produces only one of the optional desired results.

- ○   c. The proposed solution produces the required result but does not produce any of the optional desired results.

- ○   d. The proposed solution does not produce the required result.

The correct answer is b. Installing Windows NT Server into the same directory as Windows 95 is the best way to retain as much of the original configuration as possible, but this procedure is not a true upgrade path. The installation routine retains some of the configuration of Windows 95, but because of their dissimilarities, there will be more changes than you might initially expect. The layout of the Start menu will be retained, with many new additions. So, the proposed solution satisfies the required result and one of the optional desired results. The installation process does not retain local user accounts from Windows 95. Therefore, the second optional desired result is not fulfilled.

Scenario 5

Suppose the following situation exists:

Your Windows NT Server 3.51 PDC is scheduled to be migrated to Windows NT Server 4 to comply with company standards.

Required result:

- Perform an upgrade install of Windows NT Server 4.

Optional desired results:

- Repair the Registry where manual changes where made.
- Retain all users and groups.

Proposed solution:

- Launch WINNT32.EXE /b from a network share. Select to install Windows NT Server 4 into the same directory used by Windows NT Server 3.51.

Which results does the proposed solution produce?

- ○ a. The proposed solution produces the required result and produces both of the optional desired results.
- ○ b. The proposed solution produces the required result and produces only one of the optional desired results.
- ○ c. The proposed solution produces the required result but does not produce any of the optional desired results.
- ○ d. The proposed solution does not produce the required result.

The correct answer is b. Upgrading from Windows NT 3.51 to 4 is the smoothest upgrade path available for Windows NT Server. The launching of WINNT32 /b from a network share allows a complete upgrade of the system. This process retains users and groups. However, the upgrade process does not alter manual Registry edits (that is, all changes will be retained). Therefore, the proposed solution fulfills the required result and only one of the optional desired results.

Scenario 6

Suppose the following situation exists:

A Windows 95 system hosts a CD-ROM drive that functions perfectly under Windows 95 but is not compatible with Windows NT. This computer is attached to the network. It will be used as a test platform for new Windows NT Server software before being deployed on production Windows NT Server systems.

Required result:

- Install Windows NT Server onto the system.

Optional desired results:

- Configure the system to dual boot between Windows 95 and Windows NT Server.

- Provide a method or mechanism for installing CD-ROM applications onto Windows NT Server after the installation is complete.

Proposed solution:

- Boot to Windows 95.

- Copy the contents of the \i386 directory to the hard drive.

- Launch WINNT /b from the \i386 copy.

- Instruct the setup routine to install Windows NT Server into \WINNT instead of \Windows.

- After the setup is complete, delete \i386 directory.

Which results does the proposed solution produce?

- ○ a. The proposed solution produces the required result and produces both of the optional desired results.

- ○ b. The proposed solution produces the required result and produces only one of the optional desired results.

- ○ c. The proposed solution produces the required result but does not produce any of the optional desired results.

- ○ d. The proposed solution does not produce the required result.

The correct answer is a. Copying the \i386 directory to the hard drive enables the installation of Windows NT Server to complete successfully in spite of the non-Windows NT CD-ROM drive. Directing the installation routine to an alternate directory will cause the installation to establish a dual boot on the computer between Windows 95 and Windows NT. By leaving Windows 95 intact, two methods of installing software onto Windows NT from CD-ROM exist. One method is to copy the installation files from CD to the hard drive and then boot into Windows NT before launching the setup routine. The other method is to share the application CD-ROM from a CD-ROM drive elsewhere on the network and then use Windows NT to access that share. The proposed solution satisfies the required result and both optional desired results.

Scenario 7

Suppose the following situation exists:

You need to create a shared folder to store documents for access over the network. You install a new hard drive on a Windows NT Server system. You create a 4 GB partition.

Required result:

*   Create a share to host 4 GB of data.

Optional desired results:

*   Track usage of the share.

*   Allow for file-level security of the share.

Proposed solution:

*   Format the share with FAT.

*   Share the formatted partition.

*   Enable auditing success and failure of File and Object Access. Turn on auditing for the share for all reads and writes.

Which results does the proposed solution produce?

○   a. The proposed solution produces the required result and produces both of the optional desired results.

○   b. The proposed solution produces the required result and produces only one of the optional desired results.

○   c. The proposed solution produces the required result but does not produce any of the optional desired results.

○   d. The proposed solution does not produce the required result.

The correct answer is c. The proposed solution creates a share that can be used to store 4 GB of data. But because it's formatted with FAT, it cannot offer audit tracking or file-level security. Therefore, only the required result is fulfilled.

Scenario 8

Suppose the following situation exists:

You're configuring a Windows NT Server to support several types of applications.

Required result:

- Native support for OS/2, POSIX, and Macintosh files must be fully enabled.

Optional desired results:

- Allow for file-level compression.

- Allow long file names.

Proposed solution:

- Format at least one drive with NTFS.

Which results does the proposed solution produce?

- ○ a. The proposed solution produces the required result and produces both of the optional desired results.

- ○ b. The proposed solution produces the required result and produces only one of the optional desired results.

- ○ c. The proposed solution produces the required result but does not produce any of the optional desired results.

- ○ d. The proposed solution does not produce the required result.

The correct answer is a. The proposed solution of formatting a volume with NTFS provides support for POSIX file system, hosting of a Macintosh volume, supports OS/2 extended attributes, and supports file-level compression and long file names. Therefore, the proposed solution produces the required result and both of the optional desired results.

Scenario 9

Suppose the following situation exists:

You need to impose fault tolerance on your Windows NT Server. You've just installed a second SCSI drive controller and connected four hard drives to it.

Required result:

- Create a disk striping with parity configuration.

Optional desired results:

- Enable file access auditing.
- Place no restrictions on the number of files in the root directory.

Proposed solution:

- Create a disk stripe set with parity. Format the set with FAT.

Which results does the proposed solution produce?

○ a. The proposed solution produces the required result and produces both of the optional desired results.

○ b. The proposed solution produces the required result and produces only one of the optional desired results.

○ c. The proposed solution produces the required result but does not produce any of the optional desired results.

○ d. The proposed solution does not produce the required result.

The correct answer is c. The proposed solution only satisfies the required result. All RAID disk configurations supported by Windows NT can be formatted with either FAT or NTFS. FAT does not support file auditing, and it doesn't allow unlimited files in the root directory.

Scenario 10

Suppose the following situation exists:

Bob is a new user on the domain. He's working in the Sales group but has been assigned to a project from Research. The Research project involves data from both the Development Department and the Accounting Department. Group permissions on the related data shares are:

- Sales share:
  - **Sales group** Change
  - **Research group** Read
  - **Development group** Change
  - **Accounting group** Change
- Research share:
  - **Sales group** None defined
  - **Research group** Change
  - **Development group** None defined
  - **Accounting group** Read
- Development share:
  - **Sales group** No Access
  - **Research group** None defined
  - **Development group** Change
  - **Accounting group** Read
- Accounting share:
  - **Sales group** No Access
  - **Research group** None defined
  - **Development group** Read
  - **Accounting group** Change

Required result:

- Grant Bob the ability to access all data required for this project.

Optional desired results:

- Retain existing group permissions on file/folder/share objects.

(continued)

Scenario 10 (continued)

- Prevent non-Accounting division workers from changing accounting data.

Proposed solution:

- Make Bob a member of the Research and Development groups.

Which results does the proposed solution produce?

○ a. The proposed solution produces the required result and produces both of the optional desired results.

○ b. The proposed solution produces the required result and produces only one of the optional desired results.

○ c. The proposed solution produces the required result but does not produce any of the optional desired results.

○ d. The proposed solution does not produce the required result.

The correct answer is a. The proposed solution grants Bob the minimal level of access he needs to accomplish his project. The solution does not change existing group permissions on files/folders/shares, and it does not grant Bob anything more than read access to the Accounting data. The proposed solution fulfills the required result and both of the optional desired results.

Scenario 11

Suppose the following situation exists:

You must rearrange data folders on your Windows NT Server due to space problems. After adding a new 36 GB RAID drive formatted with NTFS, you begin moving files to the new storage area.

Required result:

* Retain original permissions on all files and folders.

Optional desired results:

* Reuse the old share names.

* Keep the transfer process as simple as possible.

Proposed solution:

* Use Windows Explorer to drag and drop all data folders from their original location to the new storage area.

* One at a time, delete an old share, and then create a new share from the new folder/file location using the same share name.

Which results does the proposed solution produce?

○ a. The proposed solution produces the required result and produces both of the optional desired results.

○ b. The proposed solution produces the required result and produces only one of the optional desired results.

○ c. The proposed solution produces the required result but does not produce any of the optional desired results.

○ d. The proposed solution does not produce the required result.

The correct answer is d. The proposed solution will not retain the original file/folder permissions. When files are moved or copied from one partition to another, they inherit the permissions of their new container. In this case, the inherited permissions would be Full Control for Everyone, because that is the default of newly formatted storage volumes. The best solution for this situation would be to employ the Resource Kit tool SCOPY, which will transfer the files and folders and retain their original security settings. Manual migration of the shares would still be required, but this is the simplest method available.

Scenario 12

Suppose the following situation exists:

You have a Windows NT Server 3.51 system that has hardware components listed on the Windows NT HCL 4. You want to upgrade the system to Windows NT Server 4. The data drives are formatted with HPFS.

Required result:

- Upgrade the system to Windows NT Server 4.

Optional desired results:

- Allow network clients to access the data drives via shares.

- Retain as much of the original configuration as possible.

Proposed solution:

- Perform an upgrade install by launching WINNT32 /b from the \i386 directory of the Windows NT Server 4 CD-ROM.

- Convert the HPFS drives to NTFS using the CONVERT tool from Windows NT 4.

Which results does the proposed solution produce?

- ○ a. The proposed solution produces the required result and produces both of the optional desired results.

- ○ b. The proposed solution produces the required result and produces only one of the optional desired results.

- ○ c. The proposed solution produces the required result but does not produce any of the optional desired results.

- ○ d. The proposed solution does not produce the required result.

The correct answer is b. The proposed solution will perform a successful upgrade of Windows NT Server 3.51 to Windows NT Server 4 and will retain much of the original configuration. However, Windows NT 4 does not support HPFS on any level. The CONVERT tool from Windows NT 4 does not convert HPFS to NTFS; it only converts FAT to NTFS. The CONVERT tool from Windows NT 3.51 should be used before the upgrade is initiated. Therefore, the required result and only one optional desired result is fulfilled.

Scenario 13

Suppose the following situation exists:

Your Windows NT Server is protected from device failure with a disk duplex of the system partition. For an unknown reason, the drive hosting the system partition fails. You attempt several reboots only to discover the drive will no longer power up. All drives on the system were formatted with NTFS.

Required result:

- Return the system to a functional state.

Optional desired results:

- Employ a reusable solution.

- Other than restoring operation, make no other changes to the server.

Proposed solution:

- From another Windows NT system, format and create a boot floppy. Edit the BOOT.INI file on the floppy to point to the duplexed drive.

- Boot the system with the custom boot disk.

Which results does the proposed solution produce?

○   a. The proposed solution produces the required result and produces both of the optional desired results.

○   b. The proposed solution produces the required result and produces only one of the optional desired results.

○   c. The proposed solution produces the required result but does not produce any of the optional desired results.

○   d. The proposed solution does not produce the required result.

The correct answer is a. The proposed solution will boot the machine simply by focusing the bootstrapping routine at the duplexed drive. This is a reusable solution both on the current system and on other systems—you'll have to re-edit the BOOT.INI, but that is fairly easy. Because you're employing a boot floppy, you're not making any changes to the server. At this point, you should edit the BOOT.INI on the system to point to the duplexed drive, thereby making it the primary system partition. Then, schedule downtime to replace the bad drive, and, after it's replaced, create a new duplex/mirror set.

Scenario 14

Suppose the following situation exists:

You need to protect the data on your Windows NT Server system by deploying a fault-tolerant drive configuration.

Required result:

- Protect data stored on the Windows NT Server system with a fault-tolerant drive configuration.

Optional desired results:

- Provide protection from drive controller failure.

- Provide protection from a single drive failure.

Proposed solution:

- Deploy a mirror set for all partitions that need protection, which might require the addition of hard drives to the existing drive controllers.

Which results does the proposed solution produce?

- ○ a. The proposed solution produces the required result and produces both of the optional desired results.

- ○ b. The proposed solution produces the required result and produces only one of the optional desired results.

- ○ c. The proposed solution produces the required result but does not produce any of the optional desired results.

- ○ d. The proposed solution does not produce the required result.

The correct answer is b. The proposed solution is a fault-tolerance option, but it only protects data loss from a single drive failure, not from drive controller failure. A duplexed set or a stripe set with parity would provide the protection desired. Therefore, the required result and only one of the optional desired results are fulfilled.

Scenario 15

Suppose the following situation exists:

You need to protect the data on your Windows NT Server system by deploying a fault-tolerant drive configuration.

Required result:

- Protect data stored on the Windows NT Server system with a fault-tolerant drive configuration.

Optional desired results:

- Provide protection from a single drive failure without downtime.

- Improve read and write performance.

Proposed solution:

- Deploy a disk stripe set with parity.

Which results does the proposed solution produce?

- ○ a. The proposed solution produces the required result and produces both of the optional desired results.

- ○ b. The proposed solution produces the required result and produces only one of the optional desired results.

- ○ c. The proposed solution produces the required result but does not produce any of the optional desired results.

- ○ d. The proposed solution does not produce the required result.

The correct answer is a. The proposed solution provides a fault-tolerance disk configuration that provides for single drive failure without downtime and improves the performance of drive activities. Therefore, the required result and both optional desired results are fulfilled.

Scenario 16

Suppose the following situation exists:

Your organization functions 24 hours a day, and the day is divided into 3 8-hour shifts. Most of the employees work from a central office. However, there are a few dozen telecommuters. Your system is able to support roughly only 1/3 of the total workforce without suffering from severe performance degradations. All workers are assigned specific shifts, and they do not change shifts. However, some telecommuters work additional hours at the end of their shifts to complete tasks or get ahead on work. In-house workers are unable to work extra hours, because there are only enough workstations for each shift. Each in-house worker must leave the workstation at the end of his or her shift so the next shift can log on and begin work.

All in-house users log onto the network with a common shift user account; therefore, there are three shift accounts. And all telecommuting users log into the network with a unique user account, because callback security is employed with a predefined number. All users identify themselves to the application where they perform most of their daily work.

Required result:

- Prevent telecommuters from establishing new sessions outside of their normal working hours.

Optional desired results:

- Allow workers to work beyond their assigned shifts.
- Retain existing passwords on current user accounts.

Proposed solution:

- Configure all shift accounts to have logon hours according to their shifts, for example, 8:00 A.M. through 4:00 P.M., 4:00 P.M. through 12:00 A.M., 12:00 A.M. through 8:00 A.M.
- Configure each existing telecommuter account to the appropriate logon hours for that user's shift.
- Configure the Accounts Policy so the Forcibly Disconnect Remote Users When Logon Hours Expire checkbox is not selected.
- For all future hires of telecommuters, copy an existing telecommuter account with the appropriate shift hours, and then change the callback number.

(continued)

Scenario 16 *(continued)*

Which results does the proposed solution produce?

○ a. The proposed solution produces the required result and produces both of the optional desired results.

○ b. The proposed solution produces the required result and produces only one of the optional desired results.

○ c. The proposed solution produces the required result but does not produce any of the optional desired results.

○ d. The proposed solution does not produce the required result.

The correct answer is a. The proposed solution resolves the situation correctly by allowing users to work beyond their shift hours, but prevents them from initiating new sessions. The logon hours function by preventing new connections outside of the defined hours. With the Forcibly Disconnect option disabled, users can remain connected to complete their work. The user will be sent a warning message every 10 minutes, by default, which warns them that their logon hours have expired. The proposed solution also makes no changes to the existing user accounts' passwords. Therefore, the proposed solution fulfills the required result and both the optional desired results.

Scenario 17

Suppose the following situation exists:

Several temporary workers will be using your network to perform basic word processing and send email.

Required result:

• Maintain distinct environments for each temporary user.

Optional desired results:

• Allow each user to retain customized desktop settings.

• Enable tracking of user file access.

Proposed solution:

• Create a unique user account for each temporary worker.

• Have the user accounts share the same roaming profile.

(continued)

Scenario 17 *(continued)*

Which results does the proposed solution produce?

- ○   a.   The proposed solution produces the required result and produces both of the optional desired results.

- ○   b.   The proposed solution produces the required result and produces only one of the optional desired results.

- ○   c.   The proposed solution produces the required result but does not produce any of the optional desired results.

- ○   d.   The proposed solution does not produce the required result.

The correct answer is d. The proposed solution does not maintain distinct environments for each user. Having unique user accounts does not provide for distinct environments when all users share a common roaming profile. Actually, this causes a chaotic environment in which each user's settings overwrite the previous user's changes. If all accounts share the same profile, it must be a mandatory profile. If all accounts have unique customizable environments, then each account needs its own unique roaming profile. Having unique user accounts allows the tracking of file access based on user. The proposed solution does not satisfy the required result. Unique roaming profiles for each account is the only way to satisfy all the requirements in this situation.

Scenario 18

Suppose the following situation exists:

Your network has four BDCs (BDC1, BDC2, BDC3, and BDC4) in addition to its PDC. All user accounts have logon scripts defined to map network drives and launch software updates. To spread the load of the launching of these logon scripts, you decide to employ replication. All user accounts have the logon script path defined as \logon\script1.bat.

Required result:

- •   Employ replication to distribute logon scripts.

Optional desired results:

- •   Allow the PDC and BDCs to share the workload of authentication.

(continued)

Scenario 18 *(continued)*

> • Allow the PDC and BDCs to share the workload of logon
>   script execution.
>
> Proposed solution:
>
> • Place all logon scripts into the
>   \WINNT\System32\Repl\Export\Scripts directory.
>
> • Export the \WINNT\System32\Repl\Export\Scripts
>   directory.
>
> • Import the exported directory to
>   \WINNT\System32\Repl\Import\Scripts on BDC1, BDC2,
>   BDC3, and BDC4.
>
> Which results does the proposed solution produce?
>
> ○ a. The proposed solution produces the required result and
>   produces both of the optional desired results.
>
> ○ b. The proposed solution produces the required result and
>   produces only one of the optional desired results.
>
> ○ c. The proposed solution produces the required result but
>   does not produce any of the optional desired results.
>
> ○ d. The proposed solution does not produce the required
>   result.

The correct answer is b. The proposed solution employs replication to distribute the logon scripts, but it does so incompletely. One important key to using replication is to always export to yourself. In other words, you must configure the PDC to import the exported directory so its contents will be stored in the PDC's NETLOGON share (\WINNT\System32\Repl\Import\Scripts). As the configuration stands (as proposed in the offered solution), the PDC and the BDCs share the load for authenticating users, but only the BDCs offer the logon scripts. The logon path defined in a user account automatically looks into the NETLOGON share to locate the path and file name of logon scripts. The defined path is a relative path statement within the NETLOGON share. Therefore, the proposed solution fulfills the required result and only one of the optional desired results.

Scenario 19

Suppose the following situation exists:

You need to create several shares for use by the Domain Admins. Your security policy requires that resources that users are not allowed to access should not be revealed to them.

Required result:

- Create the shares and configure access for Domain Admins only.

Optional desired results:

- Hide the shares from all users.
- Track access to files via the new shares.

Proposed solution:

- Name the shares with a $ as the last character in their NetBIOS name.
- Enable auditing on File and Object Access. On the files and folders within the share, enable auditing for read access.

Which results does the proposed solution produce?

○ a. The proposed solution produces the required result and produces both of the optional desired results.

○ b. The proposed solution produces the required result and produces only one of the optional desired results.

○ c. The proposed solution produces the required result but does not produce any of the optional desired results.

○ d. The proposed solution does not produce the required result.

The correct answer is a. The proposed solution creates hidden shares by adding the $ character to the end of the NetBIOS name. The shares will not appear in any browse list except that of Shared Directories via Server Manager—which will only be accessed by Domain Admins anyway. The proposed solution also enables auditing on the files within the shares. Keep in mind that auditing access to files requires NTFS, which is assumed in this question. Also, remember that it's not possible to audit share use but it is possible to audit files and folders on an NTFS partition. The audit events for these objects will show the client computer name and the username of the person accessing the files. Therefore, the proposed solution fulfills the required result and both the optional desired results.

Scenario 20

Suppose the following situation exists:

Your Windows NT Server network consists of a PDC and 3 BDCs, and supports 50 Windows 98 clients. You've been assigned the task of implementing security on the network.

Required result:

- Centralize control over server resources.

Optional desired results:

- Monitor access to resources.

- Ensure passwords are longer than six characters.

Proposed solution:

- Format all drives to host resources with NTFS.

- Set access permissions on resources based on groups.

- Create shares for the file and folder resources.

- Set access permissions on the shares based on groups.

- Enable auditing on all files and folders accessible through the shares.

- Set the Account policy to require passwords to be at least eight characters long.

- Revoke the Log On Locally User Right for all users on the servers.

Which results does the proposed solution produce?

- ○   a.   The proposed solution produces the required result and produces both of the optional desired results.

- ○   b.   The proposed solution produces the required result and produces only one of the optional desired results.

- ○   c.   The proposed solution produces the required result but does not produce any of the optional desired results.

- ○   d.   The proposed solution does not produce the required result.

The correct answer is a. The proposed solution provides for centralized management of resources because they are all hosted on servers. It also provides for access control, auditing of access to those resources, and minimum password length requirements. Therefore, the proposed solution fulfills the required result and both optional desired results.

Scenario 21

Suppose the following situation exists:

Your network consists of the following:

- Servers:
    - 12 Windows NT Servers
    - 4 Web-in-a-box computers
- Clients:
    - 140 Windows 98 computers
    - 45 Macintosh systems
    - 28 Sun Sparc workstations

All computers are using TCP/IP, SPX/IPX, or both. All clients use DHCP. Internet access is granted by a proxy server, which includes an IP-to-IPX gateway.

Required result:

- Improve network throughput of actual data.

Optional desired results:

- Reduce administrative overhead.
- Retain Internet access for all clients.

Proposed solution:

- Force all systems to use TCP/IP only.
- Disable the IP-to-IPX gateway.
- Deploy a WINS server.
- Deploy a DNS server. Configure it to pull DNS information from an Internet DNS server.

Which results does the proposed solution produce?

- ○ a. The proposed solution produces the required result and produces both of the optional desired results.
- ○ b. The proposed solution produces the required result and produces only one of the optional desired results.
- ○ c. The proposed solution produces the required result but does not produce any of the optional desired results.
- ○ d. The proposed solution does not produce the required result.

The correct answer is a. The proposed solution will improve the through-put of actual data over the network. The removal of an unnecessary proto-col and the deployment of a WINS server will eliminate lots of useless traffic and system overhead. The DNS server will simplify domain name resolution for internal and external hosts. The DNS server causes some additional overhead, but it's an important element on networks of this size with Internet access. Therefore, the required result and both optional de-sired results are fulfilled.

Scenario 22

Suppose the following situation exists:

Your Windows NT Server-based network uses NetBEUI, TCP/IP, and NWLink. All the clients regularly use Internet access in addi-tion to the internal network services. Most users complain that the network is slow to respond to initial resource requests.

Required result:

- Improve network performance.

Optional desired results:

- Maintain the ability for clients to access the Internet.

- Improve security for the entire network.

Proposed solution:

- Remove NetBEUI and NWLink from all servers and clients.

Which results does the proposed solution produce?

- ○ a. The proposed solution produces the required result and produces both of the optional desired results.

- ○ b. The proposed solution produces the required result and produces only one of the optional desired results.

- ○ c. The proposed solution produces the required result but does not produce any of the optional desired results.

- ○ d. The proposed solution does not produce the required result.

The correct answer is b. The proposed solution will improve performance by eliminating two unnecessary protocols. The presence of multiple un-used protocols can result in lengthy resource request response, because a timeout must be reached before the next protocol is tried, especially if the protocol used most often is not bound in priority. This solution also retains Internet access. This solution does not address security. Therefore, the proposed solution fulfills the required result and only one of the optional desired results.

Scenario 23

Suppose the following situation exists:

Your network hosts both Windows NT and NetWare servers. Some clients authenticate to Windows NT, and others authenticate to NetWare. All the Windows NT clients use TCP/IP. All the NetWare clients use IPX/SPX. You've recently added a SQL Server database to a Windows NT Server and a RAID array for file storage to a NetWare server.

Required result:

- Ensure that all clients can access the SQL Server and the RAID file storage.

Optional desired results:

- Retain existing protocol settings on all clients.

- Maintain user-specific security of all resource access.

Proposed solution:

- Install NWLink on the SQL Server host.

- Install and configure GSNW on the SQL Server host.

- Configure NetWare to allow GSNW access to the RAID file storage.

Which results does the proposed solution produce?

- ○ a. The proposed solution produces the required result and produces both of the optional desired results.

- ○ b. The proposed solution produces the required result and produces only one of the optional desired results.

- ○ c. The proposed solution produces the required result but does not produce any of the optional desired results.

- ○ d. The proposed solution does not produce the required result.

The correct answer is b. The proposed solution allows clients from either network to gain access to the SQL Server and the RAID file storage. The use of SQL Server by NetWare clients only requires a common protocol; it does not require File and Print Services For NetWare. Windows NT clients can access the RAID array through Gateway Services For NetWare. This configuration retains the original protocol settings on all clients. However, this configuration does not maintain individual user security on resource access for Windows NT clients accessing the NetWare-hosted RAID file storage. GSNW combines all NetWare access into a single user. Therefore, the proposed solution fulfills the required result but only one of the optional desired results. An alternate solution to this situation would involve installing CSNW and NWLink on all Windows NT clients. This would maintain individual security settings but alter the protocol settings on the clients. There is no solution that would satisfy both optional desired results at the same time, short of moving the RAID file storage over to a Windows NT Server.

Scenario 24

Suppose the following situation exists:

A new printer is added to your network. You want to provide print access to users and allow all managers to print documents in priority to normal users.

Required result:

- Grant all users the ability to print to the new printer.

Optional desired results:

- Enable managers to print documents in priority to all users.

- Reduce the amount of time a user must wait to continue work after submitting a print job.

Proposed solution:

- Create a logical printer. Set it to a priority of 99. Grant the Domain Users group print access to the logical printer.

- Create another logical printer. Set it to a priority of 1. Grant the Managers group print access to the logical printer.

- Set both logical printers to spool printed documents and begin printing only after the entire print job is spooled.

(continued)

Scenario 24 *(continued)*

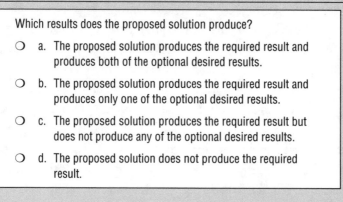

Which results does the proposed solution produce?

- ○ a. The proposed solution produces the required result and produces both of the optional desired results.
- ○ b. The proposed solution produces the required result and produces only one of the optional desired results.
- ○ c. The proposed solution produces the required result but does not produce any of the optional desired results.
- ○ d. The proposed solution does not produce the required result.

The correct answer is b. The proposed solution grants all users access to the printer and returns control of an application back to the user quickly by spooling print jobs. However, the priority of 99 will print before the priority of 1, so the priority settings are backwards. Therefore, the proposed solution fulfills the required result but only one of the optional desired results.

Scenario 25

Suppose the following situation exists:

Your network has four Windows NT Servers. Only one has an attached backup tape device. You're assigned the task of configuring an automated backup system to fully protect the data on all four servers.

Required result:

- Back up all data on all four servers regularly.

Optional desired results:

- Back up the Registry on all four servers.
- Provide a means to restore lost data as quickly as possible.

Proposed solution:

- Use the NTBACKUP tool native to Windows NT.
- Configure a full backup of all four servers to occur on Friday evenings. Be sure to select to back up the Registry.
- Configure an incremental backup of all four servers to occur every night except Fridays. Be sure to select to back up the Registry.

(continued)

Scenario 25 *(continued)*

- Use the AT command with batch files to automate the launching of these backups.

Which results does the proposed solution produce?

- ○ a. The proposed solution produces the required result and produces both of the optional desired results.

- ○ b. The proposed solution produces the required result and produces only one of the optional desired results.

- ○ c. The proposed solution produces the required result but does not produce any of the optional desired results.

- ○ d. The proposed solution does not produce the required result.

The correct answer is c. The proposed solution will protect the data on all four servers, but it will not protect the Registry of the three remote servers. In addition, this solution does not offer the quickest restore method. The AT command is required to automate the execution of NTBACKUP, because the Windows NT native backup utility does not include an internal scheduling mechanism. The NTBACKUP tool is unable to back up remote Registries. Also, a differential backup offers a faster restore method than an incremental backup. Therefore, the proposed solution fulfills the required result but neither of the optional desired results.

Scenario 26

Suppose the following situation exists:

You have a small network consisting of a Windows NT Server acting as a PDC with three Windows 98 clients. You want to provide Internet access to the clients by connecting the Windows NT Server system to an ISP.

Required result:

- Grant the clients Internet access.

Optional desired results:

- Allow clients to be assigned Internet IP addresses on demand.

- Support encrypted data transmission and authentication.

(continued)

Scenario 26 *(continued)*

Proposed solution:

- Use RAS to make a SLIP connection to an ISP.

- Configure RAS routing to support access to the entire network.

- Configure the gateway address on all clients to that of the Windows NT Server's IP address.

Which results does the proposed solution produce?

○ a. The proposed solution produces the required result and produces both of the optional desired results.

○ b. The proposed solution produces the required result and produces only one of the optional desired results.

○ c. The proposed solution produces the required result but does not produce any of the optional desired results.

○ d. The proposed solution does not produce the required result.

The correct answer is d. The proposed solution does not grant clients Internet access. Typically, SLIP is not the best choice for connecting any Windows system to the Internet. SLIP does not support DHCP or encryption. Additionally, simply establishing a connection to an ISP from the Windows NT Server does not grant access to the clients. A proxy server or individually assigned IP addresses is required. Therefore, the proposed solution does not satisfy the required result.

Scenario 27

Suppose the following situation exists:

At the Slotion Corporation, the Research Department produces book-length documents on a regular basis, yet they have all kinds of shorter documents they need to print during working hours. You've been asked to configure their print services so the shorter jobs aren't impeded by the longer, book-length printouts.

Required result:

- Set up print services so book-length jobs print during non-work hours, from 11:00 P.M. through 5:00 A.M., and short jobs print immediately.

Optional desired results:

- Configure rush orders to print ahead of all other print jobs.

- Block users who do not work in Research from using the printers.

Proposed solution:

- Install two printers in a printer pool on your print server.

- Set up the first printer for short print jobs.

- Instruct users to assign rush jobs a priority of 99, and regular jobs a priority of 1.

- Set up the second printer for long print jobs, and allow the printer to operate only between 11:00 P.M. and 5:00 A.M.

- Check permissions for both printers to make sure only members of the Research group have print access.

- Instruct users to print short and rush print jobs to the first printer, and book-length print jobs to the second printer.

Which results does the proposed solution produce?

- ○ a. The proposed solution produces the required result and produces both of the optional desired results.

- ○ b. The proposed solution produces the required result and produces only one of the optional desired results.

- ○ c. The proposed solution produces the required result but does not produce any of the optional desired results.

- ○ d. The proposed solution does not produce the required result.

The correct answer is d. The proposed solution fails to properly configure the printer subsystem to print long documents after hours. Therefore, the proposed solution fails to meet the required result. Problems with this solution include: a printer pool is not required; the devices in a printer pool cannot be configured separately; as a user, you have no control over which device in a printer pool a document will be printed on; and priorities are assigned to logical printers, not print jobs. The proper solution for this situation would be to create three logical printers for a single print device. Assign the first logical printer a print priority of 1 for regular print jobs. Assign the second logical printer a print priority of 99 for rush print jobs. Then, assign the third logical printer the working hours of 11:00 P.M. through 5:00 A.M. Configure the access permissions for these logical printers for members of the Research group. Instruct the Research group to submit their print jobs to the appropriate logical printer and assign useful names, like printnormal, printrush, and printbook.

Scenario 28

Suppose the following situation exists:

At XYZ Corporation, you've been asked to design a naming scheme for computers on a new network. Note that there are two individuals named Robert P. Smith at XYZ Corp, both of whom work in the same department and location.

Required result:

- Create a naming scheme that enables users to uniquely identify a machine's type, location, and department in the browser listing or in Server Manager.

Optional desired results:

- Ensure that user workstations are easy to identify by viewing their names.

- Ensure that users will be able to easily understand and generate names by inspecting existing names.

Proposed solution:

- Identify departments with three-letter codes at the beginning of each name.

- Identify machine types with three-letter codes, following each department code.

- Identify locations with five-letter codes, following each machine type code.

- Append an underscore followed by three initials for each user's name on user machines. Duplicate initials will have a number appended to make sure names are unique.

Which results does the proposed solution produce?

- ○ a. The proposed solution produces the required result and produces both of the optional desired results.

- ○ b. The proposed solution produces the required result and produces only one of the optional desired results.

- ○ c. The proposed solution produces the required result but does not produce any of the optional desired results.

- ○ d. The proposed solution does not produce the required result.

The correct answer is d. The proposed scheme will produce a name that is 16 characters long for the two Robert P. Smiths who work in the same department and location. A NetBIOS name can be only 15 characters long. Therefore, the proposed solution fails to produce the desired results, because some of the names will be invalid.

Online Resources

Here's a collection of online resources that might help you to prepare for your Microsoft certification exam. Many of these Web sites include sample questions, study materials, and study tips for Windows NT Server 4 and other exams.

➤ **http://209.207.167.177** is the BrainDump Heaven site, on which you can find peer discussions on topics and issues.

➤ **http://home.nycap.rr.com/blaineman/mcselinks.html** is a personal page that contains links to MCSE-related sites.

➤ **http://imedoff.virtualave.net/mcse.htm** is a personal page that contains links to MCSE-related sites.

➤ **http://leuthard.ch/mcse/** is the Checkpoint MCSE site, on which you can find free practice tests and links to MCSE-related sites.

➤ **http://stsware.com/microsts.htm** is the Self Test Software site that has practice tests for sale.

➤ **www.america.net/~dhack/mcse** is a personal MCSE page that contains links to newsgroups and other resources.

➤ **www.axxa.com/certcorner/default.asp** is the Axxa Corporation page that contains a collection of study materials, reference sites, and MCSE information.

➤ www.certificationinsider.com is The Coriolis Group's Certification Insider Press site, on which you can find information about Exam Cram/Exam Prep books and other certification products, as well as free online sample tests.

➤ www.certificationshack.com is the Certification Shack site, on which you can find general MCSE information.

➤ www.certify.com is the Cyber Pass site. You can order MCSE practice tests from this site.

➤ www.commandcentral.com is the CommandCentral site, on which you can find free practice tests.

➤ www.computingcentral.msn.com/topics/windowsnt/chat.asp is the MSN, Computing Central, Windows NT chat forum where you can ask questions of peers and experts.

➤ www.cramsession.com is the CramSession site, on which you can find study guides, free practice questions via email and online, and general certification information.

➤ www.cyber-1.com/mcse is an MCSE study group site.

➤ www.geocities.com/~mcse_mct is a personal page that contains MCSE information and resource links.

➤ www.goodground.com/index.htm is the GoodGround site, on which you can find links and free online sample tests.

➤ www.hardcoremcse.com is the HardcoreMCSE site, which contains study aids and links, and sells practice exams.

➤ www.inquiry.com is the Inquiry.com site, on which you can find general technology information.

➤ www.internexis.com/mcp is an MCSE chat and study site.

➤ www.learnquick.com is LearnQuick's site, which offers accelerated MCSE training and tons of MCSE resources.

➤ www.matisse.net/files/glossary.html contains a glossary of Internet terms that can be very helpful.

➤ www.mattscasa.com/netindex.htm is a personal site that contains free practice tests.

➤ www.mcpmag.com is the Microsoft Certified Professional online magazine.

➤ www.mcseinfo.com is the MCSEInfo.com site that includes study tips, review information, and links to MCSE-related sites.

➤ www.mcsetutor.com is the MCSETutor.com site that offers test discussions, book reviews, and links to free online tests.

➤ www.network-info.com/Links/links.html is the Network-Info.com site, on which you can find links to MCSE-related sites.

➤ www.ptek.com/links.asp is a personal page that contains many MCSE/MCP-related links.

➤ www.rad.com/networks/netterms.htm is RAD University's general networking information and reference page. It's not MCSE specific.

➤ www.saluki.com/mcp is the MCP Online site that contains questions and topical discussions. This site is the host of an MCSE mailing list.

➤ www.tekmetrics.com/cert is the e-certifications site that contains information about non-Microsoft certifications.

➤ www.testfree.com is the TestFree site that offers free practice tests.

Glossary

AATP (Authorized Academic Training Program)—A program that authorizes accredited academic institutions of higher learning to offer Microsoft Certified Professional testing and training to their students. The institutions also are allowed to use the Microsoft Education course materials and Microsoft Certified Trainers.

account—*See* user account

account operators—A group built into Windows NT; users assigned to this account have the right to add, delete, and modify user accounts.

account policy—A policy that establishes how the passwords on a domain or a workstation are going to be used.

ACL (Access Control List)—A list of security identifiers contained by system objects that defines which users and groups have what level of services for an object.

ACLCONV utility—A tool used to transform O/S2 HPFS access lists to NTFS ACLs.

administrator—The person responsible for the upkeep, management, and security of a network. When capitalized, this term refers to a built-in user in Windows NT that has full control of the system.

AppleTalk—Apple Computer's networking protocols and software.

architecture— The structure of a network—how the network is set up and how its components are connected to each other.

ASCII (American Standard Code for Information Interchange)—A way of coding that translates letters, numbers, and symbols into digital form.

assessment exam—Similar to the certification exam, this type of exam gives you the opportunity to answer questions at your own pace. This type of exam also utilizes the same tools as the certification exam.

ATEC (Authorized Technical Education Center)—The location where you can take a Microsoft Official Curriculum course taught by Microsoft Certified Trainers.

Auto Frame Type Detection—A setting of the NWLink protocol that detects the frame type being used on the network.

AUTOEXEC.BAT—A DOS batch file launched when a computer is started or booted.

backup browsers—The machines on a Windows NT network that maintain a duplicate list of the resources and act in a similar way within the Browser Service, as does the BDC within domain control.

basevideo—A command line parameter switch used on the BOOT.INI file, basevideo forces Windows NT to boot using 16-color VGA video at 640×480. This setting appears by default on the ARC name line identified by [VGA mode].

BDC (Backup Domain Controller)—A backup server that protects the integrity and availability of the SAM database. BDCs are not able to make changes or modifications, but they can use the database to authenticate users.

beta exam—A trial exam that is given to participants at a Sylvan Prometric testing center before the development of the Microsoft Certified Professional certification exam is finalized. The final exam questions are selected based on the results of the beta exam. For example, if all beta exam participants get an answer correct or wrong, that question generally will not appear in the final version.

BIOS (Basic Input/Output System)—A system that houses the buffers used to transfer information from a program to the hardware devices receiving the information.

blue screen—The screen that appears when a GPF occurs under Windows NT. This is a test display of the stop message error. Many details are included on this screen, such as the location of the error, type of error, and whether or not a memory dump is created.

blueprint survey—A part of the development process of the Microsoft Certification Exam, in which data is gathered from qualified job function experts. The blueprint survey helps decide the importance, required competence, and weighting for each individual exam objective.

boot disk—A hard drive or floppy drive that has bootstrap files on it. The bootstrap files enable an operating system to launch.

boot menu—The text menu that appears immediately after the hardware test on a Windows NT machine. It lists all the known operating systems present. The OS listed first will be booted by default when the timeout period expires, unless an alternate OS is manually selected.

BOOT.INI—One of the files placed on the system partition. This file contains the location of the system files for each OS installed on the machine. The locations are listed using ARC names.

BOOTSECT.DOS—The file containing DOS boot sector data; this file appears in the system partition only on a multiboot machine that numbers DOS, Windows 3.x, Windows 95, Windows 98, or some other near-DOS equivalent among the list of boot options in BOOT.INI.

break mirror—The first step in repairing a mirrored set. This is accomplished in the Disk Administrator utility, using the Break Mirror option in the Fault Tolerance drop-down menu.

cache—A specified area of high-speed memory used to contain data that is going to be, or recently has been, accessed.

CDFS (Compact Disk File System)—A special read-only file system supported by both Windows 95 and Windows NT 3.51 and higher, including 4. CDFS permits easy access to CDs in these operating systems.

Chart view—In Performance Monitor, this is the view that allows users to peruse realtime data in a line graph or histogram form.

client—A network user or a computer on a network used to access resources hosted by other machines on the network.

command line—A DOS prompt that accepts DOS-based commands.

computername—The name of a computer on a LAN that is specific to an individual workstation or server.

CONFIG.POL—In the NETLOGON share, this is the file where all policies are stored.

Control Panel—In Windows, this is the area where you modify settings such as fonts, screen color, SCSI hardware, and printers.

CPU (central processing unit)—The brains of your computer—the area where all functions are performed.

CSNW (Client Service For NetWare)—Designed for Windows NT Workstations that require a direct link to NetWare servers, CSNW lets Windows NT machines link up to and browse NetWare resources alongside Microsoft Windows Network resources.

cut score—On the Microsoft Certified Professional exam, the lowest score a person can receive and still pass.

database—A collection of information arranged and stored so that data can be accessed quickly and accurately.

default—A setting that is factory set and used until the user specifies otherwise.

deltree—A DOS application that deletes a directory tree and its contents.

DHCP (Dynamic Host Configuration Protocol)—A service that enables the dynamic assignment of TCP/IP network addresses, based on a specified pool of available addresses.

Dial-Up Networking (DUN)—A utility, found in the RAS Phonebook| Programs|Accessories folder of the Start menu, that controls the dial-out capabilities of RAS.

directory replication—A service designed to disseminate often-used and regularly updated data (such as user profiles, logon scripts, and system policies) to multiple computers to speed file access and improve reliability.

Disk Administrator—An administration application in the Administrative Tools group that lets an administrator create and delete stripe sets and various disk partitions, change the assignment of drive letters, and display facts about partition size and setup.

disk controller—A piece of hardware that controls how data is written and retrieved from the computer's disk drive.

disk duplexing—A fault tolerance method used by Windows NT that employs a duplicate physical and logical drive on a separate hard disk where the drive is connected to the system via a separate controller. If the original drive or controller fails, the system continues to operate using the duplexed drive.

disk mirroring—A fault tolerance method used by Windows NT that creates an exact duplicate of one physical and logical storage device on a separate physical storage device, both attached to the same controller.

disk partition—A portion of a hard disk that acts like a physically separate unit.

disk striping—A fault tolerance method used by Windows NT that stores data across multiple physical storage devices.

Display Properties—A dialog box that allows you to modify certain properties of your desktop—the background, the screen saver, settings, and more.

DLC (Data Link Control)—A protocol used to interoperate with IBM mainframes and provide connectivity to network attached print devices.

DLLs (dynamic link libraries)—Small executable program routines or device drivers stored in separate files. DLLs are loaded by the OS when called upon by a process or hardware device.

DMA (Direct Memory Addresses)—A method used by hardware adapters to get and store data from a system's RAM without involving the CPU.

DMP file—A memory dump file with the extension .DMP.

DNS (Domain Name Service)—A Windows NT service used to resolve host names into IP addresses.

domain—A group of computers and peripheral devices sharing a common security database.

domain controller—A computer that authenticates domain logons and manages the Security Accounts Manager (SAM) database.

domain database—A computer account requires 0.5 KB, a global group account requires 512 bytes for the group and 12 bytes per user, and a local group account requires 512 bytes for the group and 36 bytes for each account.

Domain Guests—A group whose members are given the minimal level of user access to all domain resources. The Guest account is automatically a member of this group.

domain model—A network setup definition used by Microsoft to describe and define organizational schemes for networks. In theory, the domain model can scale up to handle any size of network.

DOS (disk operating system)—Software that regulates the way a computer reacts with its floppy disks or hard disks.

driver—Software that binds a peripheral device to the operating system.

encryption—A method of coding data in which a person has to have a decoding key to decipher the information.

ERD (Emergency Repair Disk)—A miniature first aid kit for Windows NT. This single floppy contains all the files needed to repair the system partition and many boot partition-related problems.

ESDI (Enhanced Small Device Interface)—A pre-IDE type storage device that is low-level formatted with various values of sector per track.

Ethernet—The most widely used type of LAN; developed by Xerox.

Event log—An option in the Event Viewer in the Administrative Tools group that lets you view all of the events that have taken place on a particular computer.

Event Viewer—The application in Windows NT that displays all of the log files and lets you modify them.

Everyone—A default group that cannot be deleted or renamed and that lists each user within a domain as a member.

Exabytes—One billion Gigabytes.

Exam Preparation Guides—Guides that provide information specific to the material covered on Microsoft Certified Professional exams to help students prepare for the exam.

Exam Study Guide—Short for Microsoft Certified Professional Program Exam Study Guide, this contains information about the topics covered on more than one of the Microsoft Certified Professional exams.

FAT (File Allocation Table)—A table originally used by the DOS file system to hold information about the properties, location, and size of files being stored on a disk.

fault tolerance—The ability of a computer to work continuously, even when there is system failure.

FDISK command—A DOS command that is used to partition a hard disk.

firewall—A barrier—made of software and/or hardware—between two networks, permitting only authorized communication to pass.

firmware—A type of software that becomes part of the hardware function after it has been saved into a programmable read-only memory chip (PROM).

FPNW (File And Print Services For NetWare)—A Windows NT service that makes resources from a Windows NT Server available to NetWare clients without requiring additional software or configuration changes.

FQDN (fully qualified domain name)—The complete site name of an Internet computer system.

frames—The segments created by the access method used when packets are being sent across a network.

FTP (File Transfer Protocol)—A protocol that transfers files to and from a local hard drive to an FTP server located on another TCP/IP-based network (such as the Internet).

Full Control—In Windows NT Server, a level of permission that gives the person to whom it is assigned all of the general permissions, as well as the authority to change permissions.

gateway—The service performed by a computer that converts the protocols between different types of networks or computers.

GDI (Graphics Device Interface)—A component that provides network applications with a system for presenting graphical information. The GDI works as a translator between an application's print request and the device driver interface (DDI), ensuring that the job is rendered accurately.

global groups—Groups that apply to all computers within a network. A global group needs to be defined only once for each domain. Global groups may only have users as members.

Gopher service—An Internet service that provides text-only information over the Internet. A Gopher service is most suited to large documents with little or no formatting or images.

GPF (general protection fault)—In Windows 3.x, this is an error that occurs when two or more programs are assigned to the same area of memory. In Windows NT, this appears as a blue screen.

graphics—Pictures and images created in a computer.

groups—Collections of users defined with a common name and level of resource permissions.

GSNW (Gateway Service For NetWare)—A Windows NT service that lets Windows NT Servers map a drive to a NetWare server. GSNW provides access to NetWare server resources for Windows NT Workstations (via a gateway).

GUI (graphical user interface)—A computer setup that uses graphics, windows, and a trackball or mouse as the method of interaction with the computer.

HAL (Hardware Abstraction Layer)—In the Windows NT operating system, the HAL creates a bridge between the Windows NT operating system and a computer's CPU.

hard drive—Also called the hard disk, the hard drive is the permanent storage area for data.

hardware—The physical components of a computer system.

HCL (Hardware Compatibility List)—A list that comes with Windows NT Server; this list indicates what hardware is compatible with the software. The most updated version of this list can be found on the Microsoft Web site or on the TechNet CD.

hive—A section of the Windows NT Registry.

HPFS (High Performance File System)—The first PC-compatible file system that supported LFNs. Like FAT, HPFS maintains a directory structure, but it adds automatic sorting of the directory and includes support for special attributes to better accommodate multiple naming conventions and file-level security. HPFS is no longer supported under Windows NT 4.

HTML (Hypertext Markup Language)—Based on SGML, HTML is the markup language used to create Web pages.

HTTP (Hypertext Transfer Protocol)—The World Wide Web protocol that allows for the transfer of HTML documents over the Internet or intranets and responds to actions (such as a user clicking on hypertext links).

IDE (Integrated Device Electronics)—A type of storage device interface in which the electronics required to operate the drive are stored on the drive itself, thus eliminating the need for a separate controller card.

IEEE (Institute of Electrical and Electronic Engineers)—A group of technical professionals that sponsors technical conferences worldwide, publishes over 25 percent of the world's technical papers, and contributes significantly to the establishment of technical standards.

IIS (Internet Information Server)—Web server software by Microsoft; included and implemented with Windows NT Server.

INI files—Files that contain all of the startup information essential to launching a program or operating system.

Input/Output System—A system that requires input into an input device (such as a keyboard) and outputs.

Internet—The collection of TCP/IP-based networks around the world.

intranet—An internal, private network that uses the same protocols and standards as the Internet.

IP address—Four sets of numbers, separated by decimal points, that represent the numeric address of a computer attached to a TCP/IP network, such as the Internet.

IPC (Interprocess Communications)—Within an operating system, this is the service that facilitates the exchange of data between applications.

IPX/SPX (Internetwork Packet Exchange/Sequenced Packet Exchange)—
Novell's NetWare protocol, reinvented by Microsoft and implemented in
Windows NT under the name NWLink. It is fully compatible with Novell's
version and in many cases is a better implementation than the original.

IRQ (interrupt request line)—On a PC, IRQ is a hardware interrupt.

ISDN (Integrated Services Digital Network)—A form of digital communication that has a bandwidth of 128 Kbps.

ISP (Internet Service Provider)—An organization that charges a fee for
providing your Internet connection and other related services.

job function expert—A person with extensive knowledge about a particular job function and the software products/technologies related to that job.
Typically, a job function expert is currently performing the job, has recently
performed the job, or is training people to do this job.

kernel—The essential part of an operating system; provides basic OS services.

kernel debugger—A Windows NT application that records Windows NT's
activity during bootup and when a stop error occurs.

LAN (local area network)—A network confined to a single building or
geographic area and comprised of servers, workstations, peripheral devices,
a network operating system, and a communications link.

LAN Manager—A network operating system product developed by
Microsoft, deployed as a server application under OS/2.

Last Known Good Configuration (LKGC)—A recording made by Windows NT of all the Registry settings that existed the last time a user successfully logged on to the server.

leased line—A communication line leased from a communications provider, such as an ISP or a telephone company.

LFNs (long file names)—File names of up to 256 characters.

LMHOSTS—The predecessor to WINS, LMHOSTS is a static list of
NetBIOS names mapped to IP addresses.

local group—A group of users on a single workstation; when the group is
set up, the users are given privileges and rights. Local groups may contain
users or global groups.

lockout—In Windows NT security, lockout is a feature used to prevent compromised accounts from being used.

logical partitions—The multiple segments of a physical hard drive. Each segment can be used independently of the others, including belonging to separate volumes and hosting different file systems. Most logical partitions have a drive letter assigned to them and can be referred to by an ARC name.

logical printers—The software component used by Windows NT to direct print jobs from applications to a print server. A physical printer can be serviced by numerous logical printers.

logoff—The process by which a user quits a computer system.

logon—The process by which a user gains access or signs on to a computer system.

MAKEDISK.BAT—A utility located in the \Support\Hqtool directory that creates a bootable DOS floppy to run NTHQ (NT Hardware Qualifier) upon bootup.

Master Boot Record (MBR)—A BIOS bootstrap routine—used by low-level, hardware-based system code stored in Read-Only Memory (ROM)—to initiate the boot sequence on a PC. This in turn calls a bootstrap loader, which then commences to load the machine's designated operating system.

master browser—A computer on a Windows NT network that maintains the main list of all available resources within a domain (including links to external domains).

MCI (multiple-choice item)—An item (within a series of items) that is the answer to a question (single-response MCI) or one of the answers to a question (multiple-response MCI).

MCP (Microsoft Certified Professional)—An individual who has taken and passed at least one certification exam and has earned one or more of the following certifications: Microsoft Certified Trainer, Microsoft Certified Solution Developer, Microsoft Certified Systems Engineer, or Microsoft Certified Product Specialist.

MCSD (Microsoft Certified Solution Developer)—An individual who is qualified to create and develop solutions for businesses using the Microsoft development tools, technologies, and platforms.

MCSE (Microsoft Certified Systems Engineer)—An individual who is an expert on Windows NT and the Microsoft BackOffice integrated family of server software. This individual also can plan, implement, maintain, and support information systems associated with these products.

MCT (Microsoft Certified Trainer)—An individual who is qualified by Microsoft to teach Microsoft Education courses at sites authorized by Microsoft.

Microsoft certification exam—A test created by Microsoft to verify a test taker's mastery of a software product, technology, or computing topic.

Microsoft Certified Professional Certification Update—A newsletter for Microsoft Certified Professional candidates and Microsoft Certified Professionals.

Microsoft Exchange—An enterprise-wide messaging and mail system, developed by Microsoft.

Microsoft official curriculum—Microsoft education courses that support the certification exam process and are created by the Microsoft product groups.

Microsoft Roadmap to Education and Certification—An application, based on Microsoft Windows, that will take you through the process of deciding what your certification goals are and inform you of the best way to achieve them.

Microsoft Sales Fax Service—A service through which you can obtain Exam Preparation Guides, fact sheets, and additional information about the Microsoft Certified Professional Program.

Microsoft Solution Provider—An organization, not directly related to Microsoft, that provides integration, consulting, technical support, and other services related to Microsoft products.

Microsoft TechNet Technical Information Network (TechNet)—A service provided by Microsoft that provides helpful information via a monthly CD-ROM disk. TechNet is the primary source of technical information for people who support and/or educate end users, create automated solutions, or administer networks and/or databases.

Microsoft's NWLink—Microsoft's implementation of the Internetwork Packet Exchange/Sequenced Packet Exchange (IPX/SPX) protocols.

migration tool—An application that converts a hardware or software technology from one form to another. The Windows NT NetWare Migration Tool converts users and groups to Windows NT equivalents.

mirror set—A pair of disks that have been duplicated through the Windows NT disk mirroring fault tolerance method.

Modems Applet—An application for installing and maintaining a modem.

motherboard—The main circuit board in a computer system.

MRI (multiple-rating item)—An item that gives you a task and a proposed solution. Every time the task is set, an alternate solution is given and the candidate must choose the answer that gives the best results produced by one solution.

MSDN (Microsoft Developer Network)—The official source for Software Development Kits (SDKs), Device Driver Kits (DDKs), operating systems, and programming information associated with creating applications for Microsoft Windows and Windows NT.

multi—The designation in an ARC name of the type of hard drive; the other option is SCSI.

multicast—The transmission of a message to several recipients simultaneously.

multichannel—Having more than a single inbound or outbound communications port, link, or connection.

Multilink PPP—A Windows NT network protocol that allows you to combine the bandwidth of multiple physical links, which increases the total bandwidth that could be used for a RAS connection.

multiple master domain model—A domain model that has two or more master domains; they must trust each other via two-way trust relationships. Centralized administration of user accounts also must be provided.

multitasking—Running more than one computer application on a system at a time.

NDA (nondisclosure agreement)—A legal agreement that binds two parties to maintain secrecy regarding the subject of the agreement. This is an instrument commonly used by Microsoft to keep its partners and vendors quiet about software until it is commercially released.

NetBEUI (NetBIOS Extended User Interface)—A simple Network layer transport protocol developed to support NetBIOS networks.

NetBIOS (Network Basic Input/Output System)—Originally developed by IBM in the 1980s, this protocol provides the underlying communication mechanism for some basic Windows NT functions, such as browsing and interprocess communications between network servers.

NETLOGON—An administrative share created and used within domain controllers for authenticating users logging on to the enterprise domain.

NetWare—A popular network operating system developed by Novell.

Network Client Administrator—Located in the Administrative Tools Start menu, this is used to create a boot disk or a set of startup disks for DOS workstations.

Network Filing System (NFS)—A popular distributed file system on Unix networks.

Network Neighborhood—Within Explorer or My Computer, this is the area in which you access other computers on the network.

NIC (network interface card)—An adapter card used to connect a computer to a network. Also called a network board, network adapter, and network card.

No Access permission—A level of permission assigned to users or groups, restricting them from accessing the designated area.

nodebug—A BOOT.INI switch that informs you that no debugging information is being monitored.

NTCONFIG.POL—The file that defines a system policy as the default policy.

NTFS (New Technology File System)—The native file system of Windows NT.

NTGATEWAY—The suggested default name of the group account for GSNW.

NTHQ (NT Hardware Qualifier) disk—The disk that checks a computer against a built-in version of the HCL (except on machines with hardware newer than August 1996, which the software may not recognize).

NTLDR file—The executable program, launched by the boot files, that loads the Windows NT kernel. The name is a shortened version of Windows NT Loader.

NTOSKRNL.EXE—The executable file for the Windows NT operating system that includes all the basic capabilities and components necessary to establish a working runtime environment. This file resides in the \Winnt\System32 directory on the boot partition.

null-modem cable—An RS-232 cable used to enable two computers within close proximity to communicate without using a modem.

NWLink—Microsoft's "clean room" implementation of Novell's IPX/SPX protocol suite for NetWare networks.

operating system (OS)—A software program that controls the operations on a computer system.

OSLOADER.EXE—The OS loader program for RISC computers. This program provides all of the services and information provided by NTDETECT.COM, BOOTSECT.DOS, NTDETECT.COM, and NTLDR on PCs. This file resides wherever the nonvolatile RAM location data indicates.

/OX—The parameter switch used on WINNT.EXE or WINNT32.EXE to force setup floppy creation. If /OX appears as the only parameter, it will simply build a set of installation disks for Windows NT.

pagefile—The file used by the virtual memory manager to store segments or pages of memory temporarily to hard disk.

PAP (Password Authentication Protocol)—A clear-text authentication protocol.

parity—Redundant segments of data used to provide fault tolerance to information. Within Windows NT, this term is most commonly used when discussing stripe sets with parity. Also, a disk storage configuration where additional data is stored so that, in the event of a single drive failure, all data can be reconstructed.

partition—A portion of memory or a portion of a hard disk.

password—A word used by an individual to gain access to a particular system.

PDC (Primary Domain Controller)—The central storage and management server for the SAM database.

Per Seat—A licensing mode that allows users to connect to as many servers as they want without requiring a separate license for each connection.

Performance Monitor—A graphical application that lets you set, graph, log, and report alerts.

peripheral device—A hardware device connected to a computer.

permissions—A level of access assigned to files or folders. Permissions determine who has access rights to those files or folders.

PGP (Pretty Good Privacy)—An encryption program that is not native to Windows NT.

phonebook entry—A collection of settings used by a RAS to establish a connection with a remote dial-up server. A phonebook entry contains details such as phone number, name, password, protocol settings, and encryption type.

physical disk—The hardware component that adds additional storage space. A physical disk must be partitioned and formatted with a file system before data can be stored on it.

PING—A TCP/IP command used to verify the existence and connection to remote hosts over a network.

policies—A set of specifications or limitations that restrict the environment of a user. Windows NT has three policies: account, user rights, and audit.

POSIX—An operating system type that complies with the IEEE Std 1003.1 standard. Windows NT supports only POSIX.1.

potential browser—A computer with the ability to participate in the support of the list of resources for a domain. A potential browser will be elected to a position of backup or master browser by the browser service automatically, as needed.

PPP (Point-to-Point Protocol)—An industry-standard protocol used to establish network-protocol-supporting links over telephone lines using modems.

PPTP (Point-to-Point Tunneling Protocol)—A protocol that enables "tunneling" of IPX, NetBEUI, or TCP/IP inside PPP packets in such a way as to establish a secure link between a client and server over the Internet.

print device—The physical hardware device that produces printed output.

print driver—The software component that enables communication between the operating system and the physical printing device.

print job—A document or image sent from a client to a printer. A print job is typically coded in Windows EMF or the RAW language of the printer.

Print Operators—A default group that has full control over all printers within a domain.

print queue—The list of print jobs waiting to be sent to the printer for processing. The print queue can be viewed by opening the printer folder for any individual logical printer.

print server—The computer that hosts the spool file for a printer and/or that physically is attached to the printer.

printer—Typically refers to the logical printer (software component) within the Windows NT environment, as opposed to the physical printing device.

printer pool—A collection of identical printers served by a single logical printer.

printing device—The hardware device that creates marks on paper in the pattern dictated by the driver software.

priorities—The designation of the importance of a process to gain processing time.

process tracking—A type Audit event that records process activities, such as handle duplication, indirect object access, and process termination.

processor time—A counter in the Performance Monitor that shows you how busy the processor is.

protocol—In networking, a set of rules that defines how information is transmitted over a network.

RAID (Redundant Array of Inexpensive Disks)—A standardized method for categorizing fault tolerance storage systems. Windows NT implements Level 0, Level 1, and Level 5 RAID through software, not hardware.

RAS (Remote Access Service)—A Windows NT service that provides network communication for remote clients over telecommunication lines. RAS connections are different from standard direct network connections only in relation to speed.

rdisk—The second segment of an ARC name used with the initial segment of MULTI to indicate the ordinal number of the physical storage device. The third element in an ARC pathname.

read access—The ability to view and open a file or document.

Registry—The hierarchical database that serves as a repository for hardware, software, and OS configuration information.

replication—A service of Windows NT that automatically distributes files and directories from one server to multiple servers and workstations on the network.

Replicator group—The default group whose members have permissions to access the replication service and directories. This group is used exclusively by the Directory Replication service and the user account created for the service.

Resource Kit—The additional documentation and software utilities distributed by Microsoft to provide information and instruction on the proper operation and modification of its software products.

rights—Settings that define the ability of a user to access a computer or a domain.

RIP (Routing Internet Protocol)—A protocol that enables communication between routers on a network to facilitate the exchange of routing tables.

RISC (Reduced Instruction Set Computer)—A set of processor instructions that speeds up processing by using simple computer instructions. Also, a type of computer platform.

router—A device or a software implementation that enables interoperability and communication across networks.

RPC (Remote Procedure Call) Configuration—A programming interface that allows software applications running on separate computers on different networks to use each other's services.

RSA (Rivest-Shamir-Adleman)—An encryption technology that uses a public/private key pair.

SAM (Security Accounts Manager)—The security database of Windows NT, the SAM maintains a record of all users, groups, and permissions within a domain. The SAM is stored on the PDC and is duplicated on the BDCs.

SAP (Service Advertising Protocol)—An IPX service that broadcasts the services and addresses on a network.

SCSI (Small Computer System Interface)—A standard interface, defined by ANSI, that provides for high-speed connections to devices such as hard drives, scanners, and printers.

security—A manner of protecting data by restricting access to authorized users.

Server Manager—The Windows NT administration utility where computer accounts are managed.

Server Operators—The default group whose members can manage domain servers.

service pack—A patch or fix distributed by Microsoft after the final release of a product to repair errors, bugs, and security breaches.

share—A network construct that enables remote users to access resources located throughout a network.

share-level permissions—The setting of user/group access on a network share. The permissions of a network share must be met by users before access to the object is granted.

SLIP (Serial Line Internet Protocol)—An older industry standard for RAS communication links. It is included with Windows NT only for establishing connections with Unix systems that do not support the newer PPP standard.

SMTP (Simple Mail Transfer Protocol)—An Internet protocol used to distribute email from one mail server to another over a TCP/IP network.

SNA (Systems Network Architecture)—A widely used network architecture developed by IBM.

SNMP (Simple Network Management Protocol)—A protocol used to monitor remote hosts over a TCP/IP network.

spooler—A software component of the print system that stores print jobs on a hard drive while the jobs wait in the print queue.

SQL Server—A Microsoft product that supports a network-enabled relational database system.

Stand-Alone server—Also called a "member server," this is a server in a workgroup or a domain environment that does not participate in domain control or user authentication; therefore, it must rely on other domain controllers to service its domain logons.

stripe set—A hard disk construct in which segments of data are written in sequence across multiple drives.

subnet—A portion or segment of a TCP/IP network.

System log—The log, viewed through Event Viewer, in which general system information and errors are recorded.

System Policy Editor—The administrative tool used to create and modify system policies for computers, groups, and users.

take ownership—The command that allows you to grab Full Control authority over an object.

tape drives—Devices, used for backing up data, that employ metal film cassettes for storage.

TAPI (Telephony Application Programming Interface)—An interface and API that defines how applications can interact with data/fax/voice devices and calls.

Task Manager—A utility with which applications and processes can be viewed, stopped, and started. Task Manager also offers CPU and memory status information.

TCP/IP (Transmission Control Protocol/Internet Protocol)—The most widely used protocol in networking today, because it is the most flexible of the transport protocols and is able to span wide areas.

Telnet—A terminal emulation utility used to interact with remote computers.

Token Ring—A network topology in which the computers are arranged in a ring and a token is used to pass the privilege of communicating over the network.

trust—A link between two domains that enables pass-through authentication, so that users from one domain can access the resources of another. A trust is a one-way relationship only.

two-way trust—A link between two domains established by the creation of two one-way trusts.

UDP (User Datagram Protocol)—A TCP component that transmits data through a connectionless service. This type of transmission does not guarantee the delivery or sequencing of sent packets.

UNC (Universal Naming Convention)—A standardized naming method for networks taking the form of \\servername\sharename.

Unicode character set—An ANSI standard for encoding characters and letters shared between different languages' character sets and keyboards.

Unix—An interactive time-sharing operating system developed in 1969 by a hacker to play games. This system developed into the most widely used industrial-strength computer operating system in the world, and ultimately supported the birth of the Internet.

UPS (uninterruptible power supply)—A semi-intelligent, rechargeable battery system that protects a computer from power failures and fluctuations.

user account—The collection of information—such as name, password, group memberships, access privileges, and user rights—stored by Windows NT about a specific network user. User accounts are managed through the User Manager For Domains utility.

User Manager For Domains—The Windows NT Server administration utility controlling account management, group membership, and security policies for a domain.

user profile—The collection of desktop and environmental settings that define the work area of the local computer.

user rights—Settings that define the ability of a user to access a computer or a domain.

users group—Another term for group.

username—The human-friendly name of a user account. The username is one of the two data items used to log on to Windows NT. Windows NT does not recognize an account by the username, but rather by the SID.

VFAT (Virtual File Allocation Table)—This file system is currently supported by Windows 95, Windows NT 3.51, and Windows NT 4; VFAT provides 32-bit Protected Mode access for file manipulation.

VGA (Video Graphics Array)—A PC display standard of 640×480 pixels, 16 colors, and a 4:3 aspect ratio.

volume set—A disk construct comprised of one or more logical partitions formatted with a single file system.

VPN (virtual private network)—A WAN, provided by a common communications carrier, that works like a private network; however, the backbone of the network is shared with all of the customers in a public network.

WAN (wide area network)—A network that spans geographically distant segments. Often a distance of two or more miles is used to define a WAN. Microsoft, however, considers that any RAS connection establishes a WAN.

Windows NT Workstation—A Microsoft OS product that is a client version of the Windows NT system. It is the same as Windows NT Server, but without the ability to host multiple services and resources for a network.

WINS (Windows Internet Name Service)—A Windows network service used to resolve NetBIOS names to IP addresses.

workgroup—A collection of networked computers that participate in a peer-to-peer relationship.

World Wide Web—An information distribution system hosted on TCP/IP networks. The Web supports text, graphics, and multimedia. The IIS component of Windows NT is a Web server that can distribute Web documents.

write permissions—The ability to create or modify files and directories.

XCOPY—A command-line utility used to copy files and subdirectories while maintaining the directory tree structure.

Index

Look for All of the Exam Cram Brand Certification Study Systems

ALL NEW! Exam Cram Personal Trainer Systems

The Exam Cram Personal Trainer systems are an exciting new category in certification training products. These CD-ROM based systems offer extensive capabilities at a moderate price and are the first certification-specific testing product to completely link learning with testing.

This Exam Cram Study Guide turned interactive course lets you customize the way you learn.

Each system includes:

- A Personalized Practice Test engine with multiple test methods,
- A database of nearly 300 questions linked directly to the subject matter within the Exam Cram on which that question is based.

Exam Cram Audio Review Systems

Written and read by certification instructors, each set contains four cassettes jam-packed with the certification exam information you must have. Designed to be used on their own or as a complement to our Exam Cram Study Guides, Flash Cards, and Practice Tests.

Each system includes:

- Study preparation tips with an essential last-minute review for the exam
- Hours of lessons highlighting key terms and techniques
- A comprehensive overview of all exam objectives
- 45 minutes of review questions complete with answers and explanations

Exam Cram Flash Cards

These pocket-sized study tools are 100% focused on exams. Key questions appear on side one of each card and in-depth answers on side two. Each card features either a cross-reference to the appropriate Exam Cram Study Guide chapter or to another valuable resource. Comes with a CD-ROM featuring electronic versions of the flash cards and a complete practice exam.

Exam Cram Practice Tests

Our readers told us that extra practice exams were vital to certification success, so we created the perfect companion book for certification study material.

Each book contains:

- Several practice exams
- Electronic versions of practice exams on the accompanying CD-ROM presented in an interactive format enabling practice in an environment similar to that of the actual exam
- Each practice question is followed by the corresponding answer (why the right answers are right and the wrong answers are wrong)
- References to the Exam Cram Study Guide chapter or other resource for that topic

CORIOLIS™
Certification Insider Press